UNDERSTANDING CONTEMPORARY AFRICA

UNDERSTANDING ―――――――――――――――――
Introductions to the States and Regions of the Contemporary World
Donald L. Gordon, series editor

Understanding Contemporary Africa, second edition
edited by April A. Gordon & Donald L. Gordon

Understanding Contemporary Latin America
edited by Richard S. Hillman

SECOND EDITION

UNDERSTANDING CONTEMPORARY AFRICA

edited by
April A. Gordon & Donald L. Gordon

LYNNE
RIENNER
PUBLISHERS

BOULDER
LONDON

Cover: Betty LaDuke, who painted "Millet Rhythms,"
is an artist-traveler and professor of art at Southern Oregon State College, Ashland.

Published in the United States of America in 1996 by
Lynne Rienner Publishers, Inc.
1800 30th Street, Boulder, Colorado 80301

and in the United Kingdom by
Lynne Rienner Publishers, Inc.
3 Henrietta Street, Covent Garden, London WC2E 8LU

Library of Congress Cataloging-in-Publication Data
Understanding contemporary Africa / edited by April A. Gordon and
    Donald L. Gordon.—2nd ed.
        p. cm.—(Understanding: Introductions to the states and regions
    of the contemporary world)
    Includes bibliographical references and index.
    ISBN 1-55587-547-5 (alk. paper)
    1. Africa—Politics and government—1960– 2. Africa—Social
conditions—1960– I. Gordon, April A. II. Gordon, Donald L.
III. Series.
DT30.5.U536 1996
960.3'2—dc20   96-7581
                                                                   CIP

British Cataloguing in Publication Data
A Cataloguing in Publication record for this book
is available from the British Library.

Printed and bound in the United States of America

The paper used in this publication meets the requirements
of the American National Standard for Permanence of
Paper for Printed Library Materials Z39.48-1984.

5 4

Contents

Maps

▪ Preface ▪

The first edition of *Understanding Contemporary Africa* was the culmination of nearly three years of collaborative thought, research, and writing by a dedicated group of Africanist scholars and teachers. On the basis of informal conversations, and then in a broader survey of other Africanists teaching at the undergraduate level, we discovered that most of us were finding it difficult to locate a good, up-to-date text on sub-Saharan Africa to use in our introductory courses. Available texts were, for the most part, too discipline-oriented—created especially for history, anthropology, or political science courses; they were too advanced for students with little prior background; or they were dated. On the other hand, some introductory texts on the market tried to do too much; they were so broad in scope that they lacked the theoretical base or scholarly depth we were looking for. This left professors compelled to use multiple readings from several different books and periodicals to cover their topics. We decided that for us, as well as many other teachers of "Introduction to Africa" courses, the availability of a single text designed to address important contemporary topics and to provide background from a variety of academic subject areas would be an attractive alternative. It would save many of us from lengthy searches for material, time wasted with library reserve procedures, or an expensive panoply of required book purchases.

Addressing the above concerns provided the rationale for this book. The success of the book since its publication in 1992 confirms our belief that *Understanding Contemporary Africa,* with its broad scope, up-to-date and in-depth chapters, and attention to readability for undergraduate students, is a valuable text for both multidisciplinary African studies courses and disciplinal courses. It covers many of the most important topics and issues needed for a grasp of the reality of sub-Saharan Africa in the 1990s—e.g., the environment, women's roles, population, and urbanization—that get little or no treatment in most disciplinal texts.

The information in each chapter of the book represents the best of the current research and thinking in those fields of study, providing students and professors with a useful background on Africa, and also presenting major issues in a way students can understand. And, although each chapter is designed to stand alone, the authors have produced a well-integrated volume, referring in their own chapters to complementary ideas discussed elsewhere in the book. This allows instructors to assign readings to meet their needs—by chapter or by topic, for instance—at the same time that the book helps students to see the connections among issues or events and reinforces what they may have read earlier.

We have retained the organization of the first edition, while adding a chapter on Africa's international relations: In the introduction that follows this preface, the scope and themes of the book are discussed. Next, chapters on the geography and history of sub-Saharan Africa provide the background necessary for understanding what follows. (Readers should refer to the maps in the geography chapter when reading later chapters of the book.) The remaining chapters cover major institutions and issues confronting sub-Saharan Africa today. While each chapter provides historical background, the emphasis is on the vital concerns facing Africa now and in the future. Most central among these concerns are African political and economic systems and issues, which are discussed in Chapters 4, 5, and 6. Tied closely to political and economic policies and trends are population growth, urbanization, and environmental problems, as discussed in Chapters 7 and 8. Next we discuss African family and kinship systems; without an awareness of how Africans understand kinship, issues like tribalism and corruption are difficult to comprehend and often misconstrued by outsiders. Women in Africa are the focus of Chapter 10; as this chapter shows, social change in Africa is affecting women much differently than men, and often to the disadvantage of women. In Chapters 11 and 12, on African religion and literature, the focus shifts to the ideological sphere—to how Africans explain and attempt to grapple with the complexities of their world and their place in it.

Chapter 13 is different from the others because it deals with one country, South Africa. In recent years, South Africa has captured the attention of the outside world as its black majority struggled to break the shackles of centuries of racist oppression. Although white-ruled South Africa has been in many ways an anomaly on the continent, we think it is important that students understand the history of apartheid, the liberation struggle, and current efforts to create a new democratic South Africa in which people of all races can live together and prosper.

In a brief chapter on trends and prospects, which follows the discussion of South Africa, we assess where sub-Saharan Africa may be heading. While we do not attempt to predict any specific outcomes, we do note that many African countries are attempting political and economic reform; some are making real progress while others are teetering on the brink of disaster. In all countries, new leaders are emerging, replacing those who assumed power at independence. Whether the new generation shaping the Africa of the future will improve on the record of the past still remains very much an open question.

Writing and editing this book has left us indebted to a number of people.

Our research was aided especially by summer research grants from the

University of Florida African Studies Center under the direction of Hunt Davis, to whom we are most grateful. Prior research at the Institute of Development Studies at the University of Sussex and help from Charles Harvey were also important and appreciated.

In a different way each of us is obligated to Mark DeLancey of the University of South Carolina. Mark's leadership and professionalism as an Africanist are well known. For us both, a Fulbright program in Cameroon under Mark's direction was an academic high point. For April Gordon, Mark's introduction to Africa was the inspiration for a career focused on the continent. In addition, April owes much to several people at Winthrop University. The moral support, release time, and staff aid generously given by Jack Tucker, chair of the Sociology Department, were vital. Furthermore, Al Lyles, former dean of arts and sciences, and Betsy Brown, the current dean, approved summer stipends and release time; the Winthrop Research Council provided additional financial assistance; and former dean Robin Bowers was kind enough to fund a 1994 Council for International Education Exchange trip to Zimbabwe.

Don Gordon is obliged to many people at Furman University: A special debt is owed to Jim Guth, then chair of the Department of Political Science, for his help in arranging blocks of time for Don to concentrate on this book, and for his advice as a professional editor. In addition, Don is grateful to former vice-president and dean of Furman University, John H. Crabtree, Jr., for his strong support for research trips to Zimbabwe and Malawi and Africa Study Programs in Egypt, Kenya, and Tanzania. Don's research and travel were also underwritten by the Research and Professional Growth Committee of Furman University.

While the impetus for writing this book came from many sources, much of it can be traced to Don Gordon's long-term association with the National Model Organization of African Unity Simulation directed by Michael Nwanze at Howard University. We are both indebted to Michael, to Jack Parson of The College of Charleston, to Ed Baum of Ohio University, and to the other highly committed Africanist professors who made this educational event so successful and from whom we have learned much about how undergraduates learn about Africa.

We extend our thanks to Mary Lou Ingram at the World Bank for her generosity in providing us with most of the photographs we used in the book.

No book can be completed without considerable secretarial assistance. We have been blessed with some of the very best: Peggy Herron of Winthrop and, at Furman, Margaret Crisp and Carolyn Sims. These competent, pleasant professionals cheerfully suffered typing numerous revisions of each chapter.

This book has been significantly improved through the help of several individuals, two of whom we do not know. We gratefully acknowledge two anonymous reviewers whose comments were of considerable help in revising and improving the book, the aid of Claude Stulting of Furman for "editing the editors," and Rick Watson of North Carolina Wesleyan for reviewing several chapters.

Our gratitude to our chapter authors and other contributors to this book is as broad as the African continent. We thank them for their expertise and for their commitment to expanding an appreciation for Africa, not only in this book but in their work in the classroom.

Foremost, we thank our family: our sons, Aaron and Jared, were young children when the first edition of this book was being written. They are now old enough to realize that the time and energy the book took (sometimes away from them) was well spent. Last, we thank Lela, whose fifty years in the classroom are a model to us all.

April A. Gordon
Donald L. Gordon

▪ 1 ▪

Introduction

April A. Gordon & Donald L. Gordon

Most people know very little about sub-Saharan Africa, and most of what they do know is only partially correct or based on stereotypes or an inadequate historical or conceptual framework for understanding and interpretation. For instance, it is not uncommon to find people who believe that Africa is a land of primitive stone-age hunters and gatherers living in the jungle (the Africa of Tarzan movies). Another idea is that Africans are an especially violent people who practice cannibalism, believe in cruel religions and gods, and conduct endemic tribal warfare. At the other extreme are images of Africans as innocents unaware of modern twentieth-century life, like the "Bushman" hero of the movie *The Gods Must Be Crazy*. The media tend to reinforce these perceptions, especially with their almost exclusive focus on negative news, such as drought and famine, civil war, or widespread poverty. While these phenomena certainly exist, there is far more to Africa and its people. Moreover, where Africa is suffering from problems like drought, civil war, and poverty, it is important to know why and what has been or should be done about such tragedies.

Understanding Contemporary Africa has been written to provide the basic concepts, theoretical perspectives, and essential information that are necessary for understanding the dynamic, as well as troubled, region that is Africa today. This book is mainly about sub-Saharan Africa, Africa south of the Sahara. While some mention is made of North Africa, Africa's Asiatic communities, and white settlers (especially in South Africa), those interested in these topics will need to consult additional sources. The authors have written in depth on the most important issues and institutions in Africa. Although these writers are from different disciplines and each chapter is more or less self-contained, a broad portrait of sub-Saharan Africa is discernible.

Geographically, Africa is a massive continent, roughly three and a half times larger than the United States. Africa's range of climates, topography, and physical beauty have created conditions conducive to the formation of an immense diversity of peoples and cultures. Africa is in fact the "home" of humankind, in which every means of livelihood from gathering and hunting to industrialism can be found. At the same time, the enormity of the continent and its often harsh ecological conditions, such as extremes of oppressive heat, vast deserts, marginal soils, and expanses of subtropical vegetation, left many groups relatively isolated from other parts of the world until the last few centuries and limited the concentrations of population and resources that led to the more technologically complex societies of the "old world" and industrial Europe. Despite this relative isolation, some societies had contact with regions as distant as North Africa, India, and even China. Regardless, all developed intricate cultures with rich religious and artistic traditions and complex social and kinship relations.

As is true of other areas of the world, sub-Saharan Africa's history is fraught with episodes of upheaval, violence, and cultural challenges generated from both internal and external forces. For instance, movements of people within the continent led to cross-cultural exchange of ideas, goods, and people as well as to conflict. Foreign religions, mainly Christianity and Islam, were carried by outsiders and resulted in challenges and conflicts not only with local religious beliefs but with long-established customs and ways of life. At the same time, these religions have been incorporated into African societies, changing both in the process. There have also been periods of peace and prosperity in which Africans could live out their lives in relative security and contentment, partly because most lacked the extreme class stratification and state structures that led to so much oppression and exploitation in so-called civilized areas of the world.

Beginning in the 1500s, Africa's history began to commingle with that of an expansionist West in pursuit of trade, booty, and exotic lands and people to conquer. This eventuated in the most cruel and disruptive period in African history, starting with the slave trade and culminating in colonial domination of the continent. This reached its most extreme form in South Africa, whose African majority was ruled until recently by the white descendants of its European colonizers.

Along with its other effects, the Western penetration of Africa exposed Africans to the material riches and culture of the West. As Bohannan and Curtin (1988:16) observe, Africans were not deprived before Western penetration of their societies. Many lived fulfilling lives of great dignity, content without the "trappings of Western civilization." However, once exposed to the possibilities of Western civilization, the lure has proven to be almost irresistible in Africa and elsewhere.

The influence of the West and Western culture is the major transformative force in Africa today. By responding to the promise of acquiring Western affluence, Africans across the continent, to varying degrees, are being integrated into the worldwide network of trade and productive relationships sometimes called "the global capitalist economy." This global economy is dominated for the most part by the few rich, politically and militarily powerful countries of Europe and by the United States—countries that initially gained much of their preeminence from the exploitation of Africans (and other Third World people). As slaves or colonial subjects, Africans' labor and resources (usually obtained directly or indirectly by coercion) provided many of the low-cost raw materials for Western factories and affluent consumer lifestyles.

Since colonialism, African cash crops, minerals, and fuels have continued to be transported overseas, while Western manufactured goods, technology, financial capital, and Western lifestyles are imported to Africa. So far, the "integration" of Africa into the global economy has largely gone badly for most countries on the continent as the cost of Western imports compared to the prices of African exports has become increasingly unfavorable to Africa, leaving almost all countries in debt, their economies a shambles, and living standards spiraling downward. Only a minority of Africans have been able to acquire more than a few tokens of the promised life the West symbolizes.

Another import from the West is Western political systems. Like a hand-me-down suit never fitted to its new wearer, Western multiparty political systems, hastily handed over to Africans experienced mainly in colonial despotism, did not "fit." Most degenerated into one-party states or military dictatorships riddled with corruption and inefficiency. Opposition to the state was either co-opted or ruthlessly repressed. Expected to be the architects of development for their people, African states instead became largely self-serving, bloated bureaucracies alienated from the masses for whom "development" became a more remote prospect as economies began deteriorating from the 1970s on.

Making things worse were the unprecedented growth of population in Africa and the rapid expansion of urban areas. In part, these two related trends both reflected and exacerbated economic and political problems. Certainly, agrarian societies like Africa's value large families. Nonetheless, African family sizes are considerably in excess of those found in most other developing regions. In Africa, inadequate investment in farming, especially in food crops grown mostly by women, keeps most agriculture highly "labor intensive" (dependent on labor rather than machines). Since mainly it is men who migrate to cities for work, women need children more than ever to help them with farm chores. Moreover, as patronage relationships based on ethnicity and kinship are often vital to gaining access to resources (such as jobs, schooling, or money), children are valuable assets even in affluent urban families. For many Africans resources are shrinking because of mounting political and economic problems. Structural adjustment programs (SAPs), designed ostensibly to combat these problems, often compound the hardships instead. The neglect of agriculture and lack of opportunity in rural areas along with the expansion of wage jobs in cities inevitably attract job seekers. Unfortunately, their numbers are far greater than the capacity of cities to employ them or adequately service their needs. The resulting discontent of urbanites is frequently the basis of political opposition to whatever regime is in power and contributes to the problems of political repression and instability.

The way Africans have tried to develop their economies, often on the basis of Western development advice, has indirectly promoted population growth and urbanization by favoring industry, export production, and cities over rural areas. It has also discriminated against women and neglected their interests as producers, mothers, and individuals, with detrimental effects on the economy and social welfare. It has also contributed to environmental degradation, especially soil erosion, deforestation, and desertification. Land scarcity is affecting growing numbers of poor farmers and pastoralists. Lack of resources or technology to improve methods of production, along with lack of opportunity to make a living elsewhere, leaves many people with little recourse to cultivating or grazing their cattle on fragile or marginal land and destroying trees. Western multinational corporations and development agencies, often in league with African business or state elites, have also been guilty of pursuing economic "growth" and profits at the expense of the environment.

As gloomy as this picture of Africa looks, we must remember that African independence is only about thirty years old, or less in some cases. Africans are a practical and adaptive people, as their history and cultures clearly show. Africans have not been locked in hopelessly outmoded traditions, as stereotypes sometimes suggest. Rather, they have always taken from other traditions and cultures what they perceived to be valuable for their own. African resilience and flexibility are in evidence now as in the past. Africans have been experimenting for well over a thousand years with Islam and Christianity and more recently with secular religions such as socialism, capitalism, and Marxism-Leninism, blending them in often quixotic stews with indigenous African practices. That such experimentation produces mixed results should be expected. As Goran Hyden (1983) notes in the title of his book on Africa, there are "no shortcuts to progress," a hard lesson being learned by many Africans whose expectations for quick development have been sharply downscaled as a result of recent trends.

African cultures remain vibrant and are playing a leading role in the efforts to cope with and assess the forces affecting African societies. Questions of personal and collective identity and meaning frequently come to the fore as well as discontent with political oppression, foreign exploitation, and economic inequality and poverty. These concerns are clearly manifested in new forms of religious expression, literature, and political movements for democratization. The extended family remains a vital refuge for most Africans, although the Western nuclear family and challenges to male dominance are growing.

Until recently, it was easy and convenient to blame Africa's problems on the West, and for the most part accurate. The negative legacy of colonialism has been especially profound. Many scholars still contend that the role Africa has been assigned in the global economy as a producer of cheap raw materials continues to prevent it from achieving its economic potential. At least partial blame for Africa's political problems such as coups d'état and authoritarian rule could be laid at the West's doorstep. After all, the West often has had a major role in deciding who came to power or stayed in power. Typically, Western interference in African politics has been determined mostly by geopolitical or economic interests rather than by such lofty goals as democracy or good government. This is apparent in the support accorded dictators like Mobutu Sese Seko of Zaire as well as Western complicity (until recently) in maintaining the brutal apartheid system in South Africa.

As the colonial period recedes in time, more critical attention is being focused on Africans themselves, especially their leaders. This represents, for the most part, a growing awareness that Africans are not simply pawns in the machinations of self-interested Western multinational corporations, bankers, or governments. More Africans are acknowledging that they must address their own shortcomings and institute reforms, be they political, economic, social, or religious renewal. By themselves, such reforms are unlikely to overcome all the inequities of the global economic and political order over which Africa has little control; but only an enlightened and competent African leadership can hope to mobilize the energy and commitment of its people for the challenges that lie ahead.

As Africa approaches the twenty-first century, we must keep some historical perspective to avoid pessimism about the continent's prospects. We must remember that profound societal transformations are under way and that such change often entails considerable suffering, alienation, and disruptions that may take generations to resolve. Mao Zedong, the leader of postrevolutionary China, was once asked by author Edgar Snow what he thought was the significance of the French Revolution. Mao's sage reply was, "I think it's a little too early to tell" (in Whitaker, 1988:12). After little more than one generation of independence, it is certainly "too early to tell" about Africa.

■ **BIBLIOGRAPHY**

Bohannan, Paul, and Philip Curtin. 1988. *Africa and Africans*. Prospect Heights, IL: Waveland Press.

Hyden, Goran. 1983. *No Shortcuts to Progress*. Berkeley: University of California Press.

Whitaker, Jennifer Seymour. 1988. *How Can Africa Survive?* New York: Council on Foreign Relations Press.

■ 2 ■

Africa:
A Geographic Preface
Jeffrey W. Neff

Of all the places of the world for which we can conjure up a mental map, Africa is frequently the "blankest." For this reason, some introduction to the geography of this vast and varied continent is needed (Map 2.1, at the end of this chapter). This chapter and the maps it includes will be useful reference sources as locations and features are mentioned in subsequent chapters.

A student of geography can appreciate the size of the United States (3.6 million square miles/9.5 million square kilometers) and the cultural diversity of its very large (262 million) population. Consider this, however: Three countries the size of the United States could fit into the landmass area of Africa, with a little room to spare! In addition, more than 715 million people live in Africa (over two-thirds of them in sub-Saharan Africa). Africa's population is not only two and a half times larger than that of the United States, but it displays a greater degree of cultural complexity. Of all the world's known languages, over one-third are spoken in Africa (deBlij and Muller, 1991:394). The perception of Africa as a wild, untamed land—vast herds of wild animals, spectacular gorges and waterfalls, towering mountains, trackless forests, great deserts—needs some revision in light of these basic population characteristics.

■ THE MOVING ITCZ

Most Africans are engaged in some form of agriculture or pastoralism, either at a subsistence level (the great majority) or in commercial agriculture (a very small minority). The African economy is further driven by other products harvested or extracted directly from nature, such as forest products and minerals.

7

Nature wields a much heavier hand in Africa in directly influencing the welfare of hundreds of millions of people than it does in the industrialized world where, at least up to now, people have been insulated to some degree from the effects of drought, flood, plagues, and other natural hazards. To understand contemporary Africa, the student of Africa needs a basic knowledge of natural phenomena and processes. In my estimation, the single most powerful environmental mechanism that affects life and survival in Africa south of the Sahara is something called the Intertropical Convergence Zone, or the ITCZ (Map 2.2).

The ITCZ represents a meteorological phenomenon whereby large-scale airflows from generally opposite directions converge or meet, creating a relatively constant updraft of displaced air. The vertical movement is supplemented by buoyant heated air from the sun-soaked, warm surface conditions of the tropical regions. This rising air cools off rapidly, causing atmospheric water vapor (if present) to condense into droplets first, then precipitation (Strahler and Strahler, 1979:100–111). At least, this is the ideal chain of events, and the ITCZ is the primary rainmaking mechanism not only in Africa but throughout the tropical world. Rainfall often occurs as daily thunderstorms and can be torrential during the rainy season.

Note two very important features of Map 2.2. First, the ITCZ shifts pronouncedly from June to January. (The shift is caused by changing earth-sun

Photo: World Bank

Pastoralists in the unpredictable environment of the Sahel move their cattle in search of food and water.

relationships during the year and by the inclination of the earth's axis.) This motion is crucial for the delivery of rainfall to almost all of sub-Saharan Africa and gives most of Africa its wet-and-dry seasonality. When the ITCZ is stationed at its northward June position, the rainy season is on—or should be—and southern Africa is dry. The southward migration of the ITCZ signals rain for the south and the onset of the dry season in the north. And so it has gone, century after century. Some regions, such as the tropical forest belt, get longer rainy seasons and more rain than others, and some regions face greater unpredictability, or precipitation variation (the semi-arid Sahel). Sometimes the ITCZ "misbehaves" and does not shift when it's normally expected to or move where it usually should, bringing stress to the life that depends on it. Generally, though, farming societies throughout Africa continue to coordinate planting and harvesting with the ITCZ's rainmaking mechanism. Pastoralists move their cattle, and herds of wild animals migrate in similar response to seasonal moisture availability. Nature and people have adjusted to a life rhythm tied to this slow, unending, writhing dance of the ITCZ back and forth across the length and breadth of the continent.

■ **NATURAL REGIONS**

Map 2.2 also reveals, in a highly generalized rendition, the natural environments of Africa as depicted by vegetative patterns. The natural vegetation represents the long-term adjustment of complex plant communities to the conditions of the African climate. From a human perspective, these environmental regions possess very different capacities for life support (or carrying capacity). Awareness of the potentials and the problems of these life zones is crucial for survival; exceeding their carrying capacities promises serious penalties for the occupants, as Julius Nyang'oro details in Chapter 8.

Trouble spots abound in the drier margins. The semi-arid, grassy steppe of the Sahel and the East African desert (parts of Kenya, Somalia, and Ethiopia), plagued by an unpredictable ITCZ and burgeoning populations, have been the scenes of human misery periodically during the last two decades. The specter of mass starvation brought on by drought and desertification in the semi-arid regions of the Dry Savanna has been prominent and publicized but not surprising. Tropical wet-and-dry climates have always been problematic for their human occupants. In the twentieth century, an exploding population has exceeded beyond all reason the ability of the more fragile, marginal zones to support it.

Even the "humid" tropical forest of Africa is not immune from trouble. Here, drought and desertification are removed as threats to be replaced by rampant deforestation, primarily for hardwood harvest and plantation expansion. At current rates of cutting, much of the easily accessible forests

The semi-arid Sahel is becoming increasingly vulnerable to drought and desertification, putting villages like this one in Burkina Faso at growing risk.

of coastal West and East Africa will be gone by the year 2000. Probably only the relatively insulated interior forests of the eastern Congo (Zaire) Basin will survive into the next century. Without controls, they too will likely disappear by mid-century.

The "friendlier" Wet Savanna will come under increasing pressure as population growth and the movement of environmental refugees from the deteriorating Dry Savanna place undue strains on its carrying capacity. But almost all of tropical Africa is marked by poor, infertile, sometimes sterile soils, and the Wet Savanna has only limited agricultural potential. Only temperate South Africa is soil "rich"; however, it cannot sustain more than a fraction of Africa's future food needs.

Sub-Saharan Africa's natural regions are fragile and seem destined for continuing problems. If predicted global climatic changes affect the already erratic character and behavior of the ITCZ, the human carrying capacity of these natural regions could be reduced rapidly and massively. This is not a pleasant prospect to contemplate, but every student of Africa should be aware of the possibility. In the midst of the Sahelian drought of 1968–1974, for example, unusually large numbers of adult males in Upper Volta (now Burkina Faso) and Niger left their villages to search for jobs in more favored agricultural areas to the south or in large towns such as Abidjan and Lagos in the richer coastal countries. Such sudden movements placed heavy burdens on the meager support services and social balances of the destination areas (Caldwell, 1977:95–96).

■ **CONTINENTS ADRIFT:
AFRICA, THE "MOTHER" OF LANDMASSES**

There is another geographic attribute crucial to the understanding of Africa, and most students who have had some earth science are aware of it. Until about 100 million years ago, the earth's landmasses were bound together as a supercontinent known as Pangaea. The southern landmasses constituted Gondwana, with present-day Africa the keystone. Through the phenomenon of plate tectonics, or continental drift, Africa's "children" began to leave the nest and scatter to their present positions: North and South America, Antarctica, Australia, and India all moved away from "mother" Africa, leaving her with her distinctive present-day shape and configuration. More important, it left her with relatively sharp, steep edges on all sides where the other plates tore away. (The presence of deep rift valleys in eastern Africa suggests that this continental separation process is not yet complete; Africa may be further fractured and split along the rift zone. The Red Sea is an expanding "rift," and eastern Africa could eventually pull away from the continent.) This steep edge is known generally as the Great Escarpment, and it is very prominent in eastern and southern Africa and somewhat less pronounced, but evident, in western Africa. It commences its sharp ascent just a few miles inland from the coast and, once topped, a high plateau-like landscape unfolds. Broad coastal lowlands are generally absent (Church et al., 1977:23, 26).

There are several interesting, important, and unique phenomena associated with this continental morphology that have had direct, powerful impacts on human history and activity in Africa.

□ Carriers and Barriers

"Carriers and barriers" refers to phenomena that influence, control, channel, restrict, or enhance various human spatial processes. An analysis of the pattern of railways and navigable waterways reveals the incomplete and unconnected nature of these linkages (Map 2.3). Oddly, except for the Nile River and the lower Niger River, most river transport does not connect with the coast. Why not? Primarily because of the barriers of falls and rapids created where major rivers fall over or break through the Great Escarpment in their escape to the sea. The most navigable stretches of water occur on interior sections of African rivers. Water access from the sea to Africa's interior is now and always has been physically restricted.

Nor does the Great Escarpment stimulate railway and road building between coast and interior. Some stretches of the escarpment tower 2,000 to 4,000 feet and more above the adjacent coastal lowland, especially in southern Africa (e.g., the Drakensberg). Construction is difficult and very expensive; some rail lines were built only where access to valuable raw materials warranted the effort. Note too the dearth of natural harbors and major ports along Africa's steep, smooth, and regular coastline, highlighting the difficulty of access to the interior. Movement *within* Africa has been easier, and in regions such as western Africa, a fairly lively intraregional trade developed over the centuries prior to European contact, as both Tom O'Toole and Virginia DeLancey document in later chapters.

In fact, most of the significant states and empires that evolved within Africa through the centuries did so in the *interior* of the continent, not along the coastal margins (Map 2.4). By geographic edict, Africa's insular tendency was established long ago and was only slightly reoriented with the beginnings of the slave trade, first by the Arabs in eastern Africa, then more violently by the Europeans (sixteenth century) in western and equatorial Africa. Still, for three centuries European contact and interest remained peripheral; the walls of "Fortress Africa" were violated and permanently breached by these "invaders" only in the nineteenth century.

The Berlin Conference of 1884–1885 and the ensuing partitioning of

Photo: World Bank

The relative isolation of the African interior from the coast was reinforced during colonial times, when transportation links were determined by colonial interests. Improving infrastructure, such as roads, has been a major priority since independence.

Africa among the European powers symbolized the inevitable geographic reorientation of Africa and Africans and a wholesale dismantling of their states, societies, and livelihoods, to be replaced by European models (Betts, 1972). By the eve of World War I, a new type of fragmentation, as powerful in its own way as the Gondwana breakup 100 million years earlier, had changed the face of "the Mother of Continents" forever (Map 2.5). The historical and political dynamics of these periods are treated in great detail in Chapters 3 and 4.

☐ The Resource Base

The huge, high block of mostly metamorphic rock that became post-Gondwana Africa may have hindered outside penetration, but geologic forces created some powerful attractions for European exploiters. The ancient metamorphic rock of Africa is highly "mineralized." Map 2.3 reveals the occurrence and location of some of these mineral resources, coveted by an industrial world.

In several categories of industrial raw materials and minerals, Africa contains some highly ranked producing countries and regions. The copper-laden zone straddling the borders of Zambia and Zaire, for example, accounts for about 7 percent of the world's output of that mineral, making it the fourth-ranked production region in the world (after Chile, the United States, and Canada). Zambia and Zaire also account for roughly half the world's output of cobalt, a critical ferroalloy in jet and rocket engines, and provide the United States with over a third of its cobalt needs (*CRB Commodity Yearbook,* 1994).

Other important resource producers would include Guinea, which is second only to Australia in bauxite production (for aluminum); South Africa and Zimbabwe, which together provide nearly 30 percent of the global output of chromite, a strategic metallic mineral crucial to steel manufacturing in the industrial world; and Nigeria, which has consistently been among the top five exporters of crude oil to the United States and is Africa's top petroleum producer, ahead of both Algeria and Libya (United Nations, 1994:180–181).

As previously mentioned, many transportation lines exist primarily to provide access to these resources, not to interconnect Africa. Furthermore, many mineral sites were revealed only after the European partitioning process was completed and several mineral zones were divided between opposing states (e.g., the Copperbelt between Zaire and Zambia), contributing to tension and conflict in postcolonial Africa.

Although rich in metallic ores, Africa's geology yields only a few favored fossil fuel occurrences (coal, oil, and gas are normally associated with sedimentary rather than metamorphic rock), namely, the petroleum of the Niger River Delta, Gabon, Angola, and Algeria/Libya, and the coal of South Africa. Thus, Africa exports its metallic ores and imports much of its energy.

Another resource that exists in great potential abundance in Africa is directly related to the problematic topography of the landmass itself: water power. Although deficient in fossil-fuel energy resources (Nigeria, Gabon, Angola, and South Africa are exceptions), sub-Saharan Africa is "rich" in hydroelectric potential. The specific sites of this potential are where major rivers experience impressive drops—and therefore rapids and falls—in their escape routes from the continent's interior. Electricity generation at these sites could conceivably enhance economic development over large regions. Several noteworthy projects have been completed for just this purpose: the Nile's Aswan High Dam in Egypt; the Zambezi's Kariba Dam, shared by Zambia and Zimbabwe; and the Volta's Akosombo Dam in Ghana. In fact, Africa possesses the greatest hydroelectric potential of any continent, and the intent of these projects has been to "tap" some of it.

More intriguing than the presence of such projects, however, is their small number in Africa. Most rivers are *not* being harnessed for power generation, and few hydroelectric facilities exist. Resource abundance, large "reserves" of power, and seemingly infinite potential have not been reconfigured into actual use for a very basic economic reason: lack of markets. Africans use very little electricity. They are predominantly farmers and laborers—and they are income-poor. Industry, a big potential user of electrical power, is not a significant part of Africa's economic mix. Cities are also viable concentrated electricity markets, but most Africans are village dwellers, not urbanites. A huge capital investment is required to build dams and generating facilities, to transport the electricity great distances, and to distribute it in regional grids. Achieving a reasonable return on such an investment in Africa would be extremely difficult; therefore, this particular component of the continent's resource base remains greatly underexploited.

The long exposure of the ancient African landmass to the tropical sun and rain—and to the force of gravity—has also removed much of the original surface material by erosion. The poor tropical soil that remains holds little fertility, and alluvial soils (the deep, rich, stream-deposited sediments found on floodplains and deltas) and rich volcanic soils are uncommon on the high plateau surface. (The fertile soils of the alluvial Inland Niger Delta between Segou and Timbuktu in Mali and the volcanically derived soils of Cameroon and the Kenya highlands are examples of exceptions to this generalization.) Many of the better coastal sites are held by large plantation operations geared to products for export.

As previously mentioned, nontropical southern Africa is "richer" in soil fertility and can be considered an exception to the African rule of low soil productivity. Cooler temperatures mark this projection of the African landmass into the middle latitudes of the Southern Hemisphere. Latitudinal position and the high elevation of South Africa's Highveld combine with lower rainfall to reduce the leaching of soil nutrients, while simultaneously allowing for a thicker accumulation of organic material (humus), which is a critical factor in soil fertility. The resulting greater productivity of South African soil has supported the development of a diverse agricultural economy that is relatively free of tropical disease vectors and is grain and livestock-based (corn, wheat, sheep, and cattle). The shifting cultivation practices so typical of tropical Africa, described in Chapter 8 by Julius Nyang'oro, are replaced here by permanent and prosperous small family farms.

For most Africans, however, agriculture remains subsistence, and food supply problems have increased with the growing population, an issue treated more fully in later chapters on the economy, environment, and population.

Nature, history, and the global economic system have combined to deprive Africans of much potential wealth and well-being. In many instances, the artificially imposed unity of the colonial era exacerbated conflict. Supranationalism—multistate political and economic cooperation to identify and promote shared objectives—remains highly elusive, frustrated by a disjointed transportation system, ethnic/tribal conflicts, and an illogical political geography of too many fragmented nation-states (Map 2.6). A problematic environment, an exploding population, and the political-geographic realities of late twentieth-century Africa may ultimately conspire to quickly drain this vast continent of the vitality and energy that is still there in the form of raw material wealth, food-production capacity, and resourceful human spirit. These issues and others will be addressed in the following chapters, which explore the political, economic, environmental, and social forces determining Africa's destiny.

■ BIBLIOGRAPHY

Best, Alan C. G., and Harm J. deBlij. 1977. *African Survey.* New York: John Wiley and Sons.

Betts, Raymond F. 1972. *The Scramble for Africa: Causes and Dimensions of Empire.* Lexington, MA: D. C. Heath.

Caldwell, J. C. 1977. "Demographic Aspects of Drought: An Examination of the African Drought of 1970–1974." Pp. 93–99 in D. Dalby, R. J. H. Church, and F. Bezzaz (eds.). *Drought in Africa.* London: International African Institute.

Church, R. J. H., John I. Clarke, P. J. H. Clarke, and H. J. R. Henderson. 1977. *Africa and the Islands.* New York: John Wiley and Sons.

CRB Commodity Yearbook 1994. New York: John Wiley and Sons, Knight-Ridder Financial/Commodity Research Bureau.

deBlij, Harm J., and Peter O. Muller. 1991. *Geography: Regions and Concepts.* New York: John Wiley and Sons.

Strahler, Arthur N., and Alan H. Strahler. 1979. *Elements of Physical Geography.* New York: John Wiley and Sons.

Turner, Howard. 1986. *Africa South of the Sahara.* Burnt Mill, Harlow (Essex), England: Longman.

Udo, Reuben K. 1978. *A Comprehensive Geography of West Africa.* New York: Africana.

United Nations. 1994. *United Nations Energy Statistics Yearbook 1992.* New York: United Nations.

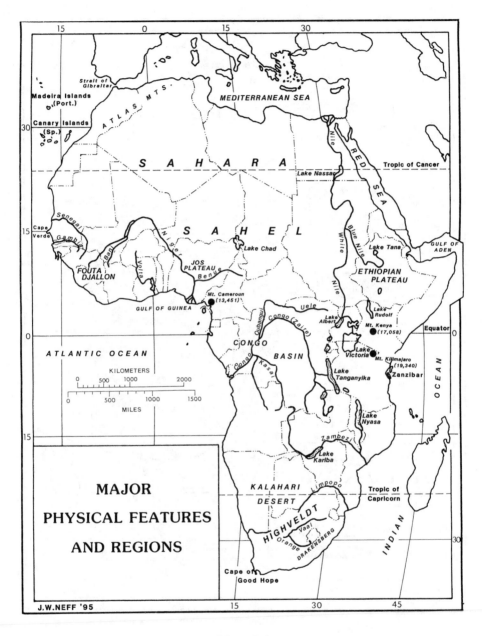

MAJOR
PHYSICAL FEATURES
AND REGIONS

J.W.NEFF '95

Map 2.1

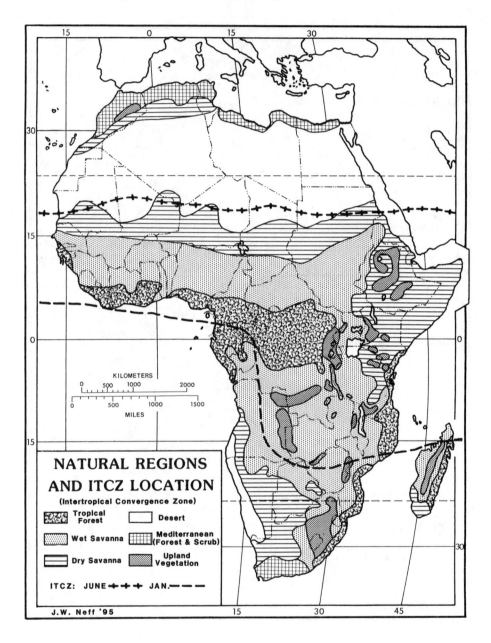

Map 2.2

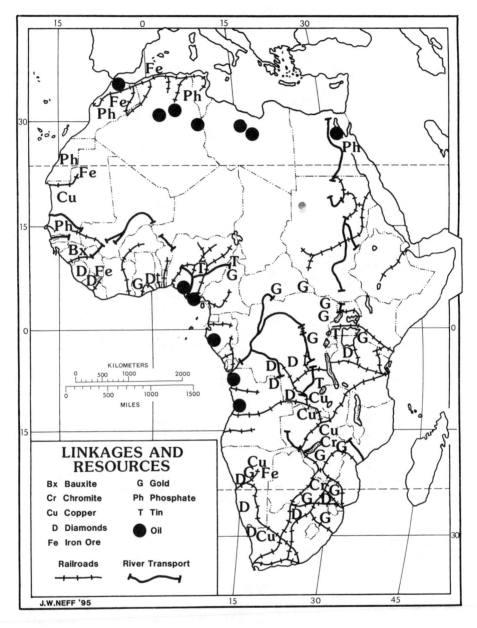

Map 2.3

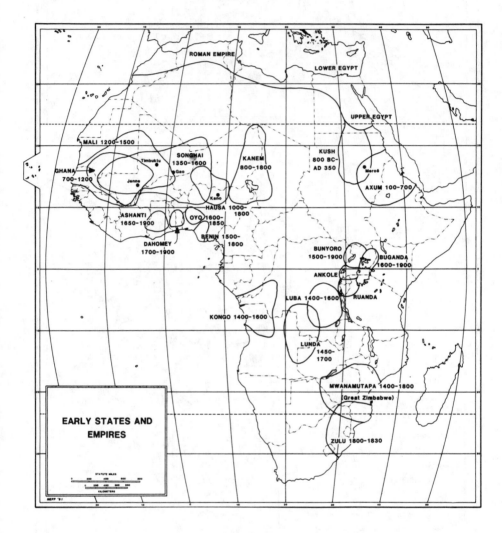

Map 2.4

Adapted from Alan C. G. Best and Harm J. deBlij, *African Survey*, New York: John Wiley and Sons, 1977, p. 64; and Reuben K. Udo, *A Comprehensive Geography of West Africa*, New York: Africana, 1978, p. xiv.

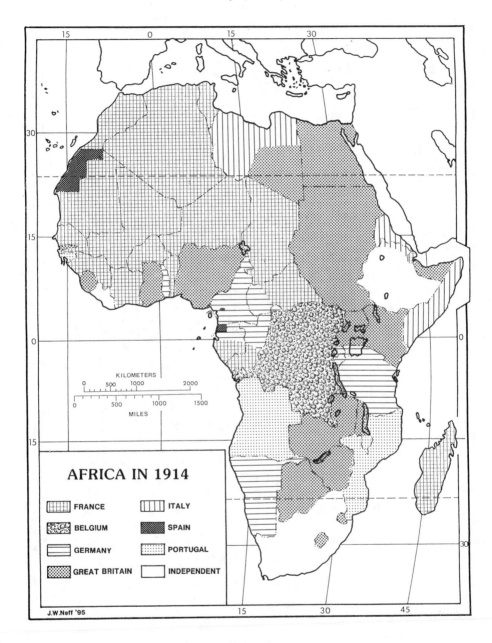

Map 2.5

Adapted from R. F. Beets, *The Scramble for Africa: Causes and Dimensions of Empire*, Lexington, MA: D. C. Heath, 1972, p. xiv.

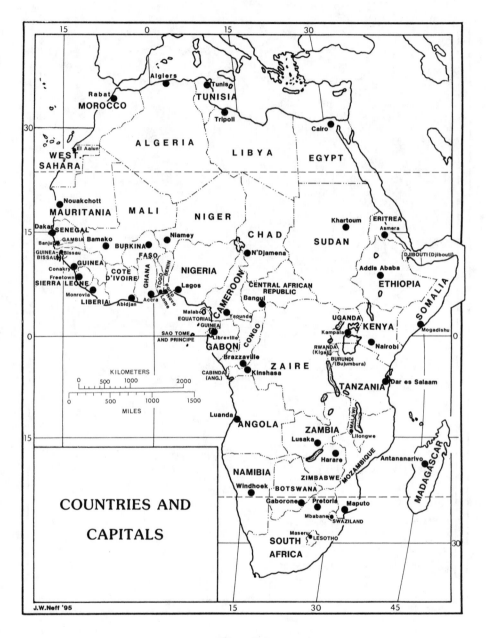

Map 2.6

Abuja, Dodoma, and Yamassoukro are the new legal capitals of Nigeria, Tanzania, and Côte d'Ivoire, respectively; but most government activities continue to be conducted in the capital cities named on this map.

▪ 3 ▪

The Historical Context
Thomas O'Toole

As Jeffrey Neff points out in Chapter 2, Africa is a huge and geographically diverse continent over three times as large as the United States and several times larger than Europe (see Map 2.1). This chapter focuses on Africa south of the Sahara, though contacts between northern and sub-Saharan Africa have been extensive. Because sub-Saharan Africa's history is distinctive in many ways from that of northern Africa, it warrants separate treatment (in the same way that South Asia is studied separately from other areas of the Asian continent). In the south of Africa, I have set the Limpopo River as the limit, because South Africa is covered in depth in Chapter 13.

I have also set some pragmatic limits on the time focus of this chapter. I begin about 200,000 years ago since that is a reasonable estimate, based on current evidence, for the presence of our species, *Homo sapiens,* on the continent. I conclude the chapter with the end of colonialism and the independence period. The postindependence period will be discussed thematically in the remaining chapters of the book.

This chapter presents a general historical background on Africa to facilitate understanding of the issues treated in subsequent chapters. Many present-day conflicts and problems in Africa stem from economic, social, and political changes associated with the establishment of European colonial rule. However, as important as colonialism is, patterns and identities established over the millennia of precolonial African history influenced the colonial experience and continue to be a powerful force shaping postcolonial Africa. To see Africa in its historical context is to grasp the complexity of the continent and to appreciate the ingenuity and dynamism of its people as they respond to the challenges posed by history. We can also appreciate, to paraphrase Karl Marx, that while Africans created and continue to create their own history, they do so under conditions that, in many cases, they do not control.

■ **THE PEOPLING OF AFRICA**

□ **The Cradle of Humankind**

The African savannas of mixed grasslands and scattered trees, which developed as part of a worldwide cooling and drying trend about 10 million years ago, are the ancestral homeland of all humankind. The toolmaking and fire-using genus *Homo* emerged on these savannas more than 2 million years ago. The earliest forms of modern humans, *Homo sapiens,* appeared in Africa between 200,000 and 100,000 years ago and from there began populating other parts of the world.

By about 100,000 years ago, regionally specialized cultural complexes of sophisticated stone tool–using populations had developed in Africa and elsewhere. On the southern border of the Mediterranean basin and in the savanna regions of eastern and southern Africa, two distinct gathering and hunting cultures seem to have emerged, with only slightly different adaptations to their savanna habitats. A third cultural complex adapting to the tropical forest environment probably was also evolving on the eastern and southern fringes of the central African forests.

It seems reasonable to identify, in a general way, three major linguistic groups in Africa with these three cultural complexes by about 12,000 years ago. The Mediterranean cultural complex can be associated with the Afro-Asiatic language family, while the eastern and southern savanna cultures generally correspond to the Khoisan ("click") language family. The tropical rainforest cultural complexes can be linked to the Niger-Congo family. A fourth major linguistic group, the Nilo-Saharan, can probably be associated with another cultural complex, highly adapted to fishing, which flourished in the entire central, south-central, and southeastern Sahara between 7,500 and 4,000 years ago, when the Sahara received far more rainfall than it does now (Shillington, 1989:5–18).

□ **Gathering and Hunting**

In general, Africans, like all other humans, made their living by gathering and hunting until about 7,000 years ago, when increasing populations and the climatic shift, which would ultimately create the Sahara Desert, made food cultivation and animal herding necessary. Archaeological evidence and comparisons with surviving gathering and hunting peoples indicate that African gatherers and hunters adapted their tools and ways of life to three basic African environments: the moist tropical rainforests with their hardwoods and small game; the more open savannas with their diversity of large game living in grasslands, woods, and forests along the rivers; and riverbank and lakeside ecologies found along major water courses or around lakes and ponds.

I must point out, though, that rainforest, savanna, and waterside habitats differed greatly from place to place, and the societies found in them differed more among themselves and were far more complex than this general overview might imply. I could easily devote a whole chapter to pointing out, in each habitat, some differences between ways and styles of life that were the products of ceaseless change over millennia. The political, social, and economic histories of each specific society, along with its history of ideas, values, and ideology, could fill whole volumes. With such diversity it is obvious that savanna dwellers, rainforest dwellers, and people in water-focused societies were not so perfectly adapted to a single environment as to be incapable of leaving one for the other. These three environmental niches are simply explanatory categories. In the real world, environments merge gradually into others, as do the societies living within them.

Despite the myriad of habitats and diversity among their inhabitants as well as the internal differences that existed within them, it still makes sense to generalize about rainforest societies. Many forest dwellers, well into the twentieth century, lived in bands of thirty to fifty individuals. Their pursuit of game and harvesting of a variety of insect, stream, and plant foods kept them on the move in a rather fixed cycle as various foods came into season at different locations in their foraging areas. Consequently, they constructed only temporary shelters of leaves and poles, very functional for a life in which more permanent structures would have been useless. Drawing equally upon vegetable and animal food sources, with the men specializing in hunting and the women in gathering, they had little need for contact with outsiders or for exploration beyond the confines of their own regular territories. In hunting and gathering societies, female economic functions along with childbearing were absolutely crucial. Women typically generated more food through gathering than did the men, who hunted animals or looked for game that had already been killed. Hunting and gathering societies appear to have developed delicately balanced social relationships that permitted necessary group decisions without the need for defined leaders. Quite likely, their moral, ethical, and artistic sensitivities resembled those of their modern descendants, the Mbuti or M'Baka (sometimes called pygmies), who still live in the rainforests of equatorial Africa.

Savanna-dwelling gatherers and hunters led similarly mobile lives but often specialized in the collection of wild cereals that grew in their grassy plains and the occasional hunting of large grass-eating animals—giraffe, zebra, warthog, and many species of antelope. In particularly favorable circumstances, savanna dwellers might congregate in groups of 300 or more during the rainy seasons, when vegetation was lush and game plentiful. They dispersed in groups of 30 to 100 during the dry months to hunt, first with sticks and game pits, and later with nets, bows and arrows, and poisons. As populations grew, their contacts with other groups intensified until territories emerged, and exotic shells, stones, feathers, and other less durable items were passed in sporadic trade over distances of hundreds of miles. Their history consisted of the gradual refinement of gathering and hunting techniques, a slow spread of new inventions from one group to another, and, probably, the very slow growth of population (Parkington, 1980:695–727).

□ Fishing

Major fishing communities in Africa predate the development of techniques of growing food crops and taming animals. Many settlements were clustered around the lakes and rivers of what are now the dry southern reaches of the Sahara. During the last great wet period in Africa's climate, from about 11,000 to 5,000 years ago, Lake Chad rose to cover a huge area many times its present size and overflowed southwestward into the Benue-Niger rivers, which empty into the Atlantic Ocean. This huge lake was fed by rivers from the Tibesti Plateau in the central Sahara. Quite probably Lake Nakaru in present-day Kenya overflowed into the Great Rift valley, while Lake Turkana was one of the headwaters of the Nile (Shillington, 1989:12–13). The inland delta of the Niger in present-day Mali was far more vast and held enormous quantities of water in permanent lakes.

In these lands of lakes and rivers lived thriving fishing communities. They carved intricate harpoon barbs and fishhooks out of bone, fired some of the earliest pottery in Africa, probably wove baskets and nets of reeds, and hunted crocodile, hippopotamus, and waterfowl. More important, these fishing peoples supported themselves without constant movement and at much higher population densities than gathering and hunting would allow. The need to cooperate in order to fish efficiently encouraged people to settle in larger and more permanent villages. The centralized coordination required in these larger settlements led to more formalized leadership structures, with experienced elders or single arbitrators making decisions. Some individuals could, for the first time, gain more wealth in the form of fishing equipment and houses than others in the village. These fishing peoples probably traded dried fish for plant and animal products offered by their gatherer-hunter neighbors. Local commercial networks developed, and new ideas spread more rapidly to larger areas. Fishing peoples probably played a crucial role in the transition from gathering and hunting to more settled ways of life (Sutton, 1980:521–524).

□ Farming and Herding

Most scholars overgeneralize when they suggest that the Agricultural Revolution was a great step forward for humankind. Only with the invention of agriculture—and in Africa, hoe-farming (or horticulture)—could the human species create the elaborate social and cultural patterns that most

Herding societies have existed in Africa for thousands of years.

Much African agriculture is hoe-farming. Agriculture was most likely invented thousands of years ago by women.

people today would recognize. And only in agricultural societies did the separation between rulers and ruled, inequality between men and women, and
the institution of slavery evolve. In Africa the move to crop raising evolved
much more slowly in most places than it did in southwest Asia, for example.
A few very functional gathering and hunting societies continued into the
twentieth century in a variety of African natural environments. Though
farming allows larger populations than hunting and gathering, the environmental realities of Africa limit its agricultural potential in most places.
Because of the continent's location on the equator, Africa generally has very
fixed wet and dry seasons. This limits agricultural production and animal
pasturing during the six or seven dry months. Three-fifths of the continent
is desert, much of the rest has large areas of poor soils, and the more humid
areas are home to the malaria-carrying mosquito and the parasitic infection–carrying tsetse fly. Africa's relatively light population density throughout history demonstrates the very real limits the continent's physical environment placed on the development of settled farming. In Africa the rainfall
and soils often meant that farming and herding peoples were more exposed
to the dangers of famine caused by natural disasters such as drought or
flood. In most African hoe-farming communities, gathering, hunting, and
especially fishing have remained important sources of food and general
livelihood (Coquery-Vidrovitch, 1988:7–18, 115–129).

For many historians of Africa, a major question is why Africans ever
turned to farming at all, given the effectiveness of the hunting and gathering
lifestyles. A logical, schematic reconstruction of what happened might be
made based on several explanations, but none based on direct knowledge.
One, which has considerable support, is given here as an example.

The fishing cultures, which evolved near lakes and rivers in the African
savannas between the Sahara and the forests and in eastern Africa after the
last Ice Age, allowed relatively large stationary populations with new skills
and populations to increase. At the same time, these peoples began to
domesticate animals, especially cattle, using skills acquired from hunting
game that gathered near watering places. Five or six thousand years ago the
Sahara was drying up, pushing to its margins large populations that could
not adapt to the change without moving. Much African agricultural innova-
tion apparently was forced upon people by the population pressures that
grew along the waterways to the south and east of this expanding desert
(Curtin et al., 1978:7–11).

How agriculture developed is much easier to guess at than it is to ascer-
tain why it developed. Women, the gathering specialists, became aware of
where particularly good crops, especially grains, grew, and they camped on
sites where these crops were plentiful. Over time, the harvested seeds were
planted, and larger and more firmly attached seed heads developed. In the
widespread African savanna, millets and sorghums were domesticated. In
the Ethiopian highlands and the Futa Djallon, *teff* and *fonio,* grasslike grains

with tiny kernels, became the respective staples. In the marshlands of the interior delta of the Niger River in present-day Mali, a type of rice was cultivated. East Africans probably planted *ensete,* a crop related to the banana. Other root crops and the native oil palm of western Africa enabled agriculturalists to penetrate the forests. Yet, for most gathering and hunting populations of southern and central Africa, there was little pressure to change from a way of life that had proven quite satisfactory for thousands of years. The growth of population, which accompanied the slow shift to agriculture, set in motion another important process in African history (Shillington, 1989:29–32).

□ Bantu Migrations

Early in the twentieth century, scholars were struck by the remarkable similarities in the languages and cultures of peoples living throughout the vast area stretching east from present-day Cameroon to Kenya and on south to the Republic of South Africa. All these peoples spoke languages having the word-stem *ntu,* or something very similar to it, meaning "person." The prefix *ba* denotes the plural in most of these languages so that *ba-ntu* means, literally, "people." The source of these languages and the farming and herding cultures associated with them and how they became so widespread in Africa were major questions by the mid–twentieth century.

One plausible—though still speculative—answer is based on linguistics, archaeology, and studies of plant origins. According to this account, about 3,000 years ago near the Benue River in the western African savannas, fairly large-scale settlements guided by councils of lineage elders had evolved based on fishing with dugout canoes, nets, fishhooks, traps, and harpoons. Cultivating yams and oil palms and raising goats, these Bantu-speaking peoples were better able to survive drought and misfortune than the small pockets of cultivators that might have developed in and south of the tropical rainforests of central Africa. Having long mastered the art of firing pottery, these Bantu speakers had learned on their own or from peoples in northern Africa to smelt iron for spears, arrows, hoes, scythes, and axes by at least 2,500 years ago. Population pressures grew along the Benue as Saharan farmers slowly moved south to escape the gradually drying desert. Pushed by growing populations, the Bantu fisherpeoples moved south and east. After reaching the Zaire (Congo) tributaries, they spread up the rivers of central Africa to the Zambezi and on south to the tip of Africa. Bantu-speaking groups intermarried with, conquered, or pushed out the Khoisan speakers and other populations they encountered. As they slowly migrated, these Bantu-speaking peoples learned to cultivate Asian yams and bananas, which had been introduced to eastern Africa by Malayo-Polynesian sailors who colonized the island of Madagascar about 1,800 years ago. In some cases, the Bantu-speaking migrants became large-scale cattle keepers. By 1,000 years ago, most of central and southern Africa was populated by iron-smelting, Bantu-speaking villagers who had virtually replaced all but scattered pockets of the original gathering and hunting peoples (Lamphear, 1986:78–86).

■ POLITICAL PATTERNS OF THE PAST

□ Stateless Societies

Until recently, most historians relied on written sources, so most history tended to be about societies with writing. Since most African societies did not develop writing, the historical record was sparse, gleaned from accounts of non-African travelers, notably the Muslims, and archaeological remains. In the past forty years, specialists in African history have learned to use historical linguistics, oral traditions, and other sources to overcome the apparent lack of evidence and develop a far better understanding of African history. Views like those voiced as late as 1965 by Hugh Trevor-Roper, regius professor of history at Oxford University, are virtually a thing of the past. Trevor-Roper said:

> Undergraduates, seduced as always by the changing breath of journalistic fashion, demand that they should be taught the history of black Africa. Perhaps, in the future there will be some African history to teach. But at present there is none, or very little: there is only the history of Europeans in Africa, The rest is darkness. . . . And darkness is not a subject for history. . . . [There are only] the unrewarding gyrations of barbarous tribes in picturesque but irrelevant corners of the globe. (Trevor-Roper, 1965:1)

Nevertheless, most world history texts continue to treat human societies without writing as "prehistoric." This is rather ironic given that even in those complex urban-centered societies called civilizations, which have had written records for more than 5,000 years, only a small minority of people were literate and most people did not live in cities. Certainly in Africa this pre-historic-historic distinction has little value. Most historians of Africa realize that a focus on written sources alone would mean virtually ignoring the histories of the vast majority of Africa's peoples, who were able to achieve through kinship, ritual, and other means relatively orderly and just societies without centralized governments or states.

In fact, until about 2,500 years ago, virtually all Africans living south of the Sahara were able to avoid relying on the bureaucratic organization called "the state" to carry out the political requirements of their societies. Even large groups created social systems based on lineage (kinship) with no single center of power or authority. Ideally, such systems could accommodate

Photo: World Bank

Most Africans have long relied on decentralized, kinship-based political systems. In Burkina Faso, male family heads meet to discuss a rural development project.

several million people. On the local level, lineage systems depended on a balance of power to solve political problems. They controlled conflict and resolved disputes through a balance of centers of cooperation and opposition, which appear to have been almost universal in human societies. (Brian Siegel explains in Chapter 9 how these systems worked in practice.) This human ethic of cooperation was especially crucial in herding and agricultural societies that existed in the often challenging physical environments of Africa (Turnbull, 1973:233–255).

Variations of lineage systems also helped Africans resist European colonial domination. For example, colonial attempts to divide Africa into districts, cantons, and even tribes were doomed to failure when most of the continent south of the Sahara was really a kaleidoscope of lineage fragments, scattering and regrouping as the need arose. Through marriage alliances and various forms of reciprocal exchanges, these networks could expand almost indefinitely. As another example, European officials erroneously assumed that their control of an important African authority figure ensured the "pacification" of a given territory. The Africans, on the other hand, could simply turn to another member of a kinship linkage and continue their struggle against the outsiders.

Africa's past demonstrates the truly remarkable ability of African peoples to resist incorporation into state political and economic organizations right up to the present (Hyden, 1980). This represents one of the most unusual aspects of the continent's history. As Siegel explains in Chapter 9, many Africans still rely on extended family organizations and call upon kinship behavior to maintain justice and cultural and territorial integrity, not only in domestic but also in wider spheres (see also Mair, 1974). And, as in the past, many Africans see any state without at least some symbolic lineage-based authority as inherently tyrannical. The continuing desire to seek and find order in institutions other than the state is very understandable in the African context.

Yet, to those accustomed to state forms of organization, African social organization based on kinship seems chaotic, and nonstate societies are seen as less civilized or lacking in sociopolitical development. To dispel the notion that Africa lacked civilization, many dedicated Africanists have focused almost exclusively on the relatively unrepresentative centralized states when portraying Africa's past. This has sometimes obscured, however, the important role of local kinship relations in maintaining peace and harmony in most African societies. But since state societies as well as nonstate societies have a long history in Africa, the significance of state societies in Africa's development will be examined next.

□ State Societies

Many of the first historians of Africa hypothesized that African states were largely the result of an idea of divine kingship diffused from Egypt (Curtin et al., 1978:30–37). Most scholars now realize that African states, like states elsewhere in the world, arose from a variety of causes and probably resulted from internal forces present in various areas of the continent. (See Map 2.4 for early states and empires.) In many parts of Africa, control over long-distance trade was an important aspect of the origin of states. Control of military force for conquest and protection was also generally present. In most cases, African states or kingdoms typically retained an element of kinship-based social organization. In fact, the process of state-building was usually a long one in which rulers gradually established special privileges for their own lineages and created a superlineage basis for authority (Freund, 1984:25–27). This caused a certain reciprocity of mutual obligations between the subjects and their rulers that persisted for generations in all but the most authoritarian states. Rulers brought prosperity to their people and organized the military to protect them, while the ruled supported their rulers with subsistence goods, labor, and even service in the military.

The first regional states in Africa were those that united independent farming communities growing up below the first cataract in Egypt about 5,500 years ago. Here the gradual drying of the Sahara Desert had forced together growing populations from the desert into a diminishing crop-growing area dependent upon the annual Nile floods. From this time until Egypt was conquered by the armies of Alexander the Great, the pharaohs, priests, and nobility of Egypt were able to extract surplus wealth from the farmers of the valley and to war with, trade with, and interact with the Nubians south of the cataract. The Egyptian ruling elite controlled irrigation and other public works and justified their rule through claims that the pharaoh was a god-king incarnate (Shillington, 1989:18–29).

Farther to the south, in a land the Egyptians called Kush, another independent political entity (though not continuously so) developed by about 3,800 years ago. Achieving its greatest power between 2,800 and 2,700 years ago, the history of Kush was closely linked to that of Egypt. In fact, Kushite kings ruled Egypt from about 700 to 500 B.C. Driven from Egypt about 2,500 years ago, the Kushite leaders pushed farther south into Meroe, where a vast iron industry flourished. The causes of the rise of Kush and the extent to which its political ideas and metallurgical techniques spread are still open to considerable discussion. Meroe's successor states adopted Coptic Christianity from Axum (Ethiopia) as a court religion, but this was replaced by Islam more than 1,000 years ago. Four hundred years ago the Sennar kingdom imposed unity over much of this area, forcing peasants to pay heavy taxes to subsidize their rulers' households. A large, literate merchant class established itself in numerous towns and played a crucial role in deepening the Islamic cultural influence so important in the northern part of the present-day republic of Sudan (Leclant, 1980:295–314; Hakem, 1980:315–346).

Still farther south in the Ethiopian highlands, Axum, another major state dating back more than 2,000 years, rose to challenge Kush. The founders of Axum migrated from southern Arabia 2,100 years ago and later extended their authority over the northern half of what are now Ethiopia and eastern Sudan. Two thousand years ago they controlled ports on the Red Sea and maintained trade relations with merchants from the eastern end of the Mediterranean who came to buy ivory, gold, and incense from the African interior. Four hundred years later Axum's rulers became Christians and expanded to control other lesser-known states that had also arisen in the central and southern highlands of Ethiopia. An Amhara-speaking state, which arose in the north-central area of the Ethiopian highlands about 700 years ago, claimed some ties to the long-collapsed Axum. This state (the ancestor of today's Ethiopia) was based on an expanding landowning class. It flourished 500 to 600 years ago, broke up, and was then substantially reunited in the eighteenth century (Oliver and Crowder, 1981:121–124, 144–145, 155, 204).

State formation in the savannas of western Africa lagged after the Roman defeat of the Phoenician-founded city of Carthage (in Tunisia). This city-state had conducted a flourishing trans-Saharan trade with sub-Saharan

Africans through Berber partners between 2,800 to 2,500 years ago. Gradually, kingdoms created by horse-mounted forces establishing control over small agricultural communities developed in the Senegambia and the middle Niger about 2,000 years ago. The first of these western African states (mentioned by travelers writing in Arabic) was Tekrur on the Senegal River. Eleven hundred years ago Muslim traders from northern Africa also described Ghana, a state centered somewhat north of Tekrur. The location of Ghana's consecutive capitals, Kumbi Saleh and Walata, in southern Mauritania on the northern edge of cultivation points, became crucial to these cities' roles as staging places to assemble and equip the caravans carrying gold shipments north as the reviving gold trade between northern Africa and the sources farther south was reestablished. Archaeological evidence suggests that Ghana was already hundreds of years old when it was visited 1,000 years ago by Arab traders searching for profits, especially this gold. The writings of these traders and other travelers about Ghana and the subsequent western African savanna kingdoms of Mali and Songhai provide little knowledge of those crucial aspects of western African society not of direct interest to commercial travelers. Ghana's decline and ultimate sacking by Berber Muslims were part of a larger shift in sub-Saharan trade centers. Trade shifted south as the spreading desert made food production around Walata much more difficult, and Arab groups pushing into the western desert prompted a shift eastward.

Trade and power passed first to Mali, a kingdom of Mande-speaking groups on the upper Niger River. Founded, according to oral traditions, between A.D. 1230 and 1235 by Sundiata, Mali not only extracted enough grain from local farmers to maintain a standing army but also traded gold and other goods for salt from the desert and other commodities from the larger Muslim world. One of Mali's rulers, Mansa Musa, established a reputation for wealth as the result of the splendor of his pilgrimage to Mecca in 1324. From 1468 on, the power of Mali passed to Songhai, located yet farther east on the Niger, under its king Sonni Ali. Songhai, which controlled the river by military canoes, was able to dominate the trading cities of Timbuktu, Jenne, and Gao until the Battle of Tondibi in April A.D. 1591, when Moroccan invaders decisively defeated an empire already in decline (Bohannan and Curtin, 1995:166–169).

With origins going back to a past almost as remote as that of Ghana, Kanem, a state near the desert edge in modern Chad, served as a trading entrepôt for centuries. More than 500 years ago Arabic sources referred to a strong successor state called Bornu, southwest of Lake Chad in what is today northern Nigeria. This southward shift probably reveals a deepening control over a fixed population of cultivators, since Bornu had no gold to sustain a large trade-based kingdom.

Two very interesting savanna states, which actually prospered as the trade north declined, were the highly centralized non-Islamic kingdoms of

Mossi (Mori-speaking) peoples in present-day Burkina Faso and the Bambara kingdoms of Segu and Kaarta (in the present nation of Mali). Though the Mossi kingdoms date back in some form more than 900 years, both of these clusters of states probably had economies based on the slave trade at the height of their power (Shillington, 1989:101, 183).

By 400 years ago, the most dynamic region in the entire western African savanna was the Hausaland plain west of Bornu. Here a high water table and numerous river valleys permitted year-round irrigated cultivation. The resulting food supply permitted an exceptionally dense population, which established a thick network of walled settlements and allowed the growth of an extensive, specialized, commodity-production economy. Surplus dyed textiles and leather goods became available for long-distance trade (Shillington, 1989:186–188).

Elsewhere in Africa there were a number of major state clusters, but none date back more than 1,000 years. Sometime about 500 years ago a process of state formation began in the region of the Great Lakes of eastern Africa. The best known is Buganda, which occupied the fertile plains northwest of Lake Victoria Nyanza. In the eighteenth and nineteenth centuries, the *kabaka,* the ruler of the Buganda, extended his authority over much of modern Uganda by gradually taking over the prerogatives of all the Ganda lineages. Besides plentiful supplies of bananas, the economic base of this state also appeared to be a lively trade in handicraft production (Freund, 1984:32).

Other states existed south of the equator. Near the mouth of the river of the same name lay the Kongo kingdom. When the Portuguese first arrived in the late fifteenth century, this kingdom, ruled by Nzinga Nkuwu, had already existed for several generations. In 1506, Nzinga Nkuwu's son Affonso, who had converted to Catholicism, defeated his brother to become *manicongo* (ruler) of this kingdom. His ascension to power marked the beginning of decline for the kingdom, since much of the ruler's authority depended upon local religious values (which were undermined by his conversion), the missionaries who surrounded him, and the expanding Portuguese influence as slave traders (Curtin et al., 1978:258–261).

Another cluster of centralized polities lay far inland in a basin particularly favored by salt and iron deposits, which assisted the development of long-distance trade. Here, in Zaire's Shaba province, a huntsman hero, Ilunga Kalala, had founded a dynasty among the Luba in the early 1400s. Other states of the southern savanna in what are now Zaire, Zambia, and Angola established the superiority of their ruling lineages by associating their founding legends with the Luba, including the Lozi state in the upper Zambezi floodplain of western Zambia, unified in the last century (Curtin et al., 1978:252–258).

Great Zimbabwe (in the modern state of the same name), the center of extensive and complex archaeological remains, dates back at least 800

Great Zimbabwe

years. These massive stone ruins were built by people ancestral to modern-day Shona speakers. It probably served as a capital for an empire that stretched from the Zambezi to the Limpopo, had linkages with widespread Indian Ocean trade networks, and encompassed an area of rich gold works. The massive stone architecture of this state indicates a complex economic and political system. The organization of the necessary labor to build these structures suggests in itself advanced social, economic, and political organization. Oral histories and firsthand descriptions of early Portuguese visitors to the area also confirm the existence of a strong centralized political system. Though the original Shona state probably broke up because of intergroup warfare after Indian Ocean traders found alternative African partners in the Zambezi valley, a successor state was established by 1420 or so under a northern Shona, Nyatsimbe Mutota, using the title *Mwene Mutapa* (Shillington, 1989:149–153).

In the forest regions of western Africa, Benin (located in the present-day nation of Nigeria) was already a strong and extensive kingdom when the Portuguese contacted it more than 500 years ago. Benin and other more recent states, like the savanna states of Mali and Songhai, which were influenced by Islamic bureaucratic techniques, derived great stimulus from outside forces. These states separately reflect the renewal of ties between the Eurasian world and much of sub-Saharan Africa's emergence from the relative isolation that existed in many areas during the previous millennium.

The oldest and best examples of these externally influenced states were the trading states of the coast of eastern Africa. Evolving from previously existing coastal fishing towns linked to farming peoples in the interior, these trading entrepôts had contacts with the Greco-Roman world as early as A.D. 100 (Curtin et al., 1978:142). Beginning gradually in the ninth century, these city-states rose and fell in concert with both the Islamized maritime cultures of the Indian Ocean and the African political systems that supplied the ivory, gold, and slaves for trade. By A.D. 1000 these local African towns, from Mogadishu (Somalia) to Sofala (Mozambique), were deeply involved in overseas commerce. Some, like Kilwa in southern Tanzania, which drew upon the Shona-controlled goldfields of Zimbabwe, traded extensively with China, India, and the Islamic world. These city-state-based, coastal-trading societies were influenced by Arab and Persian immigrants and developed a unique Swahili culture derived from both African and southwest Asian sources (Connah, 1987:150–182).

The Nigerian kingdoms of Benin and Oyo have historical origins dating back hundreds of years. Yet, it was not until 1500, when trade with Europeans on the coast contributed to the increase in the scale of organization, that other centralized political systems developed in the forests and savannas closer to the Atlantic coast of western Africa. For example, the Asante of modern Ghana rose to power after 1680 when the Asantehene (king of the Asante) Osei Tutu and his adviser and priest, Okonfo Anokye, forcefully united three smaller states into a confederation dominated by Akan-speaking peoples. The rise of the Asante state owed much to the control of the goldfields in central Ghana. The major factor, though, was the growth of military activity connected with the slave trade and the imported guns that came with this trade. The Asante fought to protect the trade routes to the coast in much the same way that the United States intervened in Kuwait to maintain what it considered its vital resources (Shillington, 1989:193–196).

Four hundred years ago the dominant state behind the coast in western Africa was the Yoruba's savanna-based state of Oyo. With far-ranging cavalry, Oyo was poised to respond to the growing demand for slaves by French, English, Portuguese, and other traders at ports such as Whydah, Porto Novo, and Badagry. By 1730, Dahomey, a tributary state of Oyo, became a major slave-trading power in its own right under King Agaja and dominated the major routes to the sea until the slave trade declined in the nineteenth century. Faced with the rise of the Muslim Sokoto caliphate to the north and the breaking away of better-armed Yoruba satellite states to the south, Oyo then declined (Curtin et al., 1978:238–244).

A very different series of events, the jihads (holy wars) of the western Sudan in the eighteenth and nineteenth centuries, was directly inspired by Islamic reforming movements introduced from northern Africa and the Arabian peninsula and by the large-scale shift in trade and production brought about by European commercial interests pressing in from the coast. The jihads of western Africa began in the highlands of the Futa Djallon in present-day Guinea when Fulani pastoralists, supported by Muslim traders, revolted against their farming rulers and created a Fulani-dominated Islamic state by about 1750 under the leadership of Ibrahima Sori. By 1776, the Fulani had produced a *shari'a*-ruled (based on Islamic law) state on the lower Senegal led by Abd al-Qadir. In the early nineteenth century, a similar Fulani-inspired revolution launched by Uthman dan Fodio on the Hausa kingdoms farther east created the Sokoto caliphate with a population of about 10 million people and the Ilorin emirate, Oyo's rival, in the 1830s. This jihad was extended into northern Cameroon by other Fulani leaders. Another Fulani jihad, inspired by that of Uthman dan Fodio, was led by Seku Ahmadu in Macina in present-day Mali. Beginning in 1852, al-Hajj Umar formed another empire on the upper Niger that united previously existing Bambara kingdoms until it fell to the French in the 1890s (Curtin et al., 1978:304–310, 362–390).

Several other state-building processes, the result of both indigenous and external forces, took place in the past 300 years. One originated in what is now South Africa but had such a large influence as far afield as Malawi that I feel it is necessary to deal with it here, even though it is covered in Patrick Furlong's chapter on South Africa. This state-building process set in motion the *Mfecane,* a period of wars and disturbances that marked the rise of the Zulu kingdom in southern Africa and the resultant migrations and conquest.

The *Mfecane,* which in the Zulu language means "the era of the crushing or breaking," was directly influenced by the presence of expanding white settlement in South Africa. Also important to the rise of the Zulu kingdom was the culmination of more profound changes, including population growth, long-distance trade in slaves and ivory, and the introduction of maize (corn) by the Portuguese centuries before.

Until the nineteenth century, the necessities of defense, irrigation, trade, and other factors, which led to the creation of states elsewhere in Africa, were apparently not as important farther south. Ecological pressures and the activities of Portuguese and Cape Colony slave traders caused an intensification of rivalries between small political groupings in the region between the Drakensberg Mountains and the Indian Ocean about 200 years ago. In that struggle for power, the most successful leader to emerge was Shaka. He refined and improved local warfare techniques and consolidated authority so effectively that between 1819 and 1828 he was able to create a military state that set in motion a series of migrations and conquests resulting in the creation of many kingdoms throughout southern Africa. This extraordinary individual trained an army that was very effective and able to expand rapidly. He was able to do this by transforming the existing system of initiation groups (an age-grade system) into cross-lineage groups, which he then was able to centrally control. This revolutionary social organization allowed him to mobilize an entire generation of young men to fight for him while the women worked to produce food to support them (Bohannan and Curtin, 1995:192–196).

This forging of a Zulu nation pushed other peoples, desperate to replace cattle stolen by the Zulu, into the interior grasslands of modern-day South Africa and far beyond, creating new political formations in what are now Zimbabwe, Malawi, Mozambique, Zambia, and Tanzania. The Sotho kingdom of present-day Lesotho and the Ndebele kingdom of modern Zimbabwe were among the results of the *Mfecane* (Freund, 1984:33–34).

■ **TRADE, EXPLORATION, AND CONQUEST**

□ **Slavery**

Apologists for the slave trade in the eighteenth and nineteenth centuries argued that slavery was intrinsic in backward African societies and that slavery in the "Christian" Americas was probably better for Africans than the situation in their "pagan" homelands. Abolitionists essentially agreed with these negative stereotypes about indigenous African societies. Most abolitionists supported "legitimate" trade, missionary activities, and ultimately colonialism, because these intrusions would put an end to slavery and the slave trade and begin the process of redeeming this "pagan" continent. African nationalists and defenders of African culture in the twentieth century argued that African civilizations, extending back to the glories of ancient Egypt, had been deformed and barbarized by the effects of the Atlantic slave trade. Some argued that the Atlantic slave trade had enriched the West at the expense of Africa and was largely responsible for Africa's relative economic backwardness (Manning, 1990:8–26; Cooper, 1979:103–125).

Slavery in Africa, as elsewhere, is as old as civilization. From the Egyptian dynasties through the Carthaginian and Greek trading states to the Roman Empire, a small number of black Africans were always part of trans-Saharan commerce. By the time the Arabs overran northern Africa in the middle of the seventh century, bondage and the slave trade were already fixtures of this part of the world. War prisoners from the Sudan, in Arabic *bilad al-Sudan,* "the land of the blacks," were sold north from at least A.D. 700. The demand for slaves in the Mediterranean world kept a persistent and substantial movement of black humans as trade goods flowing across the desert and dying on the journey well into the twentieth century (Manning, 1990:27–37, 149–164).

A variety of clientship, pawning, and sale of individuals to pay for food in times of famine have existed in many African societies for generations, as they have elsewhere in the world. Conquered peoples were absorbed into the victors' societies, often serving in a lowly status with few rights and privileges for generations before prerogatives and status distinctions between slave and free blurred. In some African states, plantation, quarry, mining, and porterage slavery were important parts of the economic base. Slave-soldiers were found in the Cayor kingdom of Senegal in the fifteenth century and in the modern Sudan as late as the 1880s (Meirs and Kopytoff, 1977:3ff).

While recent historical research no longer maintains, as serious scholars once did, that as many as 50 million Africans were taken from western Africa as part of the Atlantic slave trade, the economic and human loss to Africa of the 10 million or more slave immigrants who reached the New World was serious enough (Manning, 1990:5). More important to understand are the broader negative effects that the slave trade, the conflicts connected with it, and the rise of slavery within Africa associated with the trade had on African culture. At a time when European and American populations were growing rapidly, Africa's was in decline. While Europe and the Americas were industrializing, Africa, largely as a result of the slave trade, was involved in an exploitative and unproductive system of trade (Bohannan and Curtin, 1995:188–190).

Focus on the Atlantic slave trade should not result in less attention being paid to the Indian Ocean slave trade. This trade, though it never matched the massive numbers of the Atlantic slave trade, had disastrous consequences as far inland as the shores of Lake Malawi and those areas of Zaire west of Lake Tanganyika. The centuries-old, though relatively small, trade in

African humans to south and southwest Asia for plantation and mine workers, soldiers, and concubines reached substantial proportions beginning in the middle decades of the eighteenth century as demand for slaves grew on the French plantations on Mauritius and Réunion. This trade continued very actively into the nineteenth century, supplying slaves for Brazil and the clove plantations on the islands of Pemba and Zanzibar off the coast of eastern Africa. The nineteenth-century Afro-Arab slavers and ivory hunters penetrated swiftly and deeply inland, causing proportionately as great a loss of life and disruption in eastern African societies as the Atlantic slave trade did at its height (Alpers, 1975).

Wherever it occurred, the slave trade had far-reaching economic and social impacts. It turned African enterprise away from more productive pursuits and influenced the rise of more authoritarian rulers. Certainly one of the most important impacts of slavery and the slave trade was the resulting racism. Even now, the equation of black people and slavery persists in the minds of many people, including some blacks, to the detriment of human relations in North America and international relations between African states and the West.

□ "Legitimate" Trade

By the end of the eighteenth century, the world price of sugar was declining because of overproduction. At the same time, the price of slaves was rising because of stiffer competition among suppliers in western Africa. As a result, the power and influence of plantation owners from the British West Indies was declining in the British Parliament. The Industrial Revolution was spawning a new dominant class of industrialists in Great Britain who were finding it increasingly necessary to seek new markets abroad for the clothing, pottery, and metal goods they were producing in growing quantities. These industrialists saw that Africans in Africa could provide Europe with both necessary raw materials and new markets for their cheaply produced manufactured goods (Bohannan and Curtin, 1995:213–214).

The Haitian revolution, the abolition movement, the French domination of the sugar industry, and, perhaps, some growing acceptance of the egalitarian principles of the French Revolution and the U.S. War of Independence led the British, with the strongest navy in the world, to abandon the slave trade. Having transported half the captives from western Africa at the end of the eighteenth century, the British government set up an "anti-slavery squadron" and began using force to stop the trade by 1807 (Manning, 1990:149–157).

Beginning in the 1790s, trade in palm oil for use in soap, candles, cooking products, lubricants for looms, and other items had begun in western Africa. By the 1830s the commercial production of peanuts for the European market was well under way in western Africa. Though slaving and the "legitimate" trade in these commodities as well as gold, timber, gum arabic, skins, and spices coexisted through mid-century, it became apparent that greater profits existed in "legitimate commerce" than in slaves after the markets of Cuba and the United States were closed in the 1860s.

Large European trading firms were soon to squeeze out a number of smaller-scale entrepreneurs. Among those squeezed out were Eurafricans, groups of people of mixed European and African ancestry from the Senegambia who had promoted the peanut trade along the coast to the south, and other Eurafricans and former African slavers from Liberia to Cameroon who had become increasingly involved in palm oil commerce. Arab, Indian, and Luso-African (of Portuguese and African ancestry) intermediaries from Angola to Somalia, who had switched from trading slaves to trading ivory, gum arabic, copra, cloves, and other commodities, also suffered. Some intermediaries were reduced to becoming agents for the European companies, while others were simply driven out of business. The cloth, alcohol, tobacco, and firearms imported by the European trading houses did little to strengthen African economies, and as competition grew more fierce, European trading monopolies backed by their governments fought even harder to cut out all the African intermediaries and their European competitors. This growing European trading competition played a major role in the "scramble for Africa" in the 1870s and 1880s.

□ Exploration

It is ironic that people continue to credit European explorers of the nineteenth century with the "discovery" of rivers, waterfalls, and such in Africa when it is obvious that Africans living there already knew these things existed. Obviously, discovery simply meant that a European had verified in writing the existence of something long known to others.

With the exception of the Portuguese and perhaps a few Afrikaans-speaking people, the systematic exploration of Africa between the Limpopo River and the Sahara Desert by Europeans can be dated to Mungo Park's first expedition to the Niger in 1795. By 1885, crossings of the continent from east to west had been thoroughly documented, the extent of the Sahara was known to the European and North American public, and the major rivers in Africa had been followed and mapped by Europeans. To most Africans, though, this was of little importance, and some African rulers by the latter part of the nineteenth century were beginning to be less hospitable to wandering white men. These rulers had begun to fear the outside influence and rivalry that might weaken their control over trade, or as in the case of the Afro-Arab slave traders in central and eastern Africa, bring it to an end.

Mungo Park, for example, traveled up the Gambia River in 1795 to determine if it was linked to the Niger River, which appeared on some maps of the period as rising near Lake Chad and flowing west to the Atlantic. He did find the Niger and determined that it flowed eastward, not westward, thereby disproving the Gambia-Niger connection. Since he was then unable to follow the river to its mouth, he returned in 1805 bent on proving that the Niger actually was the Zaire River. He died on this expedition, and only in 1830 did Richard Lander demonstrate that the Niger flows into the Gulf of Guinea.

In the first half of the nineteenth century, other explorers like René Caillé, Hugh Clapperton, and Heinrich Barth traversed the western parts of Africa recording information that might be of interest to the governments, scientific groups, and missionary organizations that sponsored them. Not until the second half of the century were the sporadic efforts of Portuguese and Arab explorers penetrating equatorial Africa really taken up by Europeans. The first of these explorers, I presume, was the most famous of all, David Livingstone.

Livingstone was sent to Africa by the London Missionary Society. He arrived in Cape Town, South Africa, in 1841 and then traveled north. He roamed the interior for years, reaching the Okavango swamp and delta complex in Botswana in 1849, crossing Angola to Luanda in 1854, and reaching Victoria Falls in 1855. In 1858, he traveled up the Zambezi from its mouth and then turned north up the Shire River to Lake Malawi. His death south of Lake Bangweulu in 1873 inspired a great deal of European interest in this part of Africa, especially because of the writings of Henry Morton Stanley, who had "found" Livingstone in 1871.

For the majority of peoples in Europe and North America, the exploits of these explorers meant little more than excitement and drama set on an exotic stage. For small minorities, the diaries of these explorers and those of others, such as Richard Burton and John Speke, who sought the source of the Nile, did much to arouse their interest. Church groups and members of missionary societies were interested in "saving" the Africans. Also interested were the new monied classes spawned by the Industrial Revolution in Europe and North America. These entrepreneurs and investors urged their respective governments to act in their behalf to establish control of the "newly found" riches and regions (Brooks, 1986:104–121).

□ African Americans in Africa

During the 1900s, as European expansion into Africa increased, many former African slaves and their descendants were reestablishing ties with their African homeland in western Africa. While most attention has been paid to the activities of whites in Africa, attention should also be given to the role of African Americans as missionaries, explorers, settlers, and political opponents of colonialism.

Many ex-slaves from the Americas and some who never reached the Americas returned to Africa. For example, ex-slaves from Brazil began arriving in what are now Nigeria, Dahomey, and Togo in the 1840s. They became active in commerce and the skilled trades and, by the 1880s, dominated the inland trade from the French post in Dahomey (now Benin). The Brazilian architectural styles they brought with them can still be seen in some older homes in western Nigeria. In Freetown, Sierra Leone, Africans freed from slavery by British antislavery patrols were released. They were joined by African Americans returning from Jamaica and British North America. These Africans of many origins eventually formed a mixed African-Western "Krio" (Creole) culture. They too specialized in trade both along the coast and into the interior. Many of Yoruba ancestry moved to Lagos and Badagry in western Nigeria. When the British annexed Lagos in 1861, Krios became officials in the new colony (Bohannan and Curtin, 1995:215–216). Liberia was another refuge for ex-slaves, in this case from the United States. In 1822, the American Colonization Society transported freed slaves from the Carolinas to Monrovia, named after then president James Monroe. Alexander Crummell, a leading nineteenth-century African American intellectual, migrated to Liberia in the 1850s, and Bishop H. M. Turner was one of the leading black advocates of immigration to Africa for African Americans at the turn of the century.

All along the Guinea coast—especially in Nigeria, Sierra Leone, and Liberia—Africans and African Americans joined the Christian missionary effort. Many were Krios from Sierra Leone or Nigeria. African American missionaries also met with considerable success in other parts of western Africa, the Congo, and as far as South Africa.

African Americans helped to explore the continent. Notably, the National Emigration Convention of Colored Men sent out an all-black exploring party headed by Martin Delany, a physician, to explore the Niger valley from the coast shortly before the American Civil War (Harris, 1987:212–218).

The combined activities of African Americans and Westernized Africans were, in fact, slowly transforming many areas of Africa before European conquest and rule were imposed. As Bohannan and Curtin point out, many progressive changes that had been occurring in Africa during the 1800s were reversed during the colonial period.

> With the colonial period, Europeans reasserted their authority over the missionary movement. Europeans replaced most of the Africans who had held high posts in government administration, medical services, and the like. The African middle class of traders in Senegal, Sierra Leone, Liberia, and elsewhere found it increasingly hard to compete with large European firms in the export trade to Europe, though Africans continued to fill the role of middlemen between the African producers and the European firms. In the colonial setting, Western impact increased immensely, but with Africans

playing a diminished role as responsible participants in the process. (Bohannan and Curtin, 1995:218)

Finally, the role of African Americans in the anticolonial struggle should be mentioned. The "back to Africa" movement in the United States in the early 1800s later spawned the idea that all people of African descent should unite to promote their common interests and fight racism. The pan-African movement in the late 1800s and early 1900s protested the abuses and racism affecting Africans in such areas as Rhodesia and South Africa. While lacking the power to change colonialism, the movement was useful because it publicized the truth about colonialism to the world. African Americans influential in the pan-African movement included the West Indian, and later Liberian, diplomat Edward Wilmot Blyden and Jamaica's Marcus Moziah Garvey. In 1914 in New York, Garvey founded the Universal Negro Improvement Association, whose influence was widespread in Africa. Perhaps the most famous member of the pan-African movement was W. E. B. Du Bois, who was a founder of the National Association for the Advancement of Colored People (NAACP). Du Bois's ideas on pan-Africanism influenced many Africans, including U.S.-educated Kwame Nkrumah, the first president of Ghana. A great student of African history, Du Bois became a citizen of Ghana and was buried in Accra (Davidson, 1989:32–33; Harris, 1987:212–218).

□ Conquest and Resistance

Aided by missionaries who appealed to their home governments for various degrees of political or military "protection," by explorers who touted the riches to be found in the interior of Africa if only the local inhabitants could be "pacified," and by the owners of trading companies who wanted to eliminate competition, the political and military support for the takeover of Africa was not difficult to find in most European countries by the last decades of the nineteenth century. By 1884, at the Berlin Conference, the leaders of most European states came together and agreed on ground rules for dividing up Africa. Unfortunately, the political boundaries they drew on their largely inaccurate maps cut apart ethnic groups, kingdoms, and historically linked regions in ways that continue to cause conflicts in Africa today (Harris, 1987:158–167).

The push of the British, French, German, and other European powers into Africa in the last quarter of the nineteenth century required considerable effort. A good majority of the people of Africa, whether living in states or small-scale lineage-based societies, opposed European occupation through force of arms or nonviolently (Crowder, 1971:1–2). Well-organized, if poorly armed, Muslim armies filled with a spirit of jihad resisted British advances in Sudan, and the full subjugation of the region was not completed

until the late 1890s. In western Africa, the Tukolor empire under Ahmadu
Seku and the Maninka leader, Samory Touré, fought the French into the
1890s. Rabih, a Muslim leader from the upper Nile, resisted French expansion in what are today Chad and the Central African Republic until 1900.

Dahomey, a kingdom in present-day Benin, was not conquered until
1894 by the French using Senegalese troops. Leaders of numerous groups in
the forests of Côte d'Ivoire resisted the French for twenty years. The British
had to invade the Asante in Ghana in 1874 and 1895–1896 and again in 1900
before they could establish the Gold Coast colony. In Nigeria the British had
to launch major offensives to defeat the various peoples: Ilorin in
Yorubaland held out until 1897 as did the *oba,* or leader, of Benin City; and
the Sokoto caliphate was not completely overcome until 1903. In Uganda,
the Bunyoro used guerrilla warfare against the British until 1898; Swahili
speakers on the coast of Kenya successfully resisted the British for most of
1895 and 1896; Nandi and other Kenyan peoples fought the British well into
the 1900s.

Farther south in Nyasaland (Malawi), Yao, Chewa, and Nguni forces
fought the British in the 1890s; the Gaza empire and the Barwe kingdom
fought the Portuguese in Mozambique; and the Nama resisted the Germans
in South-West Africa (Namibia). As Furlong demonstrates in Chapter
13, South African groups resisted the imposition of British control as
well.

Even after the colonial regimes seemed to have been well established,
attempts to reassert independence broke out throughout Africa. In the 1890s,
the Shona and Ndebele rose up against the British in Southern Rhodesia
(Zimbabwe), the people of Tanganyika (Tanzania) fought the Germans in the
Maji Maji resistance in 1905–1906, and the Herero and Nama peoples
launched open warfare against the Germans in South-West Africa in
1904–1907. Throughout colonial Africa, these and other struggles, such as
the Kongo War in present-day Central African Republic (then part of French
Equatorial Africa), continued as late as the 1930s (O'Toole, 1984:329–344).

In the end, though, the superior military technology, logistic and organizational skills, and resources of the Europeans won out. All too often,
African leaders found that their inability to unite various ethnic groups and
factions against their common European enemies led to defeat. Most of
Africa north of the Limpopo River fell under European rule between 1880
and 1905.

■ THE COLONIAL PERIOD

□ Colonial Rule

The two major European powers to establish colonial systems in Africa
were Britain and France. After World War I, the limited amount of

German territory in Africa was redistributed, in most cases to France or Britain, while the Belgians and Portuguese maintained smaller areas under their nominal control. Wherever and whenever the colonial rule was established, it was essentially a paternalistic, bureaucratic dictatorship. Yet, given the vast areas occupied and the variety of African communities encountered, the colonialists were forced to recognize or to create a class of intermediaries to assist them. Somewhat oversimplified, colonial policies can be divided into direct and indirect rule, with the British portrayed as indirect rulers and the French as direct rulers (Bohannan and Curtin, 1995:230–235). In Chapter 4, on African politics, Donald Gordon discusses colonial rule from the standpoint of colonial economic interests in different regions of Africa.

The British, in particular, were often convinced that ruling through "traditional, tribal" authorities was the most efficient way to govern and to extract whatever revenue possible. This indirect rule policy, theoretically, interfered as little as possible so that Africans could advance along "their own lines." In reality, even in northern Nigeria, one place where this form of colonialism came quite close to working, the "traditional" authorities could often use their positions to extort substantial incomes, though their freedom to rule was very circumscribed. They often faced resistance from their own subjects. And any "traditional" ruler not acceptable to the colonial power was deposed and replaced by British appointees who were more amenable to the colonial regime.

The British tried to use indirect rule in several other places by reintroducing monarchy to Benin (in southern Nigeria), by restoring the Asantehene in central Ghana (Gold Coast), and by attempting to reestablish the Oyo empire among the Yoruba in Nigeria. They also were instrumental in maintaining monarchies in Swaziland, Lesotho, Uganda, and "Barotseland" in what was then Northern Rhodesia.

The French were relatively disinterested in indirect rule, though they too utilized the old ruling classes when it seemed advantageous. The French typically established administrative units that cut across traditional boundaries, created a transethnic elite, and used the French language at all levels of administration. At its extreme, French policy held that all Africans were to be completely assimilated and made equal citizens of France. More often, the highly centralized French administration maintained the necessity of deliberately creating an African elite who would accept French standards and then become "associated" with French rulers in the work of governing the colonies.

Belgian policy, like that of the French and the Portuguese, never displayed a great interest in indirect rule. Initially, the Belgians ruled through private companies, which were responsible for areas of administration. This was changed to direct rule by the 1910s because of the gross abuses committed by the companies against the local people under their control. The Belgians, unlike the French, deliberately limited African education to the primary levels and geared it entirely to semiskilled occupational training. Rather ironically, local political realities, coupled with a lack of finance for a developed system of bureaucratic control, meant that the French, Belgians, and Portuguese were often forced to rule through traditional elites in ways little different from the British.

Overall, the French colonies were as despotically ruled as any, but they did have the anomaly of the *quatre communes,* the four towns of Senegal— Dakar, Saint Louis, Gorée, and Rufisque—where all locally born residents had the legal rights of French citizenship from the time of the French Revolution and were represented after 1848 in the French chamber of deputies. Likewise, from 1910 to 1926, the Portuguese allowed a few Portuguese-speaking African Catholics from Angola, Mozambique, and Guinea-Bissau to be represented in the Portuguese parliament.

The major differences in colonial policies were regionally based rather than based on the particular colonial power that controlled the land. In most of western Africa, both the French and British refused to allocate land to European settlers or companies since local suppliers produced enough materials for trade. By contrast, in parts of British East and Central Africa, as well as in French Equatorial Africa and the Belgian Congo, land was taken from Africans and sold to European settlers and companies to ensure sufficient production for export. This difference caused a number of grave political problems in the nationalist era (Freund, 1984:122–125, 217–232).

□ Toward Independence

As Donald Gordon and Virginia DeLancey discuss in Chapters 4 and 5, during the colonial period Africans became increasingly involved in the world economy. For the seventy-plus years that countries of Europe ruled Africa, the economies of African countries were shaped to the advantage of the colonizers. Cash crops such as coffee, rubber, peanuts, and cocoa were grown for the European markets. Mining also increased during colonial times. Most cash crop economies benefited the European owners of large plantations rather than African farmers, and almost all mines produced for European companies.

In both the French- and the British-ruled areas of Africa, Western-educated African elites were active participants in some form of local government from the early decades of the twentieth century. In the 1920s, reform movements developed in British West Africa, which, apart from South Africa, were probably the earliest nationalist movements in Africa (other than in Liberia and Ethiopia, where European colonial rule was never fully established). These movements, like those led earlier by such men as J. E. Casely Hayford and John Mensah Sarbah in the Gold Coast and Samuel Lewis in Sierra Leone, originated among urban, highly Westernized populations in the cities of the coast and were directed primarily at abuses of the colonial system. Nowhere before World War II did the idea of actual political independence from colonial rule gather much momentum (Bohannan and Curtin, 1995:240–250).

The war, though, helped to raise African political consciousness. African soldiers fought in most of the same areas as their European masters. In cooperation with Charles de Gaulle and his "Free French," French West Africans and French Equatorial Africans joined in the fight against Nazi racialism. During the war, the Atlantic Charter was proclaimed and the United Nations created. The ideas therein contributed to the new visions of the right to freedom from colonial rule that Africans began to voice. After the war, national political parties took hold all over Africa. The strongest parties to emerge were those in West Africa, where no large European settler class blocked demands. From 1945 to 1960, African nationalist parties under men such as Kwame Nkrumah, Sékou Touré, Nnamdi Azikiwe, Léopold Senghor, and Félix Houphouët-Boigny developed mass support, won local elections, and pressured for more political rights and ultimately for independence (Harris, 1987:208–240).

In 1957, Ghana became the first black African nation to become independent in the twentieth century. From the capital, Accra, Ghana's first president, Kwame Nkrumah (1909–1972), set about creating a nation from the former British colony of Gold Coast. Faced with a cocoa monoculture export economy and Asante nationalism dating back to the resistance against British imperialism by the Asantehene Prempeh I in the nineteenth century, Nkrumah's advocacy of pan-African unity was never sufficient to overcome the influences of competing nationalisms and economic dependency that worked against unity.

In eastern Africa, the presence of European settlers made the struggle for independence even more difficult. In Kenya, colonized by the British between 1895 and 1963, a peaceful evolution to independence was ruled out by white settler opposition. Waiyaki Wa Hinga, a Gikuyu leader, initially welcomed Europeans and even entered into "blood brotherhood" with one early colonial administrator in 1890. Waiyaki was killed in 1892 by officials of the Imperial East African Company when he objected to the building of an unsanctioned fort in his area. Harry Thuku, Kenya's pioneer nationalist, also tried peaceful means to resist British colonialism. Concerned with improving the economic lot of Africans, he founded in 1921 a broad-based organization known as the East African Association. Advocating civil disobedience as a political weapon, he was arrested for disturbing the peace in February 1922. His arrest led to riots and the deaths of several Africans.

Independence for most settler colonies was won only through armed struggle. Like the Algerians, who fought a bitter eight-year freedom struggle against the French, Kenyans too found it necessary to resort to arms to achieve independence. The national liberation struggle in Kenya, called Mau Mau by the British, began in the late 1940s and was most strongly supported by the Gikuyu. Jomo Kenyatta (a London-educated anthropologist married to a white Englishwoman) was imprisoned by the British between 1953 and 1961 as the alleged brains behind the movement, though the actual fighting was done by such "forest fighters" as Dedan Kimathi, who was captured and executed in 1957. During the struggle, as many as 10,000 Africans (mostly Gikuyu) were killed. A growing sense of national unity against the British resulted from this conflict, and the British finally granted independence to Kenya in 1963 (Swainson, 1980).

Among the last African nations to achieve independence north of the Limpopo were the former colonies of Portugal: Angola, Guinea-Bissau, and Mozambique. After more than two decades of armed struggle, independence for the three colonies came quickly when the Portuguese government was overthrown by a military coup in 1974. Faced with South African– and U.S.-backed guerrilla oppositions, Angola was forced to struggle for survival until a peace agreement was finally reached in 1991 (unfortunately a peace that was not to last). Mozambique also faced armed opposition financed by South African and ultraconservative groups from the United States into the 1990s.

Both Zimbabwe and Namibia achieved black majority rule even later. Zimbabwe defeated the white settler government after a long liberation war and became an internationally recognized independent state in 1980. With the support of the United Nations, Namibia achieved its independence from South African control in 1990 after a protracted struggle. In 1994, Africa's last "colony," South Africa, finally attained black majority rule after the country's first racially inclusive democratic elections.

Independence did not usher in a golden era. In almost all countries, democracy degenerated into authoritarianism, and economic decline is universal. Population and environmental problems plague the continent. These and other issues will be discussed in the chapters that follow. Under the circumstances, the greatest achievement of African states since independence may be that they exist at all.

While the present appears bleak in many respects, most historians of Africa are wise enough to avoid hazarding any predictions about the future. As Coquery-Vidrovitch states so well:

> In twenty years every aspect that defines Africa today will have undergone an alteration that cannot be foretold by our present means of analysis. The pessimism undeniably called for in the short term, then, cannot validly be extended to the longer term. (Coquery-Vidrovitch, 1988:318)

■ CONCLUSIONS

African history in the last decade of the twentieth century is quite different from what it was when African studies was expanding rapidly in the early 1960s. It is no longer necessary to prove that Africa has a history. The racist and antihistorical synthesis that Africa was "discovered" by or "saved" by Europe, though still reflected in much "common knowledge," has been eliminated as an acceptable view. Professional historians have written hundreds of works about virtually every part of the continent. There are specific studies of individual African nations; regional introductory histories of eastern, western, central, and southern Africa; and general histories of the whole continent.

In this chapter I discussed four basic concept-centered goals that my teaching, reading, and writing on the broad subject of African history lead me to believe are crucial. The first goal is to enhance students' and others' awareness of the long time span and wide geographical area involved in African history. The second goal is to increase readers' understanding of the great diversity of Africa's past. Third, I wanted to make clear that both change and continuity have been integral parts of the human experience in Africa. The fourth goal I sought to weave into the chapter was a heightened awareness that all events of history have more than one cause and that the interwoven happenings that produce a given outcome are the result of complex chains of events.

Readers ought personally to pursue a fifth goal, not explicitly focused on in this chapter, as they read the other chapters in this text. That goal is to sharpen their awareness of the role Africa has played in world history. To deal with today's global realities, a marriage between the past and the present is needed. On the one hand, one needs to be introduced to humanity's collective memory, a large part of which flows from Africa. On the other hand, one needs to be sensitized to the current world. People must realize that what happens in Africa is linked to what happens to them and vice versa. As was true 200,000 years ago, we share a common humanity as members of one race—the human race. And, while Africa may no longer be our home, our destinies are still linked.

■ **BIBLIOGRAPHY**

Alpers, Edward. 1975. *Ivory and Slaves in East Central Africa*. London: Heinemann.
Bohannan, Paul, and Philip Curtin. 1995. *Africa and Africans*. Prospect Heights, IL: Waveland Press.
Brooks, George E. 1986. "African 'Landlords' and European 'Strangers': African-European Relations to 1870." Pp. 104–121 in Phyllis M. Martin and Patrick O'Meara (eds.). *Africa*. Bloomington: Indiana University Press.
Connah, Graham. 1987. *African Civilizations*. Cambridge: Cambridge University Press.
Cooper, Frederick. 1979. "The Problem of Slavery in African Studies." *Journal of African History* 2:103–125.
Coquery-Vidrovitch, Catherine. 1988. *Africa: Endurance and Change South of the Sahara*. Translated by David Maisel. Berkeley: University of California Press.

Crowder, Michael (ed.). 1971. *West African Resistance*. London: Hutchinson of London.

Curtin, Philip, Steven Feierman, Leonard Thompson, and Jan Vansina. 1978. *African History*. Madison: University of Wisconsin Press.

Davidson, Basil. 1989. *Modern Africa: A Social and Political History*. London: Longman.

Freund, Bill. 1984. *The Making of Contemporary Africa: The Development of African Society Since 1800*. Bloomington: Indiana University Press.

Hakem, A. 1980. "La civilisation de Napata et de Meroé." Pp. 315–346 in G. Mokhtar (ed.). *Histoire Générale de l'Afrique II*. Paris: UNESCO (Jeune Afrique).

Harris, Joseph. 1987. *Africans and Their History*. New York: New American Library.

Hyden, Goran. 1980. *Beyond Ujamaa in Tanzania: Underdevelopment and an Uncaptured Peasantry*. London: Heinemann.

Lamphear, John. 1986. "Aspects of Early African History." Pp. 64–86 in Phyllis M. Martin and Patrick O'Meara (eds.). *Africa*. Bloomington: Indiana University Press.

Leclant, J. 1980. "L'empire de Koush: Napata et Meroé." Pp. 295–314 in G. Mokhtar (ed.). *Histoire Générale de l'Afrique II*. Paris: UNESCO (Jeune Afrique).

Mair, Lucy. 1974. *African Societies*. Cambridge: Cambridge University Press.

Manning, Patrick. 1990. *Slavery and African Life*. Cambridge: Cambridge University Press.

Meirs, Suzanne, and Igor Kopytoff (eds.). 1977. *Slavery in Africa*. Madison: University of Wisconsin Press.

Parkington, J. E. 1980. "L'Afrique méridionale: Chasserus et Cueilleurs." Pp. 695–727 in G. Mokhtar (ed.). *Histoire Générale de l'Afrique II*. Paris: UNESCO (Jeune Afrique).

Oliver, Roland, and Michael Crowder (eds.). 1981. *The Cambridge Encyclopedia of Africa*. Cambridge: Cambridge University Press.

O'Toole, Thomas. 1984. "The 1929–1931 Gbaya Insurrection in Ubangui-Shari: Messianic Movement or Village Self Defense?" *Canadian Journal of African Studies* 18:329–344.

Shillington, Kevin. 1989. *History of Africa*. New York: St. Martin's Press.

Sutton, J. E. G. 1980. "L'Afrique orientale avant le VIIe siècle." Pp. 613–639 in G. Mokhtar (ed.). *Histoire Générale de l'Afrique II*. Paris: UNESCO (Jeune Afrique).

Swainson, Nicola. 1980. *Development of Corporate Capitalism in Kenya*. London: Heinemann.

Trevor-Roper, Hugh. 1965. *The Rise of Christian Europe*. New York: Harcourt, Brace and World.

Turnbull, Colin (ed.). 1973. *Africa and Change*. New York: Alfred A. Knopf.

■ 4 ■

African Politics
Donald L. Gordon

After thirty years of predominantly authoritarian rule, the winds of political change are sweeping Africa. Beginning in the late 1980s and gathering momentum in the 1990s, African citizens moved to challenge autocratic rule. Motivated by stifling political repression, deteriorating economies, and democratic revolutions in the Soviet Union and Eastern Europe (among other circumstances), Africans have demanded multiparty political systems, expanded civil liberties, accountable public officials, and free elections. In a wide variety of countries across the continent, existing regimes have allowed opposition parties to form and have promised open national elections. In several countries, elections among competing parties have actually taken place and new presidents have assumed office.

For many who study Africa, these moves toward democratization and the energy, euphoria, and hope that accompany them are highly reminiscent of the anticolonial struggle and the early days of independence from European rule. For then, as now, there were expectations of immediate and substantial changes not only in the political system but also in the daily lives of Africans. The transfer of power to African decisionmakers would end political oppression and allow the perceived wealth of the former colony, siphoned off to Europe, to bring quick relief and instant economic progress to African professionals, businesspeople, artisans, and the huge ranks of the poor. However, this joyous anticipation that marked the late 1950s and early 1960s soon disappeared as the new leadership grappled with the sobering aftermath of colonial rule.

Over time, more than fifty independent African states emerged. The variety of government structures and regimes virtually covered the scope of possibilities. By the 1980s in Africa, one could find monarchies and dictatorships, military regimes and civilian governments, revolutionary systems and democracies, populist administrations, and authoritarian modes of rule (Chazan et al., 1988:3–4). Yet, notwithstanding the diversity of structures, variations in political style, and professed ideological differences (from

Marxism to capitalism), the political evolution of African states since independence has been characterized by patterns that are strikingly similar.

With some exceptions, African governments became increasingly authoritarian. This trend was marked by the concentration of power in single political parties and, in many cases, in personal rule by the national president. Centralization of power was accompanied by the elimination of competitive elections, greater reliance on administrative bureaucracies, and intolerance of dissent. These systems of rule were often unstable and subject to coups d'état. Stable or unstable, most have also been characterized by inefficiency, mismanagement, and corruption.

How and why did all of this develop? Why were most African states unable to sustain democratic, multiparty political systems? What consequences has this had on Africa's people and on economic development? These are some of the central questions to be examined in this chapter. And as I will demonstrate, the structure and problems of African societies have not only been shaped by the systems of politics that have evolved, but they, in turn, have also been shaping the changes in the politics of Africa that we are now observing.

Before proceeding, however, readers need to be aware of what this chapter does not discuss as well as what it does. First, my remarks are of necessity relatively abstract and general, as it is a difficult task to synthesize given the variation and complexity of Africa's many countries. Moreover, although an attempt has been made to examine and link together the most important processes and trends, significant issues are inevitably bound to be left out or to be insufficiently detailed. Perhaps the most important issue I have not discussed in more length is the role of foreign political and economic interests in shaping—or misshaping—African political regimes and processes since independence. While foreign governments have regularly intervened to topple or support African rulers or to influence their policies, I have chosen to focus on Africans as political actors rather than as pawns of, say, superpower politics, multinational corporations, or Western development agencies. I have also largely omitted Africans' political dealings both with each other, through such organizations as the Organization of African Unity (OAU), and with the international community outside Africa. The reader should refer to Chapter 6 for a discussion of these topics. In sum, this chapter is an introduction to African politics rather than an exhaustive survey.

■ THE IMPACT OF COLONIALISM

It is surprising to many students that most of Africa was under European control for less than a century and that the Berlin Conference of 1884–1885, which initiated the European scramble for Africa, took place just over 100 years ago. Yet, in that relatively short period massive changes took place on the continent that not only established the immediate context for African politics but also continue to constrain and shape its future.

To begin, the political map inherited by the new states of Africa was based largely on the expedient economic and political strategies of imperial Europe. Superimposed over the continent were highly divergent and artificial geographical forms and the distortion of traditional social and economic patterns. For one, the physical map of Africa contrasts such sprawling giants as Sudan, Zaire, and Algeria with the ministates of Djibouti and The Gambia (see Map 2.6 in Chapter 2). Diminutive, The Gambia (4,127 square miles) could fit into Sudan more than 240 times! Substantial diversity was and is also apparent in population sizes. Nigeria, now estimated at well over 100 million people, and Equatorial Guinea, with only 244,000, provide extreme examples (Sullivan, 1989). With the creation of these artificial boundaries, cohesive social groups were separated, and logical and well-established trading areas were divided. Geographical units were developed that were landlocked or contained few if any resources or enveloped existing diverse and highly competitive cultural and political systems. As a result of these and other circumstances, the political map inherited at independence created huge differences among the various African countries in their potentials for nation-building, economic development, and stability.

While the colonial economic history of Africa and its contemporary impact is complex and variegated, European strategies and actions during the period were generally quite similar. African colonies were made politically and economically subordinate to European needs. The recently industrialized states of Europe, particularly Britain and France, required cheap raw materials and desired captive markets for manufactured goods. Over time, these governments integrated their African colonies into what many call the "international capitalist system." African territories supplied inexpensively produced agricultural commodities such as palm oil, rubber, and cotton, and such minerals and metals as copper and gold to the industries of Europe. Manufactured textiles, household goods, and farm implements sold to Africans at high profit completed the integrated economic system.

But there were differences as well as similarities in the forms colonialism took to extract Africa's wealth. Samir Amin (1972:503–521) argues that regional differences in colonial political and economic policies were determined by the nature of exploitable resources.

For instance, in the coastal territories of French and British West Africa, Amin's "Africa of the colonial trade economy," the colonial state attempted to pay for itself and to satisfy the needs of European industry by promoting cash cropping among the indigenous population. In Senegal, the Ivory Coast (Côte d'Ivoire), the Gold Coast (Ghana), and Nigeria, many traditional subsistence farmers (growing food crops for their own use) switched to producing such export crops as palm oil, rubber, cotton, cocoa, and peanuts.

Amin's "Africa of the labor reserves" describes such colonial territories as Malawi, Mozambique, and Upper Volta (Burkina Faso), which had few easily tapped material resources or had limited potential for peasant- or settler-produced agricultural exports. As a result, these colonies rather quickly became reservoirs of labor migrants, primarily for the mines of the Belgian Congo (Zaire), Northern Rhodesia (Zambia), and South Africa, and for the white settler plantations of sections of Kenya, Tanganyika (Tanzania), and Southern Rhodesia (Zimbabwe).

The former French colonies of Gabon, Congo, and the Central African Republic and the Belgian Congo (Zaire) are labeled by Amin as "Africa of the concession-owning companies." Environmental constraints and low population densities that prohibited profitable cash cropping prompted transfer of most of these areas to concessionary companies. Exploitation of available resources in the concession areas was characterized by low investment and brutality.

A fourth macroregion, "white settler Africa" (parts of Kenya, Tanganyika until 1918, and Southern and Northern Rhodesia), was, like western Africa, characterized by colonial concentration on the production of agricultural exports. Aided by colonial authorities, Europeans quickly expropriated most of the region's fertile land, displacing traditional African farming groups such as the Gikuyu in Kenya, the Chagga in Tanganyika, and the Shona in Southern Rhodesia. Peasant farmers were either legally shut off from growing most cash crops as in Kenya or deprived of suitable land.

No matter what specialized impact colonial economic decisions had on particular geographical areas, the profit-centered activities of European industrial and commercial firms, settlers, and supportive colonial administrators clearly disregarded *African* development. In no case, even after World War II, when the pressures of world opinion and decolonization were heavy, did European colonizers invest in cogent, rational programs of development designed to make African states self-sufficient. Without joining the debate about whether Europe actually "underdeveloped" Africa, it is obvious that colonial policies worked to handicap independent Africa's economic future.

On departure, colonial administrations left Africa with weak, malintegrated, severely distorted economies. These realities and others placed most of Africa into a multifaceted and tenacious dependency relationship with more economically advanced states. The decisions, strategies, and even sovereignty of emergent Africa would be contingent on *foreign* markets, industry, finance, and expertise. (A more detailed discussion of the impact of colonial economic policy on Africa is found in Chapter 5.)

It is important to note that the end of colonial rule by the British and French was accomplished with almost the same speed that had characterized its initial imposition. The achievement of independence by Ghana in 1957 and Guinea in 1958 came quickly and was for many observers unexpected

(Liebenow, 1986:21). With very few exceptions, British, French, and Belgian colonies had been granted independence by 1966, over twenty between 1960 and 1964.

Independence, therefore, was not the culmination of a long process of preparation in which the end was long known and the means carefully developed. Among the colonizing powers, only the British and French made attempts to bequeath to Africans the administrative and executive skills requisite for governing the new states (Hodder-Williams, 1984:84). Furthermore, decisions allowing Africans the possibility of more participation in voting for legislative councils with relatively significant power came almost entirely after 1950 (Hayward, 1987:7).

Within this context, the democratic governmental models developed by the French and British for their colonies were essentially alien structures hastily superimposed over the deeply ingrained political legacies of imperial rule. The real political inheritances of African states at independence were the authoritarian structures of the colonial state, an accompanying political culture, and an environment of politically relevant circumstances tied heavily to the nature of colonial rule. Imperial rule from the beginning expropriated political power. Unconcerned with the needs and wishes of the indigenous population, the colonial powers created governing apparatuses primarily intended to control the territorial population, to implement exploitation of natural resources, and to maintain themselves and the European population. For all European colonizers—British, French, Belgian, Portuguese, German, Spanish, and Italian—power was vested in a colonial state that was, in essence, a centralized hierarchical bureaucracy. Specifically, colonial rule was highly authoritarian and backed by police forces and colonial troops. Under this circumstance, power did not rest in the legitimacy of public confidence and acceptance. There was no doubt where power lay; it lay firmly with the political authorities.

Long-term experience with the colonial state also shaped the nature of *ideas* bequeathed at independence. Future African leaders, continuously exposed to the milieu of authoritarian control, were accustomed to government justified on the basis of force. The idea that government was above self-interested political activity (which only served to subvert the public's welfare) was communicated by colonial administrators. As a result, notions that authoritarianism was an appropriate mode of rule were part of the colonial political legacy (Kasfir, 1983:34).

Furthermore, at independence the politics of the new states would be shaped by at least four heavily influential societal circumstances either set in motion or amplified by colonial political decisions. First, virtually all colonial territories experienced growing inequalities between social classes as both the actions of and the location of colonial administrations created opportunities for some and obstacles for others. Second, in most colonies, particularly those under the British model of "indirect" rule through so-called tribal rulers, heightened identification with and competition between ethnic groups took place. (See the comparison of direct and indirect rule in Chapter 3.) This "tribalism" would especially mark the politics of the early independence period. Third, the context of postcolonial politics in many new states would include dramatic shifts of population from rural areas to the primary administrative city. Finally, as a result of discriminatory colonial educational policies that provided little money for or access to education for most Africans until after World War II, African countries entered independence ill-equipped to staff either the agencies of government or private business and development organizations. (For the best account of the colonial state in Africa see Young, 1994.)

■ NATIONALISM AND THE POLITICS OF INDEPENDENCE

Political freedom for most African states has come only within the last thirty-five years. For some, it is far more recent. The former Portuguese colonies of Guinea-Bissau, Angola, and Mozambique achieved independence in 1974–1975, the former French colony of Djibouti in 1977, and Zimbabwe in 1980. After years of illegal subjugation by South Africa, Namibia became independent in 1990. And while not a colony, South Africa attained majority black rule only in 1994. African states are thus very young.

The nature of the imperial response to African nationalism and the way in which power was eventually transferred to Africans influenced the ideological orientations, political practices, and economic possibilities of the new African states. Especially important here is whether the transfer of power came as a result of peaceful confrontation or whether independence was achieved only after a violent armed struggle. Our understanding of contemporary African politics requires us to look, if only briefly, at nationalism in Africa and at the politics of the independence period.

To begin, the term "nationalism" widely applied to African struggles for independence is somewhat misleading. The term was borrowed from European history, where it referred to nineteenth-century political movements in which people with a common culture, language, and historical tradition claimed the right of self-determination. As Bohannan and Curtin (1988:366–367) further state, "Europeans began with the nation which then wanted to become an independent state. The Africans had states—the existing colonial units through which the Europeans ruled—and they wanted independence for the units so that they could become nations." Yet, it is important to note that, at least initially, very few Africans pushing for autonomy from the European colonizers thought in terms of building a nation. The struggle that would become known as African nationalism was essen-

Independence rally in Luanda, Angola.

tially an anticolonial struggle, and its intensity was a reflection in large part of the degree of colonial impact on groups and individuals.

Anticolonial feelings, criticism of, and actions against imperial rule were present in Africa from the very beginnings of colonialism. Where European economic and political penetration was deepest—the white settler areas and mining centers of eastern and southern Africa—worker-initiated petitions, strikes, and minor sabotage began in the early 1900s. For the most part, however, these work actions were localized attempts to protest low wages, hard work, and harsh discipline. They were not part of a nationalist independence movement (Tangri, 1985:4–9).

In nonsettler Africa, especially in the British territories of western Africa, objections to colonial rule were primarily articulated by a small core of educated and professional Africans kept from good jobs and access to political power by the racially discriminatory practices of colonial rule. In fact, until what Freund (1984:191) refers to as the "second occupation of Africa," beginning mainly after the Second World War, most objections and actions against colonial rule were attempts to reform the system, to open it to participation by Africans. The great masses of Africans, mostly engaged in subsistence agriculture and relatively unaffected by colonial authority, were virtually uninvolved in anticolonial activity.

The end of the Great Depression and World War II marked the beginning of a period of rapid change and intense pressure on Africa. Unable to provide for their industrial and food requirements because of the war, Europeans turned to their colonial holdings. At war's end, and even more so by the late 1940s, food crop and cash crop agriculture would be dramatically increased; roads, bridges, railways, and ports would be improved and expanded; and large numbers of additional bureaucrats would be added to the rolls of African colonial administrations. These extraordinary changes in African society set the stage for expanded anticolonial activity. The changes greatly influenced the creation of new groups and classes among Africans and helped shape the conditions, opportunities, and relationships from which the new nationalist leadership emerged.

Increased colonial activity in Africa after World War II took place in a changed international environment and among the changing expectations of a growing number of Africans. A substantial number of African soldiers from such British and French colonies as Senegal, the Gold Coast, Kenya, and the Rhodesias had fought in the war. Their experiences in battle and knowledge of Japanese successes against Western forces in the Asian theater challenged ideas of white superiority. The war itself had been justified on the grounds of rejection of racial superiority and the rights of national independence. Furthermore, many Africans were aware of the new United Nations Charter, which advocated political self-determination.

Within this atmosphere of new expectations, European colonial administrators began to push new rules and regulations, especially into rural areas of Africa. In eastern Africa, particularly, a series of new regulations imposing Western-oriented agricultural methods were forced on rural farmers and cattle herders. Ostensibly imposed to protect resources, these alien measures, such as contour plowing and cattle destocking, were often coercively enforced. Though less affected, western, central, and southern African farmers were subject to new agricultural orders that provoked considerable discontent. In the Gold Coast (Ghana), the "swollen shoot program" required the cutting of huge numbers of cocoa trees. In the Belgian and Portuguese colonies, forced crop production and resettlement of farmers took place. These and other new colonial operations caused mass rural discontent across much of sub-Saharan Africa (Tangri, 1985:18).

This watershed period immediately after World War II marked the beginning of true African nationalism. The nature and pace of political activity was dramatically transformed. Anticolonial activity focused on influencing policies within the colonial system rapidly became efforts aimed at political liberation.

The prewar associations of African elites (owners of small businesses, physicians, lawyers, and other professionals in West Africa, teachers and clerks in East Africa) were limited in size and scope. Composed mainly of Western-educated "notables" with some access to colonial authorities, these groups were mainly confined to urban administrative centers such as Lagos

(Nigeria), Accra (Ghana), and Nairobi (Kenya). Their central concerns were the common interests of a relatively privileged minority.

New and more militant groups were formed by younger activists from among what Marxist analysts refer to as the "petty bourgeoisie"—traders, farmers, and low-level civil servants. Stimulated by the enthusiasm of those in the new movements, many of the old prewar elite associations were themselves transformed into nationalist organizations (Tangri, 1985:15–17).

The combination of bourgeoisie (the elites) and petty bourgeoisie groups was central to the eventual attainment of independence. To become formidable opponents of colonial rule, embryonic elite-led nationalist organizations had to tie themselves to the rural (and increasingly urban) masses of Africans. As Roger Tangri (1985:18) indicates, a litany of complaints was tapped by the nationalist politicians. These included not only disgust of subsistence and cash crop farmers over onerous new agricultural rules but also worker unrest, complaints against colonial restrictions on small businesses and cooperatives, anti–poll tax agitation, and the general revulsion over the white man's racist behavior and racial discrimination.

It must be noted that in very few instances were nationalist groups part of a unified and highly integrated movement. In fact, in most colonies the African nationalist campaign was a relatively loose linking of "different elements representing sometimes interrelated, but often diverse, economic, ethnic, and regional interests temporarily united in a struggle for independence" (Tordoff, 1984:53).

During the late 1940s and early to middle 1950s, a series of circumstances led the French and British to consider and then begin the process of decolonization. The decade of the 1950s saw substantial shifts in colonial policies over much of the continent. Among other factors, rising costs of administering the territories, pressure from the United Nations, and the growth of nationalism influenced policymakers, especially in France, England, and Belgium. In 1956, the French granted independence to the North African territories of Morocco and Tunisia and instituted the Loi-Cadre for colonies in sub-Saharan Africa. The Loi-Cadre allowed for domestic autonomy but not independence. In 1957, the British granted independence to the Gold Coast; and by 1959, along with the Belgians, they had accepted the imminence of African self-rule for all territories (Young, 1988a:52–53).

As colonial authorities began to allow consultative forums and African-elected councils to form before independence, many of the nationalist organizations placed emphasis on expanding their influence. Many, if not most, became full-fledged political parties bent on mobilizing mass support and promoting agitational politics. "As independence neared, demonstration of numerical strength became indispensable to validate the claims of a nationalist party to succeed to power" (Young, 1988b:516). It should be noted that the ideas, characteristics, and activities of politicians leading the nationalist organizations would have a significant impact on the nature of African governments after independence. Their position in the social and economic hierarchy, the methods used to recruit support, and indeed the personal goals of Africa's new nationalist leadership would all set patterns for future political activity.

Remember that only a few Africans lived outside the bounds of poverty and material deprivation during the colonial period. Although most of the nationalist leaders, especially in West Africa, were educated and somewhat better off than the masses, they were poor compared to low-level European administrators and settlers. Many were low-salaried teachers or clerical employees of the colonial government or foreign business. Others were small-time traders, contractors, or shopkeepers. Given these circumstances, a significant number of the new leaders from this economic class hoped to convert their leadership positions into social and economic gain. Common among these were, as Wolpe (1974:118) says, "men on the make," their political activities motivated by freedom from colonial domination and the desire for individual mobility. Those that rose to the top were usually charismatic, fluent speakers with organizational skills. After independence, many nationalist leaders, recognizing that political office was the only vehicle available to escape poverty, would not easily relinquish such powerful positions (see Kasfir, 1987; Tangri, 1985).

Political parties and individual politicians recognized that mass protest and wide support would not only hasten independence but also work to secure political advantage or even to ratify leadership positions at independence. Securing mass support in the circumstances African nationalists faced was not easy. Lack of money, poor communications facilities, transportation problems, and widely spread populations were obvious obstacles. Partly as a result, but more so because of familiarity and social access, politicians appealed for support from individuals and groups from their home villages and regions and from their ethnic groups. (Perhaps the best discussion of political parties in the nationalist period is found in Hodgkin, 1957.)

The networks of political affiliation that resulted would have at least two important consequences for the postindependence period. For one thing, in most of Africa this pattern of political recruitment and support worked to create political parties along "natural" lines of social cleavage. Perhaps the most blatant example of this pattern was Nigeria, where the three main parties were sharply divided along ethnic and regional lines: the Northern People's Congress (NPC) in the predominantly Hausa-Fulani north, the National Council of Nigeria and the Cameroons (NCNC) in the heavily Ibo east, and the Action Group in the mainly Yoruba west (Diamond, 1988:33–39). A second result of this form of "linkage" developed during the preindependence period. Promises of material aid to supporters for their backing or for votes created the basis for patronage relationships after independence. Called "patron-client networks" by social scientists, these political webs would become the major form of political interaction for many African countries in the postcolonial era.

■ THE TRANSFER OF POWER

When the British, French, and Belgians decided to relinquish power to their African colonies, they did so with deliberate speed. In part, the rapidity of transition reflected practical difficulties of control. Riots in the Gold Coast (Ghana) in 1948, the Mau Mau rebellion in Kenya in the early 1950s, and a breakdown of law and order in Nyasaland (Malawi) in the mid-1950s were strong hints to the British that containing nationalism would be very expensive. For the French, the defeat at Dien Bien Phu (in Vietnam) in 1954, the failure at Suez in 1956, and the Algerian rebellion were most influential (Hodder-Williams, 1984:78–79).

Many observers, however, point to more politically advantageous reasons for the colonial powers' quick exit. The main goal was to retain as much political and especially economic control as possible. Rapid decolonization lowered the level of conflict between the colonial rulers and nationalist leaders. By creating a basically smooth transition to independence (especially in West Africa), the British and French prevented the creation of radicalized political leaders and the formation of segregated, militant, and broadly based nationalist organizations. While not having complete freedom during the transfer period, the imperial powers were the dominant actors (Hodder-Williams, 1984:80–83). Essentially, they maneuvered to exclude elements of the nationalist movements perceived to be dangerous and to aid those leaders and parties friendlier to European economic interests (see Freund, 1984:202–224; Tangri, 1985:20–23). One example is Cameroon, where the French essentially eliminated the Union des Populations Camerounaises (UPC), a radical movement that played a leading role in the Cameroonian nationalist struggle. The politicians who eventually inherited power in Cameroon were moderate and conservative leaders whose roles in the struggle were insignificant (Joseph, 1977:2–3).

This strategy of a quick transition coupled with active promotion of moderate nationalist leaders had generally favorable results for the British and French. Influenced heavily by their own class and personal goals, most nationalist leaders endorsed the legitimacy of private property and other tenets of capitalism. As a consequence, in most countries the economic interests of the European powers were largely preserved (see Young, 1988b:53–55; Tangri, 1985:23).

In contrast, during the 1960s and early 1970s, Portuguese refusal to grant independence to Angola, Guinea-Bissau, and Mozambique led to armed revolt. A protracted liberation struggle provoked mass mobilization of farmers and urban workers. A revolutionary consciousness evolved that rejected most elements of Portuguese colonialism, including the capitalist economy. In addition, mass involvement of destitute populations in FRELIMO (Frente de Libertação de Moçambique) and the MPLA (Movimento Popular de Libertação de Angola) presented obstacles to leaders bent on personal gain through entrepreneurial activity (Saul, 1975:330; Tangri, 1985:24).

For the first wave of African countries to receive independence, a final legacy of colonial rule was bequeathed at independence—formal structures of democratic rule. British colonies received negotiated variations of the basic Westminster parliamentary type of government in which a prime minister is chosen from elected members of parliament and in which executive and legislative powers are fused. The French model was a president-centered form in which the legislative and executive branches are separate. Both instituted a democratic election process, political parties, separate judiciaries, and protection for citizens' rights.

The first period of decolonization, roughly 1957–1969, which saw more than thirty new African states obtain sovereignty, came at the end of more than a decade of rising commodity prices. In the words of Crawford Young (1988a:56), "The extraordinary prosperity of the 1950s contributed heavily to [a] mood of optimism and good feeling. . . . The metropolitan states looked forward to fruitful continuing partnerships with their erstwhile appendages and turned over the keys to the kingdom in a veritable orgy of self-celebration."

■ INDEPENDENCE

The early days of freedom from colonial rule were charged with excitement and full of hope. The immediately obvious burdens of racist imperial rule were gone. New flags flew over government offices, Africans rather than Europeans held political control, and the world recognized the new states as sovereign. Yet, the excitement of independence masked an enormous set of problems the leadership had to confront promptly.

From the beginning, internal conflict plagued the parties that assumed leadership at independence. The anticolonial organizations that the nationalist movements comprised differed along ethnic, regional, and ideological lines. At independence, with the overarching bond of opposition to colonial oppression weakened or removed, intraparty and interparty conflicts emerged. One divisive issue was access to positions of power in the government and ruling political party. Offices in government (whether at the national or local level) meant access to influencing decisions, to power over resources, and to personal profit (Tangri, 1985:28–33).

The anticolonialist leaders who became the national leaders in the elections of the decolonization period faced a fragile national unity. The geographical areas ruled by the colonizers were superimposed over diverse cultures, language groups, political entities, and trading areas. During the colonial period, little attempt was made to integrate or unify peoples within the colonies. Rather, as a method of control, ethnic groups were often pitted against each other.

The reality of African life, heavily oriented toward subsistence farming and tied to the land, was that most Africans identified primarily with their village and clan and secondarily to a "tribal" or ethnic group. At independence subnational loyalties were far more important than the new state, for which there were no national traditions, no national symbols, and no national consciousness. While Africans did not necessarily identify with the new state or its leadership, their expectations about what should come from the end of colonialism were high. They wanted education for their children, hospitals and health care, drinkable water, farm-to-market roads, better prices for their crops, and an instantly better life.

No matter what policy orientations the new leadership pursued, all faced bleak economic circumstances and little available capital. Most of the new states had an underdeveloped industrial structure, if any at all. Almost all states would depend on the sale of one or a very limited number of export commodities to make up their treasury. But many of the new states had few natural resources. And all were in an economically dependent relationship with Europe and the industrial countries (Ake, 1981:90–114).

In addition to this environment of meager economic resources, external vulnerability, high demands and expectations, and a political arena in flux, the new governments were shackled with inexperience. "Localization," the placing of Africans into civil service clerical positions, increased (rapidly in parts of nonsettler West Africa) immediately prior to independence. Yet, in areas of technical expertise (accounting, engineering, health), on which the new states would heavily depend, the colonial powers had provided Africans with little training. Furthermore, "the new leaders themselves had earned their positions as a result of their ability to organize and capitalize upon colonial protest. They had little, if any, experience in governing even a small area, let alone an entire country" (Chazan et al., 1988:43).

■ THE CENTRALIZATION OF STATE POWER

From the outset, the leadership of most new states felt—and indeed *were*—politically insecure. With some exceptions (such as Tanzania), most of the new governments had only a thin base of support after the unraveling of the anticolonial alliances left those in power with limited backing (often of only their own ethnic groups and regions). Any expansion of support would have to come from a quick and meaningful response to the high expectations and deep social and economic needs of the population.

The fact is that most states simply did not have the revenues to meet social needs. While most commodity prices remained relatively high during the early independence period, the enormous neglect of Africans during the colonial era would require decades for substantial improvement. Extreme poverty and the high expectations of most Africans led to enormous demands on the leadership.

Formed or heavily expanded during the openness of the waning colonial period, organized interest groups (especially trade unions, rural coopera-tives, and student organizations) became increasingly vocal and insistent on government help and action. In many countries, demonstrations and strikes among an increasing number of associational groups soon followed. In real-ity, many of the new governments were forced to spend much of their time, energy, and money on simply maintaining order (Chazan et al., 1988:44).

Most threatening to the new state rulers during the early independence period were organizations based on the mobilization of regional, religious, generational, class, and (especially) ethnic interests. During the colonial period, economic and social disparities were created in a variety of ways. People living close to colonial administrative centers, European mercantile centers or plantations, or shipping and port facilities had opportunities for wage labor or low-level public or private clerical positions or as low-ranked foot soldiers in the colonial military. Close proximity and employment also led to facility in European languages. For some, especially after World War II, it led to education in government- or mission-sponsored schools. Such circumstances not only created an embryonic political elite with tremendous advantages to gain office at independence but also left most other individu-als and groups disadvantaged. Whatever group or coalition of anticolonial groups attained power at independence, either as a dominating single party such as the Tanganyika African National Union or a winning party among several contenders, winners and losers were created. Debilitating poverty and the understanding that the only mechanism for economic development and personal gain was the state itself had prompted the politicalization of ethnicity during the preindependence election period. The rapidly forming structures of power after independence, in which the ascendant leadership was easily identifiable by group and region, were perceived generally to bring instant economic and political power for particular ethnic groups. At the same time, those groups not represented in the leadership group or on its periphery felt immensely threatened with the loss of "their" share of the government pie. Such conditions caused tumultuous political activity. Groups jockeyed for power within the ruling party, and often new parties were formed representing specific ethnic or regional interests (see Rothchild, 1981; Horowitz, 1985).

Under the circumstances, the choices confronting the governing elites were limited. They could use their positions to strengthen themselves politically, or they could operate within the colonially positioned democratic political structures and risk electoral defeat. No matter what motivations prevailed among the political elites of the continent—personal greed or selfless nationalism or some combination—there was no option. With few exceptions, the independence leadership quickly moved to consolidate power and expand political control. Across the continent, the early years of independence witnessed a strikingly similar transformation of inherited governmental and political structures. Concentration of political power and control was achieved primarily through (1) limiting or eliminating opposition and (2) expanding the bureaucratic agencies and the security (military and police) organizations, which passed to the new leadership at independence. (The works of Zolberg, 1966; Wunsch and Olowu, 1990; and Chazan et al., 1988:44–51 are particularly instructive.)

A variety of justifications for centralizing state power was offered by African independence leaders. Fundamentally, most leaders believed that a strong central government was essential to national unity and economic development. If political competition along the ethnic, regional, and religious (in areas of heavy Islamic concentration) fault lines of society were not eliminated, the resulting antagonisms would "shred the precious fabric of national accord" (Young, 1988b:495). Wunsch and Olowu (1990:44) point to other influential factors in the movement toward centralization:

1. It was part of the colonial legacy of an administrative state.
2. Outside development consultants from both Western countries and the Eastern bloc were heavily emphasizing central direction and long-term planning.
3. It complemented the expectation of potential donor agencies for "rational" planning and management of assistance programs.
4. It provided a possible solution for the very real challenges African leaders faced.

The manner in which opponents to regimes lost power and access to government involved a variety of actions and mechanisms, with regimes differing on the emphasis and degree of restrictiveness. At the outset, the main targets of government moves to eliminate political competition were rival political parties. Some states, such as Guinea and Ghana, simply declared local political parties illegal and contrary to the national interest; others (e.g., Cameroon) made it virtually impossible for opposition parties to exist. In Uganda, Angola, and Mozambique, coercive force was used to eliminate opposition parties. In any event, as Astride Zolberg's (1966:66–76) classic work *Creating Political Order* points out:

1. Competing political parties were eliminated and the government party fortified.
2. Political opponents were co-opted (drawn in by various inducements), intimidated, detained, or otherwise eliminated (imprisonment, exile, or, much more rarely, murder).
3. Electoral systems were modified to make competition unlikely or impossible.
4. Constitutions were changed to give wide authority to restrict the power of representative assemblies, including national parliaments and provincial and local assemblies.

By the late 1960s, thus, the most common political organization of the new states was the single-party state. Arguably, only Botswana and The Gambia were true multiparty exceptions. But transformation of the democratic political structures bequeathed by European political powers involved considerably more than the systematic dismantling of institutions of representation and interest expression—opposition parties, parliaments, provincial and state assemblies, and local district and city councils. Motivated by the desire for more comprehensive political control, for regime security, and for implementation of government policies, ruling groups moved hastily to fortify three main structures of government: administrative bureaucracies, the military and police, and the executive. Building on the legacy of effective colonial bureaucracies and security forces (passed on virtually intact in many instances and containing the main reservoir of skilled personnel in all African countries), the new regimes expanded both the size and function of administrative agencies (Chazan et al., 1988:48–49). While the number and size of almost all administrative bodies increased during the immediate postindependence years, the most dramatic increases were created in the ministries of economic planning, transportation, education, and social services, especially the latter two. Greatly expanded too were government bureaucracies and parastatals (relatively autonomous, state-owned corporations) involved in buying and marketing agricultural and mineral commodities, producing beer and cigarettes, and controlling railroads, airlines, and electric power.

Kept small and under heavy European control (all officers and many noncommissioned officers were European) during the colonial period, the police and especially the military were expanded. In Nigeria, Kenya, Uganda, Sudan, and Zaire, where particularly strong regional or ethnic interests either challenged the government or were perceived to be an immediate threat to the regime, the growth of coercive elements was most rapid.

Perhaps most important in the transformation and augmentation of administrative institutions was the concentration of legitimate authority in the executive. Virtually all new states in the first decolonization wave were left with mechanisms to limit, disperse, or check executive power. Yet, beginning in the early postindependence period, strong executive presidencies (supported by the creation of single-party states and the preemption of regional and local politics by bureaucracies) began to displace all independent legislative authority (Wunsch and Olowu, 1990:55–56). By the late 1960s, in governments such as Malawi, Cameroon, Mali, Tanzania, Togo, Zaire, and Zambia, presidential decree had replaced meaningful legislative debate.

The relative ease with which early postindependence African leaders consolidated power through shutting off avenues of access to government, gutting representative bodies, and extending the hold on society of the administrative branches came as a surprise to many Western observers. After all, in the 1950s Europeans had expanded social services to Africans; opened the lower branches of colonial government to African clerks; allowed trade unions, political parties, and other associations to flourish; and "given" the

Although Zimbabwe is not officially a single-party state, the ruling party, ZANU–PF, whose headquarters are pictured here, has virtually monopolized power under President Robert Mugabe since independence in 1980.

gift of democracy to Africans. Critics blamed (among other things) the "intelligence of Africans" and the "incomplete job of 'Europeanization' of Africans." Others saw in the anti-imperial slogans of the nationalist period and in the extension of the state an anticapitalist bias. When coupled with the "abandoning" of democratic institutions and heavy expansion of the state, many, Americans especially, saw the specter of socialism (easily equated in the Cold War period with communism). Ironically, while lamenting the antidemocratic trend in Africa, the United States was at the same time supporting such dictators as Mobutu Sese Seko in Zaire and other nondemocratic regimes so long as they were avowedly anticommunist.

In reality, the ease and speed with which authoritarian regimes were created were rooted in the social and economic by-products of colonial rule. Long-term colonial economic policies oriented toward commodity production and keeping labor cheap left most African states with huge peasant farmer populations overlaid by very small middle classes and minuscule upper classes. Effective opposition to the monopolization of power by political elites is most often associated with a strong middle class with investments to protect and with sources of economic and political power independent of the state. Only a large middle class would have the educational and organizational skills, the motivation, and the monetary resources to successfully challenge government actions. Furthermore, the colonial system, highly capitalistic in an international context, created conditions that made accumulation of wealth by local individuals and groups virtually impossible. Without considerable amounts of savings, significant private investment in production of new resources and goods for society cannot take place. In effect, colonial rule thwarted local capitalism; consequently, independent centers of economic and political power were severely limited. Only the new African state itself, through its taxing and revenue-creating powers, could aggregate money to finance development of the country. Those who controlled the state, therefore, not only had little effective political opposition but controlled the only source for the attainment of wealth.

■ PATRONAGE, THE PATRIMONIAL STATE, AND PERSONAL RULE

The rulers and their associates who dismantled the democratic structures left at independence were attempting to stay in power. The creation of centralized single-party systems of governance was an attempt to consolidate control over the political actions of rival interest groups. By centralizing power under the executive, the regimes also were acting to obtain compliance with government policies.

Yet, the constriction of the political arena, the often ruthless manner with which single-party governments were imposed on the populations, and the fact that the party and the central organs of government were usually closely tied to the ethnic and regional support base of the ruling elite did little to dampen opposition. Politicians who lost out in the moves that restricted access to decisionmakers and limited participation in the political process found it relatively easy to mobilize ethnic and other groups not associated with or favored by the ruling elite. As Sandbrook (1985:77–81) makes clear, ethnic politicization, or "tribalism," increased throughout the first decade of independence as ethnicity became the main vehicle for expressing grievances by those outside the system.

To maintain themselves in power, therefore, African leaders had to construct stronger bases of social support. Given the virtual monopolization of scarce economic resources by the new regimes and the elimination of restrictions on the leaders of most African countries, the answer lay in the discretionary distribution of patronage and the development of "clientelistic" ties to key individuals and groups (see Eisenstadt and Lemarchand, 1981; Fatton, 1986). While patron-client relations quickly became the main form of political exchange in postindependence Africa, "clientelism" and the swapping of favors for support were rooted in the politics of anticolonialism. Local leaders were drawn into various nationalist movements with promises of personal office and gain of aid to their villages and regions at independence.

In any event, most African rulers moved to build support and defuse opposition by a wide variety of patronage devices made possible by their control of the state. Key figures were co-opted into government by appointment to high political offices or important positions in the administrative branch or in parastatals (state-owned corporations). Among other kinds of patronage used to bind support for the regimes and rulers were import-export licenses, government contracts, monopolies over certain kinds of business, tax exemptions, the use of government houses and automobiles, and subsidizing of university educations.

The fact is that patron-client relationships permeate most African governments. Citizens "tie" themselves to patrons (from their kinship line, village, ethnic, or regional group) in government who can help them in some way. Lower-level patrons invariably are clients themselves to a more important patron who may have been responsible for securing his ethnic "brother's" job in the first place. At the upper end of patron-client networks are "middlemen" clients of the ruling elite. Using political clout, powerful positions, and access to government monetary resources made available by the rulers, these middlemen-patrons not only supply jobs in government but money for schools, health clinics, wells, storage facilities, roads, and other favors to their ethnic groups and regions. Patronage binds local constituencies not only to their network of patronage but also to support for the regime itself. Emanating from the country leader may be literally hundreds of patron-client linkages that fix support of other elites to the country's leadership and create substantial support for the regime. Acting also as a system of control, state patronage and "clientelism" served to consolidate regimes by offering access to state resources in exchange for political acquiescence (Boone, 1990b:37).

Following Max Weber, social scientists generally refer to the political process in which government office is bestowed in return for political support and personal loyalty and service as "patrimonialism" (Bendix, 1962:334–335). The essence of patrimonial rule is the personalization of power by a country's ruler. By the end of the first decade of independence, most African political systems were characterized by varying degrees of personal authoritarian rule. In some countries (such as Zaire under Mobutu in the early to mid-1970s), the personal authority of a strongman ruler became virtually synonymous with government itself. (For Zaire, see Callaghy, 1984; Young and Turner, 1985:166–184; Leslie, 1993; for personal rule generally, see Jackson and Rosberg, 1982.) A most illustrative "portrait" of a personal authoritarian ruler is one described by Richard Sandbrook:

> The strongman, usually the president, occupies the center of political life. Front and center stage he is the central force around which all else revolves. Not only the ceremonial head of state, the president is also the chief political, military and cultural figure; head of government, commander-in-chief of the armed forces, head of the governing party (if there is one) and even chancellor of the local university. His aim is typically to identify his person with the "nation." His physical self is omnipresent: as in Orwell's *1984,* Big Brother is plastered on public walls, billboards and even private homes. His portrait also adorns stamps, coins, paper money and even T-shirts and buttons often distributed to the party "faithful." Schools, hospitals and stadiums are named after him. The mass media herald his every word and action, no matter how insignificant. (Sandbrook, 1985:90)

Personal rule, of course, depends on the combination of patronage and coercion. Regimes varied in the degree of repressiveness and in the size of those sharing the resources of government. In Cameroon under Ahidjo and Côte d'Ivoire under Houphouët-Boigny, broad and relatively genuine ethnically balanced elite networks created long periods of stability. The more autocratic the personal ruler, the more likely the spoils were to be distributed only among the politically important: top bureaucrats, party officials, local notables, national and regional politicians, military officers, and trade union officials (Sandbrook, 1985:94–95). In Idi Amin's Uganda, patronage was limited to the ruler's band of close associates and his numerically small cultural group, and violent repression became virtually the only method of political and social control. In any event, what must be understood is that maintaining patronage networks and forces of coercion requires a huge amount of money. And in short order, African rulers found that to keep clients secure and the system stable, governments had to commit increasing amounts of money to patronage or allow increasing opportunities for those in government to use their positions for personal gain.

■ MILITARY INTERVENTION

As African leaders shut down rival political parties and representational bodies and closed off access to government for the vast majority of their citizens, they also increased the size of their armed forces. First used as symbols of national sovereignty and independence through the 1960s and 1970s, the military increasingly became a part of the ruling group's enforcement apparatus. Although the actual growth of the military and its relationship to African rulers varied, the armed forces in most countries became politically powerful entities (Chazan et al., 1988:55–57). As a result of their organization and control of weaponry, the armed forces were uniquely positioned to overthrow civilian regimes. As the good feeling and political openness of the nationalist period quickly disappeared in the actuality of single-party government, a variety of factors created conditions that "justified" military intervention in politics. Certainly, the amount and speed of economic improvement was not even close to public expectations. Animosity toward the government grew among those touched by increasingly repressive personal rule. Furthermore, conspicuous spending on palaces, airplanes, and

Photo: Hollandse Hoogte/Jan Boqaerts, Impact Visuals

The military is an important political actor in most African states.

personal luxury items by many of the ruling elite, contrasting with the general poverty of the masses of citizens, created resentment. While military takeovers have occurred to rid countries of unpopular and corrupt regimes, most are probably better explained by other factors such as the personal ambitions of military officers or attempts by the military to deal with low pay, poor conditions, or neglect (see Decalo, 1976; Cox, 1976).

In any event, between the 1952 overthrow of King Farouk by Egyptian colonel Gamal Abdul Nasser and 1984, seventy successful coups took place in thirty African countries (McGowan and Johnson, 1984:633–666). According to Samuel Decalo (1989:547–548), "If during the 1960s the coup d'état emerged as the most visible and recurrent characteristic of the African political experience, by the 1980s, quasi-permanent military rule, of whatever ideological hue, had become the norm for most of the continent. At any one time, 65 percent of all of Africa's inhabitants and well over half of its states are governed by military administrations."

Since independence, Benin, Burkina Faso (Upper Volta), Ghana, and Nigeria have had five or more successful coups d'état, and just twelve African states have never had civilian rule disrupted by military intervention. Only Côte d'Ivoire and Malawi have not yet experienced an attempted or successful coup d'état. While military regimes have normally claimed to be "caretakers" who would "clean up the mess" and "return to the barracks," most instead have moved to consolidate power. It is important to note that almost invariably military regimes have tended to operate much like the civilian regimes that preceded them (Ball, 1981:576–580; Young, 1988a:496–497; Meroe, 1980). Most have adopted the single-party political organization, and, usually from a small ruling group, a single ruler emerges. Furthermore, and highly important for an understanding of the continent, most military rulers share with their civilian counterparts both the use of patronage as a mechanism for gathering political support and the use of coercion to control or eliminate opposition. They also share an overall preoccupation with increasing their own economic position. Nigeria's current military ruler, General Sani Abacha, is a case in point. Along with crushing all political opposition, Abacha and his corrupt military cronies have diverted vast oil revenues for patronage and their own aggrandizement. Abacha is alleged to have stolen a billion-dollar fortune for himself (Beran, 1995:19). Finally, military and civilian rulers alike have pursued almost identical economic development policies and have reaped similar results. (For an exhaustive review of the military in Africa, see Luckham, 1994:13–75.)

■ **THE POLITICAL ECONOMY OF DECLINE**

For ordinary Africans, development is seen in personal terms. It means additional money for children's schoolbooks, usable roads that allow farmers to get their produce to market, electric lights in the village, affordable rice and flour, or a health clinic within walking distance. Development too is measured by access to land, jobs, and better housing.

But most Africans experienced little real economic progress in the post-colonial period. Resources needed for effective, broad-scale development were drained away, among other reasons, to support regime efforts to con-solidate power.

As we have seen, attempts by African regimes to enhance control over the political arena and to strengthen and extend bases of support led to remarkably similar actions. State patronage and clientelism emerged as the main methods of political control and governance. State resources that could have been committed to development were used to pull into the system the elite from a variety of politicized factions (ethnic, regional, workers' groups, student associations, women's groups). In reality, private appropriation of state resources and the use of government money to build and expand per-sonal rule lay at the very heart of the process by which most postcolonial regimes sought to govern (Boone, 1990b:36–37).

In large part because of patronage-based rule, the 1960s and 1970s (and beyond) were marked by the rapid growth of the political branch, the bureaucracies, and the parastatals. In fact, during the 1960s, the civil service in Africa grew at a rate of 7 percent per year, a rate that doubled the number of employees in ten years. The result was that by 1970 over 60 percent of all African wage earners were government employees. By 1980, at least half of *all* African government expenditures were allocated simply to pay the salaries of government employees. Furthermore, the expansion of govern-ment corporations during the first two decades borders on phenomenal. Parastatals were developed to deal with a broad range of government activ-ities. For example, state-owned companies were created to handle the con-trol and marketing of agricultural products, provide banking services, run airlines and railroads, manufacture products, and manage retail stores. As an extreme example of their number and range in a particular country, Nigeria (in the mid-1970s) had over 250 state-owned corporations (Chazan et al., 1988:52–53).

The patronage-based elaboration of the state, the expansion of the armed forces, and economic development of a country depended on the availability of substantial amounts of money. Especially needed was foreign exchange to purchase petroleum, trucks, buses, industrial parts, and a vast menu of items Africans could not produce. While some money began to flow from donor nations, most government activities would depend on money aggregated locally. Given the scarcity of indigenous private savings from which to borrow, the lack of established middle- and upper-income groups on which income taxes could be levied, the absence of an industrial base, and a heavy dependency on technologically advanced countries, most African regimes turned to the profits to be made from the export of mainly agricultural commodities. Catherine Boone's description of how African regimes moved to control highly productive areas of postcolonial commerce is highly relevant. "Building on the regulatory apparatus of the colonial state, post-colonial governments licensed wholesalers and importers, controlled imports through tax and tariff regimes and fixed the process of agricultural commodities, agricultural imports, and staple consumer goods" (Boone, 1990b:26). The result was that throughout most of the continent, substantial profits were "earned" by African regimes by paying rural agricultural commodity producers low prices and marketing the commodities at considerably higher prices (Bates, 1981). The consequence for farmers and rural areas of Africa was that the promise of development turned into the harsh reality of subsistence living. For increasing numbers, the hope for a better life centered on the already well-traveled path of migration to the cities.

In fact, government economic policies that handicapped farmers were heavily reinforced by the reactions of rulers to major population growth in urban areas. By the early 1960s, "primate cities" (capitals and ports) often were growing at rates as high as 10 percent per year. For example, between 1958 and 1970, the population of Kinshasa, Zaire, increased from 389,000 to 1,323,000 (Young and Turner, 1985:81), and Douala, Cameroon, grew from 54,000 in 1957 to over 313,000 in 1976 (Government of Cameroon, 1977). Early within the first decade of independence in most African capitals, massive conglomerations of under- and unemployed Africans existed in sprawling squatter settlements with no city services. In some instances, they already formed the bulk of cities' populations. (An analysis of urbanization and population growth in Africa is found in April Gordon's Chapter 7.)

From the earliest days of independence, African leaders were aware of the potential danger of large urban concentrations of the poor and unemployed. Many regimes had experienced urban-based strikes, demonstrations, and even violence during moves to centralize the state or as disappointment grew over slow progress toward meeting the needs and expectations of various interest groups. As a result, most leaders acted to cut the potential of "instability" of large concentrations of urban poor by holding down food prices in the cities. In effect, urban areas were subsidized by requiring food crop farmers (mostly women) to accept low prices from government monopoly wholesalers or by setting price caps on food sold in urban areas.

In order to extract profits from rurally produced agricultural commodities and to keep food costs low for urban residents, government policies caused the deterioration of rural economies, pushed the rate of rural to urban migration dramatically upward, and added to the growing inequality between rural and urban areas. Furthermore, farmers, in large numbers where access was available, began to sell their crops in the black market economy outside government control (see Bates, 1981).

For much of Africa, then, development of the rural areas was sacrificed to finance patrimonial states. These patronage-based systems created opportunities for all those connected to government through patron-client networks. For the elite, appointed by rulers to the highest party, administrative, and parastatal positions, state office and political influence created amazing legal and illegal advantages for personal gain. And in virtually all states, those in positions of power (and their patrons) moved to use their influence for economic profit (Young, 1988b:503).

It is the way in which the state-based elite used their profits that is most important for an understanding of a political economy of decline. For the most part, money legally or illegally secured from government position was either used to buy luxury import items or placed into speculative real estate development, taxis and trucks, or retail and wholesale commercial ventures (Boone, 1990a:427). For a variety of reasons, very little investment took place in ventures that created substantial employment, boosted industrial capacity, or generally helped develop the country (see Sandbrook, 1985).

Given the circumstances of government economic policies that virtually devastated rural areas and pushed urbanization, the expansion of the state and the huge costs of personnel and patronage, and the essentially nonproductive and wasteful use by the elite of public resources, almost all African states were in economic decline by the early 1970s. During the mid- to late 1970s, a combination of external and internal political, economic, and social factors moved the continent from decline into crisis.

■ STATE AND SOCIETY IN CRISIS

The political agendas that created costly government superstructures and siphoned money into the hands of a relatively nonproductive elite class inhibited the development of most African countries. In many regimes, inefficiency, mismanagement, and corruption wasted public resources. Moreover, most of the wealth that flowed to the dominant classes was not spent on capital investments, investments that help a country to produce more and that ultimately promote development.

As a result of these and other factors, the economic growth rate of the continent declined. Data taken from Nafziger (1988:16–34) help chart the path of African economic stagnation and descent. From a growth rate of approximately 1.3 percent per year in the decade prior to independence, economic growth dropped to 0.2 percent yearly for the period from 1965 through 1984. Between 1980 and 1985, Africa's real gross domestic product (GDP) per capita fell an average of 2.3 percent yearly. By the mid-1980s, the "great descent" had become an internationally recognized tragedy of crisis proportions. While the economic impact of political decisions by African rulers was a major factor in creating crisis conditions, other factors generally outside the control of rulers contributed substantially.

The relatively high prices that commodities brought in the waning colonial years began to drop in the early independence period. During the 1970s, and continuously since, prices for virtually all of the continent's main agricultural and mineral commodities have declined. At the same time, costs of goods imported from the more technologically sophisticated countries have risen steadily. Machine parts, automobiles and trucks, industrial tools, and luxury items have become increasingly more expensive.

Even more disadvantageous changes in the "terms of trade" for African states were caused by the oil shocks from the mid-1970s to the early 1980s. With the exception of oil producers such as Nigeria, Angola, and Gabon, sub-Saharan African states were staggered by the high costs of petroleum products.

While changes in the international economy placed most African countries in increasing jeopardy, population changes within Africa created conditions that would hinder any hope of economic progress. From the relatively slow population increases of the colonial period, population growth rates in independent Africa simply exploded. By the mid-1980s, the continental population growth average rose to a yearly rate of over 3.0 percent. At this rate of growth, populations double in size in little more than twenty years (World Bank, 1990a:229).

The scope of the crisis can be understood by the number of Africans relegated to absolute poverty. By 1985, the number of absolute poor grew to 180 million people—47 percent of the population. Rapid population growth and slow economic growth will increase the number of poor by an additional 100 million by the year 2000. This means that Africans will constitute 30 percent of all the poor in the developing world as compared to only 16 percent in 1985 (World Bank, 1990b:5, 29). (A comprehensive description and analysis of the current economic crisis is found in Chapter 5.)

In any event, the fact is that by the early 1980s most African states simply did not have the capacity to meet rapidly growing budgetary requirements. Most often, among other results, there was an overall weakening of the government's ability to carry out essential public services. Over time, roads and rail systems deteriorated. Services to agriculture were abandoned. School systems (already shocked by huge increases in the under-fifteen population) found little money available for school construction or teacher salaries. Furthermore, as the state "softened" (Hyden, 1983:60–63), even the most essential government tasks, such as tax collection, became problematic.

As the administrative capacity of governments decreased, decay within regimes increased. In many states, corrupt practices among strategically placed politicians and bureaucrats became so habitual as to be institutionalized. Under these circumstances, citizens expected to pay bribes; and they viewed politicians' raiding of government treasuries as simply "the way things are done." The term "kleptocratic" has been applied to states such as

Zaire, where corruption has been systematically practiced at all levels (Young and Turner, 1985:183). Yet, even in countries with a traditionally professional civil service, the economic crisis created conditions or "structured" incentives for corruption. In Ghana, for example, "where hyper-inflation rapidly outran increases in salaries, demanding a bribe (or a higher one than previously) was an understandable reaction of junior or middle-ranking government officials to the problem of feeding their families" (Jeffries, 1989:80).

For individual Africans, strategies for survival are registered in such rational acts as the following: a decision to sell cocoa not to the official government agency but on the black market for twice the government price; a move to avoid the possibility of losing money on an export peanut crop by "retreating" into subsistence agriculture (for own use); or the decision (made by many) to invest time and work in one or a variety of mutual aid organizations that operate to help finance a farmer's seeds, repair a road, build a school, or even protect a village from thieves.

Since the early 1980s, the actions of African "civil society" have had a substantial impact on African regimes. Basically, two major patterns have emerged. First, although varying by country and regime, large numbers of Africans have disengaged themselves from the state or have been partially successful in avoiding state laws and officials (see Rothchild and Chazan, 1988). Second, a resurgence and expansion of voluntary organizations and associations have taken place, even within coercive states (see Bratton, 1989b; Fatton, 1992; and Harbeson et al., 1994). While both developments have significant ramifications for African regimes, withdrawal from the state and its power to tax has been most difficult for rulers to control and has added most immediately to the state in crisis.

Disengagement from the state denies regimes their expected revenues in two significant ways. First, the economic foundation of most African states rests on revenues produced from selling agricultural exports. When farmers simply stop growing export crops, the fiscal base of regimes (already weakened by a continuing slide in commodity prices) is further eroded. Certainly, less foreign exchange is accrued and the economic crisis deepens. Disengagement from the state also takes place when people turn to clandestine economic transactions for survival or profit. These black market activities are remarkably alike throughout the continent and primarily involve

1. Hoarding and exchanging scarce goods above both official and justified market prices;
2. Smuggling lucrative cash crops, precious metals, or manufactured foods, either into or out of the country; and
3. Engaging in illegal currency transactions to avoid monetary exchange controls or exchange rates.

These and other activities are a major part of the parallel or informal economy, which creates incomes and assets that largely escape government regulations and taxes. African governments lose huge amounts of money in this
manner, weakening the fiscal basis of the state even further (MacGaffey,
1988:177–185; Lemarchand, 1988:160–166; Sandbrook, 1985:139–149).

In any event, as revenues stagnated or declined, as treasuries were
drained, and as terms of trade for imported goods and services became
increasingly disadvantageous, African governments borrowed heavily to
maintain themselves. Unfortunately, many commercial loans were secured
when rates were high. Because of Africa's heavy dependence on Europe,
Japan, the United States, the Soviet Union, and other industrial nations for
money, sub-Saharan Africa had by 1990 compiled debts so huge that over 40
percent of export earnings needed to be spent each year simply to pay interest (World Bank, 1990b). Economists generally agree that with economies
further deteriorating, few African states have the ability to ever pay debt
principal, and a significant number cannot meet interest payment schedules.
Under these circumstances, economic credit from virtually all major lenders
dried up, leaving only the World Bank/International Monetary Fund loan
packages with their grinding austerity measures to ward off the virtually
complete economic collapse of many (if not most) African governments.

■ STRUCTURAL ADJUSTMENT AND
THE REORDERING OF THE STATE

For the first twenty to twenty-five years, independent rule in most
African states was based on a relatively standard political and economic
structure. In the most simple terms, an autocratic leader emerged and consolidated political control through patronage and a heavily expanded state.
As a result of government employment and opportunities, connections, and
favors, a dominant group formed. Over time, as this urban-based group co-
alesced, government policies increasingly focused on maintaining their support.

Patronage networks, massive bureaucracies, and the economic needs of
a dominant class require a large and steady stream of money. As the economic crisis of the late 1970s reached cataclysmic proportions in the mid-
1980s, most African regimes were forced into the desperate gamble of
"structural adjustment" loans from the International Monetary Fund (IMF).

What must be understood is that African regimes have consistently
avoided IMF loans. Conditions tied to them require countries essentially to
reorder society by adjusting the structure of internal economic relationships.
Structural adjustment is controversial in Africa, as Virginia DeLancey discusses in Chapter 5, and for authoritarian patrimonial states, they are truly
last-ditch agreements. Most such agreements require countries to

1. Devalue currencies so that exports will be cheaper to foreign buyers;
2. Reduce deficits by freezing government salaries;
3. Quit setting agricultural prices and eliminate subsidies to urban consumers;
4. End import restrictions;
5. Privatize state-owned enterprises; and
6. Increase bank interest rates to encourage savings to generate capital investment.

Countries that have accepted these loans accept close surveillance of their economies by the Bank. Lofchie (1989:122) states that "at the level of government officer, structural adjustment has transferred effective operational authority from African civil servants to staff members of these international lending agencies." By 1989, all but five of forty-four sub-Saharan African states were borrowers from the IMF (Kraus, 1991:211–212).

From a political standpoint, the significance of these developments should not be underestimated, because for most countries the sweeping economic reforms required to receive IMF monies change the context of political relations not only between the rulers and the ruled but within regimes themselves.

At the outset, structural adjustment policies have a major impact on the urban areas, which rulers have often pacified by subsidizing foodstuffs. Deregulating agricultural prices has caused food costs to rise dramatically. In the major cities, where relatively little food is grown for personal use, price increases for such staples as rice, flour, and meal are often devastating. While the vast urban population made up largely of nonsalaried, underemployed, or unemployed poor feels the full effect of structural adjustment austerity, lower- and middle-range government employees are also affected substantially. Across the continent, opposition to food price increases has been especially bitter and has led to demonstrations and riots in many countries.

While allowing agricultural prices to rise and eliminating subsidies increased the scope and intensity of opposition to many African regimes and further undermined any remaining legitimacy, other austerity measures associated with structural adjustment threatened to unravel the very basis of regime existence. As governments froze salaries and sold off government corporations, money for patronage was drastically reduced, and positions connected to the system were eliminated. Furthermore, virtually bankrupt regimes slashed services and were increasingly unable to meet the pay schedules of teachers, public health workers, and other low- and medium-level civil servants. In other words, the patronage systems that in most African states tied together and supported an essential socioeconomic-political elite were either substantially weakened or began to break apart. (See

Chakoadza, 1993; Olukoshi, 1993; Onimode, 1989 for the social and political impact of SAPs.)

In many African countries, regimes in political and economic retreat faced variations of an increasingly common scenario:

1. Associational groups such as self-help organizations, cooperatives, churches, vigilante groups, and professional organizations, which had increased as the economic crisis worsened, expanded further under structural adjustment. Deeply rooted in society, these groups formed the basis of popular dissent toward the regime (see Bratton, 1989a, 1989b:29–33; Hyden, 1989:4–5; Shaw, 1990).
2. Civil servants and trade union members—whose living standards and incomes were most threatened by the economic crisis and austerity measures—began demanding political reforms ("A Chance for Africa," 1991:2; Neavoll, 1991:40; Press, 1991:4; Henry, 1991).
3. College students, graduates, and professors facing cutbacks and poor job prospects actively worked against the regime (Morna, 1990, 1991). They, along with civil servants and trade unionists, led popular demonstrations against the government.

As autonomous centers of power formed and opposition to regimes increased, many regimes faced additional pressures from outside the continent as well. The extraordinary political upheaval that brought democratization to the Soviet Union and Eastern Europe resulted in political accord between the superpowers and ended the Cold War. Under these new conditions, the strategic importance of Africa was greatly diminished. Among the consequences, the United States and the Soviet Union began to cooperate in foreign policy and to reduce both military and economic aid. Countries tied to the Soviet Union and Eastern Europe for aid and technology (such as Mozambique, Ethiopia, and Angola) had monies cut off and were pressured to accommodate political change. For client states of the United States (especially Zaire and Kenya), cutbacks in U.S. aid and the consequent new attention paid by the United States to human rights abuses by those states brought new and heavy pressures on rulers (see Hull, 1991:193–196, 233–234). In West Africa, former French colonies (Benin, Gabon, Côte d'Ivoire, and Chad) long dependent on French aid and troops to support single-party states and authoritarian rulers were subject to change in the foreign policy of France. New assistance from France apparently required regimes to be responsive to citizens' demands for political reform (Whiteman, 1991; see also Chapter 6).

All of these events created an atmosphere for change and heightened expectations Africans had for political transformation. Under these circumstances, the last decade of the twentieth century began.

■ BEYOND AUTOCRACY:
DEMOCRATIZATION IN AFRICA

By late 1989, in countries as different as Algeria and Zaire, Gabon and Madagascar, and Benin and Togo, open challenges to incumbent regimes became commonplace. At first, spontaneous demonstrations, strikes, and riots were focused on government austerity measures. Shortly thereafter, protest escalated rapidly into widespread and strident demands for the end of single-party rule, for accountable political officials, and for free elections (Bratton and van de Walle, 1992:27–38).

Most African regimes responded first with repression. However, shaken by the scope and intensity of protest and pressured by conditions and countries outside the continent, many African rulers moved reluctantly to actual or promised reform (see Kraus, 1991).

Beginning approximately with the new decade (1990), a period of remarkable political change began to take place. Within eighteen months, a large number of states had either publicly committed themselves to a multiparty political system or already allowed opposition parties to form. Among those that had legalized multiple political parties by late 1991 were Angola, Burkina Faso, Cameroon, Congo-Brazzaville, Guinea, Mozambique, Niger,

The democratization movements sweeping Africa are resulting in multiparty elections for the first time in many years. In 1990 multiparty elections were held in Côte d'Ivoire.

Sierra Leone, Togo, Zaire, and Zambia. Two others, Côte d'Ivoire and
Gabon, had allowed competitive elections with opposing parties to take
place by late 1990. Also during this period, President Robert Mugabe
retreated from his attempts to impose one-party rule on multiparty
Zimbabwe, and the Nigerian military government announced the formation
of a two-party system (though subsequent presidential elections were
annulled) (*African Demos,* 1991; Diamond, 1995:458).

During 1990 and 1991, several authoritarian regimes fell as the result of
either wars of liberation or peaceful elections. For example, after decades of
illegal occupation and rule by South Africa and a bloody liberation struggle,
Namibia (formerly South-West Africa) received independence in March
1990. And in the Horn of Africa, the highly repressive regimes of Siad Barre
in Somalia and Mengistu Haile Mariam of Ethiopia fell to liberation movements during the first half of 1991. In West Africa, political pressures led to
open democratic presidential elections in February and March 1991 in Cape
Verde, São Tomé and Principe, and Benin. In each case, a new president was
elected over the former ruler, and a peaceful transfer of power took place
(*African Demos,* 1991:vol. 4:8). In November 1991, Kenneth Kaunda,
leader of Zambia since independence, was soundly defeated in a relatively
problem-free presidential election by trade union leader Frederick Chiluba.
And, most remarkedly, on May 10, 1994, Nelson Mandela, leader of the
African National Congress (ANC), was sworn in as South Africa's first
black president. Altogether between 1990 and 1995, over thirty competitive
national elections were held across the continent, fourteen of which resulted
in peaceful transfers of power (Doro, 1995:245).

Clearly, a political transformation is taking place on the African continent. In a wide variety of states, power is being decentralized, political liberties are being expanded, and new individuals and groups are entering the
political arena. This thrust toward democratization is strengthened by the
loss of credibility of ideologies that legitimated autocracy (particularly the
Leninist version of Marxism); by the growth of local African and international human rights movements; and by expectations and the will to act
prompted by democratic revolutions elsewhere in the world (Diamond et al.,
1995:1–2). Increasingly, democratization is both prompted and underwritten
by "political conditionalities" placed on loans from the World Bank/IMF
and many donor countries that require regimes to implement democratic
reform in their countries before monies are released to them.

Yet, notwithstanding the democratic impulse, the social and economic
context that shaped the political trajectory of Africa over the past thirty years
remains substantially intact. Illiteracy and disease abound, unemployment
and poverty continue unabated, and inequalities between classes are far
worse than at independence. Furthermore, in most countries, divisive ethnic,
regional, religious, and even subethnic cleavages tear at the social fabric
(see Adediji, 1995:134). Interclan civil war in Somalia, genocide in Rwanda,

and religious tensions in Nigeria are notable cases in point. Therefore, as promising as these movements toward democratization in Africa might appear, it is premature to conclude that genuinely competitive multiparty democracies can easily be built or, with Africa's myriad problems, that they can survive.

These uncertainties have led to considerable debate among Africanist scholars. Can these fragile democracies become "consolidated"—i.e., gain respect over an extended period of time? (See *African Demos*, 1991.) Are they compatible with the harsh economic reforms currently taking place in Africa? Is Western-style democracy (as practiced in the United States and Europe) a workable idea in Africa with its host of problems and diverse cultures? Three perspectives currently dominate the debate on these issues.

One perspective is that, while Africa needs democracy, it must turn to its own precolonial traditions of rule to build authentic, workable democratic institutions. According to Adediji,

> The failure of African leaders to recover, proudly acknowledge, and act upon their continent's accumulated wisdom—whether social, economic, or political—largely accounts for the endemic crisis that has been Africa's plight since independence. Cut off from its history, postcolonial Africa has spawned no culture capable of nurturing internal dynamism and stability. (Adediji, 1995:138)

Another criticism is that Western models of democracy, with their strong focus on creating systems of political opportunity, are normally dominated by relatively small economic elites. Western democracy is seen as divisive and leading to class cleavages and voter disaffection. To survive in Africa, "winner-take-all" electoral politics must be replaced by democratic systems that include a much wider range of people and groups, that reward cooperation rather than conflict, and that build into the system mechanisms that promote participation and consensus building (Adediji, 1995:135–136).

Others see such efforts to turn to the precolonial past for some "utopian African form of democracy" as "naïve" (Callaghy, 1995:149) and "impractical" (van de Walle, 1995:158). Sandbrook (1993:92–94) points out that Africa's precolonial past offers relatively little guidance for the multiethnic, complex nation-states Africans now inhabit. There were many systems of rule in Africa's past, varying from highly centralized, autocratic states (e.g., among the Hausa-Fulani) to highly decentralized, egalitarian communities (e.g., among the Igbo). While there were often rudiments of democratic practice in these societies, the politics of patronage and conflict were commonplace, while such democratic values as tolerance of opposition and freedom of association were not.

Calling proposals to build African forms of democracy "back to the future," Callaghy (1995:149) dismisses them for ignoring the hard economic and international realities Africa faces. That is, given the current economic crisis in Africa, Africa's dependence on Western financial assistance, and Western insistence on economic and political liberalization along Western lines, there is little likelihood that such political experimentation will be feasible.

In fact, Callaghy (1995; Callaghy and Ravenhill, 1993:521–563) is not optimistic that Western-style democratic reforms can survive in more than a handful of African countries or that democracy will enable them to sustain necessary, but often painful, economic reform. Africa needs strong, capable states (not necessarily democratic ones) able to insulate themselves from both popular political pressures and narrow interest groups that would divert scarce public resources to meet current needs at the expense of long-term investments in development (see also Qadir et al., 1993).

The last perspective is that democracy is both needed and desirable in Africa. Democracy has advantages over the strong, authoritarian state and is better, not less, able to carry out economic reform. Among these advantages is that democracy compels governments to be more open to public scrutiny. This makes it easier to expose and curb incompetence and corruption. Another benefit is that ending single-party dominance will strengthen the professional bureaucracy and technocrats, thereby helping to eliminate politics from the decisionmaking process so that decisions will be more "rational." Also as governments become more open and inclusive, citizens perceive them as more legitimate. This can facilitate convincing the public of the need to undergo or sustain painful but (in the long run) beneficial reforms (see van de Walle, 1995:155–156; Diamond et al., 1995:9–19). Extending this argument, Clapham (1993:435) proposes that democracy may be the only way to avoid disintegration and chaos in African countries (e.g., Zaire) where both political and economic systems are in severe decline. Eventually, such states will have no choice but to appeal to popular support if they hope to survive.

Although the above perspectives on the desirability and viability of democracy in Africa differ, all agree on one thing: No state in Africa—be it authoritarian or democratic—will long survive without a measurable and sustainable improvement in economic development for Africa's long-suffering people.

■ BIBLIOGRAPHY

Adediji, Adebayo. 1995. "An Alternative for Africa." Pp. 126–139 in Larry Diamond and Marc F. Plattner (eds.). *Economic Reform and Democracy.* Baltimore: Johns Hopkins University Press.
African Demos. 1991. Vols. 1, 2, and 4 (January, March, and May).
Ake, Claude. 1981. *A Political Economy of Africa.* Burnt Mill, Harlow (Essex), England: Longman.

Amin, Samir. 1972. "Underdevelopment and Dependence in Black Africa: Origins and Contemporary Forms." *Journal of Modern African Studies* 4:503–521.

Ball, Nicole. 1981. "The Military in Politics: Who Benefits and How." *World Development* 9 (6):569–582.

Bates, Robert. 1981. *Markets and States in Tropical Africa.* Los Angeles: University of California Press.

Bendix, Reinhard. 1962. *Max Weber: An Intellectual Portrait.* Garden City, NY: Doubleday.

Beran, Paul. 1995. "The Only Way to Dislodge Nigeria's Dictator." *Christian Science Monitor* (November 24):19.

Bohannan, Paul, and Philip Curtin. 1988. *Africa and Africans.* Prospect Heights, IL: Waveland Press.

Boone, Catherine. 1990a. "The Making of a Rentier Class: Wealth Accumulation and Political Control in Senegal." *Journal of Development Studies* 26:425–449.

———. 1990b. "States and Ruling Classes in Post-Colonial Africa: The Enduring Contradictions of Power." Paper presented at the 33d annual meeting of the African Studies Association, Baltimore, November 1–4.

Bratton, Michael. 1989a. "Beyond Autocracy: Civil Society in Africa." Pp. 29–33 in *Beyond Autocracy in Africa.* Atlanta: The Carter Center of Emory University.

———. 1989b. "Beyond the State: Civil Society and Associational Life in Africa." *World Politics* 41:407–430.

Bratton, Michael, and Nicholas van de Walle. 1992. "Towards Governance in Africa: Popular Demands and State Responses." Pp. 27–55 in Goran Hyden and Michael Bratton (eds.). *Governance and Politics in Africa.* Boulder: Lynne Rienner Publishers.

Callaghy, Thomas M. 1984. *The State-Society Struggle: Zaire in Comparative Perspective.* New York: Columbia University Press.

———. 1995. "Africa: Back to the Future?" Pp. 140–152 in Larry Diamond and Marc F. Plattner (eds.). *Economic Reform and Democracy.* Baltimore: Johns Hopkins University Press.

Callaghy, Thomas M., and John Ravenhill. 1993. "How Hemmed In? Lessons and Prospects of Africa's Responses to Decline." Pp. 520–564 in Thomas M. Callaghy and John Ravenhill. *Hemmed In: Responses to Africa's Economic Decline.* New York: Columbia University Press.

"A Chance for Africa." 1991. *Africa News* 34 (May 20):2.

Chazan, Naomi, Robert Mortimer, John Ravenhill, and Donald Rothchild. 1988. *Politics and Society in Contemporary Africa.* Boulder: Lynne Rienner Publishers.

Chakoadza, Austin M. 1993. *Structural Adjustment in Zambia and Zimbabwe: Reconstruction or Destruction?* Harare: Third World Publishing House.

Clapham, Christopher. 1993. "Democratisation in Africa: Obstacles and Prospects." *Third World Quarterly* 14:423–438.

Cox, Thomas S. 1976. *Civil-Military Relations in Sierra Leone: A Case Study of African Soldiers in Politics.* Cambridge: Harvard University Press.

Decalo, Samuel. 1976. *Coups and Army Rule in Africa: Studies in Military Style.* New Haven: Yale University Press.

———. 1989. "Modalities of Civil-Military Stability in Africa." *Journal of Modern African Studies* 27:547–578.

Diamond, Larry. 1988. "Nigeria: Pluralism, Statism, and the Struggle for Democracy." Pp. 33–91 in Larry Diamond, Juan J. Linz, and Seymour Martin Lipset (eds.). *Democracy in Developing Countries: Africa.* Boulder: Lynne Rienner Publishers.

———. 1995. "Nigeria: The Uncivic Society and the Descent into Praetorianism."

Pp. 417–491 in Larry Diamond, Juan J. Linz, and Seymour Martin Lipset (eds.). *Politics in Developing Countries: Comparing Experiences with Democracy.* Boulder: Lynne Rienner Publishers.

Diamond, Larry, Juan J. Linz, and Seymour Martin Lipset (eds.). 1995. *Politics in Developing Countries: Comparing Experiences with Democracy.* Boulder: Lynne Rienner Publishers.

Doro, Marion E. 1995. "The Democratization Process in Africa." *Choice* (October):245–257.

Eisenstadt, Stuart N., and René Lemarchand. 1981. *Political Clientelism, Patronage and Development.* Beverly Hills: Sage Publications.

Fatton, Robert, Jr. 1986. "Clientelism and Patronage in Senegal." *African Studies Review* 29:61–78.

———. 1992. *Predatory Rule: State and Civil Society in Africa.* Boulder: Lynne Rienner Publishers.

Freund, Bill. 1984. *The Making of Contemporary Africa: The Development of African Society Since 1800.* Bloomington: Indiana University Press.

Government of Cameroon. Central Bureau of the Census. 1977. *Main Results of the April 1976 General Population and Housing Census.* Yaounde: Ministry of Economic Affairs and Planning.

Harbeson, John W., Donald Rothchild, and Naomi Chazan (eds.). 1994. *Civil Society and the State.* Boulder: Lynne Rienner Publishers.

Hayward, Fred M. 1987. "Introduction." Pp. 1–23 in Fred M. Hayward (ed.). *Elections in Independent Africa.* Boulder: Westview Press.

Henry, Neil. 1991. "Will Freedom Finally Follow Independence?" *The Washington Post National Weekly Edition* (June 3–9):18.

Hodder-Williams, Richard. 1984. *An Introduction to the Politics of Tropical Africa.* London: George Allen and Unwin.

Hodgkin, Thomas. 1957. *Nationalism in Colonial Africa.* New York: New York University Press.

Horowitz, Donald L. 1985. *Ethnic Groups in Conflict.* Berkeley: University of California Press.

Hull, Richard. 1991. "The Challenge to the United States in Africa." *Current History* 90:193–234.

Hyden, Goran. 1983. *No Shortcuts to Progress.* Berkeley: University of California Press.

———. 1989. "Community Governance and 'High' Politics." Pp. 2–7 in *Beyond Autocracy in Africa.* Atlanta: The Carter Center of Emory University.

Jackson, Robert H., and Carl J. Rosberg. 1982. *Personal Rule in Black Africa.* Berkeley: University of California Press.

Jeffries, Richard. 1989. "Ghana: The Political Economy of Personal Rule." Pp. 75–98 in Donald B. Cruise O'Brien, John Dunn, and Richard Rathbone (eds.). *Contemporary West African States.* Cambridge: Cambridge University Press.

Joseph, Richard A. 1977. *Radical Nationalism in Cameroon: Social Origins of the UPC Rebellion.* Oxford: Oxford University Press.

Kasfir, Nelson. 1983. "Designs and Dilemmas: An Overview." Pp. 25–47 in Phillip Mawhood (ed.). *Local Government in the Third World: The Experience of Tropical Africa.* Chichester, England: John Wiley and Sons.

———. 1987. "Class, Political Domination, and the African State." Pp. 35–61 in Zaki Ergas (ed.). *The African State in Transition.* New York: St. Martin's Press.

Kraus, John. 1991. "Building Democracy in Africa." *Current History* 90:209–212.

Lemarchand, René. 1988. "The State, the Parallel Economy and the Changing Structure of Patronage Systems." Pp. 149–170 in Donald Rothchild and Naomi

Chazan (eds.). *The Precarious Balance: State and Society in Africa.* Boulder: Westview Press.

Leslie, Winsome J. 1993. *Continuity and Change in an Oppressive State.* Boulder: Westview Press.

Liebenow, Gus J. 1986. *African Politics: Crisis and Challenges.* Bloomington: Indiana University Press.

Lofchie, Michael F. 1989. "Reflections on Structural Adjustment in Africa." Pp. 121–125 in *Beyond Autocracy in Africa.* Atlanta: The Carter Center of Emory University.

Luckham, Robin. 1994. "The Military, Militarization and Democratization in Africa." *African Studies Review* 37:13–75.

MacGaffey, Janet. 1988. "Economic Disengagement and Class Formation in Zaire." Pp. 171–188 in Donald Rothchild and Naomi Chazan (eds.). *The Precarious Balance: State and Society in Africa.* Boulder: Westview Press.

McGowan, Pat, and Thomas H. Johnson. 1984. "African Military Coups d'Etat and Underdevelopment: A Quantitative Historical Analysis." *Journal of Modern African Studies* 22:633–666.

Meroe, Isaac J. 1980. *The Performance of Soldiers as Governors.* Washington, DC: University Press of America.

Morna, Colleen Lowe. 1990. "Africa's Campuses Lead Pro-Democracy Drive." *The Chronicle of Higher Education* (November 28):A1, 40.

———. 1991. "Cutting Back on Campus." *Africa Report* 36(March-April):61–63.

Nafziger, Wayne F. 1988. *Inequality in Africa.* Cambridge: Cambridge University Press.

Neavoll, George. 1991. "A Victory for Democracy." *Africa Report* 36(May-June): 39–40, 42.

Olukoshi, Adebayo (ed.). 1993. *The Politics of Structural Adjustment in Nigeria.* Portsmouth, NH: Heinemann.

Onimode, Bade (ed.). 1989. *The IMF, the World Bank and the African Debt: The Social and Political Impact.* Vol. 2. London: Zed.

Press, Robert M. 1991. "Africa's Struggle for Democracy." *The Christian Science Monitor* (March 21):4.

Qadir, Shahid, Christopher Clapham, and Barry Gills. 1993. "Sustainable Democracy: Formalism vs. Substance." *Third World Quarterly* 14:415–422.

Rothchild, Donald, and Naomi Chazan (eds.). 1988. *The Precarious Balance: State and Society in Africa.* Boulder: Westview Press.

Rothchild, Joseph. 1981. *Ethnopolitics.* New York: Cambridge University Press.

Sandbrook, Richard. 1985. *The Politics of Africa's Economic Stagnation.* Cambridge: Cambridge University Press.

———. 1993. *The Politics of Africa's Economic Recovery.* Cambridge: Cambridge University Press.

Saul, John. 1975. "The Revolution in Portugal's African Colonies: A Review Essay." *Canadian Journal of African Studies* 9:321–340.

Shaw, Timothy M. 1990. "Popular Participation in Non-Government Structures in Africa: Implications for Democratic Development." Pp. 5–22 in *Africa Today.* Denver: Africa Today Associates.

Sklar, Richard L., and C. S. Whitaker. 1991. *African Politics and Problems in Development.* Boulder: Lynne Rienner Publishers.

Sullivan, Jo. 1989. *Global Studies: Africa.* Guilford, CT: Dushkin Publishing Group.

Tangri, Roger. 1985. *Politics in Sub-Saharan Africa.* London: James Currey and Heinemann Educational Books.

Tordoff, William. 1984. *Government and Politics in Africa.* Bloomington: Indiana University Press.

van de Walle, Nicolas. 1995. "Crisis and Opportunity in Africa." Pp. 153–166 in Larry Diamond and Marc F. Plattner (eds.). *Economic Reform and Democracy.* Baltimore: Johns Hopkins University Press.

Whiteman, Kaye. 1991. "The Gallic Paradox." *Africa Report* 36 (January-February):17–20.

Wolpe, Howard. 1974. *Urban Politics in Nigeria: A Study of Port Harcourt.* Berkeley: University of California Press.

World Bank. 1990a. *World Debt Tables, 1989–1990: Supplemental Report.* Washington, DC: World Bank.

———. 1990b. *World Development Report.* New York: Oxford University Press.

Wunsch, James S., and Dele Olowu. 1990. *The Failure of the Centralized State: Institutions and Self-Governance in Africa.* Boulder: Westview Press.

Young, Crawford. 1988a. "The African State and Its Colonial Legacy." Pp. 25–66 in Donald Rothchild and Naomi Chazan (eds.). *The Precarious Balance: State and Society in Africa.* Boulder: Westview Press.

———. 1988b. "Politics in Africa." Pp. 487–538 in Gabriel Almond and G. Bingham Powell, Jr. (eds.). *Comparative Politics Today: A World View.* Glenview, IL: Scott Foresman.

———. 1989. "Beyond Patrimonial Autocracy: The African Challenge." Pp. 22–24 in *Beyond Autocracy in Africa.* Atlanta: The Carter Center of Emory University.

Young, Crawford. 1994. *The African Colonial State in Comparative Perspective.* New Haven: Yale University Press.

Young, Crawford, and Thomas Turner. 1985. *The Rise and Decline of the Zairian State.* Madison: University of Wisconsin Press.

Zolberg, Aristide R. 1966. *Creating Political Order: The Party-States of West Africa.* Chicago: Rand McNally.

■ 5 ■

The Economies of Africa
Virginia DeLancey

■ PRECOLONIAL ECONOMIES

The earliest economies in sub-Saharan Africa were based on hunting, fishing, and gathering food. Economic activity varied, however, depending upon geographic location. In some regions of the continent, populations moved continually to search for food as the seasons changed. In regions where conditions were favorable year-round, populations were relatively sedentary (Clark, 1962:211–214). (See Chapter 2 for more on the relationship between Africa's geography and economic activities.)

Hunting and gathering societies persist today, such as the San of the Kalahari Desert in southern Africa and the Mbuti and the M'Baka of equatorial Africa. Pastoral societies are even more prevalent, particularly in the Sahel (areas bordering the Sahara Desert) and the savanna lands (grasslands) throughout the continent. The Fulani (Fulbe) of West Africa and the Maasai, the Somali, and the Turkana of East Africa are examples of pastoral peoples. Nevertheless, over time, populations became increasingly sedentary. As livestock and crops, especially cereals such as millet and sorghum, became domesticated, populations began to permanently occupy lands that previously could support only temporary settlements. Their economies became based upon agriculture or on agro-pastoralism (Wickins, 1986:33–36).[1]

Although societies became more sedentary over time, they did not necessarily become more isolated. On the contrary, the change to crop cultivation and/or livestock management meant that it was no longer necessary to search constantly for food. It provided both the opportunity to produce surplus food and the possibility to specialize in the production of food or other commodities for exchange in the market. It also allowed time to develop commercial networks. As a result, although many economies were basically self-sufficient—producing all necessary food, clothing, household objects, and farm equipment—many economies also included trade.

Markets developed for the exchange of food crops and livestock as well

91

as for household and farm equipment within local economies and among neighboring communities. Trade developed over very great distances as well. Gold from western Africa was traded internationally beginning as early as the eighth century (Fage, 1959:15, 47; Herskovits and Harwitz, 1964:299–300). Spices and tropical products were traded between eastern Africa and the Middle East. During the Middle Ages, gold, salt, and slaves, as well as many other products, continued to be traded along the trans-Saharan caravan routes that connected sub-Saharan Africa, especially western Africa, with northern Africa (Neumark, 1977:127–130). Clearly, African economies were interdependent and based on long-distance trade long before contact with the Europeans (Davidson, 1972:84). It was not until the 1400s, when Europeans began to explore the coasts of Africa, that African economies began to have major interaction with the economies of Europe.

Precolonial contacts with the international economy beyond the continental borders developed in eastern Africa as a result of trade along the perimeter of the Indian Ocean with the Middle East and Asia. Some of the earliest references to this trade occurred about A.D. 150. Because of the use of sea transport rather than camels, the products traded were less restricted to luxuries, although ivory was the most important commodity until the end of the nineteenth century. Other African commodities that entered the trade were slaves,[2] mangrove tree poles for house construction, iron, and gold (Austen, 1987:59).

Beginning about 1500, first the Portuguese and then the Omani attempted to control the Indian Ocean trade along the coast of eastern Africa, although other countries continued to trade as well (Austen, 1987:60–62).

In the nineteenth century, the British succeeded in gaining political dominance over the coast of eastern Africa. They attempted to destroy the slave trade but were not successful immediately. However, ivory, resins, cloves, and other "legitimate" products were also exported from as far south on the continent as Mozambique through Zanzibar in exchange for manufactured goods from Britain, France, and the United States. During this time, there was considerable expansion of trade far into the interior of the continent in commodities such as foodstuffs, iron (and iron implements), copper, salt, and other export goods such as cloves, cowries, gum copal, copra, and cereals (Austen, 1987:60–63).

In western Africa, the Portuguese voyages of exploration, beginning in the fifteenth century, brought the coastal societies into contact with the international economy. Over time, economic relations increased from Senegal to Angola, although Europeans seldom settled on this part of the continent because of the harsh climate and the associated health risks. Instead, European traders, who relied on African intermediaries to reach the hinterland, established permanent trading posts, called "factories," on shipboard (Austen, 1987:81–84).

Although certain commodities such as ivory, timber, gum, and wax were staple exports from the African continent, there were other commodities that were especially important at different periods of time. The Portuguese, then later the Dutch, British, and the Danish, came to search for gold. The trade in gold reached its peak in the sixteenth and seventeenth centuries and then declined, either because of the inability to mine additional gold with the technology of that era or because of the increase in demand for slaves.

The demand for slaves arose with the development of European-owned sugar plantations. After 1600, as the Dutch, British, and French opened plantations in the New World, the demand for slaves increased rapidly, reaching its peak in the 1800s. Between 1810 and 1870 the slave trade was declared illegal for Europeans and North Americans, although it continued for many more years.

The most immediate economic impact of the slave trade was the loss of an enormous source of productive human labor and the resultant redistribution of the population of the continent. The civil disruption associated with slaving also had economic effects. Many of those who were not captured died during the raids or went into hiding to escape being caught. Agricultural production must have decreased, in part because of the difficulty of farming during the raids. In addition, the strongest young men and women were forced to leave their farms, or disappeared on their own initiative until danger subsided. Health was also affected, as a result of new diseases such as cholera and smallpox, which were introduced by the movement of peoples through the continent. Susceptibility to disease also increased, resulting from the poor diets and reduced food consumption that occurred with the disruption of agriculture. This surely lowered productivity for physical reasons as well as for psychological reasons.

"Legitimate" trade of vegetable oils such as palm oil, palm kernels, and peanuts began to increase from the beginning of the nineteenth century, while trade of wild rubber developed later in the century. The Industrial Revolution continuing in Europe during the nineteenth century provided the opportunity for shifting from the illegal trade in slaves to trade in the raw materials that were needed for European industry (Austen, 1987:85–87).

■ THE INFLUENCE OF COLONIALISM

The partition of Africa among the European powers in the late 1800s had both economic and political origins. Although imperialism may have spread to protect strategic transport routes and to demonstrate national power and prestige, perhaps its most immediate purpose was to protect economic interests that had been developing over the past several centuries. The Berlin Conference of 1884–1885 marked the beginning of this new era of economic as well as political relationships between Europe and Africa.

The economic impact of colonialism was significant and varied. It affected production, distribution, and consumption on the continent. As the Industrial Revolution spread throughout Europe, increased quantities of raw materials were required for the growth of production in the recently established factories. The trade in primary commodities that had begun earlier in the century expanded to include other commodities as a result of successful experimentation with crops introduced from other parts of the world. Among these were cotton and other fibers introduced for export to the new European textile mills. Coffee, tea, and cacao were introduced for the production of beverages and sweets for wealthy Europeans. Cultivation of these export crops brought many African farmers into the cash economy either as smallholders or as wage employees on plantations.

Following the European assumption that only men were farmers, production of these crops was introduced mainly to men, even though African women have always been important farmers. As a result, African men became the most important export crop producers, while women continued to produce food crops to sustain their families. However, when women were able to produce a surplus of food crops, they often sold them in local markets to earn extra cash. This pattern has persisted until today and has continued to affect the sexual division of labor in African agriculture, as April Gordon discusses in Chapter 10.

Where climate and other conditions were favorable, some Europeans migrated to Africa. They established their own farms or plantations, settling some of the best, most fertile land, particularly in eastern, central, and southern Africa. This has had both economic and political repercussions over time, with South Africa representing the extreme (see Chapter 13).

The European factories craved not only agricultural crops but also minerals. Copper, diamond, and gold mines, as well as mines for cobalt, manganese, and other minerals, were established, mainly in central and southern Africa. The demand for labor in these mines led to distinct patterns of migration to supply that labor.

Young men left home and even migrated across borders to work in the mines of the Rhodesias and South Africa. Many young men also migrated from the poor, landlocked hinterland to work for wages on the coastal plantations in western Africa. They went either permanently or for long periods of time, alternating with short visits home. This changed the role of the wives and families who were often left behind. The women attempted to farm without the assistance of their men, often taking over the agricultural tasks formerly done by men. Sometimes they received seasonal assistance from the men when they were able to take leave from their wage employment to return home to help with the heaviest work of preparing the land for the next farming season or harvesting the crops.

Where migration did not occur naturally, the movement of people was sometimes "assisted." Forced labor was not uncommon; it was often demanded by colonial governments to build roads and railroads or to work on the plantations.

The increased production of export commodities not only caused population movement but also affected the infrastructure of the continent. It led to the development of new distribution systems. Roads and railroads were built to evacuate the commodities from the hinterland to the coast for export to Europe. However, they did not connect and integrate countries on the continent. This too is a pattern that persists today and has been a constraint upon the ability of countries to implement regional economic integration. (See Map 2.3 in Chapter 2.)

Colonialism affected consumption as well. The new industries of Europe sought not only sources of raw materials from their colonies but also markets for the products they produced. Colonies provided "captive consumers"; the special trade preferences that were often set up between the colonial powers and their colonies remain strong today. As African workers entered the money economy, they began to desire imported consumer goods that were not produced domestically or luxuries such as bicycles and radios. Increasing numbers of Africans entered the money economy during the colonial years either as cash crop farmers or as wage earners. They worked to earn income not only to purchase goods but also to pay required taxes. Because colonial administrations were responsible for financing much of their budget in each country, they had to find sources of revenue. As a result, various forms of taxation were instituted, including taxation of individuals as well as taxation of export production and imports.

In sum, colonialism did not originate to assist African countries to develop economically. It originated to benefit European countries. That is not to say that African countries did not receive any benefits, but the growth or development that occurred in those countries was mainly peripheral to the growth and development of Europe. Only as it became clear that the colonies would soon seek independence did European countries begin to guide some of their colonies toward the goal of developing their own economies. In doing so, they began to establish a few domestic industries (usually fledgling import-substitution industries for simple-to-produce goods such as matches, plastic shoes, beer and soft drinks, and textiles) in addition to continuing production of primary commodities for export. These efforts were minimal, however, and did little to make African economies self-sufficient. By the 1960s, the colonial administrations were being dismantled rapidly across the continent—but many economic ties to the former colonial powers remained.

■ **POSTCOLONIAL DEVELOPMENT STRATEGIES**

In the years following World War II, European countries realized that soon they would have to grant their colonies independence and began to take definite steps toward the conclusion of their political rule. Britain and

France especially began to draw up long-term development plans for their colonies. Following independence in the 1960s, nearly every sub-Saharan African country continued to prepare (with mixed success) medium- to long-term economic development plans, usually covering time spans of three to five years.

In the early days of independence, Africans were optimistic that the plans would succeed in achieving the objective of promoting rapid economic growth as well as economic development within a few years. Alas, as the First Development Decade ended at the close of the 1960s, it was clear that the objective was not much closer to being achieved than at the beginning of the decade. This was especially difficult to accept, as it had been widely believed at the time of independence that as soon as the colonial powers left the continent and countries were able to take charge of their own economies, they would prosper. It was difficult to deal with rising aspirations that were not being satisfied.

There were several reasons why initial development efforts failed to bring about the desired results. Recent experience in rebuilding Europe after World War II showed the success of the Marshall Plan in channeling large quantities of foreign aid to the European countries, but Europe had already been developed prior to its destruction. The infrastructure and capital had already existed. There was an educated, skilled labor force and experienced management. Foreign aid was used simply to rebuild and replace what had already existed. In Africa the situation was different. The physical infrastructure during colonial days was minimal and was designed mainly to produce and export primary commodities to Europe and to support the colonial administration. Thus, new road systems had to be built as well as water, electric, and telephone networks. Furthermore, appropriate educational systems had to be designed and human resources trained. Not only was the literacy level low, but the educational system that existed then, and that exists in many countries even today, was not relevant to the needs of society. In addition, few Africans had been trained in management or public administration, and few had much experience in the practical aspects of running a government or operating a large-scale business or industry.

At independence, most countries were still agrarian. However, it was widely believed at that time that industrialization was the best strategy to achieve development. As a result, the agricultural sector was ignored in many development plans and emphasis was placed upon building industries. Most of the initial attempts were aimed at setting up import-substitution industries to produce previously imported goods. It was believed that this would be beneficial because it would save foreign exchange. It was forgotten, however, that if these industries took the place of industries that could produce for export, the countries would lose the opportunity to earn foreign exchange, which was required to import necessary capital (e.g., technology) for development. In addition, import-substitution industries do not always save foreign exchange as planned, because they often must import the required production equipment, spare parts, and sometimes even the raw materials to go into the production process. Consequently, the emphasis on industrialization did not necessarily improve the economies of Africa.

The drive to industrialize, in fact, hurt the economies of many countries, particularly the agricultural sectors. It stimulated rural-urban migration, yet there were insufficient jobs in the cities to absorb those who had left the countryside. And, as will be discussed in greater detail below, the net emigration rate from the rural areas was one of the causes of the decrease in food production that has led to the continentwide food crisis.

During the Second (1970s) and Third (1980s) Development Decades, African countries began to recognize that there were problems in the agricultural sector, but few of them invested heavily in that sector. During those decades, many African countries also recognized that political independence was a necessary, but not a sufficient, condition for taking control of their destiny. They realized that it was necessary to have economic independence but that they had not been able to achieve it.

Latin American economists had been the first to develop the theory of economic "dependency," but African countries soon discovered that it was applicable to them as well. For example, they were still tied to their former colonial powers through preferential trade agreements and bilateral aid. That is, their exports continued to be primary commodities, and trade (both exports and imports) was still directed toward the former colonizers. In addition, many countries had monocrop economies, where they depended primarily on one commodity for their export earnings. For example, in 1990–1991, Burundi received 78 percent and Uganda received 71 percent of the value of their exports from coffee. Burkina Faso received 63 percent and Chad received 62 percent from cotton, Réunion received 71 percent from sugar, and Malawi received 71 percent from tobacco. Other countries gained most of their foreign earnings from a single mineral export. Guinea, for instance, received 82 percent of its export earnings from nonferrous ores, Zambia received 88 percent from copper, and Niger received 72 percent from uranium. Nigeria received 95 percent and Angola received 92 percent from crude petroleum.

Such undiversified economies left African countries at the mercy of not only their former colonial masters but also the whims of the international market. When the international price of their one export product dropped, the revenues for their development plan suffered. In addition, over time the international "terms of trade" for their exports deteriorated. That is, African countries found that they had to export more and more of their primary commodities simply to earn enough foreign exchange to purchase the same quantity of manufactured goods as in the past.

Table 5.1 Africa's Commodity Dependence,[a] Selected Countries

Algeria ($10.5 billion)
Petroleum products   35.6
Crude petroleum   31.6
Gas   30.2

Angola ($3.7 billion)
Crude petroleum   91.8
Natural abrasives   5.6
Petroleum products   1.5

Burkina Faso ($0.1 billion)
Cotton   62.5
Hides, skins   5.4
Live animals   3.8

Burundi ($0.1 Billion)
Coffee   78.2
Tea   9.7

Cameroon ($2.0 billion)
Crude petroleum   3.6
Cocoa   13.2
Wood, rough   7.2

Central Afr. Rep. ($0.1
billion)
Precious/semiprecious
  stones   60.5
Coffee   9.7
Wood, shaped   7.8

Chad ($0.2 billion)
Cotton   60.8
Live animals   18.2
Crude vegetable
  materials   1.6

Congo ($1.0 billion)
Crude petroleum   68.7
Wood, rough   11.1
Precious/semiprecious
  stones   10.6

Côte d'Ivoire ($2.9 billion)
Cocoa   32.5
Wood, shaped   7.5
Coffee   7.4

Ethiopia ($0.2 billion)
Coffee   51.3
Hides, skins   17.8
Vegetables, fresh/
  preserved   6.0

Gabon ($2.4 billion)
Crude petroleum   76.1
Wood, rough   10.4
Base metal ores   9.1

Ghana ($1.1 billion)
Cocoa   37.0
Aluminum   17.5
Precious/semiprecious
  stones   8.7

Guinea ($0.6 billion)
Base metal   82.2
Precious/semiprecious
  stones   6.7
Live animals   2.3

Kenya ($1.0 billion)
Tea   23.9
Coffee   15.3
Petroleum products   6.5

Liberia ($0.3 billion)
Wood, rough   23.4
Iron ore   17.5
Natural rubber   12.4

Madagascar ($0.3 billion)
Spices (cloves)   26.3
Shellfish, fresh/
  frozen   15.2
Coffee   11.6

Malawi ($0.4 billion)
Tobacco   71.3
Tea   9.5
Sugar, honey   6.4

Mali ($0.3 billion)
Cotton   51.5
Live animals   23.1
Precious/semiprecious
  stones   9.4

Mauritania ($0.04 billion)
Iron ore   56.8
Fresh fish, shellfish 38.3
Petroleum products   1.2

Mauritius ($1.2 billion)
Clothing   48.7
Sugar, honey   28.8
Watches, clocks   2.4

Niger ($0.03 billion)
Uranium   71.7
Live animals   13.5
Coffee   1.0

Nigeria ($12.6 billion)
Crude petroleum   94.9
Petroleum products   1.3
Cocoa   0.9

Réunion ($0.2 billion)
Sugar, honey   71.2
Fresh fish, shellfish 4.3
Alcoholic beverages   2.7

Rwanda ($0.1 billion)
Coffee   64.7
Tea   8.9
Crude vegetable
  materials   2.7

Senegal ($0.7 billion)
Fish, shellfish, fresh/
  preserved   30.1
Vegetable oils   14.1
Petroleum products   14.0

Sierra Leone ($0.1 billion)
Precious/semiprecious
  stones (diamonds)   41.6
Base metal ores   40.5
Fish, shellfish, fresh/
  frozen   5.3

Somalia ($0.6 billion)
Live animals   35.6
Fresh fruit   26.0
Fish, shellfish, fresh/
  frozen/preserved   17.0

Sudan ($0.6 billion)
Cotton   46.2
Crude vegetable
  materials   16.9
Seeds for vegetable
  oil   5.6

Togo ($0.3 billion)
Fertilizers   46.4
Cotton   21.3
Coffee   5.2

Uganda ($0.2 billion)
Coffee   71.3
Hides, skins   6.9
Cotton   5.6

Zaire ($0.9 billion)
Copper   39.6
Precious/semiprecious
  stones   19.6
Crude petroleum   10.5

Zambia ($0.8 billion)
Copper   87.5
Nonferrous base
  metals   5.2
Precious/semiprecious
  stones   1.5

Zimbabwe ($1.4 billion)
Tobacco   28.1
Pig iron   9.8
Nickel   6.8

Source: UNCTAD, *Handbook of International Trade and Development Statistics,* 1993:196–218.
Note: a. Value of total exports and percentage of total exports of three leading items 1990/91

African economies are highly dependent on export crops, like tea, whose prices have fallen drastically since the 1970s.

Not only did these former colonies remain dependent upon their former colonizers, but they also became dependent upon the wealthy, developed nations in general. Because of the unequal and exploitative power relationships in the international capitalist system that dominates the world, according to dependency theory or center-periphery models of development, the wealthy, developed countries (the "center") prevent the poor countries (the "periphery") from developing. Instead, the gap between the rich and poor countries remains or even widens as most of the benefits of trade go to the already developed countries.

Moreover, within the peripheral countries, the members of certain elite groups, especially government officials, military leaders, and certain entrepreneurs, cooperate with the institutions of the powerful center such as multinational corporations, as well as bilateral and multilateral foreign aid donors. In doing so, the elite promote their own interests, especially financial interests, but they also help to maintain themselves and their country in a dependent relationship with those powerful international institutions.

As the 1980s began and African countries entered the Third Development Decade without much progress toward achieving their goals, considerable controversy arose as to the direction that renewed development efforts should take. Determined to take the initiative for their continent's development and to have some input into the development strategy for the next United Nations Development Decade, the Assembly of Heads of State and Government of the OAU adopted the Monrovia Declaration in 1979. The strategy emphasized self-reliant development.

In April 1980, the UN Economic Commission for Africa (UNECA) and the OAU adopted the Lagos Plan of Action (LPA). It identified actions that needed to be taken to implement the objectives of the Monrovia Declaration. More specifically, the LPA set food self-sufficiency as its primary goal. It also urged self-reliance in industry, transport and communications, human and natural resources, and science and technology. The Final Act of Lagos (FAL) pressed for subregional economic integration with the goal of establishing an African Economic Community by the end of the century.

In the fall of 1979, while the LPA was being finalized, the African finance ministers, in their capacity as the African governors of the World Bank, sent a memorandum to the president of the World Bank. They requested that a special report be written on the economic problems of sub-Saharan African countries—a report that would include suggestions for solving those problems. The result was the preparation of *Accelerated Development in Sub-Saharan Africa: An Agenda for Action* (World Bank, 1981), more commonly known as the Berg Report (after Elliot Berg, the coordinator of the group that wrote the report).

The Berg Report stated that it accepted the long-term objectives of African development as expressed in the Lagos Plan of Action (based on the Monrovia Declaration); however, it foresaw the need for alternative short- and medium-term action to respond to Africa's economic difficulties. One of its most important recommendations urged that aid in real terms be doubled in order to stimulate a renewal of economic growth.

The central theme of the Berg Report stressed that more efficient use of scarce resources—human and capital, managerial and technical, domestic and foreign—was essential for improving economic conditions in most African countries. It pointed out that public sector organizations would have to build the infrastructure and provide education, health care, and other services. That would create enormous demand for capable administrators and managers, the scarcest resources in those countries; therefore, the report recommended that African governments seek ways to make public sector organizations more efficient and place greater reliance on the private sector to fulfill those needs.

The report also emphasized the interdependency of countries throughout the world and maintained that African countries should pursue their "comparative advantage" by striving to improve production of their export products. In effect, this meant that African countries should continue to export primary commodities like coffee and use their foreign exchange earnings to import essential manufactured goods and even their food requirements. This was unacceptable to African governments, and it initiated a heated debate. African governments believed that implementation of such a policy would most certainly leave their countries in a permanent state of dependency and poverty and prevent them from solving their ever increasing problems of feeding their rapidly growing populations. Pursuing their comparative advantage in production and export of primary commodities would make them dependent upon the developed world for their food supplies as well as for capital goods (e.g., technology) and many manufactured consumer goods. Even worse, those capital and other manufactured goods were becoming increasingly expensive as long-term deterioration in the terms of trade between manufactured goods and primary commodities occurred. Even the cost of imported food requirements, such as wheat, was becoming increasingly expensive.

In response to criticism of the Berg Report by African governments, the World Bank issued several follow-up reports,[3] including *Sub-Saharan Africa: From Crisis to Sustainable Growth* (World Bank, 1989b:xi–xii). The latter affirmed:

1. Most African countries have embarked upon structural adjustment programs designed to transform their economies and make them more competitive.
2. To achieve food security, provide jobs, and improve living standards, African economies must achieve a growth rate of 4–5 percent.
3. For growth to be sustainable, major efforts must be made to protect the environment.
4. Economic growth must be based upon agriculture for at least the next decade.
5. Agriculture must expand twice as fast as at present in order to feed the rapidly growing population and decrease malnutrition.
6. The key to food security is to develop and apply new technology while slowing population growth rates.

An important theme of the report is that sound macroeconomic policies and an efficient infrastructure are necessary for the productive use of resources, but that they are not sufficient to transform the structure of African economies. Major efforts are needed to build African capacities; to produce a better-trained, healthier population; and to strengthen the institutional framework within which development can take place. The report supports the call made by the UNECA, the United Nations Development Programme (UNDP), and the United Nations International Children's Emergency Fund (UNICEF) for a human-centered development strategy.

The report also stresses that good governance is important, that there must be an efficient public service, a judicial system that is reliable, and an administration that is accountable to its public. There must be a better balance between the government and the governed. (Donald Gordon explains in Chapter 4 how African political systems have hindered economic development.) The report contains proposals to give ordinary people, and especially women, greater responsibility for improving their lives. This can be achieved best through grassroots organization that nurtures rather than obstructs informal sector enterprises and that promotes nongovernmental organizations (NGOs) and intermediary bodies. In other words, development must be more bottom-up and less top-down; it must include more participation, particularly in the planning stages, by those who will benefit from it.

Because the difficulties facing Africa are so formidable, the report encourages joint action among all the partners in development—African governments and multilateral institutions, the private sector and the donors, official and nongovernmental organizations. It maintains that by working together, African governments will be able to achieve more rapid progress toward regional cooperation and integration, the central theme of the Lagos Plan of Action as well as the African Development Bank.

The earlier World Bank reports as well as this one call for increased aid. They note, however, that aid must be accompanied by improved policies because, in the long run, dependency on aid must be reduced and eliminated. Moreover, in the short run, ways must be found to mobilize resources, including measures to reduce African debt (World Bank, 1989b:xii).

■ CURRENT ISSUES

Since the 1960s, when most sub-Saharan African countries gained political independence, the continent has experienced persistent economic problems. These economic problems, in turn, have affected the social aspects of development, that is, the health, education, and general quality of life.

Throughout the continent, economic growth[4] has averaged about 3 percent since 1961, although it has varied by country. The existence of economic growth, even rapid economic growth, however, does not mean that economic development is also occurring. For example, economic growth may increase income inequality within countries if the wealthy control the resources and reap the benefits of increased production. Economic growth may also result in environmental degradation in the race to increase production. Neither of these consequences of economic growth can be considered economic development. Neither of these consequences improves the overall quality of life of the people in terms of reducing poverty, increasing the equality of income distribution, and decreasing unemployment, some of the most important goals of economic development. Yet, if economic growth is slow, it is more difficult to achieve the goals of development. This is particularly true if population growth is also rapid. It would be extremely difficult to achieve development if population growth is more rapid than economic growth, because this would cause the gross national product (GNP) per capita to actually decline. In fact, the worst scenario has occurred in sub-Saharan Africa; overall economic growth has decreased over the decades since independence while the population growth rate has increased.

Economic growth in sub-Saharan Africa has also varied over time. From 1961 to 1972, per capita income increased. Those were optimistic years immediately after independence when there was a net positive inflow of foreign investment and assistance, and when population growth was lower than it is today. From 1973 to 1982, economies stagnated, at least partly from the impact of adverse external factors. For example, in 1973 when the Organization of Petroleum Exporting Countries (OPEC) agreed to a dramatic increase in oil prices, it immediately affected the supply of foreign exchange of African countries. The increased prices benefited the few African petroleum exporters (Nigeria, Gabon, Angola, and Congo) by increasing their supply of foreign exchange. However, it was an economic disaster for most African countries. It severely depleted their reserves of foreign exchange or increased their already heavy burden of debt as they attempted to continue to maintain imports of petroleum necessary for continuing their previously determined development plans.

The impact of the oil crisis was compounded by a severe drought that stretched across the entire Sahelian region in 1972–1973. Hundreds of thousands of refugees fled the drought-stricken areas, flocking to the cities or seeking new pastures, often crossing borders into other countries. Agricultural production decreased drastically, and livestock starved to death. The affected countries required immediate supplies of imported food and food aid to prevent mass starvation of their populations. This put a further burden on foreign exchange reserves and increased the debt of many countries.

These mainly external factors in combination with domestic policy shortcomings resulted in a slowing of economic growth. A similar oil crisis in 1978 and declining world prices for the primary commodity exports of Africa, along with continued domestic policy deficiencies, led to a period of actual economic decline in the 1980s and the first half of the 1990s. Estimates of annual GNP per capita growth from 1980 to 1993 vary from −0.8 percent to −1.8 percent, although there are predictions of at least a temporary return to positive growth in 1995 (Katsouris and Bentsi-Enchill, 1995:1, 10; World Bank 1995b:163; UNDP, 1995:195).

Today, sub-Saharan Africa is in the depths of an economic crisis. This crisis is characterized by weak agricultural growth, a decline in industrial output, poor export production, disintegration of the productive and infrastructural facilities, increasing debt, deteriorating social indicators and institutions (especially education, public health and sanitation, housing, and potable water), and destruction of the environment (World Bank, 1989b:2;

Photo: World Bank

In many African countries, much of the infrastructure of roads, railways, and ports has deteriorated—a symptom of the economic crisis gripping the continent.

Photo: Thomas O'Toole. Reprinted from The Central African Republic: The Continent's Hidden Heart, Thomas E. O'Toole, 1986, by permission of Westview Press, Boulder, Colorado.

United Nations, n.d.:i). As a result of this crisis, the standard of living of most Africans has declined in recent years, and there is increased poverty throughout the continent.

Some of the most important issues that have affected sub-Saharan African economies in the 1980s and first half of the 1990s include the following:

- Rapid population growth and declining per capita income
- Weak agricultural growth rates and the food crisis
- Urbanization and unemployment
- Marginalization of women in the development process
- The impact of AIDS
- Role of the public sector: state-owned corporations and control of the price system
- Debt crisis
- Deforestation and environmental degradation
- Economic integration
- Structural adjustment: the role of the World Bank, the IMF, the United Nations, and the UNECA

While some of these topics are discussed in other chapters (see especially Chapters 4, 6, 7, 8, and 10), each will be discussed briefly below to emphasize its economic significance.

□ Rapid Population Growth and Declining Per Capita Income

In precolonial and colonial days, birthrates were high in Africa, as they were in Europe and the United States when the latter economies were still mainly agrarian. Since World War II, and especially since independence, many new medicines have been developed, public health measures have been expanded (such as providing clean water), and African populations have slowly gained greater access to trained health officials and medical facilities. As a result, death rates have dropped dramatically across the continent, although this has been more true in urban than in rural locations. Birthrates have remained high, however, producing increased population growth rates in some countries.

One of the important economic implications of an increase in the population growth rate is that it becomes increasingly difficult for countries to maintain or increase the amount of food production per person. That is, if population is growing at a rate faster than that of food production, people will experience a decrease in the amount of food they can consume unless countries begin to import food or resort to food aid. If countries attempt to close the food gap by importing food, they must pay for it with foreign exchange, which presents further problems, because most African countries already suffer from severe balance of payments problems and thus shortages of foreign exchange. In addition, if countries resort to food aid, they increase their dependency on other countries.

A second economic implication of an increase in the population growth rate is that it requires an expansion in services and infrastructure such as schools, hospitals, and roads as well as supplies of water and electricity. Yet, African governments have had difficulty maintaining the services and infrastructure that now exist.

A third economic implication of an increase in the population growth rate is that GNP must be divided among an increasing number of people if the growth rate of the population is greater than that of the GNP. Although a declining GNP per capita does not necessarily mean that development is decreasing, it suggests that development may be increasingly difficult to achieve. For example, if one goal of development is to increase the equality of incomes throughout the economy, then it may be necessary to redistribute income from the rich to the poor if national income is not growing, a politically difficult task. Similarly, if another goal is to decrease unemployment, it may be difficult to find new jobs for individuals if production is not increasing. In general, it will be more difficult to eradicate poverty in a stagnant or declining economy. In fact, from 1980 to 1993, twenty-three of the thirty-eight sub-Saharan African countries for which data are available showed negative growth rates of GNP per capita, and five others had growth rates lower than 1 percent. Thus, nearly three-fourths of the countries had either stagnant or declining economies on a per capita basis during that time period. It should not be unexpected, then, that the average growth rate of GNP per capita from 1980 to 1993 for sub-Saharan countries was also negative (between –0.8 and –1.8 percent) (World Bank, 1995b:162–163; UNDP, 1995:195).

□ **Weak Agricultural
Production and the Food Crisis**

Although the economies of most sub-Saharan African countries remain based upon agriculture, their agricultural sectors are not healthy. They have recorded weak growth rates of agricultural production. Since 1965, the overall growth rate of agriculture in sub-Saharan Africa has been less than that of population. In fact, while the population growth rate has increased from 2.6 percent to 2.9–3.0 percent, the overall growth rate of agricultural production has decreased from 2.2 percent to 1.7 percent. At the country level, the findings are similar. Among the individual countries, 5 out of 35 had a negative average annual growth rate of agricultural production over the period 1980–1993. Moreover, the growth rate of agriculture was greater than that of population in only eleven countries; it was lower than that of population in nineteen countries (World Bank, 1995b:164–165, 210–211; World Bank, 1989a:222, 269). In effect, agricultural production per capita declined.

Within the agricultural sector, food production also was weak. The average annual growth rate of food production during the period 1979–1993 was negative for twenty-six out of thirty-five countries. It was positive for only seven countries, and it was zero for two countries. This means that the populations of almost three-fourths of the sub-Saharan African countries had access to less per person on the average in 1993 than they did in 1979 (World Bank, 1995b:168–169).

In the United States, only 2 percent of the labor force produces enough food to feed the U.S. population, sell large quantities on the world market, and still supply food aid to Third World countries, including many of those in Africa. The percentage of the labor force working in agriculture in Africa has decreased from 78 percent in 1965 to 67 percent in 1990–1992 (UNDP, 1995:177). This is a problem, however, because those remaining have been unable to produce enough to feed the populations of their countries. Every country in sub-Saharan Africa imported cereals in 1993, and the total amount imported had more than tripled from 4,108,000 metric tons in 1974 to 13,157,000 metric tons (World Bank, 1990:184; World Bank, 1995b:168–169). Furthermore, every country (for which data were available) had received food aid in 1992–1993, and that aid had increased to more than five and a half times what it had been in 1975–1976, from 910,000 metric tons to 5,079,000 metric tons (World Bank, 1989b:234, 277; World Bank, 1995b:168–169).

There are many reasons agricultural production is weak. Rural-urban migration, as discussed above, is only symptomatic of the deeper problems that exist in the agricultural sector. Reasons for weak agricultural production include low levels of rural services such as access to water, cooking fuel, and electricity, and deficient infrastructure, particularly farm-to-market roads and other marketing channels. Other reasons for low agricultural production include lack of sufficient and relevant agricultural research and extension of the results of that research, especially new agricultural methods and technology. The reasons include, as well, uncertainty brought about by recent changes in land tenure legislation and the risk-averse reaction of reluctance to invest in the land. Finally, they include continued lack of attention to the important role of women in African agriculture, especially in food production for domestic consumption, and consequent failure to assist women farmers to increase their production.

Government macroeconomic policies have also hurt the agricultural sectors of African countries. Development policies in the past have emphasized other sectors of the economy to the neglect of agriculture. Recall that in the 1960s, development policies emphasized industrialization. When it was realized that industrialization did not necessarily lead to development, governments began to pay lip service to promoting the Green Revolution in agriculture, though they continued to initiate development projects in the cities. It is not uncommon for the agricultural sector in many less developed countries (LDCs) to contribute a higher percentage of GNP than is invested in that sector. In sub-Saharan Africa, excluding South Africa, agriculture on the average contributed 30 percent of gross domestic product in 1993, although it ranged as high as 60 percent in Ethiopia, 56 percent in Tanzania, 53 percent in Uganda, and 50 percent in the Central African Republic (World Bank, 1995b:166–169). Yet, national investment in agriculture in sub-Saharan Africa did not approach that percentage. One study of development plans, which provided reasonably comparable data for seventeen sub-Saharan African countries, found that in thirteen of them the agricultural sector contributed a higher percentage to GDP than was reinvested in that sector. Planned investment was greater than the percentage contributed by that sector to GDP in only four of them (Metra Consulting, 1988). In sum, throughout sub-Saharan Africa, rural areas have often been exploited for the benefit of the urban areas, not only during colonial times but also since independence.

Investing heavily in the urban areas makes political sense. It is difficult for farmers who are physically separated from each other and distant from the urban-based politicians to form a united front to lobby for improved services and infrastructure and for higher prices for their products. The ever increasing numbers of urban constituents have immediate access to the government to pressure for their interests, including low food prices.

Government policies to regulate the prices and marketing channels of agricultural products, especially for export crops and domestic staples, have affected production as well. In colonial days, government marketing boards were set up for individual crops to consolidate the export production of individual producers for sale on the international market. The marketing boards were designed to serve a price stabilization function as well. That is, when prices were high on the world market, they paid farmers a fixed price for their crop that was lower than the world market price. The difference between the producer price and the world market price was to be invested in the development of that crop and its marketing channels, and some was to be set aside in a price stabilization fund. When world market prices were low, the stabilization fund was to be used to maintain the prices paid to the farmers by supplementing the world market price. These marketing boards were maintained after independence, but their price stabilization function seldom worked well. The prices paid to farmers have nearly always been below the world market prices for the products, even when world market prices were low. Large proportions of the resources received from export sales have often been channeled into the development of urban areas rather

Photo: World Bank

Government control over prices paid to farmers has been a major factor in declining food and export crop production.

than into the stabilization fund or into rural development in general. Many of these marketing boards are now being dismantled.

It has also been common to regulate prices and marketing channels for domestic staples such as rice and maize. Governments know that farmers must receive prices that are high enough to provide the incentive to produce. They also know that if those higher prices are passed on to the consumers, a small increase in urban food prices might touch off riots that could topple the government. Heavy pressure in the urban areas to maintain low food prices has generally been translated into low incomes for the farmers (often women) who produce that food, and the farmers have responded.

Farmers are rational, price-responsive human beings. When they fail to receive prices for their crops that will provide them with a minimal standard of income, they refuse to produce those crops. Some alter their production and plant other crops that are more lucrative. Government price policies may even encourage a trade-off of production from domestic food crops to export crops, even though producer prices for exports are also exploitative. The trade-off may occur if the prices paid for export crops are raised relative to those paid for domestic food crops. However, feeling exploited in general, some farmers simply give up farming altogether and try to find other ways of earning a living, or they migrate to the city.

These are some of the important reasons there is a food crisis throughout Africa today, insufficient food is being produced to feed African populations, and there has been increasing dependence on food imports and food aid.

☐ Urbanization and Unemployment

Young people, especially educated young men, have been leaving the rural areas and moving to the cities in increasing numbers. By 1993, 30 percent of the population of sub-Saharan Africa lived in urban areas, and the urban population has been increasing at an annual rate of at least 4.8 percent since 1970 (World Bank, 1995b, 222–223). This is not only because life is difficult and incomes are low in the countryside but also because the migrants expect that conditions will be better in the city. Development strategies emphasizing industrialization have caused many to leave the countryside in hopes of finding employment in industry, which is usually located in or near the cities. But industry has succeeded neither in achieving economic development for most countries nor even in providing employment for all the hopeful applicants. In fact, it has been found that a small increase in the number of jobs available may stimulate migration to such an extent that unemployment actually increases as a result. In sum, providing employment for labor-abundant economies is particularly difficult when capital-intensive (highly mechanized) industrialization strategies are pursued. Not only does migration to the cities not always provide the migrants with anticipated benefits, it has often exacerbated the problems in the agricultural sector.

As urbanization has interacted with high rates of population growth, economies have been unable to create sufficient jobs in the cities. For lack of other formal wage employment opportunities, uncounted numbers have looked for survival to the informal sector, where petty trading, commodity production, or services afford a typically meager income. Many have also migrated to other countries. This may be beneficial if it relieves unemployment at home, increases the standard of living of those who migrate, and provides remittances to family members who remain at home. But it may also be detrimental, particularly if those who migrate are the most skilled or the most educated, thus creating an international brain drain. It may also be a disaster if external events, such as wars, cause the migrants to flee back to their country of origin, causing an immediate unemployment crisis.

Many of those who are unemployed in the cities are those who have migrated from the rural areas. Although they may have migrated because they concluded that their expected income in the city would exceed that in the rural areas, according to one prominent theory of migration,[5] they now find themselves without an income, unable to produce their own food, and required to purchase food from the rural areas. But it is becoming increasingly difficult for those who remain in the rural areas to maintain food production, as the most able young people are the ones who departed for the cities, leaving the farming to their aging parents or to wives who remain behind. Consequently, while there is an increasing need for food in the cities, there are fewer people remaining in the countryside to produce it; and many of those who continue to farm are becoming older and potentially less productive.

□ The Marginalization of Women in the Development Process

Women's economic productivity and independence is a long-established tradition in much of Africa. Not only do women grow most of the food and assist with cash crops, they are also actively involved in marketing foodstuffs. In the informal sector, where many nonagricultural workers pursue their livelihood, women can be found providing valuable economic services and products. In the markets of West Africa, for instance, some women have become wealthy as cloth merchants, and some of them have used their profits to become owners of vehicles for long-distance transport services. In wage jobs in the formal economy, women help support themselves and their families.

Despite the important contributions women have made to African

The Informal Sector

Photos: April Gordon

economies, the role of women is often underrated in official economic statistics, and women's interests are ignored, if not purposely undermined, by African governments and the international financial and donor community. The neglect of women has especially hurt agricultural production, but it also negatively affects other areas of the economy, as sex discrimination lessens women's opportunities to contribute their talents and skills to the development effort.

The World Bank summarizes well the economic plight of women:

> "Modernization" has shifted the balance of advantage against women. The legal framework and the modern social sector and producer services developed by the independent African nations (and also most externally sponsored development projects) have not served women well. Legal systems have discriminated in land titling. . . . It is often more difficult for women to gain access to information and technology, resources, and credit. Agricultural extension and formal financial institutions are biased toward a male clientele. . . . There is a wide gender gap in education. . . .
>
> As a result, women are less well equipped than men to take advantage of the better income-earning opportunities. . . . In industry and trade women have been confined to small-scale operations in the informal sector; . . . despite the trading empires built up by the most successful female entrepreneurs, women's average incomes are relatively low. Women are also handicapped in access to formal sector jobs by their lower educational attainments, and those who succeed are placed in lower-grade, lower-paid jobs. (World Bank, 1989b:86–87)

☐ The Economic Impact of AIDS

In Chapter 7, April Gordon discusses the impact of AIDS on Africa's population. AIDS is a health problem that has the potential for making a significant impact on the economies of sub-Saharan African countries. It is estimated that there are between 2 and 2.5 million cases of AIDS in Africa today, and that more than 10 million African adults have contracted HIV since the late 1970s. Almost two-thirds of the HIV infections occur in the under-twenty-five age group. The mode of transmission is heterosexual, and in some locations HIV rates are five times higher among girls than among boys between the ages of fifteen and nineteen. In the worst-hit areas, 5 percent of the girls between ten and fourteen are infected ("AIDS," 1994:40).

The impact of HIV/AIDS is broad and multifaceted. Overall, at this time, the greatest impact is at the micro (household) level, but it is progressing toward the macro (national) level:

1. Initially, those who are HIV positive may have to deal with the stigma of the infection and subsequent disease, not only affecting friend-

ships and familial relationships, but also making it difficult or impossible to obtain employment.

2. Within the household, the death of a spouse may cause family income to decrease dramatically, and it may also alter the division of labor, requiring the remaining spouse either to take over the household duties of the deceased spouse her/himself or find a substitute. The latter may be paid household labor or a member of the extended family, who must still be compensated in some way, which will increase the expenses of the surviving spouse.

3. Because of the heterosexual transmission, there is a strong likelihood of both husband and wife dying, leaving increasing numbers of orphans. This may have a further impact on the children's standard of living and chances for education, and it will place an increased burden on the family members who absorb them into their households.

4. As the number of infected women increases, the percentage of children born HIV positive will increase, and the child mortality rate will increase.

5. The largest numbers of AIDS cases tend to be among men and women in the most productive age groups. As the disease continues to spread, it could have a profound impact on the supply of labor, reducing the size and productivity of the labor force, including the highly trained sector.

6. In rural areas, there may be a reduction of the number of adults who can produce food, and there may be a significant change in the gender-based division of labor on the farm. The death of a spouse will make it difficult for either remaining spouse to farm by her/himself.

7. Finally, the increased cost of hospital or outpatient care and medicine and also the cost of education campaigns will drive up the health care budget requirements of countries.

□ The Role of the Public Sector: State–Owned Corporations and Control of the Price System

Postindependence development strategies emphasized industrialization in most African countries. In order to achieve industrialization, however, the state became increasingly involved in the industrial sector, especially through the establishment of state-owned corporations (often called parastatals). The World Bank maintains that, in general, public sector employment is one-half of all modern sector employment in sub-Saharan Africa, compared to only one-third in Asia. Furthermore, controlling for country size, state-owned corporations are more numerous than in most other developing countries, and they are involved in a wider range of activities. In sum, public investment accounts for the bulk of investment in the formal sector

(World Bank, 1986:21). For example, by the 1970s the proportion of public entrepreneurial capital formation was 50 percent in Côte d'Ivoire, 37 percent in Kenya, and 74 percent in Tanzania (Austen, 1987:238). Furthermore, in Senegal and Tanzania, state-owned corporations produced more than 75 percent of annual output in natural resources. In Ethiopia they contributed more than 60 percent of value added in manufacturing. Overall, they produced 20 to 30 percent of domestic output in Senegal and Guinea and almost 40 percent of output in Ghana and Zambia (World Bank, 1983, figs. 5.4, 5.5).

There are many reasons state-owned corporations have been established in developing countries. One of the most important reasons is to promote investment when it is believed that private savings are very low. A second reason is that it is believed that private investors are reluctant to invest because of high risks, especially if the market is small or sources of supply are unreliable. Some state-owned corporations are established to maintain control over strategic sectors of the economy such as defense, transport, utilities, and communications or to prevent monopolization by multinational corporations. Others are created to produce goods that have a high social benefit but that the state wishes to price at below cost. They may be established in certain sectors or geographic locations to improve national distribution of income. They may also be set up to take over important private industries that have recently gone bankrupt. Ideological orientation of the government is another factor (Todaro, 1989:567–568). Once established, they, along with the civil service institutions, have often been used to absorb surplus labor to reduce the official, open unemployment rate.

Although there are many reasons for establishing them, state-owned enterprises often have been accused of constraining economic development. The World Bank, one of the most powerful critics, maintains that the rapid growth of the public sector, along with its inefficient management and over-ambitious investment programs, is an important reason for the economic difficulties facing African countries. It also maintains that the scope of public sector activities and the operating subsidies of these enterprises have acted to stifle private enterprise in agriculture, industry, and commerce (World Bank, 1986:21).

State-owned enterprises have been accused of wasting resources and operating inefficiently with low profitability or even financial deficits. In fact, it may be difficult for them to pursue both profitability targets as well as social benefit goals of the government. Centralized decisionmaking often leaves little opportunity for managers to exercise flexibility in day-to-day operations. Managers and laborers, as state employees, often receive little incentive to increase their productivity. Attempts to resolve the unemployment problem by increasing employment in the public sector have also resulted in an increase in underemployed persons who further contribute to inefficient bureaucracies and unprofitable public sector enterprises. It is not surprising, then, that a 1983 study of four African countries (Ghana, Senegal, Tanzania, and Zambia) found that most state-owned corporations in those countries were showing losses (Killick, 1983:57–88). Not only were labor and capital productivity lower than in the private sector, but the use of capital-intensive technology prevented achieving the goal of decreasing unemployment.

The World Bank and many other foreign donors have suggested that the solution to the problems of state-owned corporations in Africa is to emphasize privatization of the public sector. This is based on the belief that private enterprise promotes greater economic efficiency through market-oriented competition, with resultant increased production and lower costs. Increasingly, donors have emphasized privatization as a condition for additional aid.

African countries have challenged the unconditional demand for increased privatization by donors. While they have recognized the economic drain of many inefficient state-owned enterprises, they continue to see a role for them under certain circumstances. They recommend establishing a pragmatic balance between the public and private sector, with the main criteria being the availability of local entrepreneurial capability and the optimum social and economic rates of return on investment (United Nations, n.d.:35). They note that there are areas in which the public sector has a role to play. These include the building of the physical, human, and institutional infrastructure; environmental protection and conservation; and the provision of essential services. At the same time, they agree that where the state has overextended itself, particularly in non–social service and nonstrategic sectors, selective privatization should be considered.

□ The Debt Crisis

The debt crisis is not unique to African countries; however, it has affected their economies particularly severely. The actual amount of debt has increased rapidly and by a significant amount. Debt in sub-Saharan Africa increased from $6 billion in 1970 to $84.3 billion in 1980 and to $200.4 billion in 1993. It was projected to be $210.7 billion in 1994. The latter is equal to 82.8 percent of its GNP in that year and 254.5 percent of its export earnings (World Bank, 1989a:20; World Bank, 1994b:216). The debt/export ratio varies significantly, however, among the individual countries. For example, it has ranged from 42.9 percent in Lesotho to 2850.9 percent in Guinea-Bissau, and twenty-eight countries had debt/export ratios of over 200:1 by the end of 1994 (World Bank, 1995b:206–207; Katsouris, 1995:11).

Most sub-Saharan African countries have had great difficulty servicing their debt.[6] Despite the problem, creditors have not taken much action until recently. This is because much of the debt is public debt, owed to other governments or international organizations. It is also because Africa's commercial debt is only about 10 percent of that of total developing country debt, too little to threaten the international banking system. Overall, debt service obligations were 43 percent of export revenues in 1992 (World Bank, 1995a:176). That is, nearly one-half of the income earned from exports should have been used simply to make annual repayments of principal and interest on the debt. This would have left little foreign exchange for imports of development capital and, for most African countries, for imports of food to meet the food crisis.

The debt of African countries originated in the same way as that of other highly indebted countries. It resulted from a complex combination of events:

1. In 1973/74 and again in 1979/80, OPEC members announced unexpected, sharp increases in the price of oil. As mentioned above, these price increases were beneficial to the few oil-exporting countries of sub-Saharan Africa; however, they were a catastrophe for the majority of countries that are oil importers. For those few petroleum exporters on the continent, the increase in the price of oil led to balance of payments surpluses; however, it led to huge balance of payments deficits for most of the countries that had to continue to import oil to keep their economies on a growth path.

2. The economies of the oil-importing countries slowed down. These included the economies of some of the industrialized countries. As the latter countries sought to restructure their own economies to reduce the balance of payments and inflationary impacts of the oil price increases, they reduced expenditures on nonessential imports, foreign travel, and foreign aid. These cutbacks had repercussions on the economies of sub-Saharan Africa.

3. As foreign aid from the oil-dependent developed countries was reduced, commercial bank credit was made readily available. This resulted from a large portion of the oil profits of the oil exporters being deposited into bank accounts; those funds were then recycled as "petrodollar" loans, particularly to LDCs. During the 1970s, African countries turned to such commercial loans, at market rates of interest. This was not much of a problem during the late 1970s because interest rates were low, often negative in real terms.[7]

4. Some of those loans were used for nonproductive purposes such as the import of nonessential consumer goods or for investment in projects with low rates of return, especially public sector investments. This use of the loans failed to generate the foreign exchange required to service the debts.

5. In addition, during the 1980s the terms of trade of sub-Saharan African countries declined as a result of both low world market prices for the primary commodities exported by African countries and rising import prices.[8] Overall, by 1986 the terms of trade (using 1980 as the base year) had

declined from 100 to 72. By 1988 they had declined to 65, and by 1993 they were down to an estimated 58 (United Nations, 1994:46). The significance of the declining terms of trade is that it began to take a greater and greater quantity of African exports (usually primary commodities such as agricultural products and minerals) to pay for their imports. Those imports included petroleum products, manufactured goods, and capital goods required for further development. Facing low or negative real interest rates, African countries continued to succumb to the temptation to borrow from commercial sources that were actively competing for their business.

6.   The economic stabilization policies of developed countries continued to affect African countries during the 1980s. By 1984, foreign aid had stagnated at $7 billion. During that same year, net private investment decreased by $480 million (Todaro, 1989:596). As a final blow, interest rates rose, causing the debt service burden of borrowers to increase.[9] This was significant for African countries because, by that time, they had a much greater proportion of their debt from commercial and other private sources. Since banks operate on the principle of profits, they required regular debt service payments. The combination of increased debts and increased debt service burdens led rapidly to a debt crisis. Sub-Saharan African countries, along with other LDCs, suddenly found that they were unable to continue to make their scheduled payments. Mexico was the first to announce the inability to service its debt in 1982, but African countries followed soon after. Unable to pay their debts, most African countries were compelled to seek various forms of debt relief and to implement structural adjustment programs (SAPs).

□ Deforestation and Environmental Degradation

As population increases, forests are cut down for urban expansion, new farmlands, and household uses such as cooking fuel. But in sub-Saharan Africa, deforestation is also taking place in many countries because of the economic crisis. In an effort to increase exports to earn foreign exchange, to reduce the international debt burden, and to maintain imports, forests are being slashed, and rough unprocessed timber is being exported, with little enforcement of reforestation laws where they exist. While estimates vary widely, deforestation is significant in some countries. The UN estimates that the highest rate of deforestation occurs in Côte d'Ivoire (5.2 percent), but that rates are significant also in Malawi (3.5 percent), Mauritius (3.3 percent), and the Comoros (3.1 percent). Rates in The Gambia, Guinea-Bissau, Liberia, Mauritania, Niger, Nigeria, and Rwanda are all higher than 2 percent as well (UNDP, 1995:188–189).

The destruction of the forests has multiple repercussions on the economies of countries. The trees that are most valuable are the tropical hardwoods. Once gone, they cannot be replaced in the near future. Moreover, removal of the forests leads to problems of soil erosion and general degradation of the land, as well as to changes in climate, which in turn affect agriculture. Deforestation also affects rural dwellers, who may depend on the forests for subsistence products such as cooking fuel, food, medicines, and building materials.

In addition to deforestation, there are also other environmental concerns. One of the most important in some countries, such as Nigeria, has been the pollution of land and water resulting from production of petroleum. These and other environmental issues are examined by Julius Nyang'oro in Chapter 8. While current disregard for the environment often reflects short-term economic interests, in the long run, environmental degradation will be ruinous for Africa's future. In its *1992 Development Report,* the World Bank (1992:178) argues that economic efficiency and sound environmental management go hand in hand. The Bank and other agencies, such as the U.S. Agency for International Development (USAID), recognize, however, that economic pressures on governments, poverty, and rapid population growth are the root problems that must be addressed if Africa's environment is to be preserved to sustain the economic needs of future generations (see Green, 1994).

□ Economic Integration

Since independence, African countries have realized that one of the most important means of achieving greater economic independence is through regional integration of economies on the continent of Africa.[10] A major step toward integrating the economies of the entire continent was taken at the OAU summit in Abuja, Nigeria, in June 1991. African leaders adopted a treaty to establish an African Economic Community by the year 2025 (Harsch, 1991:12). This treaty became effective on May 12, 1994 (Harsch, 1994:30).

It is essential for Africa to counterbalance the increasing economic power of the developed world, as Peter Schraeder discusses in Chapter 6 on African international relations. This is especially important as Europe becomes more united in the 1990s. However, as seen from the failure of many previous attempts at integration in Africa (e.g., the East African Community, or the proposed Ghana-Guinea-Mali Union), it is not easy to distribute the benefits of integration to the satisfaction of the constituent countries, and it is not easy for a sovereign nation to relinquish prerogatives to a superimposed governing body. Nevertheless, most countries of sub-Saharan Africa know that they must begin to make sacrifices now for their long-run survival.

☐ **Structural Adjustment Programs:**
   The Role of the World Bank,
   the IMF, and the UNECA

The World Bank, supported by bilateral and multilateral foreign aid donors, stresses that the solutions to sub-Saharan Africa's economic problems must be solved by long-run structural adjustment programs. Moreover, most donor organizations require implementation of structural adjustment policies prior to negotiations for various forms of debt relief and before provision of increased loan support. The main objectives of World Bank SAPs include the following:

- Reduction in the size of the public sector and improvements in its management
- Elimination of price distortions in various sectors of the economy
- Increasing trade liberalization
- Promotion of domestic savings in the public and private sectors

The main policy instruments the World Bank and the IMF have used to achieve the above objectives are:

- Exchange rate adjustment, especially devaluation
- Interest rate policies to encourage domestic savings and achieve appropriate allocation of resources
- Control of money supply and credit
- Fiscal policies to reduce government expenditures and deficit financing
- Trade and payments liberalization
- Deregulation of the prices of goods, services, and factor inputs

Most African countries have recognized the problems that such policies create, at least in the short run. These include increased costs for imports, including essential imports of resources, supplies, and capital to promote economic growth. They also include increased prices of domestic goods after subsidies are removed and prices are deregulated. The increased prices of domestic goods often have immediate impact on the welfare of the poorest members of society, especially if they affect food prices, costs of education, and payment for medical services. In many cases, price increases have led to political instability as citizens express their dislike of the changes. African countries fear that they may never have the opportunity to enjoy the promised long-term benefits of structural adjustment programs if they are unable to survive the short-run problems that are certain to occur. They believe, therefore, that they must move at a deliberate pace if they agree to proceed with structural adjustment, because their constituencies generally will not allow such extensive changes at one time.

In March 1989, a World Bank–UNDP report concluded that the more than thirty sub-Saharan African countries that have adopted SAPs were performing better than those that had not (World Bank, 1989a:iii). African countries disagree. They believe that the World Bank has used a biased analysis to push through "doctrinaire privatization" and promote "excessive dependence on market forces." Moreover, they believe that the SAPs have been unduly harsh in effect and that they have not been producing the desired results. They complain that World Bank SAPs as well as IMF stabilization programs follow only one formula, rather than individualizing programs for each country. As a result, SAPs do not meet the needs of the people or the differing conditions of their economies. They believe that many World Bank policy prescriptions are not appropriate and that they will never lead to self-sustained growth and development but only to continued marginalization and dependency.

On the basis of these criticisms, African countries have jointly prepared programs that counter the policy prescriptions and provide alternatives to those of the World Bank. The first of those major programs was the Lagos Plan of Action, discussed earlier, which emphasized self-reliant development. In 1985, African countries devised another alternative, Africa's Priority Programme for Economic Recovery 1986–1990 (APPER), which was adopted by the OAU. In APPER, Africans took some of the responsibility for their economic failures and stressed the need for economic policy reforms, but of their own design. This was the African contribution to the more general UN Programme of Action for African Economic Recovery and Development (UNPAAERD), under which developed countries agreed to support African efforts, especially with increased aid (approximately $46 billion) and greater debt relief. UNPAAERD initially was considered by donors and African countries alike to be a major breakthrough in providing increased development assistance for Africa. Economic performance, however, continued to be poor, and the final reviews of UNPAAERD determined that it was a failure. It had little impact on African economies, and Africans were poorer in 1991 than they were in 1986.

In 1989, under the auspices of the UNECA, African countries prepared yet another document, this one entitled *African Alternative Framework to Structural Adjustment Programmes for Socio-economic Recovery and Transformation (AAF-SAP)*. It looks beyond short-term adjustment and proposes a long list of policy reforms that are intended to direct countries eventually toward long-term, balanced development and fulfillment of human needs. It recommends, for example, greater limits on debt service payments, multiple exchange rates, selective subsidies and price controls, and a decrease in defense expenditures. It also advocates differential export subsidies and limited use of deficit spending for productive and infrastructural investments. As in the earlier documents, it emphasizes that African governments must take responsibility for determining their own economic programs rather than allowing donor agencies to dictate them (United Nations, n.d.).

Another attempt by sub-Saharan African countries to solve their own problems developed at a conference organized by the UNECA and NGOs in Arusha, Tanzania, in February 1990. Participants unanimously agreed that the absence of full democratic rights was the primary cause of Africa's decade-long economic crisis (Lone, 1990:1). Thus, the African Charter for Popular Participation in Development and Transformation, which was adopted at the conference, states that "there must be an opening up of political processes to accommodate freedom of opinion, and tolerate differences. In this regard, it is essential to establish independent people's organizations that are genuinely grassroot and democratically administered."

On December 18, 1991, the international community renewed the commitment to Africa it made five years earlier in the UNPAAERD by entering into a stronger accord, the UN New Agenda for the Development of Africa in the 1990s (UN-NADAF). The agenda set specific goals, including:

- Average real growth rate of GDP of 6 percent per year
- Provision of $30 billion in net Official Development Assistance (ODA) in 1992, with 4 percent growth of that amount in each succeeding year
- Preparation of a study on the need for and feasibility of a "diversification fund" to help free African economies from heavy dependence on exports of primary commodities
- Solution to the African debt crisis by commitment of creditors to further cancellation or reduction of ODA debt, additional relief for official bilateral debt, and encouragement to write off or swap commercial debt

For their part, African countries promised to transform the structure of their economies by continuing with necessary reforms and pursuing improvement of domestic economic management, including effective mobilization and utilization of domestic resources. They would do the following (Lone, 1991:1, 18–23):

- Pursue regional and subregional economic cooperation and integration with the ultimate goal of establishing the African Economic Community
- Intensify the process of democratization
- Create an enabling environment to attract foreign and domestic investment and promote the participation of the private sector

- Protect the environment through sustainable development
- Continue to integrate population factors into development programs
- Improve policies to support agriculture, rural development, and food security

By mid-1995, action to support the commitments of the international community for the UN-NADAF were very weak. The first step toward implementation was to be the establishment of a Commodity Diversification Fund for Africa in 1994. The resolution adopted by the UN General Assembly was a compromise, however, without practical and financial support for concrete steps toward diversification (Bentsi-Enchill, 1994:9).

More promising is the contribution of the UNDP, which established the Futures Project, based in Abidjan, Côte d'Ivoire, in 1992. The aim of the project is to promote long-term, strategic planning in Africa after years of crisis management. The project offers assistance and training in the elaboration of national, long-term perspective studies (NLTPS). By mid-1995, twenty-nine countries had asked for such assistance. Six had set up national teams to conduct the studies, and twelve planned to do so ("Africa Strives," 1995:1, 4).

In the midst of generally discouraging economic indicators for Africa, the World Bank (1994a) published its latest study of Africa, *Adjustment in Africa*. That study focused on twenty-nine sub-Saharan African countries that had adjustment programs in place during 1987–1991. It concluded that in the countries that had undertaken and sustained major policy reforms, adjustment was working; of the twenty-nine countries, the six with the most improvement in macroeconomic policies during the periods 1981–1986 and 1987–1991 (Ghana, Tanzania, The Gambia, Burkina Faso, Nigeria, and Zimbabwe) enjoyed the strongest resurgence in economic performance in terms of GDP per capita growth. The countries were more successful in improving their macroeconomic, trade, and agricultural policies than their public and financial sectors, and no African country had achieved a sound macroeconomic policy stance, meaning inflation under 10 percent, a very low budget deficit, and a competitive exchange rate. Moreover, the reforms that were undertaken were fragile and were merely returning Africa to the slow-growth path of the 1960s and 1970s. Finally, the report maintains that while adjustment can work in Africa, adjustment alone will not put countries on a sustained, poverty-reducing growth path, because long-term development also requires more investment in human capital (i.e., people), infrastructure, and institution building, along with better governance (World Bank, 1994b:1–2).

At nearly the same time, at a May 1994 conference of the UNECA, the African ministers of economic and social development and planning approved a "Framework Agenda for Building and Utilizing Critical Capacities in Africa," and mandated the preparation of a financing plan for the 1995–2005 first phase of an action program at national, subregional, and regional levels. The Framework Agenda identified eight priority areas that have been integral to previous development strategies over the past two decades. These include building critical capacities that support good governance, human rights, and political stability; creating capacities for effective socioeconomic policy analysis and management; developing entrepreneurship for public and private sector management; building and utilizing physical infrastructure; building capacities to exploit natural resources and diversify African economies into processing and manufacturing; strengthening food security and self-sufficiency; and mobilizing and efficiently allocating domestic and external financial resources (Harsch, 1994:1, 30).

In summary, African countries have made a critical examination of their constraints on development and have evaluated the recommendations or demands made by international donors. While recognizing the external causes of underdevelopment and admitting their own responsibility for lack of development, they continue to propose strategies for achieving development. By doing so, they hope to promote economic development of their own countries on their own terms. We must now look to the future to observe whether such initiatives will be successful.

■ **NOTES**

1. Agro-pastoralists cultivate crops during the growing season but move with their livestock during the dry season, in sometimes well-established patterns of transhumance, in search of pasturage.

2. It has been estimated that about 5 million slaves were exported from eastern Africa between the years 650 and 1500 (Austen, 1987:59).

3. *Sub-Saharan Africa: Progress Report on Development Prospects and Programs,* 1983, and *Toward Sustained Development in Sub-Saharan Africa: A Joint Program of Action,* 1984.

4. Growth of GNP, measured by growth of the value of all goods and services produced by a country within a year.

5. According to the Todaro theory, the decision to migrate depends upon expected urban-rural real wage differentials, where the expected differential is determined by the interaction of two variables, the actual urban-rural wage differential and the probability of successfully obtaining employment in the urban sector (Todaro, 1989:278–281). That is:

Expected income = (actual wage or salary) $\times$ (probability of finding a job).

6. Debt service is a combination of the periodic: (a) repayment of principal (amortization) of a loan, as well as (b) payment of interest on it.

7. The real interest rate is equal to the market rate of interest minus the rate of inflation.

8. The "terms of trade" for a country usually refers to the ratio of an index of its export prices to an index of its import prices. Therefore, if the terms of trade decline, it means that the ratio decreases as a result of either the index of export prices declining and/or the index of import prices rising.

9. Debt service is the required repayment of principal and interest on a loan.

10. Many attempts at regional integration in Africa have been made over the years, some more successful than others. The major groups at this time are:

CEAO Communauté Economique de l'Afrique de l'Ouest (West African Economic Community):
Benin, Burkina Faso, Côte d'Ivoire, Mali, Mauritania, Niger, Senegal

CEPGL Communauté Economique des Pays des Grands Lacs (Economic
(ECGLS) Community of the Great Lakes States):
Burundi, Rwanda, Zaire

COMESA Common Market for East and Southern Africa (Marché Commun d'Afrique de l'Est et d'Afrique Australe):
Angola, Burundi, Comoros, Djibouti, Ethiopia, Kenya, Lesotho, Malawi, Mauritius, Mozambique, Namibia, Rwanda, Somalia, South Africa, Sudan, Swaziland, Tanzania, Uganda, Zaire, Zambia, Zimbabwe

ECCAS Economic Community of Central African States (Communauté
(CEEAS) Economique des Etats de l'Afrique Centrale):
Burundi, Cameroon, Central African Republic, Chad, Congo, Equatorial Guinea, Gabon, Rwanda, São Tomé and Principe, Zaire

ECOWAS Economic Community of West African States (Communauté
(CEDEAO) Economique des Etats de l'Afrique de l'ouest):
Benin, Burkina Faso, Cape Verde, Côte d'Ivoire, The Gambia, Ghana, Guinea, Guinea-Bissau, Liberia, Mali, Mauritania, Niger, Nigeria, Senegal, Sierra Leone, Togo

MARIUN Mano River Union (Union du Fleuve Mano):
(UFM) Guinea, Liberia, Sierra Leone

SADC Southern African Development Community (Communauté de Développement de l'Afrique Australe):
Angola, Botswana, Lesotho, Malawi, Mozambique, Namibia, South Africa, Swaziland, Tanzania, Zambia, Zimbabwe

UDEAC Union Douanier et Economique de l'Afrique Centrale (Customs and Economic Union of Central Africa):
Cameroon, Central African Republic, Chad, Equatorial Guinea, Gabon

UMA Union du Maghreb Arabe (Union of the Arab Maghreb):
(UAM) Algeria, Libya, Mauritania, Morocco, Tunisia

■ **BIBLIOGRAPHY**

"Africa Strives to Move from Crisis Management to Strategic Thinking." 1995. *Africa Recovery* 9 (November):1, 4–7.

"AIDS Rising in Africa, but Even Faster in Asia." 1994. *Africa Recovery* 8 (April-September):40.

"Approaches to Debt Reduction." 1989. *Finance and Development* (September):16.

Austen, Ralph. 1987. *African Economic History: Internal Development and External Dependency.* London: James Currey; Portsmouth, NH: Heinemann.

Bentsi-Enchill, Nii K. 1994. "Diversification Gets Faint Donor Support." *Africa Recovery* 8 (December):9.

Clark, J. Desmond. 1962. "The Spread of Food Production in Sub-Saharan Africa." *Journal of African History* 3. Reprinted in Z. A. Konczacki and J. M. Konczacki (eds.). *An Economic History of Tropical Africa*. Vol. l. Pp. 3–13. London: Frank Cass, 1977.

Davidson, Basil. 1972. *Africa: History of a Continent*. New York: Macmillan.

Fage, J. D. 1959. *Ghana: A Historical Perspective*. Madison: University of Wisconsin Press.

Green, Cynthia P. 1994. *Sustainable Development: Population and the Environment*. Washington, DC: USAID.

Harsch, Ernest. 1991. "Africa Seeks Economic Unity." *Africa Recovery* 5 (June): 12–13, 32.

———. 1994. "Building Africa's Economic Capacity." *Africa Recovery* 8 (April-September):1, 30–31.

Herskovits, Melville J., and Mitchell Harwitz. 1964. *Economic Transition in Africa*. Chicago: Northwestern University Press.

Katsouris, Christina. 1995. "Naples Debt Deal Falls Short of Needs." *Africa Recovery* 9 (June):11–12.

Katsouris, Christina, and Nii K. Bentsi-Enchill. 1995. "Africa Under Pressure from Falling Aid, Rising Debt." *Africa Recovery* 9 (June):1, 10, 12.

Killick, Tony. 1983. "The Role of the Public Sector in the Industrialization of African Developing Countries." *Industry and Development* 7:57–88.

Lone, Salim. 1990. "Africans Adopt Bold Charter for Democratization." *Africa Recovery* 4 (April-June):14–17.

———. 1991. "New Africa Agenda Adopted at U.N." *Africa Recovery* 5 (December):1, 18–23.

Metra Consulting. 1988. *Handbook of National Development Plans*. 2 vols. London: Graham and Trotman.

Neumark, S. Daniel. 1977. "Trans-Saharan Trade in the Middle Ages." Pp. 127–131 in Z. A. Konczacki and J. M. Konczacki (eds.). *An Economic History of Tropical Africa*. Vol. l. London: Frank Cass. Reprinted in Daniel Neumark. *Foreign Trade and Economic Development in Africa: An Historical Perspective*. Stanford: Food Research Institute, Stanford University, 1964.

Todaro, Michael P. 1989. *Economic Development in the Third World*. New York: Longman.

United Nations. Conference on Trade and Development. 1994. *Handbook of International Trade and Development Statistics 1993*. New York and Geneva: United Nations.

United Nations. Economic Commission for Africa (UNECA). N.d. *African Alternative Framework to Structural Adjustment Programmes for Socio-Economic Recovery and Transformation (AAF-SAP)*. E/ECA/CM.15/6/Rev. 3.

United Nations Development Programme (UNDP). 1995. *Human Development Report 1995*. New York: Oxford University Press, for the UNDP.

Wickins, Peter. 1986. *Africa 1880–1980: An Economic History*. Cape Town: Oxford University Press.

World Bank. 1981. *Accelerated Development in Sub-Saharan Africa: An Agenda for Action*. Washington, DC: World Bank.

———. 1983. *World Development Report*. New York: Oxford University Press.

———. 1986. *Financing Adjustment with Growth in Sub-Saharan Africa, 1986–90*. Washington, DC: World Bank.

———. 1989a. *Africa's Adjustment and Growth in the 1980s*. Washington, DC: World Bank.

———. 1989b. *Sub-Saharan Africa: From Crisis to Sustainable Growth: A Long-Term Perspective Study*. Washington, DC: World Bank.

———. 1990. *World Development Report*. New York: Oxford University Press.

————. 1992. *World Development Report*. New York: Oxford University Press.

————. 1994a. *Adjustment in Africa: Reforms, Results, and the Road Ahead*. A World Bank Policy Research Report. New York: Oxford University Press.

————. 1994b. *World Debt Tables 1994–95*. Vol. 1. Washington, DC: World Bank.

————. 1995a. *African Development Indicators 1994–95*. Washington, DC: World Bank.

————. 1995b. *World Development Report*. New York: Oxford University Press.

■ 6 ■

African
International Relations

Peter J. Schraeder

Three watershed events have transformed African international relations since the late nineteenth century. In the aftermath of the Berlin Conference of 1884–1885, independent Africa (except for Ethiopia and Liberia) ceased to exist, and African international relations were controlled by the European colonial powers. A second watershed event—the independence of Libya in 1951—marked the beginning of the end of colonial rule and the return of control over African international relations to Africans. African international relations, however, were often subject to the vagaries of Cold War competition between the United States and the Soviet Union or to the interests of the former European colonial powers. The third watershed event—the fall of the Berlin Wall in 1989—signaled the end of the Cold War but not the end of international rivalry in Africa. As African leaders approach the end of the twentieth century, they must manage their countries' international relations in an environment marked by the growing competition among today's economic superpowers; the United States, Japan, France, Germany, and China.

This chapter is devoted to exploring African international relations in the aftermath of Europe's partition and eventual granting of independence to the fifty-four countries that currently constitute the African continent. After briefly outlining the major themes of what has been called the dependency-decolonization debate, I explore in the remainder of the chapter a variety of factors that are critical to understanding the evolution of African international relations. The topics discussed include (1) the formulation and implementation of African foreign policies; (2) pan-Africanism and the Organization of African Unity; (3) regional economic cooperation and integration; (4) the role of foreign powers in African international relations; and (5) the United Nations and international financial institutions.

■ THE DEPENDENCY–DECOLONIZATION DEBATE

Although the independence of Libya in 1951 marked the beginning of the end of "formal" colonial rule—a process largely culminating in 1994 when elections in South Africa led to black majority rule[1]—both African and foreign observers began an ongoing debate over the degree to which these newly independent countries truly control their international relations. According to one group of observers who belong to what has become known as the *dependency school of thought,* the granting of legal independence did little to alter the constraining web of economic, political, military, and cultural ties that bound African nations to their former colonial masters (Amin, 1973). This conceptualization of African international relations—often referred to as neocolonialism (Nkrumah, 1965)—is especially prominent in writings about the relationship between France and its former colonies, primarily due to active French policies designed to maintain what French policymakers refer to as their *chasse gardée* (literally, an exclusive hunting ground) in francophone Africa (Suret-Canale, 1975). Even in those former colonies where the European power was either too weak (e.g., Spain) or uninterested (e.g., Britain) to preserve privileged ties, the rise of the Cold War and superpower intervention are said to have ensured the gradual replacement of neocolonial relationships centered in Europe with a new set of ties dominated by Moscow and Washington (Laïdi, 1990). Simply put, direct colonial rule was merely replaced by a series of neocolonial ties that permitted the continued external domination—albeit in a more subtle form—of African international relations.

A second group of observers who belong to what has become known as the *decolonization school of thought* argue instead that legal independence was but the first step of an evolutionary process permitting African leaders to assume greater control over their countries' international relations (Zartman, 1976; see also Shaw and Newbury, 1979). According to this school of thought, although external influences may have been extremely powerful in the immediate postindependence era, layer upon layer of this foreign control is slowly being peeled away with the passage of time. Carefully underscoring that individual African countries can follow different pathways, proponents of the decolonization school argue that the most common pattern begins with legal independence followed by efforts to ensure national sovereignty in the military, economic, and (perhaps most important) cultural realms. "In this view, each layer of colonial influence is supported by the others, and as each is removed, it uncovers and exposes the next underlying one, rendering it vulnerable, untenable, and unnecessary," explains Zartman (1976:326–327). "Thus, there is a natural progression to the removal of colonial influence: its speed can be varied by policy and effort, but the direction and evolution are inherent in the process and become extremely difficult to reverse."

The end of the Cold War has ushered in a radically changed international environment with important implications for the dependency-decolonization debate. Donald Gordon discusses in Chapter 4 how the fall of communist regimes in the former Soviet Union and Eastern Europe—the intellectual heartland of single-party rule—reinforced a democratization trend in Africa. In many cases this has led to the replacement of authoritarian regimes with newly elected democratic leaders less enamored of their former foreign patrons (see Schraeder, 1994b). According to optimistic interpretations of the impact of this transforming event, Africa is undergoing a "second independence" or a "second national liberation" in which a second generation of African leaders will assume greater control over the international relations of their respective countries (e.g., Joseph, 1994). However, observers associated with the dependency school equate the end of the Cold War with the rising marginalization of African international relations. They imply that African leaders will enjoy less, rather than more, options in the post–Cold War international system (e.g., Shaw, 1991). Focusing on aggressive foreign efforts to promote democratization and economic reform, some observers have even suggested that the "recolonization" or "second scramble" for Africa is occurring (Ake, 1995).

■ THE FORMULATION AND IMPLEMENTATION OF AFRICAN FOREIGN POLICIES

The principal theme of early studies of African foreign policy is that foreign policy begins and ends with the desires of African presidents (Korany, 1986). The primary reason for what has become known as the "big man" or "big leader" syndrome of African foreign policy is that the majority of the first generation of African presidents, who assumed power during the initial independence decade of the 1960s, systematically suppressed and dismantled all centers of power capable of challenging the foreign policy supremacy of the presidential mansion. The various efforts undertaken by this first generation included the stifling of a free press, the suspension of constitutions, the banning of opposition parties, the jailing of vocal political opponents, the dismantling of independent judiciaries, and, finally, the cooptation or jailing of legislative opponents to create "rubber stamp" parliaments (Chazan et al., 1993). In short, the institutional actors associated with democratic governance who made their voices heard in the foreign policy making process were often marginalized in the name of creating single-party regimes capable of promoting unity and development.

The net result of what in essence constituted a highly centralized foreign policy machinery was the promotion of "personalized" foreign policies derivative of the interests and idiosyncrasies of individual presidents (Jackson and Rosberg, 1982). In the case of Zaire, for example, Mobutu

Sese Seko assumed power in 1965 through a military coup d'état supported by the U.S. government and gradually concentrated all power around the office of the president (Young and Turner, 1989). Often unwilling to listen to his foreign policy experts within the Ministry of Foreign Affairs and having effectively silenced other potential centers of opposition, most notably by disbanding the Zairian National Assembly, Mobutu is known for declaring policies that create international controversy. During a presidential visit to the United States during 1973, for example, Mobutu made a speech before the United Nations General Assembly in which he announced his decision to rupture all diplomatic ties with Israel. This decision was notable in that it was made without any warning to the Nixon White House and effectively derailed State Department efforts to win congressional passage of a Zairian foreign aid bill.[2]

A second outcome associated with the centralization of the foreign policy apparatus is that the first generation of African presidents often pursued foreign policies strongly tied to those of the former colonial powers. In addition to the variety of formal ties (e.g., military treaties) that bound the newly independent countries to the former colonial powers, the primary reason for what proponents of the dependency school would characterize as "dependent" foreign policies (e.g., Shaw and Aluko, 1984) was the shared culture

Photo: Abubari, Impact Visuals

Mobutu Sese Seko of Zaire, leaving the State Department in 1986, after meeting with U.S. Secretary of State George Shultz. Autocratic leaders like Mobutu have often maintained their power by seeking assistance from the superpowers.

and political values of colonially trained African presidents and their European counterparts. Moreover, although they had actively campaigned for political independence, several first-generation presidents benefited from colonial efforts designed to ensure the victory of leaders sympathetic to European concerns. In the case of Senegal, for example, former president Léopold Sédar Senghor—often described by his compatriots as "more French than Senegalese"—married a Frenchwoman, retired to a home in France, and carries the distinction of being the only African to be inducted into France's highly prestigious and selective Académie Française, the national watchdog of French language and culture (see Markovitz, 1969).

The most important outcome of the rise to power of the first generation of African presidents is that these leaders would often be more responsive to the foreign policy concerns of their external patrons than to the popular demands of their own peoples. Especially in the case of francophone Africa, the first generation of African presidents signed a variety of defense agreements with France that, rather than ensuring protection from threats from abroad, in reality were designed to ensure their political longevity. From 1963 to 1993, France intervened militarily at least thirty times in its former colonies, often at the request of presidents either under threat from internal opposition movements or seeking to be reinstated in power after being overthrown. Even in cases where pro-French leaders were overthrown by military coups d'état during the decade of the 1960s, the guiding principle of French involvement was the willingness of a particular leader to support French foreign policy objectives. For example, when asked why France did not militarily intervene when David Dacko, the democratically elected president of the Central African Republic, was overthrown in a military coup d'état in 1966, Jacques Foccart (1995:287), architect of France's policies toward francophone Africa under Presidents Charles de Gaulle and Georges Pompidou, noted in his memoirs that the new leader, Jean-Bedel Bokassa, "after all was a very pro-French military man."

The combination of the end of the Cold War and the rising strength and intensity of prodemocracy movements is contributing to the "democratization" of African foreign policies. The importance of this democratization trend—especially in the countries where multiparty elections have ensured a relatively peaceful transfer of power from one ruling elite to another—is its reinforcement of the rise to power of a new generation of African presidents less tied to their former foreign patrons and more willing to pursue increasingly independent foreign policies. In the case of Senegal, for example, President Abdou Diouf, like many of his second-generation counterparts, is taking advantage of growing economic competition among the industrialized Western democracies in the post–Cold War era to lessen his country's foreign policy dependence on France (Diop and Diouf, 1990). In a sharp departure from past policies, President Diouf withstood intense French pressures and signed contracts with South African and U.S. companies in 1995 to exploit oil fields discovered off the southwestern coast of Senegal.

The democratization process has also significantly altered the centralized foreign policy structures in several African countries. In some cases, democratization has been accompanied by the implementation of policies designed to decrease both the size of the military establishment and its involvement in governmental affairs, including in the realm of foreign policy. In South Africa during the 1980s, for example, the military strongly argued in favor of the Afrikaner regime's decision to undertake destabilization policies against its immediate neighbors (Grundy, 1986). In the wake of the country's first multiparty elections in 1994, however, the new government headed by Nelson Mandela has pledged to restore greater government control over a military force that had become too prominent in both domestic and foreign policies (Mandela, 1993; see also Crawford, 1995).

The democratization process has also led to the strengthening of institutional actors, most notably vocal, powerful, and independent national legislatures capable of challenging the presidency in the foreign policy realm. Indeed, if one can call the 1960s the "decade of the military" due to the explosion of military coups d'état during this period, observers in the future will perhaps call the 1990s the "decade of the African legislature." The primary reason behind this newfound legislative role is the creation of democratic political systems that embody the concept of separation of powers between the various branches of government. Newly empowered legislatures are beginning to reserve separate legislative budgets that allow them to adequately carry out their constitutionally mandated roles.[3] It is still an open question whether these new legislatures will largely restrict themselves to the national arena or if they will continue to have a growing voice within the realm of foreign affairs (e.g., Alderfer, 1995).

The democratization process also portends greater popular input into the foreign policy making process as the policies of the second generation of African leaders are increasingly held accountable to public opinion. Even during the Cold War era, public opinion played an influential, albeit intermittent, role in African foreign policies. For example, it has been argued that public opinion, fueled primarily by radio broadcasts by Radio France Internationale, was the primary factor that led to bloody clashes between Senegal and Mauritania in 1989 (Parker, 1991; see also Pazzanita, 1992). Despite the fact that this conflict was neither desired nor promoted by President Diouf of Senegal or President Ould Taya of Mauritania, both these leaders, despite their best efforts to contain public passions, were confronted by violent clashes that spiraled out of control. In a sense, both leaders, as well as the foreign policies of their respective countries, became "prisoners" of public opinion.[4]

The role of religion in African foreign policy, especially the impact of the rise of a variety of Islamist movements, constitutes a final element of civil society increasingly confronting today's African leaders. Sudan, Egypt, and Algeria are three countries in which Islamist movements play a key role either in supporting or opposing government policies in the post–Cold War era. Even during the Cold War, however, religion played a key role in African foreign policies in many countries. In the case of Senegal, Islamic leaders known as *marabouts* constitute an integral part of the domestic political system and play both informal and formal roles in the making of foreign policy (Villalón, 1995). The *marabouts* played a critical informal role in reducing tensions between Senegal and Mauritania in the aftermath of the 1989 border conflict by shuttling back and forth across the river that separates the two countries. In a formal sense, one of President Diouf's closest advisers is Moustaffa Cisse, a *marabout* who was a former ambassador to Egypt and to Saudi Arabia. In short, if one wants to completely understand the formulation and implementation of Senegal's foreign policy, as well as that of other African countries with sizable Muslim populations, one must take into account the role of religion. (See Chapter 11 for more on the role of Islam in African politics.)

■ PAN-AFRICANISM AND THE ORGANIZATION OF AFRICAN UNITY

Inspired by the anticolonial and antiracist activities of peoples of African descent living in North America and the West Indies during the nineteenth and twentieth centuries, African nationalists sought to promote a unified African front against colonial rule. What subsequently became known as the "pan-African ideal" was most forcefully enunciated for the first time at the 1945 meeting of the Pan-African Congress held in Manchester, England. There participants adopted a Declaration to the Colonial Peoples that affirmed the "rights" of all colonized peoples to be "free from foreign imperialist control, whether political or economic," and "to elect their own governments, without restrictions from foreign powers" (Ajala, 1988:36). In a separate Declaration to the Colonial Powers, participants further underscored that if the colonial powers were "still determined to rule mankind by force, then Africans, as a last resort, may have to appeal to force in the effort to achieve freedom" (Ajala, 1988:36).

The pan-African ideal gained momentum during the heady independence era of the late 1950s and early 1960s. In an opening address to a gathering of independent African nations held in 1958 in Accra, Ghana, President Kwame Nkrumah proclaimed: "Never before has it been possible for so representative a gathering of African Freedom Fighters to assemble in a free independent African state for the purpose of planning for a final assault upon imperialism and colonialism" (in Ajala, 1988:39). According to

Nkrumah, the realization of the pan-African ideal required a commitment between African leaders and peoples to guide their countries through four stages: (1) "the attainment of freedom and independence"; (2) "the consolidation of that independence and freedom"; (3) "the creation of unity and community between the African states"; and (4) "the economic and social reconstruction of Africa" (Ajala, 1988:30).

Despite overwhelming agreement among African leaders that the promotion of pan-Africanism required the creation of a transcontinental organization, sharp disagreement existed over the proper structure and goals of such an organization. According to Nkrumah and other leaders who belonged to what became known as the Casablanca Group (named after the famed Moroccan city), the success of pan-Africanism required a *political union* of all independent African countries patterned after the federal model of the United States of America. In speech after speech, Nkrumah would promote the two key themes—"Africa must unite!" and "Seek ye first the political kingdom!"—that became the hallmark of this international vision (see Rooney, 1988).

A second group of African leaders who belonged to what became known as the Monrovia Group (named after the capital of Liberia) rejected the idea of political union as both undesirable and unfeasible, primarily due to the assumption that African leaders would jealously guard their countries' newfound independence. Led by Alhaji Abubakar Tafawa Belewa, prime minister of Nigeria, the Monrovia Group instead called for the creation of a *looser organization* of African states. According to this vision of African international relations, African countries would guard their independence but promote growing cooperation and the harmonization of policies, particularly as concerns social and economic development.

On May 25, 1963, thirty-one African heads of state largely embraced the Monrovia vision of African international relations by launching the Organization of African Unity (OAU), the first pan-African, intergovernmental organization of independent African countries based on African soil. Currently numbering fifty-four members, the OAU is headquartered in Addis Ababa, Ethiopia, and is headed by a secretary-general elected by member states. All major decisions and resolutions are formally adopted by the annual Assembly of Heads of State and Government in the aftermath of biannual meetings of the Council of Ministers. The sovereign equality of all member states is an important guiding principle of the organization and stands in sharp contrast to great-power domination of the UN by the five permanent members of the UN Security Council: China, Great Britain, France, Russia, and the United States.

Although the creation and continued functioning of the OAU have been described as a "victory for pan-Africanism" (Olusanya, 1988:67), both critics and analysts sympathetic to the role of the OAU have questioned the organization's ability to play an effective role in African international relations. In a special issue of the *Nigerian Journal of International Affairs* that assessed the OAU's continued relevance on the "Silver Jubilee" (twenty-fifth) anniversary of the organization's creation, one Nigerian scholar expressed "sadness" over the fact that, despite the best of intentions, "Africa remains today the least developed continent in the world—a continent plagued by famine, hunger, diseases, illiteracy, heavy indebtedness, a pathetic poverty and high mortality rate" (Olusanya, 1988:70). Such statements by Africans reveal an underlying pessimism about the OAU's ability to move beyond rhetoric and take the lead in African international relations.

The OAU's effectiveness can be tentatively assessed by exploring four elements of the OAU Charter, each of which holds important implications for the dependency-decolonization debate. The most important theme of the OAU Charter is respect for the *territorial integrity of frontiers* inherited from the colonial era. Due to the multiethnic nature of most African states, African leaders remain fearful that changing even one boundary will open a Pandora's box of ethnically based secessionist movements and lead to the further "balkanization" of the African continent (i.e., the splitting of countries into ever smaller and unviable economic and political units) (see Davidson, 1992).

In the case of the Nigerian civil war (1967–1970), for example, the OAU not only refused to sanction the provision of aid to Biafra, the secessionist southeast portion of the country, but voted a series of resolutions that underscored official support for the central Nigerian government (Bukarambe, 1988:98). This decision was particularly upsetting to human rights activists and several African countries aiding the secessionist government because the military-dominated Nigerian government was using very effective starvation methods to bring the Biafrans—government and general population alike—to their knees (see Stremlau, 1977).

As ethnic tensions and separatist movements intensify in the post–Cold War era, the second generation of African elites remains firmly committed to maintaining borders inherited from the colonial era. Although the OAU recognized in 1993 the sovereignty of Eritrea after a UN-sponsored referendum in that country resulted in overwhelming popular support for independence, African leaders subsequently noted that this process did not call into question the hallowed concept of the inviolability of frontiers. Unlike the majority of African countries, Eritrea was federated to Ethiopia in the *aftermath* of independence from colonial rule and therefore enjoyed the legal right to withdraw from that voluntary union (see Iyob, 1995). However, in similar cases of voluntary federation that have unraveled in the post–Cold War era, such as northern Somalia's unilateral declaration of independence as the Somaliland Republic in 1991 and disgruntled southern Sudan's search for independence through military arms, the OAU continues to reaffirm the concept of territorial integrity (see Omaar, 1994).

The second most important guiding principle of the OAU Charter is *noninterference in the internal affairs* of member states. In the early years of the organization, African leaders debated whether to allow military leaders who had illegally deposed their civilian counterparts to maintain their OAU seats. This debate was resolved in favor of recognizing whatever group controlled the reins of power within a particular country (Akindele, 1988b:82–85). More significant was the silence among African leaders concerning human rights abuses in OAU member states. "Increased repression, denial of political choice, restrictions on the freedom of association, and like events occurred, with rare murmurs of dissent," explains Claude Welch, Jr., a specialist on human rights in Africa. "The OAU seemed to function as a club of presidents, engaged in a tacit policy of not inquiring into each other's practices" (Welch, 1991:537). A notable example of this in the 1970s was the election of the notorious Idi Amin as OAU chair, despite his personal involvement in "politically sanctioned repression and murders" while he was president of Uganda (Welch, 1991:538).[5]

Despite a tacit unwillingness to criticize their counterparts, African leaders are beginning to accept a growing role for the OAU in addressing human rights abuses. In 1981, the annual Assembly of Heads of State and Government held in Banjul, Gambia, adopted the African Charter on Human and Peoples' Rights (popularly referred to as the Banjul Charter). This human rights code officially entered into force in October 1986 and has served as the guiding principle for a variety of human rights groups that began emerging in the 1980s in a trend that has intensified in the post–Cold War era (Welch, 1991). In addition to encompassing "first-generation" rights (civil and political liberties usually associated with the Western world), as well as "second-generation" rights (economic and social rights usually associated with the socialist world), the Banjul Charter has been described as "breaking some new ground" through the adoption of "third-generation" rights intended to protect the rights of individual peoples or ethnic groups (Welch, 1991:538–539).

Despite the ratification of the Banjul Charter, the OAU's response to events in Nigeria during 1995 demonstrate the continued difficulty of translating human rights rhetoric into policy action. In response to an uprising among the Ogoni ethnic group in southeastern Nigeria that began in 1990 over control of that region's vast oil resources, the military-dominated Nigerian government unleashed a brutal campaign of repression that culminated in November 1995 with the execution of Nobel Peace Prize candidate Ken Saro-Wiwa and eight other Ogoni activists on trumped-up murder charges (French, 1995:E3; see also Osaghae, 1995). Although OAU secretary-general Salim Ahmed Salim expressed "disappointment" over the fact that the Nigerian generals failed to "respond positively" to OAU appeals for clemency, the organization did not adopt concrete measures to punish or internationally isolate the Nigerian regime (in French, 1995:E3).

The *peaceful settlement of all disputes* by negotiation, mediation, conciliation, or arbitration constitutes a third guiding principle of the OAU. Yet, strict adherence to the first two principles—support for territorial integrity and noninterference in internal affairs—historically has impeded the OAU's ability to mediate either internal conflicts or those between two or more member states. In the case of the 1967–1970 Nigerian civil war, automatic support for the territorial integrity of Nigeria seriously called into doubt (at least from the viewpoint of the secessionist Biafrans) the OAU's ability to serve as an impartial negotiator. It is precisely for this reason that the OAU Commission of Mediation, Arbitration and Conciliation was "stillborn" (Zartman, 1995b), and the majority of African-initiated arbitration efforts have been carried out on an ad hoc basis by African presidents. For example, Djiboutian president Hassan Gouled Aptidon utilized his country's stature as the headquarters for the Intergovernmental Authority on Drought and Development (IGADD) to mediate the conflict between Ethiopia and Somalia. According to Zartman (1995a:241), such efforts have led to success in only 33 percent of roughly twenty-four cases, and this success was often only temporary in nature as warring parties returned to the battlefield.

The capacity to respond with either peacekeeping or peacemaking forces once a conflict has broken out constitutes a critical aspect of peacefully resolving disputes. The OAU founding fathers attempted to prepare for this eventuality by planning the creation of an OAU defense commission composed of military contingents from several African countries. Although the defense commission was never actually created, in 1981 the OAU did construct an all-African military force in an attempt to resolve civil conflict in Chad that had become internationalized after the introduction of Libyan troops. Composed of approximately 4,800 troops from Nigeria, Zaire, and Senegal, the OAU force "failed to achieve any concrete solution" due to financial, logistical, and political difficulties and within a few months was "forced to withdraw" (Gambari, 1995:229). As discussed later in this chapter, the ineffectiveness of the OAU within this realm favors continued diplomatic and military intervention by external powers.

In an attempt to reinvigorate the OAU's ability to play a more proactive role in African conflicts in the post–Cold War era, the 1993 Assembly of Heads of State and Government adopted a resolution creating a Mechanism for Conflict Prevention, Management and Resolution (Zartman, 1995a:243). Building on a conference convened in 1991 by former Nigerian president Olusegun Obasanjo that produced a forward-thinking document, "Towards a Conference on Security, Stability, Development and Cooperation in Africa" (popularly referred to as the Kampala Document), the 1993 OAU meeting also considered but ultimately rejected a proposal to create a Council of Elders composed of former African presidents who could serve as mediators in African conflicts.[6] The OAU has even discussed the possibility of reviving the defunct African Defense Commission as part of a comprehensive approach to peacemaking in Africa. However, these discussions remain at an exploratory stage, and the Mechanism for Conflict Prevention, Management and Resolution has yet to be seriously tested in any African conflict.

The final and most successful principle embodied within the OAU Charter revolves around *unswerving opposition to colonialism and white minority rule.* Principally concerned with the former existence of white minority–ruled regimes in Rhodesia (currently Zimbabwe), Namibia, South Africa, and the Portuguese-controlled territories of Angola, Mozambique, Guinea-Bissau, and São Tomé and Principe, the OAU established a Liberation Committee based in Dar es Salaam, Tanzania, to aid liberation movements with both economic and military assistance (see Akindele, 1988a). Although disagreements often arose over which tactics would best ensure transitions to black majority–ruled governments (e.g., should one support "dialogue" with the white regime or fund a guerrilla insurgency?), every OAU member expressed public opposition to the continued existence of white minority–ruled governments. In this regard, the work of the Liberation Committee largely came to an end when South Africa in 1994 made the transition to a multiracial, multiparty democracy.

■ REGIONAL ECONOMIC COOPERATION AND INTEGRATION

Inspired by the success of the European Union (EU) and encouraged by the UN-sponsored Economic Commission for Africa (ECA) based in Addis Ababa, Ethiopia, the first generation of African leaders sought to create regional entities capable of promoting regional cooperation and integration. This vision of African international relations was best captured in 1981 by the OAU's publication of a document, *Lagos Plan of Action for the Economic Development of Africa, 1980–2000,* which proposed the "eventual establishment of an African Common Market (ACM) as the first step towards the creation of an African Economic Community (AEC) by the year 2000" (Martin, 1992:70). According to the *Lagos Plan of Action,* the creation of intergovernmental economic organizations in each of Africa's five major regions—North, East, West, Southern, and Central Africa—is the best means for ensuring the ultimate creation of a transcontinental AEC. (See Chapter 5 for information on the economic crises that have inspired these efforts.)

The flourishing of experiments in regional cooperation and integration during the postindependence era demonstrated the firm commitment of the first generation of African leaders to this economic dimension of the pan-African ideal. By the end of the 1980s, it was estimated that at least 160 intergovernmental economic groupings existed on the African continent, with thirty-two such organizations in West Africa alone (Martin, 1992:73).

Among the most notable and far-reaching economic groupings in each of Africa's major regions are the Economic Community of West African States (ECOWAS), created in 1975; the Union of the Arab Maghreb (UAM) in North Africa, created in 1989; the Southern African Development Coordination Conference (SADCC), created in 1980 (now the Southern African Development Community [SADC]); the Economic Community of Central African States (ECCAS), created in 1983; and the Intergovernmental Authority on Drought and Development (IGADD) in northeast Africa, created in 1986. These regional organizations are complemented by a few larger groupings, such as the Lomé Convention, which promotes preferential trade links between the European Union and dozens of countries from Africa, the Caribbean, and the Pacific (the so-called ACP countries)(see Ojo, 1985:146–150).

African leaders offer three rationales for seeking regional cooperation and integration. The simplest is the firm belief that there is strength in numbers. To effectively compete within an increasingly competitive international economic system dominated by economic superpowers (e.g., the United States and Japan) and powerful regional economic entities (e.g., the EU and the North American Free Trade Agreement [NAFTA] zone), African nations must band together and pool their respective resources. A second rationale revolves around the desire to promote self-sustaining economic development and particularly the industrialization of the African continent. Struggling with the reality that many of their countries are economically impoverished and lack the tools for the creation of advanced industries, African leaders believe that they can build upon the individual strengths of their neighbors to forge integrated and self-sustaining regional economies.

Most important, regional economic schemes are perceived as the best means for creating self-reliant development to reduce the ties of dependency inherited from the colonial era (Asante and Chanaiwa, 1993:741–743). For example, African leaders are rightfully concerned that national control over the evolution of their respective economies is constrained by Africa's trade dependency on Europe at the expense of intraregional trade links with African countries. It is precisely for this reason that the primary objective of early regional economic schemes was to promote intraregional trade with neighbors who theoretically share a common set of development objectives—because of special geographic features, historical ties, or a common religion, such as Islam in North Africa (e.g., see Grundy, 1985). By strengthening these ties with like-minded neighbors, a stronger African economic entity is expected to emerge that will be capable of reducing foreign influence and strengthening Africa's collective ability to bargain with foreign entities on a more equal basis.

Early optimism began to wane in the aftermath of the launching of several regional integration efforts that included the creation of supranational authorities and formal economic unions designed to promote intraregional trade and investment. In the case of the original East African Community (EAC), the 1967 decision of Kenya, Tanzania, and Uganda to create a common market with common services coordinated by a supranational governing body collapsed less then ten years later and was followed in 1978–1979 by Tanzania's military intervention in Uganda to overthrow the dictatorial government of Idi Amin (Potholm and Fredland, 1980). As concisely explained by Olatunde Ojo (1985), a specialist on regional cooperation and integration in Africa, several factors that contributed to the EAC's decline clarify why other similar efforts from the 1960s to the 1980s either failed or demonstrated minimal progress at best.

The first problem that led to the breakup of the EAC was the *polarization of national development and the perception of unequal gains* (Ojo, 1985:159–161). As typically occurred in other cases in Africa where the creation of a common market served as the cornerstone of the regional grouping, the most industrialized country (Kenya) usually reaped the benefits of economic integration, while the poorest country (Uganda) became increasingly marginalized. For example, Kenya's share of intracommunity trade increased from 63 percent in 1968 to 77 percent in 1974, whereas Uganda's share decreased from 26 to 6 percent during the same period. In addition, despite the fashioning of a common policy toward the establishment of new operations by multinational corporations (MNCs), the majority of these firms decided to locate their base of operations in Kenya due to its more advanced economy and workforce as well as its extensive infrastructural network of roads, railroads, ports, and airports.

A second factor that led to the EAC's decline was the *inadequacy of compensatory and corrective measures* (Ojo, 1985:161–166). In every integration scheme, some countries inevitably benefit more than others. As a result, policymakers can implement a series of measures, such as the creation of regional development banks or the disproportionate sharing of customs revenue, to correct the imbalance and compensate those countries expected to lose out in the short term. In the case of the EAC, a regional development bank was created to disburse funds in the following manner to the three members: Kenya (22 percent), Tanzania (38 percent), and Uganda (40 percent). However, in this and other cases of integration in Africa, even the richest members are usually incapable of subsidizing bank operations. The actual finances provided to the most needy members, therefore, never even begin to approach true development needs or completely compensate for losses incurred.

A third factor that led to the EAC's decline was *ideological differences and the rise of economic nationalism* (Ojo, 1985:168–169). Simply put, ideological differences often ensure a radically different approach to the concept of development, which in turn can significantly hinder regional integration. In the case of Kenya, a pro-West capitalist regime was very open to private enterprise, the introduction of foreign investment with few restrictions, and a very liberal policy concerning the activities of MNCs. In sharp contrast, the socialist-oriented regime of Tanzania opted for a self-help strategy known as *ujamaa* (the Kiswahili term for brotherhood) that denounced private enterprise as exploitative, restricted the flow of foreign investment, and strongly controlled MNCs. When combined with the growing public perception of unequal gains between the two countries, these ideological differences led to often acrimonious public debate between President Jomo Kenyatta of Kenya and President Julius Nyerere of Tanzania and to the rise of economic nationalism in both countries.

A fourth element that contributed to the EAC's decline was the *impact of foreign influences* (Ojo, 1985:169–171). Whereas Kenya developed close relationships with the Western bloc nations (e.g., the United States and Great Britain), Tanzania pursued close links with the socialist bloc (particularly the People's Republic of China) and Uganda sought links with the former Soviet Union and the Arab world. These links ensured that the EAC became embroiled in the Cold War rivalry of the 1960s and the 1970s and contributed to the creation of a "strategic image" that prompted EAC member states to look "outward" toward their foreign patrons rather than "inward" toward their natural regional partners.

The failure and stagnation of classic integration schemes prompted the first generation of African leaders to undertake looser forms of regional *economic cooperation* in a variety of functionally specific areas, such as transportation infrastructure (e.g., regional rail links), energy (e.g., hydroelectric projects on common rivers), and telecommunications (see Aly, 1994). The logic of pursuing this form of regionalism is that it does not require the creation of supranational authorities that can become the arena for acrimonious political debate, nor does it require policymakers to sacrifice national control over the sensitive areas of foreign trade and investment. This looser form of economic cooperation is gathering strength in the post–Cold War era, particularly as second-generation elites assume power and seek to promote cooperation with other democratically elected governments within the region.

The transformation in 1992 of the Southern African Development Coordination Conference into the renamed SADC provides a good example of this growing trend in African regional relations. Originally conceived as a vehicle for reducing the economic dependence of the Frontline States[7] on South Africa during the apartheid era, the newly reformed SADC now counts South Africa among its members and is seeking to enhance traditional cooperation in a variety of functional realms, most notably transportation. The new SADC stands poised at "the threshold of a new era" according to a report recently published by the African Development Bank in conjunction with the World Bank and the Development Bank of South Africa. "Although its effects and the inequities it has embedded will linger for a long time to come, the demise of apartheid opens up prospects unimaginable even a few years ago," explains the report. "New opportunities have emerged in every sector of economic activity for expanded trade and mutually beneficial exchanges of all kinds among the countries of southern Africa" (Morna, 1995:65).

Three factors are essential to understanding the optimism surrounding SADC's newfound status as a model for economic cooperation in Africa, particularly in terms of reducing southern Africa's dependence on foreign economic interests and creating the basis for self-sustaining, autonomous development in the post–Cold War era (see Blumenfeld, 1992). First, the inclusion of a highly industrialized South Africa provides SADC with an engine for growth that will potentially reinvigorate the entire region. In this regard, South Africa is envisioned to play a leadership role similar to that enjoyed by Germany in the EU, the United States in NAFTA, and, to a lesser degree, Nigeria in ECOWAS. Second, except for the cases of Angola and Mozambique, which are former Portuguese colonies, the remainder of SADC's membership (eight countries) share a common British colonial heritage. Although the importance of a similar colonial past should not be overstated (e.g., all the EAC member states were former British colonies), it nonetheless facilitates such technical matters as which language should serve as the official language of communication (in this case, English).

A third facilitating factor revolves around the decline in ideological differences between SADC member states that accompanied the end of the Cold War. Angola, Mozambique, and Zimbabwe have discarded in varying degrees their adherence to Marxist socialist principles of development, South Africa has officially renounced its apartheid ideology, and Tanzania and Zambia have dismantled significant portions of their formerly socialist economies. In essence, there exists a growing consensus among SADC member states that effective regional economic cooperation must be based on a shared commitment to some variant of the liberal capitalist model of development.

Finally, SADC's greatest strength is a regional commitment to conflict resolution and to the promotion of shared democratic values (Ohlson and Stedman, 1994). In the aftermath of the end of the Cold War and its subsequent impact on the rise of democratization movements throughout the African continent, civil wars have largely abated in Angola and Mozambique, and each of the SADC member states except Angola has held democratic elections. As demonstrated by the conditions that characterized the birth and expansion of the EU, most notably the existence of elites with a shared commitment to social democracy, the election of a second generation of African elites who share a firm commitment to the consolidation of democracy is critical to the strengthening of regional cooperation. Toward this end, the annual Consultative Conference of SADC members held in Lilongwe, Malawi, in 1995 considered the possibility of institutionalizing cooperation in the new functional area (officially referred to as a sector) of

Political Cooperation, Democracy, Peace and Security (Morna, 1995:67). In a statement applicable to all regions of the African continent, the 1992 Windhoek Treaty (named after the capital of Namibia), which created the restructured SADC, underscored that attentiveness to the political dimension of regional relationships is critical to the continued expansion of economic cooperation. More precisely, the treaty states that southern African leaders "must find a more abiding basis for continuing political solidarity and cooperation, in order to guarantee mutual peace and security in the region; and to free resources from military to productive development activities" (in Morna, 1995:67).

■ **THE ROLE OF FOREIGN POWERS IN AFRICAN INTERNATIONAL RELATIONS**

From the Berlin Conference of 1884–1885 to the fall of the Berlin Wall in 1989, France was the only former colonial power that maintained and expanded its presence throughout Africa, most notably in what is still referred to as "francophone Africa"[8]—those former French and Belgian colonies where French serves as an "official language of administration and education" (Martin, 1995b:163; see also Martin, 1995a). French officials, from the conservative Charles de Gaulle and the recently elected Jacques Chirac to socialist president François Mitterrand, have consistently claimed that historical links and geographical proximity justify placing significant portions of Africa within France's traditional sphere of influence (Wauthier, 1995). "According to this French version of the Monroe Doctrine," explains Guy Martin (1995b:168), a noted observer of French foreign policy toward Africa, francophone Africa is perceived as "constituting a natural French preserve (*domaine réservé,* or *pré carré*), off limits to other foreign powers," regardless of whether they constitute "friends" (e.g., the United States) or "foes" (e.g., the former Soviet Union).

In sharp contrast, Britain's official interest in maintaining formerly privileged colonial ties (rivaled only by those of France) dramatically waned during the postindependence era, except in the case of South Africa (Legum, 1994). Other, traditionally less powerful colonial powers, such as Spain, were never important diplomatic players due to the lack of extensive colonial holdings (Segal, 1989), or they at best demonstrated sporadic interest in their former colonies during times of crisis. For example, Belgium and Italy mustered only intermittent interest in resolving a series of crises in Central Africa (Zaire, Rwanda, and Burundi) and the Horn of Africa (Somalia, Ethiopia, and Eritrea), respectively (Ercolessi, 1994). Although less actively involved in the political realm, Germany continues to foster unique trade relationships throughout Africa (consistently serving as either the second or third most important trading partner of the majority of African countries) (Hofmeier, 1994; 1986). Finally, Portugal has demonstrated a renewed interest in strengthening cultural ties with its former colonies and played an important role in promoting the resolution of civil wars in Angola and Mozambique during the 1990s (MacQueen, 1985).

Despite extensive involvement during the Cold War era, the former Soviet Union and the People's Republic of China drastically reduced their presence on the African continent (Patman, 1990; Snow, 1988). Other socialist bloc nations that once enjoyed privileged relations with the African continent either completely disappeared (e.g., the former East Germany, which now constitutes part of a reunified Germany) (Winrow, 1990) or became marginalized (e.g., Cuba and North Korea) due to their pariah status within the international system and a drastic reduction in aid formerly provided by their socialist patrons (Mesa-Lago and Beikin, 1982). An important result of socialist bloc involvement in Africa from the 1950s to the 1980s is that it prompted extensive U.S. involvement in countries perceived as threatened by communist influence (Schraeder, 1994b). As discussed below, these relationships are significantly changing as the United States attempts to refashion its former Cold War–oriented foreign policy.

A variety of middle-range powers also play varying roles on the African continent. Canada and the Nordic countries, most notably Sweden, demonstrate a strong humanitarian interest, particularly in the area of famine relief in the Horn of Africa and southern Africa (e.g., Stokke, 1989). During the height of the Arab-Israeli conflict, Israel pursued an aggressive policy that exchanged Israeli technical aid for continued or renewed diplomatic recognition of the state of Israel (Chazan, 1987). Other Middle Eastern powers, such as Saudi Arabia, pursue religiously based policies toward the predominantly Muslim states of North and northeast Africa (Creed and Menkhaus, 1986). Iran especially seeks to foster links with Islamist regimes and movements in Sudan, Egypt, and Algeria; and Iraq's previously expanding relationships with several African countries, most notably Mauritania, were sharply curtailed after Iraq was defeated in the 1991 Gulf War (Lesser, 1993). Finally, India, Japan, and, to a lesser extent, Brazil and Chile, are fostering the expansion of economic relations with a variety of African countries (Badejo, 1987; Nester, 1992:235–255; Payne, 1992:97–124).

The specific impact of foreign powers can be illuminated by analyzing the evolving policies of the two countries—France and the United States—that remain the most active on the African continent. During the Cold War era, the foremost element of French Africa policies was the *rayonnement* (radiation) of such "exceptional" French values as the French language, intellectual traditions, and way of life (Kolodziej, 1974:479). Also referred to as the cultivation of *la francophonie* (a greater French-speaking community), this policy is best characterized by the regular Franco-African summits attended by the presidents of France and francophone Africa, the eighteenth of which was held in Biarritz, France, November 8–9, 1994 (Guillou, 1993).

The promotion of economic interests was integral to the promotion of French culture during the Cold War era. An example of this element of French policy was the decision by thirteen former French colonies[9] and Equatorial Guinea (a former Spanish colony) to accept membership in *la zone franc* (the franc zone), a supranational financial system, the Communauté Financière Africaine (CFA), in which France serves as a central bank and underwrites a common currency. The CFA franc is tied to the French franc and guaranteed by the French treasury (Vallée, 1989; Guillaumont, 1984). While the members of the franc zone gained financial stability and achieved levels of economic performance "no worse than that of other developing countries and significantly better than the average for sub-Saharan Africa" (Ravenhill, 1995:108), they nonetheless lost a significant degree of autonomy over domestic macroeconomic policy (Martin, 1986). For example, one of the most effective tools for promoting exports—devaluation of the national currency—is deferred to French authorities and thus unavailable to member states.

The third major determinant of French policies was the promotion of security interests. To protect French security interests, French leaders signed numerous defense accords, provided arms and military *coopérants* for training purposes, and authorized numerous interventions by French military forces to ensure maintenance of the status quo (Chipman, 1989). Consequently, when francophone regimes tried to renounce their special relationship with France, as Guinea did in 1958 when it voted in a referendum against the creation of a revised French community of states, French retribution was swift (in this case, all aid was cut off by an angry de Gaulle). But as long as these countries maintained close ties with France, even their most authoritarian leaders were unlikely to find themselves under heavy pressure from Paris to democratize.

In the case of the United States, the rise of the Cold War and superpower rivalry marked the beginning of widespread U.S. involvement in Africa and other regions of the Third World (Spanier and Hook, 1995). Throughout the Cold War era, the White House expected its European allies—most notably France—to take the lead in their former colonial territories (Schraeder, 1994b:14–15, 26–28). As succinctly summarized by George Ball (1968:240), undersecretary of state in the Kennedy administration, the United States recognized Africa as a "special European responsibility," just as European nations were expected to recognize "our [U.S.] particular responsibility in Latin America." In short, the White House intended for its European allies to take responsibility for thwarting communist and other "radical" powers from exploiting instability in Africa.

Direct U.S. involvement in Africa was driven by a combination

Only after he committed large-scale atrocities against his own people, including allegedly beating some schoolchildren to death, did France in 1979 finally turn against and depose "Emperor" Jean-Bedel Bokassa, its client ruler in the Central African Republic.

of ideological and security interests (Schraeder, 1994b). The importance of ideology was illustrated by the fact that whereas capitalist countries received on average 88 percent of U.S. aid to Africa during the 1980s, Marxist and socialist countries received on average only 6 percent each. The United States also sought special relationships with strategically important regional actors, such as Morocco, that offered special military access rights or maintained important U.S. technical facilities (e.g., telecommunications stations) on their territories. An overriding preoccupation with anticommunism led Washington policymakers to downplay rising economic deterioration and politico-military repression as long as African leaders were willing to support U.S. containment policies (Clough, 1994:76–100).

The end of the Cold War and the rise of democratization movements throughout Africa led French and U.S. policymakers to reassess their policies toward Africa. France's initial response to these events suggested that democratization would become the guiding principle of policy toward Africa. At the sixteenth Franco-African summit held in La Baule, France, in June 1990, President Mitterrand announced that France henceforth would favor those countries that were either democratic or promoting democratic change. According to what became known as the La Baule Doctrine or the "Paristroïka" of francophone Africa (Boulaga, 1993), French policymakers urged their francophone allies to initiate a process of democratization if they intended to maintain privileged ties with France. As demonstrated by the distribution of French aid in the 1990s, however, the idealist goals associated with Paristroïka were never intended to replace the more traditional goals of preserving and strengthening *la francophonie* (Agir Ici et Survie, 1995; Bayart, 1991). In Côte d'Ivoire, the Mitterrand administration rewarded President Félix Houphouët-Boigny's co-optation of the democratization process by providing their favored client with over $1.46 billion in foreign aid from 1990 to 1992—a dramatic increase from the already high level of $549 million received during the preceding three-year period.[10]

The unwillingness of France to strongly embrace democratization movements accompanied by instability was underscored at the seventeenth Franco-African summit held in Libreville, Gabon, October 5–7, 1992. The French prime minister, Pierre Bérégovoy, stated that when confronted with the simultaneous and potentially conflicting goals of promoting democracy, ensuring development, and maintaining security, francophone African leaders were expected to adhere to the following order of priorities: first and foremost, security; followed by development; and, finally, democratization (Glaser and Smith, 1994:102).

The end of the Cold War was also accompanied by the intensification of a continental economic crisis—the so-called crisis of the African state—that increasingly made it difficult for the first generation of African leaders to respond to the day-to-day needs of their populations (Callaghy and Ravenhill, 1993; Sandbrook, 1993). Given that the CFA franc had not been devalued since the creation of the franc zone in 1948, the member states that convened for a conference in Dakar, Senegal, on January 10–11, 1994, were obviously surprised when informed by French officials that their currency would be devalued by 50 percent—and consequently the purchasing power of their economies would be cut in half—beginning on January 12. According to Guy Martin (1995a:18), "The deepening economic and financial crisis in francophone Africa, coupled with a severe recession in the former metropole [France], led to the sobering realization that France could no

longer afford to foot the bill." Interestingly enough, but clearly not by accident, the French decision to devalue the CFA franc was announced and
implemented only after the death in December 1993 of President
Houphouët-Boigny of Côte d'Ivoire (Whiteman, 1994). Before his death,
Houphouët-Boigny could be counted on by other francophone leaders to utilize his diplomatic clout to squelch any French attempts at devaluation. The
decision to devalue the previously sacred CFA franc clearly suggested the
rising importance of economic factors in French calculations in the
post–Cold War era.

The French response to the genocidal conflict in Rwanda in 1994 is
especially instructive for understanding how French security interests have
evolved since the end of the Cold War (Krop, 1994). Due to a conscious
effort to more effectively integrate the former Belgian colonies of Central
Africa into the French sphere of influence, the Mitterrand administration
during the decade of the 1980s provided significant amounts of foreign aid
to Zaire ($461 million), Burundi ($243 million), and Rwanda ($199 mil-
lion). The last figure is noteworthy in that the annual amount (approximately
$20 million) provided during the 1980s was doubled to an average of $40
million during the initial three years of the 1990s. The strategic significance
of maintaining *la francophonie* served as one of the central reasons for the
increase in French aid to Rwanda, as well as for the series of French military interventions both before (Opération Noroit) and after (Opération
Turquoise) President Juvenal Habyarimana's death in 1994 and the subsequent slaughter carried out by extremist members of his Hutu ethnic group.
Specifically, the Mitterrand administration unsuccessfully sought to stem
the invasion and steady advance beginning in October 1990 of the Rwandan
Patriotic Front (RPF), a predominantly Tutsi guerrilla army supported by
Uganda and perceived by French policymakers as "hostile to France"
(Smith, 1995:452).

According to some French officials, the RPF's military victory constituted the first time a francophone country had "fallen" to Anglo-Saxon
influence—a reference to the threat posed by the intrusions of anglophone
countries that use English as the language of international diplomacy and
business. Moreover, Rwanda was perceived as the first in a series of regional
dominos that eventually could bring Burundi and an independent Shaba (the
southeastern province of Zaire) under Anglo-Saxon domination to the
"detriment" of France and *la francophonie* (Glaser and Smith,
1994:182–185). According to this culturally inspired theory, Central Africa
could become a Trojan horse projecting Anglo-Saxon influence throughout
the remainder of francophone Africa. Indeed, French hostility toward the
new RPF regime—despite the fact it neither initiated nor participated in the
genocide that ultimately ended when it achieved military victory—was
underscored by the Mitterrand administration's refusal to invite Rwanda to
the Franco-African summit held in Biarritz, France, in November 1994 (special edition of *Jeune Afrique*, 1995).

Despite official pronouncements to the contrary, the end of the Cold War reinforced the historical tendency among U.S. policymakers to treat Africa as a back-burner issue. Adopting a play on words of the Reagan administration's much-debated policy of "constructive engagement," Michael Clough, a specialist on U.S. foreign policy toward Africa, poignantly argued that the manifestation of this historical tendency during the Bush administration was a policy of "cynical disengagement" guided by three principles: (1) "Do not spend much money [on Africa] unless Congress makes you." (2) "Do not let African issues complicate policy toward other, more important parts of the world." And, above all else, (3) "Do not take stands that might create political controversies in the United States" (Clough, 1992:1). Although some argue that the Clinton administration's neglect of Africa, like that of previous administrations, is not cynically motivated (Schraeder, 1995), each of these guiding principles appears to characterize Washington's approach to Africa in the post–Cold War era.

The Clinton administration's avoidance of policies that might create domestic controversies was clearly demonstrated by its initial response to events in Rwanda in 1994. Fearful of recreating the politically damaging domestic uproar that accompanied the killing in October 1993 of eighteen U.S. soldiers taking part in Operation Restore Hope in Somalia (Schraeder, 1995:57–60), the White House initially blocked the dispatch to Rwanda of 5,500 peacekeeping troops requested by UN Secretary-General Boutros Boutros-Ghali. In addition, U.S. spokespersons were instructed to avoid labeling the unfolding ethnic conflict as "genocide," lest such a label inflame public sympathy and cause Americans to demand U.S. intervention as in Somalia during the Bush administration (Des Forges, 1995). While a variety of Africanist groups, such as Human Rights Watch/Africa (1994:2), claimed that the administration's foot-dragging contributed to the deaths of thousands of civilians, Clinton's decision nonetheless matched growing popular sentiment against U.S. involvement in UN-sponsored "peacemaking" operations.

The avoidance of financial commitments to Africa constitutes the consensus viewpoint within both the White House and the Congress as of 1996. Regardless of whether the president has been a Democrat or a Republican, U.S. foreign aid since the mid-1980s has been steadily cut due to popular pressures to trim the budget deficit and enhance spending for domestic social programs. From 1985 to 1995, bilateral aid to Africa declined in both aggregate terms (from $1.87 to $1.08 billion) and as a percentage of the U.S. foreign aid budget (from 10.3 to 6.03 percent). Although military and other security-related forms of assistance, such as Economic Support Funds (ESF), were almost totally abolished and account for the majority of these cuts, the Republicans who in 1995 controlled both the Senate and House of Representatives have vowed to severely slash even development aid due to the lack of U.S. strategic interests in Africa (see Chapter 14).

Yet, regardless of whether the levels of foreign aid significantly change, the form of even limited U.S. commitments since the end of the Cold War, coupled with new directions in foreign policy toward Africa, have contributed to growing tensions with France (see Smith, 1994). The promotion of democracy is the foremost element of this changed U.S. policy. In numerous countries throughout Africa, relatively small but effective amounts of aid from the United States have been designed to facilitate the transition to democracy (e.g., sending representatives to monitor elections), as well as to consolidate successful transitions that have already taken place. In the case of Benin, the United States provided $41 million in aid during the election year of 1991 and $14 million during 1992 after the installation of a democratically elected government (Diamond, 1995).[11]

Unlike their French counterparts, U.S. policymakers often have little to lose in strongly denouncing francophone administrations that clearly manipulate the transition to a new political order. To the consternation of some French diplomats, the State Department condemned President Paul Biya's clear-cut manipulation of the 1992 Cameroonian elections and subsequently suspended U.S. aid (Huband, 1993:42). In contrast, the Mitterrand administration, which provided Cameroon with over $400 million in aid in 1992, "sent a letter to Biya congratulating him on his victory" (Huband, 1993:43). The cases of Benin and Cameroon are not unique, but rather indicative of calculations by U.S. policymakers that the promotion of democracy (most notably the emergence of a second generation of ruling elites) throughout francophone Africa is a very low-cost strategy with potentially high returns (i.e., a new, more pro-U.S. regime may be installed). Similar to the case of France, however, the United States has been much more reluctant to strongly pressure its traditional African allies, such as Mobutu Sese Seko of Zaire, especially when such pressure is expected to lead to instability and therefore threaten U.S. interests (e.g., Kelly, 1993; Schatzberg, 1991).

The gradual decline of ideologically based policies in favor of the pursuit of economic self-interest is a second important element of changing U.S. involvement in Africa in the post–Cold War era.[12] A contradiction seemingly exists, however, between official U.S. government actions and increasing U.S. support for the private sector. Specifically, when the Republican majority in Congress was vowing in February 1995 to slash already reduced levels of aid as a result of Africa's strategic and economic unimportance, Herman Cohen, former assistant secretary of state for African affairs under the Bush administration, was presiding over a conference in Libreville, Gabon, designed to strengthen U.S.-African trade and investment. Despite their hesitation to provide the African continent with financial assistance at the same levels as their French counterparts, few if any in Congress would disagree with the central theme of Cohen's opening presentation that the concept of a *chasse gardée* in Africa has no place in the post–Cold War world. "The African market is open to everyone," explained

Cohen. "We must accept free and fair competition, equality between all actors" (in Vernet, 1995:40). Toward this end, U.S. policymakers increasingly agree that foreign policy should serve as the facilitator of U.S. private enterprise in all regions of the world, including Africa.

The net result of this evolving economic component of U.S. policy is to strengthen further the small but growing expansion into Africa of certain key U.S. industries, most notably oil and telecommunications, that has accompanied the end of the Cold War. In the eyes of many French policymakers, however, it constitutes "at best an intrusion" and "at worst an aggression" into their *chasse gardée* when U.S. policymakers aggressively pressure francophone leaders to sign preferential contracts with U.S. companies (Glaser and Smith, 1994:186). The seriousness with which this issue is treated at the highest levels of the French government was demonstrated by the public admission of Michel Roussin, minister of cooperation, that a series of meetings had been held on the theme of how best to "defend" French interests, including those within the economic realm, against those of the United States (Glaser and Smith, 1994:187).

The so-called oil war between the government of the Congo, Elf-Aquitaine (the French oil corporation), and the Congo division of Occidental Petroleum Corporation (Oxy), a U.S.-based oil company, serves as an excellent example of the potential future stakes involved in rising French-U.S. economic competition. Desperately in need of funds to pay the salaries of 80,000 civil servants prior to rapidly advancing legislative elections, the newly elected president, Pascal Lissouba, "naturally turned for help to Elf-Aquitaine, which controls 80 percent of the country's oil production." When its French manager refused to approve a $300 million mortgage on the future production of three promising new offshore oil deposits, Lissouba initiated secret negotiations with the U.S.-based Congo-Oxy. The net outcome of these negotiations was a signed agreement—ultimately renounced by the Lissouba administration eight months later due to "intense French pressure"—that resulted in a cash payment of $150 million in return for 75 million barrels of oil originally promised to Elf-Aquitaine (Martin, 1995a:15–16).

Rising economic competition between the United States and France holds important implications for the dependency-decolonization debate. In sharp contrast to the Cold War era when the West (especially the United States) sought to strengthen and enhance France's privileged role in francophone Africa as a bulwark against communism, the end of the Cold War has heightened great-power competition within the political and (especially) economic realms among the nations of the West. As a result, French policymakers increasingly claim that the United States and Japan, and to a lesser degree Germany and Canada, pose economic and political threats to French interests in francophone Africa. According to Stephen Smith (1994), the

Africa correspondent for the French daily *Libération,* such statements are indicative of a growing duel within the West over Africa, particularly between Washington and Paris.

From the viewpoint of the second generation of African leaders, this rising economic competition provides an opportunity to lessen previously privileged ties of dependence and pursue special relationships and especially economic contracts with countries willing to provide the best offer. Although the ultimate resolution in favor of France of the "oil war" in the Congo suggests that the ties of dependency are not automatically broken by the end of the Cold War, the Lissouba government nonetheless was able to obtain a better agreement from the French as a result of "playing the American card." In other cases, such as Senegal's decision to offer lucrative exploration rights to U.S. and South African companies at the expense of previously privileged ties with the French oil industry, the second generation of African leaders are successfully utilizing their increased independence within the international system to acquire the best deals for their respective countries, thereby ensuring future electoral victories in democratic political systems where public support—not authoritarian force—increasingly is the key to power.

■ THE UNITED NATIONS AND INTERNATIONAL FINANCIAL INSTITUTIONS

The relationship of African countries to the UN and to a host of international financial institutions is critical to understanding the relevance of the decolonization-dependency debate. During the independence era of the 1960s, a variety of factors suggested that membership in the UN was facilitating the ability of the first generation of African leaders to assume greater control over the international relations of their respective countries (Mathews, 1988). In addition to serving as a concrete symbol of African independence, membership in the UN provided African leaders with an important international forum for promoting African views on a variety of international issues, such as unequivocal support for complete decolonization, opposition to apartheid in South Africa, the promotion of socioeconomic development, and the need for disarmament and attention to regional security. Most important, the UN provides a unique forum for diplomatic negotiations. Financially unable to maintain embassies throughout the world, let alone throughout the African continent, African diplomats take advantage of the fact that almost all countries maintain a permanent mission in New York to carry out the day-to-day business of diplomacy.

In an era when it has become fashionable for Americans and other Westerners to criticize their countries' involvement in the UN as providing little if any tangible economic or political benefits, it is important to recognize that UN agencies often play a critical role in most African countries. Indeed, a visitor to an African capital is immediately struck by the importance of a variety of UN offices whose budgets and staffs often approach those of their counterparts within the host government. In Dakar, the capital of Senegal, for example, the visitor will find offices representing a variety of UN agencies, including the United Nations Development Programme (UNDP), the United Nations International Children's Emergency Fund (UNICEF), the United Nations High Commissioner for Refugees (UNHCR), the World Health Organization (WHO), the International Labour Organisation (ILO), and the United Nations Educational, Scientific, and Cultural Organization (UNESCO). Capturing the sentiment of African policymakers during the 1960s, a Senegalese diplomat noted that "these agencies were perceived as critical to the fulfillment of African development goals during the initial independence era, and provided a source of hope especially for those impoverished countries lacking both the resources and the expertise to implement the studies and programs pursued by each of these agencies."[13]

In the post–Cold War era of the 1990s, however, a growing segment of African intellectuals and policymakers increasingly criticize the UN as synonymous with foreign intervention and the imposition of Western values. The primary reason for this development is the UN's increased involvement in a variety of largely ethnic-based crises, such as in Somalia and Rwanda, which seemingly have intensified in the post–Cold War era. As succinctly summarized by Zartman (1995a:1–14), these crises often occur against the backdrop of "collapsed states"—the temporary disintegration of the legitimate, sovereign authority of the nation-state that is responsible for maintaining law and order within its territory. This collapse can be complete, as was the case in Somalia when civil war engulfed the country in the aftermath of the overthrow of Somali dictator Mohamed Siad Barre in 1991; or it can entail the breakdown of effective central authority over the majority of the country despite the fact that the ruling regime remains in power, as is currently the case in Zaire under the dictatorial rule of Mobutu Sese Seko.

The cornerstone of debate over the proper role of the UN in the post–Cold War era revolves around an emerging Western consensus that downplays the international legal norms of sovereignty and nonintervention in the affairs of UN member states "in favor of human rights protection and humanitarian intervention," particularly to save refugees and other peoples threatened by civil conflict and starvation (Deng et al., 1996:5). As summarized by UN Secretary-General Boutros Boutros-Ghali (1992:9), "The time of absolute and exclusive sovereignty . . . has passed; its theory was never matched by reality." It is for this reason that the UN sponsored a series of humanitarian interventions, including the U.S.-led military operation in 1992 known as Operation Restore Hope, despite the lack of an official invitation from any legally constituted Somali authority and in direct opposition to heavily armed militia groups who shared a historical mistrust of UN intentions and operations dating back to the colonial era (Hirsch and Oakley, 1995).[14] From the perspective of the UN, however, the civil war, which had intensified in the aftermath of the collapse of the Somali state, not only was spilling over into the neighboring territories of Kenya, Ethiopia, and Djibouti, but also had contributed to the creation of a humanitarian crisis in which approximately 330,000 Somalis were at "imminent risk of death" (Lyons and Samatar, 1995:24). According to this logic, the UN could justify international intervention—even in the absence of an official invitation by a legally constituted authority—on the grounds of "abatement" of a threat to international peace (Joyner, 1992).

The Somali case, extreme but not unique, constitutes part of a growing international trend of prompting even internationally recognized governments to accept UN-sponsored humanitarian intervention (Deng, 1993). In the case of Sudan, for example, a combination of civil war and drought-induced famine that led to the deaths of over 500,000 civilians since 1986 prompted the United Nations Office of Emergency Operations in Africa (OEOA) to undertake a humanitarian intervention in 1989 known as Operation Lifeline Sudan (Deng and Minear, 1992). Constituting one of the largest peacetime humanitarian interventions ever undertaken in the history of the UN, Operation Lifeline Sudan was made possible only by mounting international pressure on the Sudanese regime to recognize the scope of the problem and to accept UN-sponsored intervention. Ultimate acceptance, however, did not ensure ultimate happiness on the part of the Sudanese regime. "Even when the initial issues of involvement are resolved, relations between the donors and the recipient country or population are never entirely harmonious," explains a group of specialists on conflict resolution that includes Francis M. Deng, a Sudanese national who served as Special Representative of the United Nations Secretary-General for Internally Displaced Persons. "The dichotomy expressed between 'us' and 'them' becomes inevitable as the nationals feel their pride injured by their own failure and dependency, while the donors and relief workers resent the lack of gratitude and appreciation" (see Deng et al., 1996:11).

An even more important development from the perspective of the dependency-decolonization debate is the rising impact of "conditionalities" on African economies by international financial institutions. This trend emerged in full force in 1981 with the publication of a World Bank (1981) study, *Accelerated Development in Sub-Saharan Africa: An Agenda for Action,* which argued that wrongheaded policy decisions of the first generation of African elites were the primary cause of the mounting economic crisis of the 1980s. To resolve this crisis, the World Bank and the IMF proposed linking any future development aid to the willingness of African countries to completely restructure their economies according to what have become known as structural adjustment programs, discussed in more depth in

Chapters 4 and 5. Simply put, this orthodox economic strategy argued that African nations needed to pursue an export-oriented strategy of economic growth that promoted the private sector and systematically dismantled many forms of government intervention in their economies. In case after case, the IMF and World Bank oversaw the application of policy reforms (i.e., no reform, no aid) that demanded an end to food subsidies, the devaluation of national currencies, the trimming of government bureaucracies, and the privatization of parastatals (state-owned corporations) (Commins, 1988; Campbell and Loxley, 1989).

The end of the Cold War has had a dramatic effect on the role of conditionalities in African economic relations. The terms of the debate have shifted away from Cold War–inspired questions such as whether Marxism or an African variant of socialism is favorable to capitalism, or whether single-party or multiparty regimes can better promote the welfare of their respective peoples. The main issue now is how to facilitate and institutionalize the liberalization of African economic and political systems (i.e., create capitalist, multiparty systems in the Western image). The orthodox economic and political conditionalities of the IMF and the World Bank are largely accepted and promoted by the major Western powers; they allow the second generation of African elites only limited room to determine their own economic priorities.

Whereas cautiously optimistic interpretations of the potential impacts of SAPs in the post–Cold War era suggest that the second generation of African leaders will find themselves "hemmed in" by these externally imposed conditionalities that restrict policy choices but do not necessarily prevent policy success over the long term (Callaghy and Ravenhill, 1993), more pessimistic interpretations suggest that African countries "desperate for access to international capital" are now "uniquely vulnerable" to the demands of the IMF and the World Bank. "While dependency analysts long argued that international capitalist structures provided the context within which development in Africa occurred," explains Reed (1992:85), "it was only as Africa approached the 1990s that international financial institutions—controlled by the leading capitalist powers and designed to bolster the international capitalist economy—were able to impose policy prescriptions directly upon African governments." One of the harshest critiques of the impact of conditionalities draws upon the involvement of the international financial and donor communities in restructuring the formerly Marxist-inspired political and economic systems of Mozambique:

> Recent developments in Mozambique and elsewhere suggest that the most likely successor to post-colonial sovereignty will be neo-colonial vassalage, in which the Western powers assume direct and open-ended control over the administration, security, and economic policies of "deteriorated" states under the banner of the UN and various donors. The interests of many Africans may have been poorly served in nation-states ruled by aid-sponsored despots, but there is no reason to suppose that they will be bet-

ter served in a world governed by UN proconsuls, U.S. marines, and World
Bank economists. (Plank, 1993:430; see also Hanlon, 1991)

■ TOWARD THE FUTURE

The end of the Cold War and the rise of democratization movements
served as transforming events in the evolution of the international relations
of the African continent. These events in turn allow us to draw some tentative conclusions about the dependency-decolonization debate. Although neither approach was completely supported or rejected by the analysis, two
trends—the democratization of African foreign policies and rising competition among Western powers—suggest the increased ability of the second
generation of African leaders to assume greater control over the international relations of their respective countries. Yet, proponents of the dependency approach can point to the increasingly pervasive nature of intervention on the part of the UN and international financial institutions as
supportive of their vision of international relations. Moreover, despite some
promising developments related to SADC and ongoing discussions within
the OAU about the possible creation of African regional mechanisms to promote democracy and regional security, neither the OAU's pursuit of pan-
Africanism nor regional experiments in economic cooperation and integration offer compelling evidence to resolve the dependency-decolonization
debate. A common element in all five of the topics we have discussed, however, is the importance of the democratization process and its impact on the
rise of a second generation of African leaders committed to democratic principles. Although it is perhaps too early to tell, one can hypothesize that if
democratization succeeds, it will facilitate the peeling away of another layer
of dependency and allow the second generation of African leaders to assume
greater control over the international relations of their respective countries.

■ NOTES

    1. The only remaining territorial questions revolve around the future disposi-
tion of Western (Spanish) Sahara (partitioned by Morocco and Mauritania), and
Spain's continued control over the enclaves of Ceuta and Melilla, both of which are
claimed by Morocco.
    2. Aware that the State Department was seeking to guide a Zairian aid pack-
age through an intransigent Congress that surely would not look favorably on
Mobutu's hostile act toward Israel, Kissinger, in a private meeting with Mobutu, is
said to have sarcastically made clear his distaste for the Zairian president's actions:
"Well, Mr. President, you certainly know how to reach the American people" (quoted
in Schraeder, 1994a:82).
    3. For example, although the Senegalese constitution underscores the inde-

pendent role of the National Assembly, few if any financial resources are provided to legislators, who have no staffs and have to share offices without such basic tools as telephones.

4. Interview with Elhadj Mbodj, professor of law and international studies at Cheikh Anta Diop University, Dakar, Senegal.

5. When Amin was overthrown in 1979, after Tanzanian troops under President Julius Nyerere invaded Uganda, many African governments condemned Nyerere's actions.

6. Among those who volunteered their services were Léopold Senghor of Senegal, Julius Nyerere of Tanzania, Aristide Pereira of Cape Verde, and Olusegun Obasanjo of Nigeria.

7. These countries are Angola, Botswana, Lesotho, Malawi, Mozambique, Swaziland, Tanzania, Zambia, and Zimbabwe.

8. For the purposes of this chapter, francophone Africa includes twenty-five independent states from the following regions: Central Africa (Burundi, Cameroon, Central African Republic, Chad, Congo, Gabon, Rwanda, and Zaire); East Africa (Djibouti); Indian Ocean (Comoros, Madagascar, Mauritius, and Seychelles); North Africa or the "Maghreb" (Algeria, Morocco, and Tunisia); and West Africa (Benin, Burkina Faso, Côte d'Ivoire, Guinea, Mali, Mauritania, Niger, Senegal, and Togo). Our definition of francophone Africa therefore is inclusive of both Sub-Saharan and Saharan Africa (i.e., "trans-Saharan" Africa or the entire continent) rather than the more exclusionary set of sub-Saharan African countries.

9. These countries are Benin, Burkina Faso, Cameroon, Central African Republic, Chad, Comoros, Congo, Côte d'Ivoire, Gabon, Mali, Niger, Senegal, and Togo.

10. Figures compiled from Organization for Economic Cooperation and Development (OECD), *Geographic Distribution of Financial Flows to Developing Countries.* Paris: OECD, 1990–1994.

11. Ibid.

12. The classic understanding of the Cold War era is that U.S. foreign policy was primarily driven by ideologically inspired goals and interests. For an economically based interpretation that, although recognizing the importance of ideological factors, nonetheless argues that economic interests predominated even during the Cold War era, see Gibbs (1991).

13. Personal interview, Dakar, Senegal, January 1995.

14. Somali distrust of the UN stems from the decision of that international body to support the reimposition in 1950 of Italian colonial rule over what is currently known as the Republic of Somalia.

■ **BIBLIOGRAPHY**

Agir Ici et Survie. 1995. *L'Afrique à Biarritz: Mise en examen de la politique française (Biarritz 8 et 9 novembre 1994).* Paris: Karthala.

Ajala, Adekunle. 1988. "Background to the Establishment, Nature and Structure of the Organization of African Unity." *Nigerian Journal of International Affairs* 14, 1:35–66.

Ake, Claude. 1995. *Democracy and Development in Africa.* Washington, DC: Brookings Institution.

Akindele, R. A. 1988a. "The Organization of African Unity and Conflict Situation in Southern Africa." *Nigerian Journal of International Affairs* 14, 1:124–154.

. 1988b. "The Organization of African Unity: Four Grand Debates Among African Leaders Revisited." *Nigerian Journal of International Affairs* 14, 1:73–94.

Alderfer, Philip W. 1995. "Legislators' Attitudes in a New Democracy: The Zambian Experience." Paper presented at the 38th annual meeting of the African Studies Association, Orlando, Florida, November 3–6.

Aly, Ahmad A. H. M. 1994. *Economic Cooperation in Africa: In Search of Direction.* Boulder: Lynne Rienner Publishers.

Amin, Samir. 1973. *Neo-Colonialism in West Africa.* Harmondsworth, England: Penguin.

Asante, S. K. B., with David Chanaiwa. 1993. "Pan-Africanism and Regional Integration." Pp. 724–743 in Ali A. Mazrui (ed.). *General History of Africa.* Vol. 8. *Africa Since 1935.* Paris: UNESCO; Oxford: Heinemann; Berkeley: University of California Press.

Badejo, Babafemi A. 1987. "India's African Policy." Pp. 237–254 in Olajide Aluko (ed.). *Africa and the Great Powers in the 1980s.* Lanham, MD: University Press of America.

Ball, George. 1968. *The Disciples of Power.* Boston: Little, Brown.

Bayart, Jean-François. 1991. "La problématique de la démocratie en Afrique noire: 'La Baule' et puis après." *Politique Africaine* 43:5–20.

Blumenfeld, Jesmond. 1992. *Economic Interdependence in Southern Africa: From Conflict to Cooperation?* New York: St. Martin's Press.

Boulaga, F. Eboussi. 1993. *Les conférences nationales en Afrique noire: Une affaire à suivre.* Paris: Karthala.

Boutros-Ghali, Boutros. 1992. *An Agenda for Peace: Preventive Diplomacy, Peace-Making, and Peace-Keeping.* New York: United Nations.

Bukarambe, Bukar. 1988. "Regional Order and Local Disorder: The OAU and Civil Wars in Africa." *Nigerian Journal of International Relations* 14, 1:95–111.

Callaghy, Thomas M., and John Ravenhill (eds.). 1993. *Hemmed In: Responses to Africa's Economic Decline.* New York: Columbia University Press.

Campbell, Bonnie K., and John Loxley (eds.). 1989. *Structural Adjustment in Africa.* New York: St. Martin's Press.

Chazan, Naomi. 1987. "Israel and Africa in the 1980s: The Dilemma of Complexity and Ambiguity." Pp. 201–236 in Olajide Aluko (ed.). *Africa and the Great Powers in the 1980s.* Lanham, MD: University Press of America.

Chazan, Naomi, Robert Mortimer, John Ravenhill, and Donald Rothchild. 1993. *Politics and Society in Contemporary Africa.* Boulder: Lynne Rienner Publishers.

Chipman, John. 1989. *French Power in Africa.* Cambridge, MA: Basil Blackwell.

Clough, Michael. 1992. "The United States and Africa: The Policy of Cynical Disengagement." *Current History* 91:193–198.

. 1994. *Free at Last? U.S. Foreign Policy Toward Africa and the End of the Cold War.* New York: Council on Foreign Relations Press.

Commins, Stephen K. (ed.). 1988. *Africa's Development Challenges and the World Bank: Hard Questions, Costly Choices.* Boulder: Lynne Rienner Publishers.

Crawford, Neta C. 1995. "South Africa's New Foreign and Military Policy: Opportunities and Constraints." *Africa Today* 43, 1–2:88–121.

Creed, John, and Kenneth Menkhaus. 1986. "The Rise of Saudi Regional Power and the Foreign Policies of Northeast African States." *Northeast African Studies* 8, 2–3:1–22.

Davidson, Basil. 1992. *The Black Man's Burden: Africa and the Curse of the Nation-State.* London: James Currey.

Deng, Francis M. 1993. *Protecting the Dispossessed: A Challenge for the International Community*. Washington, DC: Brookings Institution.

Deng, Francis M., and Larry Minear. 1992. *The Challenges of Famine Relief: Emergency Operations in the Sudan*. Washington, DC: Brookings Institution.

Deng, Francis M., et al. Forthcoming 1996. *Sovereignty as Responsibility: Conflict Management in Africa*. Washington, DC: Brookings Institution.

Des Forges, Alison. 1995. "Face au génocide, une réponse désastreuse des Etats-Unis et des Nations Unies." Pp. 455–464 in André Guichaoua (ed.). *Les crises politiques au Burundi et Rwanda (1993–1994): Analyses, faits et documents*. Paris: Karthala.

Diamond, Larry. 1995. "Promoting Democracy in Africa: U.S. and International Policies in Transition." Pp. 250–277 in John W. Harbeson and Donald Rothchild (eds.). *Africa in World Politics*. Boulder: Westview Press.

Diop, Momar Coumba, and Mamadou Diouf. 1990. *Le Sénégal sous Abdou Diouf: État et société*. Paris: Karthala.

Ercolessi, Maria Cristina. 1994. "Italy's Policy in Sub-Saharan Africa." Pp. 87–108 in Stefan Brüne, Joachim Betz, and Winrich Kühne (eds.). *Africa and Europe: Relations of Two Continents in Transition*. Münster and Hamburg: Lit Verlag.

Foccart, Jacques, with Philippe Gaillard. 1995. *Foccart parle: Entretiens avec Philippe Gaillard*. Vol. 1. Paris: Fayard/Jeune Afrique.

French, Howard D. 1995. "Nigeria Comes on Too Strong." *New York Times* (November):E3.

Gambari, Ibrahim A. 1995. "The Role of Foreign Intervention in African Reconstruction." Pp. 221–233 in I. William Zartman (ed.). *Collapsed States: The Disintegration and Restoration of Legitimate Authority*. Boulder: Lynne Rienner Publishers.

Gibbs, David N. 1991. *The Political Economy of Third World Intervention: Mines, Money, and U.S. Policy in the Congo Crisis*. Chicago: University of Chicago Press.

Glaser, Antoine, and Stephen Smith. 1994. *L'Afrique sans Africains: Le rêve blanc du continent noir*. Paris: Editions Stock.

Grundy, Kenneth. 1985. "The Impact of Region on Contemporary African Politics." Pp. 97–125 in Gwendolen M. Carter and Patrick O'Meara (eds.). *African Independence: The First Twenty-Five Years*. Bloomington: Indiana University Press.

———. 1986. *The Militarization of South African Politics*. Bloomington: Indiana University Press.

Guillaumont, Patrick and Sylvianne. 1984. *Zone franc et développement africain*. Paris: Economica.

Guillou, Michel. 1993. *La francophonie: Nouvel enjeu mondial*. Paris: Hatier.

Hanlon, Joseph. 1991. *Mozambique: Who Calls the Shots?* Bloomington: Indiana University Press.

Hirsch, John L., and Robert B. Oakley. 1995. *Somalia and Operation Restore Hope: Reflections on Peacemaking and Peacekeeping*. Washington, DC: United States Institute for Peace.

Hofmeier, Rolf. 1986. "Aid From the Federal Republic of Germany to Africa." *The Journal of Modern African Studies* 24:577–601.

———. 1994. "German-African Relations: Present and Future." Pp. 71–86 in Stefan Brüne, Joachim Betz, and Winrich Kühne (eds.). *Africa and Europe: Relations of Two Continents in Transition*. Münster and Hamburg: Lit Verlag.

Huband, Mark. 1993. "Cameroon: A Flawed Victory." *Africa Report* 38 (January-February): 41–43.

Human Rights Watch/Africa. 1994. "Human Rights in Africa and U.S. Policy: A Special Report by Human Rights Watch/Africa for the White House Conference on Africa held June 26–27, 1994."

Iyob, Ruth. 1995. *The Eritrean Struggle for Independence: Domination, Resistance, Nationalism, 1941–1993.* Cambridge: Cambridge University Press.

Jackson, Robert, and Carl G. Rosberg. 1982. *Personal Rule in Africa: Prince, Autocrat, Prophet, Tyrant.* Berkeley: University of California Press.

Joseph, Richard. 1994. "Africa: The Rebirth of Political Freedom." *Journal of Democracy* 2, 4:11–24.

Joyner, Christopher C. 1992. "International Law." Pp. 229–246 in Peter J. Schraeder (ed.). *Intervention into the 1990s: U.S. Foreign Policy in the Third World.* Boulder: Lynne Rienner Publishers.

Kelly, Sean. 1993. *America's Tyrant: The CIA and Mobutu of Zaire.* Washington, DC: American University Press.

Kolodziej, Edward A. 1974. *French Foreign Policy Under de Gaulle and Pompidou: The Politics of Grandeur.* Ithaca: Cornell University Press.

Korany, Bahgat (ed.). 1986. *How Foreign Policy Decisions Are Made in the Third World: A Comparative Analysis.* Boulder: Westview Press.

Krop, Pascal. 1994. *Le génocide franco-africain: Faut-il juger les Mitterrand?* Paris: Editions Jean-Claude Lattès.

Laïdi, Zaki. 1990. *The Superpowers and Africa: The Constraints of a Rivalry, 1960–1990.* Chicago: University of Chicago Press.

Legum, Colin. 1994. "Britain's Policy in Africa." Pp. 5–69 in Stefan Brüne, Joachim Betz, and Winrich Kühne (eds.). *Africa and Europe: Relations of Two Continents in Transition.* Münster and Hamburg: Lit Verlag.

Lesser, Ian O. 1993. *Security in North Africa: Internal and External Challenges.* Santa Monica, CA: RAND Corporation.

Lyons, Terrence, and Ahmed I. Samatar. 1995. *Somalia: State Collapse, Multilateral Intervention, and Strategies for Political Reconstruction.* Washington, DC: Brookings Institution.

MacQueen, Norman. 1985. "Portugal and Africa: The Politics of Re-Engagement." *The Journal of Modern African Studies* 23:31–51.

Mandela, Nelson. 1993. "South Africa's Future Foreign Policy." *Foreign Affairs* 72, 5:86–97.

Markovitz, Irving L. 1969. *Léopold Sédar Senghor and the Politics of Negritude.* New York: Atheneum.

Martin, Guy. 1986. "The Franc Zone: Underdevelopment and Dependency in Francophone Africa." *Third World Quarterly* 8:205–235.

———. 1992. "African Regional Cooperation and Integration: Achievements, Problems and Prospects." Pp. 69–100 in Ann Seidman and Frederick Anang (eds.). *21st Century Africa: Towards a New Vision of Self-Sustainable Development.* Trenton, NJ: Africa World Press.

———. 1995a. "Continuity and Change in Franco-African Relations." *Journal of Modern African Studies* 33:1–20.

———. 1995b. "Francophone Africa in the Context of Franco-African Relations." Pp. 163–188 in John W. Harbeson and Donald Rothchild (eds.). *Africa in World Politics.* Boulder: Westview Press.

Mathews, K. 1988. "The African Group at the UN as an Instrument of African Diplomacy." *Nigerian Journal of International Affairs* 14, 1:226–258.

M'Bokolo, Elikia. 1992. "Conquêtes européennes et résistances africaines, *ca.* 1880–*ca.* 1910." Pp. 278–282 in Elikia M'Bokolo (ed.). *Afrique noire: Histoire et civilisations.* Vol. 2. *XIXe et XXe siècles.* Paris: Hatier.

Mesa-Lago, Carmelo, and June S. Beikin (eds.). 1982. *Cuba in Africa.* Pittsburgh: Center for Latin American Studies, University of Pittsburgh.

Morna, Colleen Lowe. 1995. "Southern Africa: New Era of Cooperation." *Africa Report* 40 (May-June):64–67.

Nester, William R. 1992. *Japan and the Third World: Patterns, Power, Prospects.* New York: St. Martin's Press.

Nkrumah, Kwame. 1965. *Neo-Colonialism: The Last Stage of Imperialism.* New York: International Publishers.

Ohlson, Thomas, and Stephen John Stedman, with Robert Davies. 1994. *The New Is Not Yet Born: Conflict Resolution in Southern Africa.* Washington, DC: Brookings Institution.

Ojo, Olatunde. 1985. "Regional Co-operation and Integration." Pp. 142–183 in Olatunde J. C. B. Ojo, D. K. Orwa, and C. M. B. Utete. *African International Relations.* London: Longman.

Olusanya, G. O. 1988. "Reflections on the First Twenty-Five Years of the Organization of African Unity." *Nigerian Journal of International Affairs* 14, 1:67–72.

Omaar, Rakiya. 1994. "Somalia: One Thorn Bush at a Time." *Current History* 93:232–236.

Osaghae, Eghosa E. 1995. "The Ogoni Uprising: Oil Politics, Minority Agitation and the Future of the Nigerian State." *African Affairs* 94, 376:325–344.

Parker, Ron. 1991. "The Senegal-Mauritania Conflict of 1989—A Fragile Equilibrium." *Journal of Modern African Studies* 29:155–171.

Patman, Robert G. 1990. *The Soviet Union and the Horn of Africa: The Diplomacy of Intervention and Disengagement.* Cambridge: Cambridge University Press.

Payne, Richard J. 1992. *The Third World and South Africa: Post-Apartheid Challenges.* Westport, CT: Greenwood Press.

Pazzanita, Anthony G. 1992. "Mauritania's Foreign Policy: The Search for Protection." *Journal of Modern African Studies* 30:281–304.

Plank, David N. 1993. "Aid, Debt, and the End of Sovereignty: Mozambique and Its Donors." *Journal of Modern African Studies* 31:407–430.

Potholm, Christian P., and Richard A. Fredland (eds.). 1980. *Integration and Disintegration in East Africa.* Lanham, MD: University Press of America.

Ravenhill, John. 1995. "Dependent by Default: Africa's Relations with the European Union." Pp. 95–126, in John W. Harbeson and Donald Rothchild (eds.). *Africa in World Politics.* Boulder: Westview Press.

Reed, William Cyrus. 1992. "Directions in African International Relations." Pp. 73–103 in Mark W. DeLancey (ed.). *Handbook of Political Science Research on Sub-Saharan Africa: Trends from the 1960s to the 1990s.* Westport, CT: Greenwood Press.

Rooney, David. 1988. *Kwame Nkrumah: The Political Kingdom in the Third World.* New York: St. Martin's Press.

Sandbrook, Richard. 1993. *The Politics of Africa's Economic Recovery.* Cambridge: Cambridge University Press.

Schatzberg, Michael G. 1991. *Mobutu or Chaos? The United States and Zaire, 1960–1990.* Lanham, MD: University Press of America.

Schraeder, Peter J. 1994a. "Elites as Facilitators or Impediments to Political Development? Some Lessons from the 'Third Wave' of Democratization in Africa." *Journal of Developing Areas* 29:69–90.

———. 1994b. *United States Foreign Policy Toward Africa: Incrementalism, Crisis and Change.* Cambridge: Cambridge University Press.

————. 1995. "The Clinton Administration's Africa Policies: Some Comments on Continuity and Change at Mid-Term." Pp. 47–72 in Centre d'Etudes d'Afrique Noire (ed.). *L'Afrique politique 1995: Le meilleur, le pire et l'incertain.* Paris: Karthala.

Segal, Aaron. 1989. "Spain and Africa: The Continuing Problem of Ceuta and Melilla." Pp. A71–A77 in Colin Legum and Marion E. Doro (eds.). *Africa Contemporary Record: Annual Survey and Documents 1987–88.* Vol. 20. New York: Africana.

Shaw, Timothy M. 1991. "Reformism, Revisionism, and Radicalism in African Political Economy During the 1990s." *Journal of Modern African Studies* 29:191–212.

Shaw, Timothy M., and Olajide Aluko (eds.). 1984. *The Political Economy of African Foreign Policy: Comparative Analysis.* New York: St. Martin's Press.

Shaw, Timothy M., and Catherine M. Newbury. 1979. "Dependence or Interdependence: Africa in the Global Political Economy." Pp. 39–89 in Mark W. DeLancey (ed.). *Aspects of International Relations in Africa.* Bloomington: Indiana University Press.

Smith, Robert S. 1989. *Warfare and Diplomacy in Pre-Colonial West Africa.* Madison: University of Wisconsin Press.

Smith, Stephen. 1994. "Afrique noire: Le duel Washington-Paris." *Politique Internationale* 63:355–367.

————. 1995. "France-Rwanda: Lévirat colonial et abandon dans la region des grands lacs." Pp. 447–453 in André Guichaoua (ed.). *Les crises politiques au Burundi et Rwanda (1993–1994): Analyses, faits et documents.* Paris: Karthala.

Snow, Philip. 1988. *The Star Raft: China's Encounter with Africa.* Ithaca, NY: Cornell University Press.

Spanier, John, and Steven W. Hook. 1995. *American Foreign Policy Since World War II.* Washington, DC: Congressional Quarterly Press.

Special edition of *Jeune Afrique.* 1995. "Biarritz: Les dessous du sommet." No. 1767 (November 13–17).

Stokke, Olav (ed.). 1989. *Western Middle Powers and Global Poverty: The Determinants of the Aid Policies of Canada, Denmark, the Netherlands, Norway and Sweden.* Uppsala, Sweden: Scandinavian Institute of African Studies (in cooperation with the Norwegian Institute of International Affairs).

Stremlau, John J. 1977. *The International Politics of the Nigerian Civil War, 1967–1970.* Princeton: Princeton University Press.

Suret-Canale, Jean. 1975. *Difficultés du néo-colonialisme français en Afrique tropicale.* Paris: Centre d'Etudes et de Recherches Marxistes.

Vallée, Olivier. 1989. *Le prix de l'argent CFA: Heurs et malheurs de la zone franc.* Paris: Karthala.

Vernet, Henri. 1995. "La potion libérale de l'oncle Sam." *Jeune Afrique.* No. 1783 (March 9–15).

Villalón, Leonardo A. 1995. *Islamic Society and State Power in Senegal: Disciples and Citizens in Fatick.* Cambridge: Cambridge University Press.

Wauthier, Claude. 1995. *Quatre présidents et l'Afrique: De Gaulle, Pompidou, Giscard d'Estaing, Mitterrand.* Paris: Editions du Seuil.

Welch, Jr., Claude E. 1991. "The Organization of African Unity and the Promotion of Human Rights." *Journal of Modern African Studies* 29:535–555.

Whiteman, Kay. 1994. "The Party's Over." *Africa Report* 39 (March–April):13–18.

Winrow, Gareth M. 1990. *The Foreign Policy of the GDR in Africa.* Cambridge: Cambridge University Press.

World Bank. 1981. *Accelerated Development in Sub-Saharan Africa: An Agenda for Action.* Washington, DC: World Bank.

Young, Crawford, and Thomas Turner. 1989. *The Rise and Decline of the Zairian State*. Madison: University of Wisconsin Press.

Zartman, I. William. 1976. "Europe and Africa: Decolonization or Dependency?" *Foreign Affairs* 54:325–343.

——— (ed.). 1995a. *Collapsed States: The Disintegration and Restoration of Legitimate Authority*. Boulder: Lynne Rienner Publishers.

———. 1995b. "Inter-African Negotiation." Pp. 209–233 in John W. Harbeson and Donald Rothchild (eds.). *Africa in World Politics: Post–Cold War Challenges*. Boulder: Westview Press.

▪ 7 ▪

Population Growth and Urbanization

April A. Gordon

The twentieth century has been the setting for the most explosive growth of human population in history. Whereas it took about 130 years for population to double from 1 billion in the early 1800s to 2 billion in 1930, it took only 43 years for population to double again to 4 billion in 1973. An estimated 6 billion or more will be alive in the year 2000. Most of this growth has occurred among the world's so-called developing countries. By contrast, the world's industrial nations have had, with the exception of the post–World War II baby boom, declining growth rates. In fact, most industrial nations are growing at less than 1 percent a year, and some countries of Europe are actually experiencing negative rates of growth.

A related trend is the revolutionary transition of the world's people from primarily rural agriculturalists to urban dwellers. This change is most advanced in the industrial nations, where 78 percent live in urban areas. Urbanization in the developing countries is not nearly as advanced; only 38 percent are urban (World Bank, 1995:223). The problem is that while industrial societies can provide employment and relatively high living standards for most urban dwellers, the opposite is true in developing countries. Jobs do not expand nearly fast enough to meet the need, and relentless poverty rather than improved living standards is the lot of most. Employment problems are compounded by the rapid rate of urban growth in developing societies, about 3.3 percent per year since 1980 (World Bank, 1995:223). At this rate of growth, cities would double in size every twenty-one years. Governments, already strapped for resources, find it impossible to expand or even maintain the current stock of houses, infrastructure, or services under such conditions.

As ominous as these trends are in the Third World as a whole, they are worse in sub-Saharan Africa. Overall, sub-Saharan Africa's population is growing at a rate of 3 percent a year, the highest in the world. This is an increase from the 2.7 percent average between 1965 and 1980. What's more, this rate of growth is not expected to decline significantly until the twenty-first century. Consequently, sub-Saharan Africa's population will grow from 586 million in 1995 to over 1.3 billion by 2025 (World Population, 1995; Green, 1994:37).

The growth rate of sub-Saharan Africa's cities is also high, averaging about 4.8 percent a year since 1980. Africa has sixteen of the twenty countries with the fastest rate of urbanization in the world, and the percentage of population living in urban areas has doubled since 1965—from 14 percent to 30 percent. By 2025, an estimated 54 percent of the population will live in cities (World Bank, 1995:223; 1986:10; Green, 1994:61). Most of this growth is occurring in one or two cities within each country rather than being more evenly distributed among cities and towns of varying sizes. One result is that the proportion of urban population living in cities of more than half a million (28 in 1980 versus 3 in 1960) has jumped from 6 percent in 1960 to 41 percent in 1980, and a third of the urban population lives in cities of 1 million or more (often the capital) (World Bank, 1995:223; 1990:239). It is estimated that Africa will have at least thirty such "megacities" by 2010 (Green, 1994:64).

These statistical indicators reveal only the quantitative parameters of Africa's population and urban growth trends. They do not reveal why or how

Photo: World Bank

Like most of Africa's large cities, Nairobi has experienced explosive population growth since independence.

the current situation came to be nor what can or should be done about it. There is no consensus on the issues either. For example, there are currently three basic views on the issue of rapid population growth.

One view is that family planning and education are needed to lower birthrates, slow urban growth, and ease population pressure on the land (see Montgomery and Brown, 1990:86). The claim is that family planning is the major reason birthrates have fallen so rapidly in other areas of the Third World ("Reproductive," 1992:11). Also, the fact that Africa has the world's highest birthrates and the lowest rate of contraception usage is seen as evidence that fertility might fall dramatically in Africa if family planning services were more available (Lutz, 1994:14; "Reproductive," 1992:8, 10–11).

Another view is that economic development is the solution to high rates of population growth. After all, fertility and population growth rates were already below African levels long before the advent of modern contraceptives or family planning services (see Sai, 1988). In other words, poverty is the root cause of high birthrates; family planning under such conditions as exist in Africa can achieve only moderate fertility reductions at best.

The third view, one expressed by some women's groups, is that the emphasis on population growth as a "problem" and birth control the "solution" puts the blame on women for Africa's development woes by implying they are having too many children. Framing the issue this way may lead to the sacrifice of women's human and reproductive rights in overzealous efforts to achieve population "control." One suspicion is that such programs, if implemented at the expense of women's overall welfare, become a means for the industrialized world to continue to disproportionately benefit from global economic activities that exploit poor countries and degrade the environment (Lutz, 1994:35; Ashford, 1995:7).

Each of these three views has some limited validity, but population issues in Africa are complex, and analyzing current population trends requires some understanding of African history and culture and some understanding of the political and economic constraints on the development of the conditions necessary for a widespread decline of either population growth or urban concentration. Sub-Saharan Africa's population problems are not abstract demographic problems amenable to a technological fix like family planning. Population trends are the result of individual responses to political and economic forces that are both historical and current. The major historical forces still influencing population dynamics include precolonial social institutions (which have survived in modified form to the present day), slavery, and colonialism. Since independence, the fortunes of Africa have been increasingly shaped by highly bureaucratic African states attempting to transform their societies within a global economy in which Africa has faced many disadvantages. It is also true that the extremely high rates of population and urban growth in Africa—far in excess of rates that occurred in industrializing Europe—impose tremendous hardships on struggling countries. It would be irresponsible to ignore the need for conscious efforts to control and manage population as part of an overall development strategy. There is now widespread agreement with this perspective both within and outside of Africa, as will be discussed later in this chapter.

■ PRECOLONIAL AND COLONIAL PERIODS

Many people unfamiliar with Africa perceive African societies to have been small and village-based, lacking any urban civilization before Europeans came. African scholars have altered this view by describing the many thriving commercial and/or political centers of considerable antiquity in Africa. Along the east coast from Mogadishu to Sofala, numerous commercial towns were developed by Arabs and Africans with a trading network that extended from the interior of Africa to as far away as China. Many miles from the coast in southern Africa, the massive stone ruins of Great Zimbabwe give witness to an ancient, wealthy state that thrived for centuries before the astonished Portuguese set eyes on it in the sixteenth century. In western Africa's Sahel region bordering the Sahara, major cities—Gao, Jenne, and Timbuktu—flourished along the trans-Saharan trade routes. In the forest regions of western Africa, the artistic and religious center of Yorubaland was the city of Ile-Ife, in what is now Nigeria. Kano in Hausaland was a major manufacturing city renowned for its textiles and leather goods. Even the slave trade provided the impetus for the growth of towns such as Kumasi, capital of the Asante in Ghana.

Sub-Saharan African cities never achieved the great size of the major industrial cities of Europe, nor did more than a small minority of the population live in towns or cities. Most retained a horticultural or pastoral way of life. The most likely reason for this is that Africa is so vast that population pressure could be released by migrating to new land rather than through intensification of productive technologies or the adoption of new modes of production. Low population densities, difficulties of transport, and the prevalence of largely self-sufficient communities limited the development of markets for goods and services. This, in turn, along with limited productive capacity, limited the growth of cities.

The Atlantic slave trade played a role, too, by depopulating many regions and promoting ruinous warfare among African communities. This, plus a growing reliance on cheap manufactured goods from Europe, retarded, if not completely aborted, the industrial development that would stimulate urbanization (Rodney, 1974; Mahadi and Inikori, 1987; Gupta, 1987; Davidson, 1959).

Although data for precolonial Africa are sketchy, there is good evidence that regulation of fertility (childbearing) was a common and accepted practice in most African societies, even those few that were hunter-gatherers such as the San (Bushmen) of the Kalahari. The most common methods of birth regulation involved an approximate one- to two-year period of postpartum abstinence and extended breast-feeding. The latter is well known to retard the onset of ovulation once a baby is born. Another custom in many societies deemed it unseemly for a grandmother to become pregnant. Since most females married in their mid-teens, this effectively shortened their childbearing years to the middle or late thirties. Age-grade systems in many countries of eastern Africa often led to later ages of marriage due to late male and female initiation. In Tanzania, males usually married between the ages of twenty-five and thirty. The cost of bridewealth also forced many males throughout Africa to marry fairly late. These practices, among others, resulted in effective child spacing and lowered the number of children born per woman to well below the biological maximum. Polygyny (having more than one wife) made these practices workable, since there was less pressure on a woman to be sexually and reproductively active when there was more than one wife in the household. Along with fairly high mortality rates, regulated fertility (high but not maximum) resulted in slow population growth (Newman and Lura, 1983; Page and Lesthaeghe, 1981; Jewsiewicki, 1987; Valentine and Revson, 1979).

Some scholars contend that the Atlantic slave trade and later colonial policies drastically upset the demographic balance in Africa, promoting both higher birthrates and mortality as well as urban concentration (e.g., O'Brien, 1987; Jewsiewicki, 1987; Page and Lesthaeghe, 1981; Dawson, 1987). Slave raiders sometimes captured whole villages and marched their unfortunate captives to the coast where slave ships awaited them. An estimated 10 to 20 million Africans were lost to the Americas or to death in transport. Untold others lost their lives resisting the slavers or from the economic and social disruption the slave trade caused. Major migrations and wars occurred as a result of people either escaping from slave raiders or pursuing the trade in human flesh themselves. The prime victims of the traffic in slaves were young men and women and children—Africa's aborted reproductive and productive future. The disruptions and mixing of peoples also resulted in a rise in disease, including venereal disease, and higher mortality. In central Africa, venereal and other diseases produced high rates of subfecundity and sterility in such countries as present-day Cameroon, Gabon, Zaire, and Central African Republic. With a reduced stock of young reproductive-age women and depleted populations, greater pressures were put on families—on women—to increase their fertility.

In the 1800s and 1900s, colonialism further altered the African landscape. Whereas mercantile capitalism in previous centuries valued Africa for its slaves, newly industrializing capitalism abolished the exploitation of slavery, replacing it with the exploitation of Africa's cheap labor and cheap raw materials. The colonial system incorporated Africa into the emerging global capitalist economy, but Africa did not yield willingly. Unable to secure voluntary labor for plantations, farms, and mines in a continent of self-sufficient farmers and pastoralists, colonial policies such as the hut tax were used to force young males to leave their farms and migrate to towns or other areas where they could earn cash in the colonial economy. Women were usually left in the rural areas to bear and raise children, to farm, or to occasionally earn cash as farm laborers, petty traders, or commodity producers. With fewer men to help with the farm labor, more of the burden fell on women.

Cash cropping, introduced to men by the colonialists to supply desired exports for Europe, also increased women's burdens in the fields. Left to grow most of the food by themselves, women were often compelled to work on their husband's cash crop farms as well. Forced labor, the loss of male migrant labor, and emphasis on cash cropping all threatened food production. Rising infant mortality and morbidity (disease) due to food shortages were not uncommon under the colonial regime (Jewsiewicki, 1987). According to Dawson (1987), mortality rose and population actually declined between 1900 and 1930. The economic pressures created by colonialism created the conditions for higher fertility, children became even more important as sources of farm labor and wages to be remitted to their parents, and high rates of infant and child mortality reinforced high fertility to ensure that some would survive to adulthood.

European Christianity and missionary education also inadvertently encouraged larger families. Missionaries, as well as other colonial agents, promoted Western Victorian ideas of women's "proper role" as dependent wives and mothers rather than encouraging women's productive activities outside the family. Christianity also undermined polygyny in favor of the Western monogamous family. With only one wife to work and reproduce the children necessary for family survival, the old mechanisms of child spacing broke down. Weaning occurred earlier, and postpartum abstinence was increasingly ignored or shortened. Again, the result was higher fertility (Turshen, 1987).

Contrary to the typical pattern in which urbanization (an indicator of "modernization") promotes declining fertility, in Africa the opposite occurred. Primarily male migrants, the inhabitants of colonial towns were now often able to earn the bridewealth payment necessary to acquire a wife at an earlier age. Cultural controls that limited access to wives and hence moderated potential fertility broke down. Because of the expense of maintaining more than one household, monogamy increased in the towns but so did fertility (Dawson, 1987; Turshen, 1987). Retention of rural high fertility patterns also occurred because most migrants retained land or rights to land back in their villages. Residence in cities was usually temporary, as most returned home after some years in the city. Indeed, to date, much of the growth of urban areas in Africa has been due to high birthrates, not simply migration (Montgomery and Brown, 1990:86; El-Shakhs and Amirakmadi, 1986:15–17).

■ POSTINDEPENDENCE TRENDS

The restructuring of African economies to serve the colonial capitalist economy produced growing populations and migration to cities. These trends mostly reflected hardships imposed on most Africans, not opportunities of modernization and development. After all, extracting Africa's wealth, not promoting economic prosperity for Africans, was the colonial goal. The ensuing poverty and exploitation made families highly dependent on their children both as sources of labor and income and as caretakers when they—the parents—were old.

One would expect that independent Africa, the chains of colonial oppression broken, would embark upon an economic and social transformation that would produce the fabled "demographic transition" to low birthrates and low rates of population growth characteristic of developed countries. According to transition theory, as urbanization and other aspects of modernization grow and families become less dependent on children as a source of labor, smaller families become the "rational" choice of parents. Economic growth should have the effect of altering the pronatalist motivational environment as the costs of rearing children (e.g., educational expenses) increase and new wants (e.g., consumer goods) compete with the desire for children.

So far, none of these expectations has been borne out. The birthrates in every region of the world have gone down since 1965 except in sub-Saharan Africa. This includes other Third World regions. Development trends that are purported to be associated with declining fertility have produced strikingly different results in Africa. In addition to urbanization, these trends include declining mortality (both infant and overall), higher life expectancy, widespread access to formal education, and rising per capita incomes.[1] Despite these trends, birthrates and population growth rates in almost all countries of sub-Saharan Africa have remained high or even climbed; crude birthrates (births per thousand population) average forty-four in sub-Saharan Africa compared to twenty-six in Latin America and sixteen in the United States (World Bank, 1995:213).

Especially confounding is that even in urban areas, where fertility is supposed to drop first as "development" occurs, birthrates are still little different from those of the surrounding rural areas. Equally puzzling is that among the urban affluent, usually the leading group in the move toward the

**Table 7.1   Selected Development and Demographic Trends
for Sub-Saharan Africa (SSA) and Less Developed
Countries (LDCs)**

| | SSA | | LDCs | |
	1965	1993	1965	1993
Per capita GNP ($)	—	520	—	1090
% urban	14	30	24	38
Primary education enrollment (%)	41	67[a]	78	102[a]
Infant mortality[b]160	93	117	55	55
Crude birthrate[c]	48	44	41	27
Crude death rate[d]	22	15	15	9
Rate of population growth (%)	2.6	2.9	2.6	1.6
Total fertility rate[e]	6.6	6.2	6.1	3.4
Life expectancy (female)	43	53	52	66
(male)	41	50	50	63

Source: World Bank, 1990; 1995
Notes:
a. For 1992
b. Deaths per 1,000 infants in the first year of life
c. Births per 1,000 population
d. Deaths per 1,000 population
e. Expected average number of children per woman at the end of her childbearing years

small family, large families remain the norm. In all social strata and regions, studies repeatedly show minimal motivation for small families and often little or no effort to regulate fertility (e.g., "Reproductive," 1992; Sindiga, 1985; Olusanya and Purcell, 1981; World Bank, 1986; Faruqee and Gulhati, 1983; Caldwell, 1994).

Looking beyond the demographic data to the overall conditions in African societies can help us understand current fertility and urbanization patterns. Postindependence Africa is still largely locked in patterns inherited from both its precolonial and colonial past. Combined with Africa's disadvantageous position in the global capitalist economy, societal transformations that would compel alterations of current demographic patterns are embryonic.

More specifically, most Africans are still tied to rural areas and a largely subsistence mode of production characterized by Hyden (1983) as the "economy of affection" or by others (e.g., Cordell et al., 1987) as the "domestic mode of production." Within this mode of production, land and other productive assets such as cattle are owned by related families, with rights to *use* these assets accorded to members. A major goal is to ensure that all adults have access to the means of producing food and goods, which are used to meet the basic needs of all. While all members have assured rights and obligations within the system, the division of labor by age and gender benefits the elders most, especially males, since they usually control access to most family resources and have more rights to the labor and fruits of the labor of other members of the family. Family prosperity depends on having many family members to work and to reproduce future family members. This is the major way accumulation of assets occurs.

The Western capitalist mode of production has only partially eroded the domestic mode of production through the introduction of such things as medium to large government or privately owned commercial farms or businesses. During colonial times, commercial farms and businesses were dominated by whites. Africans were incorporated into the colonial capitalist economy mostly as menial wage labor or cash crop farmers. The vast majority were left to farm or raise cattle in more or less customary ways. Indeed, the colonial system tried to use rather than destroy the domestic mode of production for its own ends—by converting much family subsistence production to cash crop production and relying on women's food crop production to feed poorly paid wage laborers and their children. As mentioned earlier, large families were major assets to both the colonial capitalist economy (ensuring a continual labor supply) and to the economy of affection (ensuring survival).

Capitalism works quite differently. It individualizes ownership of productive assets such as land, cattle, or a business, giving rights to keep, profit from, or sell such assets as the owner sees fit. Such a system eventually creates, on the one hand, an ownership class and, on the other hand, a growing mass of wage labor no longer having access to land or other economic assets. The relationships between family members change as kinship becomes less linked to production and no longer ensures access to productive assets. No longer able to rely on land or other family resources in rural areas, the urban migrant increasingly becomes dependent on himself or herself and wage employment. Temporary migration becomes permanent, weakening ties to rural family and friends. Reciprocal obligations among even distantly related kin are gradually replaced by a focus on the conjugal family and household. As education becomes more vital to success in the capitalist economy, children become more expensive to their parents and less able to contribute to the family's financial welfare. Even in rural areas, the successful farms are becoming commercial farms that rely more on capital inputs such as mechanization and less on wage and family labor. Here too the need for many children begins to decline.

As production becomes transformed by capitalism, consumption also changes. Fewer families are self-sufficient, subsistence producers. Especially in urban areas, there is increasing reliance on the market to provide food, clothing, housing, and so on. Moreover, new wants are stimulated by the capitalist economy for recreational activities, goods, and services previously nonexistent or unaffordable. Insofar as these must be acquired through the individual's or family's income, a trade-off between the number of children and satisfying new wants or acquiring necessities alters reproductive decisions in the direction of smaller and smaller families.

To be sure, this discussion simplifies the role of capitalism in transforming production and reproduction. The effects of capitalism are highly variable by country and region and by such factors as class, religion, and ethnicity. The timing and extent of changes also differ. Nonetheless, in broad outline, the patterns outlined above are widely applicable.

What about in sub-Saharan Africa? Is it just a matter of time before capitalism breaks down the economy of affection (or domestic mode of production)? Will fertility and population growth begin to slow along with rapid urbanization?

The answers to these questions are speculative at this point, but current information provides a basis for only minor optimism for the foreseeable future. The main reason for such a pessimistic conclusion is that the vast majority of African economies, whether more or less capitalist, are facing serious problems of spiraling debt and declining or minimal economic growth. Capitalism, whether in the form of multinational corporations, African entrepreneurs, or state-owned enterprises, has so far been able to only partially transform Africa's economies. Socialism has also failed to produce sustainable economic growth for its citizens. Modern sector (wage) employment absorbs only a small minority of workers and at mostly low wages. This reinforces reliance on the extended family for most people. Most urban migrants still ultimately plan to go back home to the rural areas. Oftentimes their wives and children remain on the farm, and kinship obligations are retained.

Despite current efforts to liberalize and "privatize" African economies, it is politically difficult for most governments to promote private ownership of land if this undermines lineage-based land tenure practices that ensure land for every family needing land. This is understandable given the lack of employment alternatives to farming. Indeed, many African societies pride themselves on the fact that most farmers are smallholders and that a rural aristocracy of large commercial landowners hasn't developed. While this is a tribute to equity compared to most societies, many of these smallholders are too marginal and poor to operate as "modern producers." Unable to afford or utilize many capital inputs to increase production, family labor is essential (Hyden, 1983).

As long as urban employment fails to provide alternative means of livelihood for the rural poor, pressure to ensure land for everyone and maintain lineage- and ethnic-based control of land will continue, as will the desire for large families. Urban employment for the poor majority depends so far on informal sector jobs such as petty trader, food vendor, or artisan. In many cases, such employment benefits from child labor. Since many children who go to school do not attend beyond the primary level, and since educational costs are largely borne by the government, parents still find

Children are a vital economic resource in Africa's extended family systems. Most women want large families, and only a small percentage use modern forms of contraception.

children to be a paying investment rather than a financial liability. Some may even get a good wage job and share their resources with others in the family.

Even among the more affluent—those who do have well-paid jobs in government, business, or the professions—children are seen as essential to the expansion and prosperity of the wider kin network. Responsibility for children is still widely shared as older women, relatives, and friends help in the care of children. The conjugal family does not bear this burden from its own resources alone. It is a common practice in urban households to find rural relatives working as housekeepers, cooks, and baby-sitters in exchange for room and board or an education. Sometimes such work is performed for kinsmen until a good wage job opens up—often with the help of other kin or ethnic group members. Another way families share the cost of children is through the practice of "fostering" (see Green, 1994:56–57). In parts of West Africa, one-third of children are living with their relatives rather than with their parents (Dasgupta, 1995:42).

What is happening so widely in Africa is that, rather than being undermined, the economy of affection that undergirds high birthrates is an essential means of competing and surviving in the modernizing quasi-capitalist economy. The more extensive a person's kinship system, the more potentially beneficial connections she or he has. This, in turn, enhances access to scarce resources and services. Small, conjugal families—whether rich or poor—are for the most part at a distinct disadvantage (Fapohunda, 1982; Mbacke, 1994).

It must be mentioned that the processes briefly outlined above both reflect and reinforce the inadequacies of African economies. Those inadequacies were largely imposed on Africa by the colonial system. They include dependence on a few raw materials exports; little if any industry, or foreign-dominated industry and business; illiteracy; and dependence on European rather than domestic or trans-African market linkages. Since independence, the type of development Africa has been encouraged to pursue— i.e., capital-intensive (highly mechanized), import-substitution industrialization largely supported by taxation of an export-oriented agricultural sector—has continued to encourage both high fertility and migration to cities. To squeeze the profits of agriculture to fund development of urban-based industries, below–market value prices have been paid to farmers. This has made it very difficult for most farmers to make a livelihood as farmers, and it increases reliance on kinship networks and children; many become migrants to the cities. In their efforts to promote industry, government and foreign investment manifested a significant "urban bias": electricity, clean water, housing, infrastructure, schools, health facilities, and industries are mostly located in the one or two major cities of the country, as are most of the highly coveted government jobs. The gap in rural-urban living standards and incomes is quite pronounced and is an almost irresistible motivation for out-migration from the rural areas. Yet, most of those who come to the city find that good jobs are scarce and that they must continue to rely on their kin and children to survive. In sum, from the standpoint of most families, the overall economic situation continues to make large families "rational" if potentially ruinous for the nation.

■ THE BIRTH CONTROL CONTROVERSY

There has been considerable controversy over the impact of high fertility and population growth rates on Africa, and until recently these controversies have resulted in virtual inaction on the part of most African nations in formulating any real population policies as part of their development planning. Until recently Africans pointed out that most African countries have very low population densities and small populations. They are, as a result of artificial boundaries set during colonial times, "micro states," as Goliber (1985) calls them. African officials contended that to increase the labor force and internal markets and to develop their countries' resources required a larger population.

By contrast, development agencies and family planning proponents—mostly from capitalist industrial nations—countered that unless rapid population growth is checked, increasing demands for such necessities as food, services, land, and jobs will overwhelm the fragile economies of all but a few African countries (World Bank, 1986; 1989a). It is also pointed out that while enormous areas of Africa are sparsely populated and underdeveloped, much of this land is unsuitable for intensive human use without costly investment. And given the current population pressure on land and resources in Africa, severe or even irreversible ecological damage is already undermining the environment upon which Africa's development and future populations will depend. Although much of the damage can be attributed to abuses associated with extractive industries and government policies, the expanding poor's need for wood for fuel, water, grazing land, income, or land for crops is also part of the equation. Symptomatic of the environmental damage are extensive deforestation, destruction of wildlife, desertification, and soil erosion in many parts of Africa, as Julius Nyang'oro discusses in Chapter 8. The pressures of population, it is claimed, threaten to reverse Africa's development efforts. Population control measures must be implemented if development is to take place (see Brown and Postel, 1987).

Only since the 1970s have any sub-Saharan African governments expressed concern over their population growth rates or requested assistance in developing family planning services. When the International Family Planning Foundation set up the African Regional Council in 1971, only eight countries were involved: Mauritius, Kenya, Tanzania, Liberia, Ghana, Sierra Leone, Nigeria, and The Gambia (Sai, 1988:270). At the 1974 World Population Conference in Bucharest, only three African countries expressed a desire to slow their population growth—Kenya, Ghana, and Botswana. Only half of sub-Saharan countries supported family planning even as a health measure. None provided extensive services (World Bank, 1986:1).

By December 1975, Mauritius, Kenya, Ghana, and Botswana had official policies to reduce growth. A few others, such as Tanzania, Nigeria, and Zaire, issued statements encouraging "responsible parenthood." Notably, Tanzania has tried to incorporate population with economic and social planning without an official population policy. This includes efforts to promote maternal and child health, birth spacing, increased age of marriage for women (to fifteen years!), and maternity leave (Henin, 1979). By 1976, Africa was receiving 13 percent of United Nations Fund for Population Activities (UNFPA) funds (Johnson, 1987:263).

African governments' attitudes changed markedly in the 1980s. At the Second African Population Conference, sponsored by the UN at Arusha, Tanzania, in 1984, the watershed Kilimanjaro Programme of Action on Population was adopted. It recommended that population be seen as a central component in formulating socioeconomic development plans. Governments should ensure access to family planning services to all couples and individuals freely or at a subsidized cost. At the UN International Conference on Population held in Mexico in 1985, African population growth was an issue of great concern. Vice-president of Kenya Mwai Kibaki discussed the need to stabilize Kenya's population and recommended that stabilizing world population within the next fifty years should be a major commitment. Also in 1985, leaders from forty African countries met in Berlin with World Bank officials to discuss population control (Johnson, 1987:263). By 1986, only Chad, Côte d'Ivoire, Gabon, Guinea-Bissau, and Mauritania did not support family planning. By 1989, on the other hand, Ghana, Mauritius, Nigeria, Uganda, and Zambia had declared target fertility reductions backed by explicit policies (World Bank, 1989a:71).

Interest in population growth is at an all-time high in the 1990s. By 1991 about 60 percent of African governments said their population growth was too high (versus only 30 percent in 1976). Even governments unconcerned about population growth now support family planning as part of broader maternal and child health care (Green, 1994:34). Seventeen countries have formal population policies; many others are in the process of developing them (World Population, 1993). Symbolically important, the 1994 World Population Conference was held in Africa—in Cairo, Egypt. One hundred and eighty countries, many of them African, agreed to a Program of Action to stabilize world population and to provide universal access to family planning and reproductive health services by 2015 (Ashford, 1995:2, 33).

There are indications that contraceptive use is increasing in at least some sub-Saharan African countries, especially among more educated urban dwellers. For instance, as early as 1981, studies showed contraceptive use slowly rising in such Nigerian cities as Ibadan and Lagos among those with at least secondary education and white-collar jobs and income (Olusanya and Purcell, 1981; Page and Lesthaeghe, 1981). Late 1980s data indicate that contraceptive use in Africa ranges from 43 percent among married women in Zimbabwe and 35 percent in Botswana to only 4–5 percent of women in Mali, Niger, and Uganda. Despite the increases in some countries, the use of contraception is about 20 percent lower in African countries than would be expected of countries at similar levels of socioeconomic development ("Reproductive," 1992: 8, 10).

Lack of access to family planning services is one reason contraceptive usage is so low. Family planning programs remain weak or virtually nonexistent in most countries, and only six countries—Botswana, Ghana, Kenya, South Africa, Zambia, and Zimbabwe—have programs rated "moderate" to "strong" (Green, 1994:34). Therefore, many experts believe that if African governments expanded services, many more women, even rural women, would use them (Mbacke, 1994:191; "Reproductive," 1992:8).

The major problem is not access to contraception, however. Quite simply, African women want more children than women elsewhere in the world.

The average number of children born to African women is 6.5 compared to 3.2 in Asia and Latin America (Ashford, 1995:14). As Green (1994:40) reports, the younger, more educated, urban African women who are most likely to be contraceptive users still want four to six children. While this is two to three children fewer than older women desire, it still represents very high fertility.

Although the process of fertility decline is likely to remain gradual and uneven, there is evidence that sub-Saharan Africa is beginning to embark on the road to "demographic transition" from high to low fertility. The increase in contraceptive usage and somewhat smaller family size among younger women are two such signs. Surveys in many countries also show a greater interest in family planning and a reconsideration of the benefits of a large family (Green, 1994:40; Mbacke, 1994:188–189). Some researchers conclude that despite constraints on a broad, regional reduction in birthrates, "nearly all the traditional supports for high fertility in Africa . . . have been eroding," and "it may be only a matter of time before the fertility transition takes place" ("Reproductive," 1992:8).

■ **URBAN POPULATION POLICY**

Quite clearly, urban population growth from both natural increase (high birthrates) and migration of rural population far exceeds the wage sector's abilities to absorb it. For this reason, 40 percent or more of an African city's labor force is employed in the informal sector. The oversupply of workers tends to depress wages, making it more difficult to achieve higher living standards. Because the poor have little purchasing power, the private sector fails to respond to their housing or other needs, and government budgets are insufficient to extend most services to more than a lucky minority. As bad as conditions have been in most African cities, they are getting worse, not better. As Becker et al. observe,

> As of the early 1990s, . . . the prospects for Africa's cities appear to be exceptionally bleak. Services have decayed terribly; no country can provide formal sector employment to match the growth in job seekers; industrial production is shockingly low; any increased dynamism of the private sector remains on the distant horizon; and social problems, including rising crime and HIV incidence, have become increasingly pervasive. In short, urban living standards have fallen greatly in the past decade, both for the poor and for many of the wealthy. (Becker et al., 1994:22)

Despite such grim descriptions, controversy over what to do, if anything, about urban population trends exists. Some free-market advocates contend that, however unsalutary such growth appears, it is actually more economical to concentrate industry than to decentralize in countries of relatively small population size, such as most countries in sub-Saharan Africa. Economies of scale are maximized in that industries have better access to markets and labor, and supportive infrastructure and services are more cheaply provided (Brennan and Richardson, 1986). As incomes and government revenues improve, better housing, services, and so on will increase accordingly. Others add that such urban patterns are an inevitable consequence of urban economic development and rural stagnation rather than a negative force to be suppressed. Migrants rationally perceive opportunities to be better in the city. Moreover, urban concentration ("primacy") is not excessive in Africa by world standards, as the share of total population in large cities is not usually above 10 percent. Furthermore, such primacy tends to fall as countries become more developed (Becker et al., 1994:58–60).

Critics counter that such growth may be economical from the standpoint of the foreign firms that dominate so many African countries, but they perpetuate backwardness and inequality for most of the host countries' people. Intervention and planning are called for in order to promote more balanced and equitable development throughout the country (Rondinelli, 1983). Even those less alarmed by urban concentration agree that urban decentralization could be a desirable by-product of current structural adjustment policies designed to promote rural development, shrink government, and promote exports (Becker et al., 1994:60–61).

While not agreeing on what to do about their cities, most African governments recognize that uncontrolled urban growth is problematic. Consequently, various interventionist strategies have been used throughout the continent to deal with rapid urbanization. They fall into two basic categories: (1) measures to discourage migration to the major cities and (2) policies to improve conditions in the cities. Unfortunately, these two strategies often work at cross-purposes, since improving urban conditions makes cities even more attractive to potential migrants. There are other problems as well, as will be discussed below.

Category one, discouraging migration, includes efforts to upgrade conditions in the rural areas to prevent out-migration to the cities. In Cameroon, for example, after years of neglect of the rural areas, the government in the 1980s began to pay farmers higher prices, provide more training programs, and increase aid to young farmers. The government also planned to invest more in such infrastructural improvements as road building, rural electrification, school construction, and expanded public health centers (Gordon and Gordon, 1988:13). Although rural development is a desirable goal in its own right, Stren and White (1989:307) conclude that rural development projects have not been very successful, nor have they had much effect on migration.

Some African governments used to try removing unwanted migrants from the city and destroying squatter settlements as a means of controlling overcrowding and public health hazards. These efforts also failed because

Squatters construct their homes in a settlement in Lusaka, Zambia.

migrants typically returned to the city, and their makeshift dwellings were reconstructed on the same or similar sites. Tearing down squatter housing also added to urban overcrowding by putting even more pressure on what housing was available (see Morrison and Gutkind, 1982). Squatter settlements are now major features of every large African city as the influx of poor people from the countryside continues. In Kinshasa, Zaire, for instance, about 70 percent of all housing is squatter or slum housing (El-Shakhs and Amirakmadi, 1986).

Countries such as Kenya, Ethiopia, Tanzania, and Nigeria have attempted resettlement programs as rural development strategies. Some resettlement programs are part of regional development plans designed to promote the growth of towns and cities outside of the one or two main cities. In Ethiopia, industry location policies were used to encourage the growth of medium-sized cities (Brennan and Richardson, 1986). In Cameroon, medium-sized cities have been promoted through the decentralization of government activities to regional cities throughout the country (Gordon and Gordon, 1988). Some African countries are building new capital cities as a means of decentralizing their urban populations. Examples here are Abuja in Nigeria, Dodoma in Tanzania, and Yamassoukro in Côte d'Ivoire. Abuja is expected to have 1.6 million people by the year 2000. It was designed to reduce pressures on Lagos, Nigeria's largest city, and to promote more migration to Nigeria's sparsely populated interior. So far, these regional development policies have had little impact on migration to the largest cities, according to White (1989).

Under category two, improving the cities, various policies have been tried in an attempt to maintain the livability of overextended cities. Since independence, much of the investment made by African governments has gone to cities to provide essentials like roads, housing, water and electricity, and sewage disposal. There was, in addition, an "urban bias" in government policies that resulted in cheap imported or locally produced food for urbanites and cheap housing for middle-class civil servants. IMF-imposed structural adjustment programs have forced many governments to cut such subsidies to the cities along with other government spending. Higher prices, declining urban living standards, and deteriorating social services and maintenance of public works have followed. In Dakar, Senegal, and Ibadan, Nigeria, for example, water supplies are periodically cut off because cities don't have the foreign exchange to pay for chemicals to treat the water (White, 1989:5–6, 13). Cuts in government subsidies for basic foodstuffs have led to riots in some cities, such as in Sudan and Zambia (O'Connor, 1991:117).

Because cities are growing so rapidly, providing simple housing and basic services has become a major problem. Both the government and most migrants lack the financial resources to provide anything but substandard, squatter housing. New residents to the city are often compelled by their circumstances to settle on unclaimed or unoccupied land and to scavenge for wood, corrugated metal, and other building materials. Basic services such as piped water, sewers, and electricity are usually lacking. UN data indicate that a large percentage of Africa's urban dwellers lack safe drinking water and sanitation services. In the worst case, Central African Republic, only 19 percent of urban residents have safe water; more typical is Malawi, where 40 percent are without safe water. Adequate sanitation is unavailable to 86 percent of Lesotho's urban residents, but even in such countries as Ghana, Côte d'Ivoire, Zambia, and Zaire, between 19 and 54 percent of all urban dwellers lack adequate sanitation (United Nations, 1995:58–59).

Until recently, a "sites and services" policy replaced removal of migrants and destruction of their settlements as the preferred way to deal with the urban poor. "Sites" are first cleared for housing; streets and lots are marked off; then "services" such as water points are provided, with electricity hookups and sewage disposal available. Residents build on these prepared sites, improving them and adding electricity and other improvements as their incomes allow. Because of Africa's economic crisis in the 1980s and 1990s, however, most governments have stopped providing free services to the poor. Individuals and communities have been left to fend for themselves to provide private water connections, self-help housing, and private household electric generators. Many of the poor must do without (White,

1989:19). Unfortunately, as O'Connor (1994:121) predicts, "there is no doubt whatever that the housing conditions for most poor people in African cities will continue to be appalling for the foreseeable future."

Efforts to increase urban employment opportunities are vital to improving conditions in Africa's cities. Unfortunately, too often this has meant the proliferation of unnecessary civil service jobs since other wage jobs are lacking. Many of these jobs are now being cut due to the squeeze on government budgets. Expanding private sector jobs has been attempted through providing credit and technical assistance to local entrepreneurs and small businesses. Many of these small businesses are in the informal sector, which currently employs an estimated 39 percent of sub-Saharan Africa's labor force (World Bank, 1989a:138). There is a growing interest in providing assistance to informal sector and other small businesses as a way to create jobs and expand private enterprise in Africa (cf. World Bank, 1989a:136–143; MacGaffey and Windsperger, 1990).

Affordable food is another concern in urban areas. Improving marketing, storage, and transport facilities and stimulating food production in the rural areas are crucial. Past government subsidies to ensure cheap local or imported food are becoming a thing of the past. As governments move to increase prices paid to farmers in order to increase food production, urban dwellers will pay more for their food. The hope is that ultimately prices will fall as food supplies become more abundant. In the meantime, dependence on imported food and foreign food aid is increasing (see World Bank, 1995:168–169).

Despite their concerns about urban growth trends and problems, most African governments have done relatively little about them over the years. According to findings of the UN Population Inquiry in 1983, two-thirds of sub-Saharan Africa's governments had policies of some kind to decelerate rural-urban migration. But most policies to alter or accommodate migration trends were rarely executed (Adepoju and Clarke, 1985). Current budget constraints make such policies unlikely for the foreseeable future. As long as the economy in Africa remains in disarray and population growth rates remain high, there is little reason to believe the future will bring significant relief from the myriad problems of Africa's cities.

The bottom line, as White (1989:6) concludes, is that cities will continue to grow. As bad as they are, they are better than the rural areas.

■ AIDS IN AFRICA

Complicating the picture of African population growth and urbanization trends is AIDS. The statistics are grim. At the end of 1990, the World Health Organization estimated that there were 8–10 million people in the world infected with the AIDS virus. Sub-Saharan Africa, with only 10 percent of the world's population, had 25–50 percent of all the AIDS-infected population (Chin, 1990:223). At the Eighth International Conference on AIDS in Africa, held in Marrakech, Morocco, in 1994, the WHO upped the estimated infected population to over 15 million. The largest number of new cases were in Africa—with more than 1.5 million. This brings the total in Africa to 10 million ("WHO Address," 1994). In 1995, the number of people with HIV worldwide has reportedly increased again—to 17.6 million, with 44 percent of new infections (1.6 million) in sub-Saharan Africa ("Women," 1995:3). In mid-1988 there were 100,000 official cases of full-blown AIDS in Africa (Goliber, 1989: 21); in 1993 there were 2 million (out of 3 million worldwide) ("WHO Address," 1994). In 1994, almost 1.3 million Africans died of the disease (Ashford, 1995:27). Although central and eastern Africa—the so-called AIDS belt—are most affected by AIDS, the rate of infection is rising in many other countries as well.

The ultimate demographic impact of AIDS is uncertain, but what is currently known is frightening. For example, in 1993, Ethiopia reported a half million cases of HIV/AIDS. In many Nigerian clinics that treat sexually transmitted diseases, up to 22 percent of men have the virus. In Francistown, Botswana, a third of women seeking antenatal care are HIV-infected ("WHO Address," 1994). AIDS is now the leading cause of death for adolescent males and the second leading cause of death for adolescent females in Côte d'Ivoire (Ashford, 1995:27). In Zimbabwe, a staggering 20–25 percent of the sexually active population is infected with HIV (Taylor, 1995). Recent data also suggest that the period between HIV infection and death from AIDS is much shorter in Africa than in Western Europe—five versus eleven years. And since most Africans are infected in late adolescence or in their twenties, many are dead before the age of thirty (many women become infected at younger ages than men and are dead before age twenty-five) (Gregson, 1994; "WHO Address," 1994). The rate of HIV infection is expected to grow from 1 percent of the total African population in 1990 to 8 percent by 2015 (Roudi, 1991:4).

As the above data indicate, in Africa AIDS is largely a heterosexual disease that afflicts women as much as men. It is also far more common in cities than in rural areas. Migration and other population movements are a major source of spread of the disease. This plus the disproportionate concentration of males in the cities encourages casual and commercial sex ("WHO Address," 1994).

Indeed, casual sex, often involving prostitutes (many of whom are poor women who have no other way to earn a living), is the major factor in HIV transmission (Press, 1991:12). In Lusaka, Zambia, and Nairobi, Kenya, for instance, tests show that 90 percent of the prostitutes have HIV (O'Connor, 1991:114). Not only is the rate of infection high among prostitutes, but the men who frequent prostitutes then spread the disease to other prostitutes,

Photo: World Bank

Mothers and their young children in Africa are at high risk of getting AIDS.

their wives, or girlfriends (Press, 1991:12–13). One group of men susceptible to HIV infection from unsafe sex is the African soldier. While not necessarily true in other countries of Africa, more than 50 percent of
Zimbabwe's 50,000 soldiers are reported to have HIV/AIDS (Taylor, 1995).

Africa is the one region of the world where more women than men have
HIV/AIDS. Globally, 73 women get HIV per 100 men. In sub-Saharan
Africa, 110 women get HIV per 100 men ("Women," 1995). By some estimates between 1.5 and 3 million women in central and eastern Africa's
AIDS belt will die from AIDS in the 1990s (Roudi, 1991:13). In 1994 alone,
of the almost 1.3 million Africans dying of AIDS, 40 percent were women,
37 percent were men, and 23 percent were children ("Women," 1995).

The number of children dying from AIDS is perhaps the greatest
tragedy of this terrible disease. Most of the women infected with HIV are of
reproductive age. In a WHO survey of mostly urban women in the AIDS belt
of central and eastern Africa, 25–30 percent tested positive for HIV
(Goliber, 1989:19–21). Infected women, if they become pregnant, have a
15–45 percent chance of passing the virus to their infants before, during, or
shortly after birth (Roudi, 1991:13; Chin, 1990:222). The enormity of the
problem is indicated by the fact that AIDS has become the number one killer
of African children (d'Adesky, 1990:69).

Mothers are not the only source of HIV infection of children, however.
In some countries, such as Kenya, blood transfusions are commonly used to

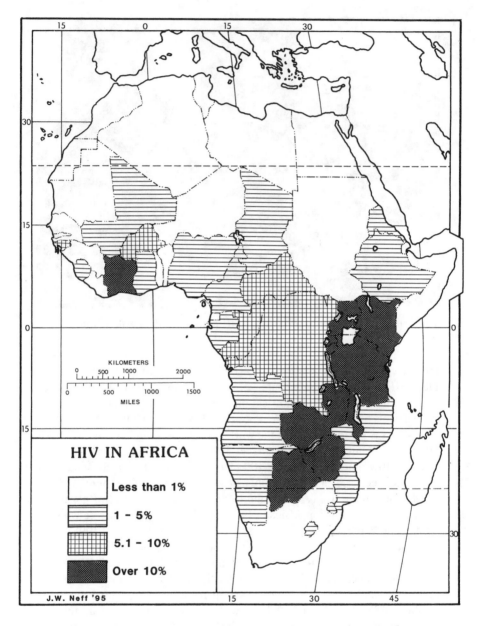

Map 7.1

HIV–1 and HIV–2 infection rates among low–risk urban populations, 1992, compiled from *The Impact of HIV/AIDS on World Population*, United States Department of Commerce, Economics and Statistics Administration, Bureau of the Census, May 1994.

treat such childhood diseases as malaria and malnutrition because the country cannot afford imported drugs. The problem is that even though efforts are made to screen blood supplies, the AIDS virus may still evade detection. The risk of receiving contaminated blood and contracting the disease increases where transfusions are used frequently ("Treating Malaria," 1990:8–10).

So far, AIDS is found mostly in urban areas, where it threatens to decimate the more educated and skilled young adults upon whom Africa's future so depends. The rate of infection in many central African cities is over 40 percent of the thirty- to forty-year-old age group (and 5–10 percent of infants). AIDS may already be the leading cause of death among adults in the most severely affected cities (Chin, 1990:223–224). In Kinshasa, Zaire, one of these severely affected cities, over 7 percent of the city's 3 million people are estimated to have AIDS (Press, 1991:13).

Although it is more prevalent in the cities, AIDS is spreading to villages and rural areas, especially those close to the cities or on connecting roads (Chin, 1990:224). In Zaire, for instance, at Kimpese, a village near Kinshasa, 5 percent of the population now has AIDS. In other more outlying villages, the incidence of AIDS is 2 percent (Press, 1991:13).

Public health campaigns to educate the public, distribute or encourage the use of condoms, safeguard blood supplies, and discourage risky sexual activity have been launched across the continent. In fact, Africa is considered to be in many ways a pioneer in AIDS prevention as a result of its creative radio and TV campaigns and efforts to promote safe sex and condom use ("WHO Address," 1994). In Zaire, for example, a vigorous prevention program is in place. Along with public education about the disease, the use of condoms by prostitutes has been successfully promoted. The sale of condoms has mushroomed from 900,000 in 1989 to 9 million in 1990. Expected sales for 1991 were 15 million condoms (Press, 1991:13). Cameroon, Côte d'Ivoire, Kenya, Malawi, and Zimbabwe have also launched ambitious education and prevention programs. Many African countries, with the help of numerous NGOs, have also developed successful home care programs for victims of the disease and programs to help survivors as well ("WHO Address," 1994).

While such efforts are vital in the war against AIDS, they are unlikely to stop the relentless advance of the disease for some time to come. There are still too many African countries with too few resources to educate the public, provide condoms, treat sexually transmitted diseases, and safeguard their blood supplies. If every country had such programs in place, it could save an estimated 4.5 million infections by the year 2000 alone ("WHO Address," 1994). Most experts do not foresee a leveling off of AIDS for another one or two decades. Predictions are that in urban areas, 16 percent of the population will be infected with HIV by 2015 (Roudi, 1991:4). Infant and child mortality in many cities may be as high as 30 percent, while the overall adult mortality rate could double or even triple (Chin, 1990:224;

d'Adesky, 1990). As a result, hard-won gains in life expectancy since independence may well be sharply reversed, with life expectancy dropping by six years in many cities (Chin, 1990:224).

The AIDS epidemic will have consequences in sub-Saharan Africa far beyond the tragic loss of human life. The devastating toll of death and illness will be an overwhelming strain on Africa's already limited health care systems as scarce medical resources are diverted to prevention of the disease and treatment of the afflicted. There are also questions about whether communities and extended families will be able to absorb and meet the needs of the large number of children orphaned by AIDS deaths among their parents, many of these children themselves stricken with the disease. In Zimbabwe, for example, a projected one-third of all children will be orphans by 2010 (Taylor, 1995). The economic costs and consequences are at this point incalculable, but the loss of so many of Africa's youngest and brightest will certainly be felt, as Virginia DeLancey observes in Chapter 5.

Ironically, AIDS is not expected to have more than a "moderate" effect on sub-Saharan Africa's overall population growth rate (perhaps lowering it by as much as 1 percent) (Roudi, 1991:4; Gregson, 1994). Although declining somewhat, birthrates and family sizes are likely to remain high, thus mitigating the impact of rising mortality. Growing awareness of the AIDS threat throughout Africa is being reflected in more caution with regard to high-risk sexual practices, thus slowing the spread of the disease and ultimately mortality rates. Migrants motivated by the same economic forces as their predecessors will continue to flood Africa's major cities, replacing in most cases AIDS victims who are dead or dying. Rather than being a draconian solution to the population explosion, the major long-term legacy of AIDS may be that it will have intensified and prolonged the misery of an already suffering continent.

■ **NOTE**

1. After rising in the 1960s and 1970s, per capita GNP in sub-Saharan Africa dropped during the 1980s from $560 in 1980 to only $330 in 1988. Infant mortality rates went up between 1985 and 1986 from 107 to 113 (World Bank, 1989b:146, 165). Both of these disheartening statistics reflect Africa's current economic crisis. World Bank (1995) data for 1993 indicate that GNP has now rebounded, while infant mortality rates have fallen.

■ **BIBLIOGRAPHY**

Adepoju, Aderanti, and John I. Clarke. 1985. "The Demographic Background to Development in Africa." Pp. 1–19 in John I. Clarke, Mustafa Khogali, and Leszek

A. Kosinski (eds.). *Population and Development Projects in Africa.* Cambridge: Cambridge University Press.

Ashford, Lori S. 1995. "New Perspectives on Population: Lessons from Cairo." *Population Bulletin* 50 (March). Washington, DC: Population Reference Bureau.

Becker, Charles M., Andrew M. Hamer, and Andrew R. Morrison. 1994. *Beyond Urban Bias in Africa.* London: James Currey.

Brennan, Ellen M., and Harry W. Richardson. 1986. "Urbanization and Urban Policy in Sub-Saharan Africa." *African Urban Quarterly* 1:20–42.

Brown, Lester, and Sandra Postel. 1987. "Thresholds of Change." Pp. 3–19 in Lester R. Brown et al. (eds.). *State of the World.* New York: W. W. Norton.

Caldwell, John C. 1994. "Fertility in Sub-Saharan Africa: Status and Prospects." *Population and Development Review* 20 (March):179–187.

Chin, James. 1990. "Current and Future Dimensions of the HIV/AIDS Pandemic in Women and Children." *Lancet* 336 (July 28):221–224.

Cordell, Dennis D., Joel W. Gregory, and Victor Piche. 1987. "African Historical Demography: The Search for a Theoretical Framework." Pp. 14–32 in Dennis D. Cordell and Joel W. Gregory (eds.). *African Population and Capitalism: Historical Perspectives.* Boulder: Westview Press.

d'Adesky, Anne-Christine. 1990. "Pediatric AIDS Now Considered a Global Threat. Millions Expected to Become Orphans." *UN Chronicle* 27 (December): 69.

Dasgupta, Partha S. 1995. "Population, Poverty and the Local Environment." *Scientific American* (February):40–45.

Davidson, Basil. 1959. *The Lost Cities of Africa.* Boston: Little, Brown.

Dawson, Marc H. 1987. "Health, Nutrition, and Population in Central Kenya, 1890–1945." Pp. 201–220 in Dennis D. Cordell and Joel W. Gregory (eds.). *African Population and Capitalism: Historical Perspectives.* Boulder: Westview Press.

El-Shakhs, Salah, and Hooshang Amirakmadi. 1986. "Urbanization and Spatial Development in Africa: Some Critical Issues." *African Urban Quarterly* 1:3–19.

Fapohunda, Eleanor R. 1982. "The Child-Care Dilemma of Working Mothers in African Cities: The Case of Lagos, Nigeria." Pp. 277–288 in Edna G. Bay (ed.). *Women and Work in Africa.* Boulder: Westview Press.

Faruqee, Rashid, and Ravi Gulhati. 1983. *Rapid Population Growth in Sub-Saharan Africa: Issues and Policies.* No. 559. Washington, DC: World Bank.

Goliber, Thomas J. 1985. "Sub-Saharan Africa: Population Pressures on Development." *Population Bulletin* 40.

Gordon, April A., and Donald L. Gordon. 1988. "Cameroon's Urban and Rural Problems: Flipsides of the Same Coin." Paper presented at the Joint Southeast Regional Seminar for African Studies Meeting, "Cameroon Day" Symposium, African Studies Center, University of Florida, Gainesville, Florida.

Green, Cynthia P. (ed.). 1994. *Sustainable Development: Population and the Environment.* Washington, DC: USAID.

Gregson, Simon. 1994. "Demographic Impact of HIV in Sub-Saharan Africa." *Zimbabwe AIDS Information Network News Bulletin* 2 (March):4–5.

Gupta, Dhruba. 1987. "Urbanization in Precolonial West Africa." *Africa Quarterly* 22:27–40.

Henin, Roushdi A. 1979. "Government Approaches to the Population Issue." Pp. 184–199 in Reuben K. Udo (ed.). *Population Education Source Book for Sub-Saharan Africa.* Nairobi: Heinemann.

Hyden, Goran. 1983. *No Shortcuts to Progress.* Berkeley: University of California Press.

Jewsiewicki, Bogumel. 1987. "Toward a Historical Sociology of Population in Zaire:

Proposals for the Analysis of the Demographic Regime." Pp. 271–280 in Dennis D. Cordell and Joel W. Gregory (eds.). *African Population and Capitalism: Historical Perspectives.* Boulder: Westview Press.

Johnson, Stanley P. 1987. *World Population and the United Nations: Challenge and Response.* New York: Cambridge University Press.

Lutz, Wolfgang. 1994. "The Future of World Population." *Population Bulletin* 49 (June). Washington, DC: Population Reference Bureau.

MacGaffey, Janet, and Gertrude Windsperger. 1990. "The Endogenous Economy." Pp. 81–90 in *The Long-Term Perspective Study of Sub-Saharan Africa.* Vol. 3. Washington, DC: World Bank.

Mahadi, Abdullahi, and J. E. Inikori. 1987. "Population and Capitalist Development in Precolonial West Africa: Kasar Kano in the Nineteenth Century." Pp. 62–73 in Dennis D. Cordell and Joel W. Gregory (eds.). *African Population and Capitalism: Historical Perspectives.* Boulder: Westview Press.

Mbacke, Cheikh. 1994. "Family Planning Programs and Fertility Transition in Sub-Saharan Africa." *Population and Development Review* 20 (March):188–193.

Montgomery, Mark R., and Edward K. Brown. 1990. "Accommodating Urban Growth in Sub-Saharan Africa." Pp. 74–88 in George T. F. Acsadi, Gwendolyn Johnson-Acsadi, and Rodolfo A. Bulatao (eds.). *Population Growth and Reproduction in Sub-Saharan Africa.* Washington, DC: World Bank.

Morrison, Minion K. C., and Peter C. W. Gutkind (eds.). 1982. *Housing the Urban Poor in Africa.* Syracuse, NY: Maxwell School of Citizenship and Public Affairs.

Newman, James L., and Russell Lura. 1983. "Fertility Control in Africa." *Geographical Review* 73:396–406.

O'Brien, Jay. 1987. "Differential High Fertility and Demographic Transition: Peripheral Capitalism in Sudan." Pp. 173–186 in Dennis D. Cordell and Joel W. Gregory (eds.). *African Population and Capitalism: Historical Perspectives.* Boulder: Westview Press.

O'Connor, Anthony. 1991. *Poverty in Africa: A Geographical Approach.* London: Belhaven Press.

Olusanya, P. Olufemi, and Donald E. Purcell. 1981. *The Prospects of Economic Development in Nigeria Under the Conditions of Rapid Population Growth.* Ibadan: Nigerian Institute of Social and Economic Research.

Page, Hilary J., and Ron Lesthaeghe. 1981. *Child-Spacing in Tropical Africa: Traditions and Change.* London: Academic Press.

Press, Steven. 1991. "Zaire Leads Africa in Fight Against AIDS." *Christian Science Monitor* (April 19):12–13.

"The Reproductive Revolution: New Survey Findings." 1992. *Population Reports.* Series M, no. 11 (December).

Rodney, Walter. 1974. *How Europe Underdeveloped Africa.* Washington, DC: Howard University Press.

Rondinelli, Dennis A. 1983. *Secondary Cities in Developing Countries.* Beverly Hills: Sage Publications.

Roudi, Nancy. 1991. "AIDS Gains Momentum in the 1990s." *Population Today* 19 (June):3–4.

Sai, Fred T. 1988. "Changing Perspectives of Population in Africa and International Responses." *African Affairs* 87: 267–276.

Sindiga, Isaac. 1985. "The Persistence of High Fertility in Kenya." *Social Science and Medicine* 20:71–84.

Stren, Richard E., and Rodney R. White. 1989. "Conclusion." Pp. 305–312 in Richard E. Stren and Rodney R. White (eds.). *African Cities in Crisis: Managing Rapid Urban Growth.* Boulder: Westview Press.

Taylor, Paul. 1995. "Zimbabwe's Sophistication No Match for AIDS." *Charlotte Observer* (April 21):22A.

"Treating Malaria, Causing AIDS." 1990. *Africa News* 33 (June 11):8–10.

Turshen, Meredith. 1987. "Population Growth and the Deterioration of Health: Mainland Tanzania, 1920–1960." Pp. 187–200 in Dennis D. Cordell and Joel W. Gregory (eds.). *African Population and Capitalism: Historical Perspectives.* Boulder: Westview Press.

United Nations. 1995. *The World's Women 1995: Trends and Statistics.* New York: United Nations.

Valentine, Carol H., and Joanne E. Revson. 1979. "Cultural Traditions, Social Change, and Fertility in Sub-Saharan Africa." *Journal of Modern African Studies* 17:453–472.

White, Rodney R. 1989. "The Influence of Environmental and Economic Factors on the Urban Crisis." Pp. 1–19 in Richard E. Stren and Rodney R. White (eds.). *African Cities in Crisis: Managing Rapid Urban Growth.* Boulder: Westview Press.

"WHO Address to Marrakech Conference." 1994. *Zimbabwe AIDS Information Network News Bulletin* 2 (March):11–12.

"Women, Children, and AIDS." 1995. *Population Today* 23 (April):3.

World Bank. 1986. *Population Growth and Policies in Sub-Saharan Africa.* Washington, DC: World Bank.

———. 1989a. *Sub-Saharan Africa: From Crisis to Sustainable Growth: A Long-Term Perspective Study.* Washington, DC: World Bank.

———. 1989b. *World Development Report.* New York: Oxford University Press.

———. 1990. *World Development Report.* New York: Oxford University Press.

———. 1995. *World Development Report.* New York: Oxford University Press.

World Population Data Sheet. 1993. Washington, DC: Population Reference Bureau.

■ 8 ■

Africa's
Environmental Problems

Julius E. Nyang'oro

In recent years, terms such as "acid rain," "the greenhouse effect," "chloro-fluorocarbons (CFCs)," "toxic waste," and "environmental degradation" have become part of our everyday vocabulary. In part, the popularization of these terms stems from citizens' increased awareness that there is some-thing wrong somewhere when government authorities or scientists warn pregnant women not to drink water from a certain river or not to eat fish from a certain lake. These warnings are usually issued after careful study by scientists of the effects of, say, the discharge of known cancer-causing chemicals into rivers, streams, and underground sources for drinking water and/or other domestic use. (See, for example "Troubled Water," 1990.) In the United States, different state governments have gone to court seeking injunctions against companies from other states to prevent these companies from discharging chemical waste into shared rivers. This was the case, for example, in 1988, when the state of Tennessee sought to prevent a North Carolina paper mill from discharging chemicals into the Pigeon River, which flows through both Tennessee and North Carolina ("Paper Mill," 1989).

Most of the concern for the environment in developed countries arises from the effects of industrialization on both the environment itself and on the peoples who inhabit the environment. Indeed, any discussion of the envi-ronment would be seriously inadequate if it did not address the question of the mutual relationship between the environment and humankind. Lynton Caldwell argues that concern about the environment compels us to look at humanity as it lives in two realities:

> The abiding reality is that of *earth* the planet—independent of man and his works; the other reality—the transient reality—is that of the *world,* which is a creation of the human mind. The earth and its biosphere form a grand synthesis of complex interactive systems within systems, organic and inor-

ganic, animate and inanimate. The world is the way humanity understands and has organized its occupancy of the earth: an expression of imagination and purpose materialized through exploration, invention, labor and violence. (Caldwell, 1984:8)

In this regard, the interconnectedness of environmental issues and humanity should receive appropriate attention. Indeed, this interconnectedness was one of the major issues addressed by the Earth Summit on the environment, which took place in Rio in July 1992. Therefore, in this chapter, we will consider the issue of the environment in Africa in relation to economic development, humanity's struggle with the environment itself, and how the environment has been affected by this interaction. This approach is dictated by the recognition that the environment in Africa, like environments elsewhere, suffers from the dilemma that Caldwell and others worry about: how to reconcile human needs and activity with sound protection of the environment to allow for future sustainability and development (Brown, 1981).[1] Issues such as deforestation, desertification, soil erosion, and industrial pollution must be understood with this dilemma in mind.

It is worth noting that concern over Africa's environment is not necessarily a recent phenomenon. As Ayodele Cole (1986) has noted, colonial Africa was endowed with legislation and regulations on environmental health and sanitation, which were sometimes vigorously enforced in both urban and rural areas if it was deemed to be in the best interests of the colonial government. In another example, as early as 1935, E. P. Stebbing wrote a pioneering article to warn the colonial governments about the "encroaching Sahara" as one of the principal environmental problems facing the West African colonies. Stebbing's article was concerned about, among other things, the dwindling fertility of the Sahel as a result of the spread of the Sahara Desert farther south.

Some of the measures undertaken in the Sahel region to alleviate problems arising from the drought of the 1970s, such as the planting of trees and the restricting of animal grazing to protect the thinning grasslands, would have greatly benefited from the historical lessons Stebbing and others addressed more than five decades ago. But as it is, international concern over the Sahel region seems to have assumed significance in the 1970s only when it became apparent that large populations in West Africa were on the verge of starvation because of dwindling rainfall, reduced soil fertility for crop cultivation, and other environmental decay (Eckholm and Brown, 1977).

Yet, it must be added that in comparative terms, the relative neglect of environmental concerns that characterized the Sahel region up to the early 1970s essentially reflected a general neglect of the environment by governments across the globe (Pirages, 1978). In the context of Africa, governments were more concerned with economic growth than with environmental protection, even though economic development had a direct impact on environmental quality (Dixon et al., 1988; Leonard, 1985). Unfortunately, the need for environmental management has been viewed as a constraint on attempts to achieve rapid economic growth. In many cases, this has led to economic growth being achieved at the cost of the environment, which has resulted in irreparable environmental damage (WCED, 1987; Kabeberi, 1988). The viewing of economic development and environmental management as two conflicting objectives raises questions that are central to the concerns about the environment in Africa today (Berntsen, 1995).

The 1972 United Nations Conference on the Human Environment in Stockholm, Sweden, gave a momentum to a global concern for environmental protection that has helped put environmental management in the forefront of both domestic and international policy. As Caldwell has noted:

> The U.N. Conference on the Human Environment (1972) was a watershed event in human relationships with the Earth. The conference epigram "Only One Earth" symbolized a change in human perception that would become a new factor in the development of ethics and in the evaluation of alternatives in policies affecting the environment. (Caldwell, 1984:1)

The establishment of the United Nations Environmental Programme (UNEP), with its headquarters in Nairobi, Kenya, should be seen as arising directly from the 1972 Stockholm conference. What should be of significance here is the recognition that the environment in Africa is closely tied to environments elsewhere in the world, and that any attempt at treating one part of the global environment in isolation from the rest would be grossly inadequate (Berntsen, 1995).

Although we have noted that there is "Only One Earth," analytically it is still possible to examine one part of the global environment in more detail. In this chapter, the principal region of concern will be Africa. We will note at appropriate places, however, the interrelationship between the African environment and the rest of the global environment.

■ THE ENVIRONMENT IN AFRICA:
CONTINUITY AND CHANGE

Geologically speaking, the African continent is an old one. According to Lewis and Berry (1988:36–70), many of the general features of the African landscape have evolved over long geologic periods without being submerged under changing sea levels, without being changed dramatically by glaciation, and without major tectonic upheavals. In comparison, Europe and North America have been affected dramatically by glaciation and tectonic upheavals, which means that they are much younger continents. This difference in geologic history has had serious consequences in terms of current environmental concerns such as soil erosion. According to Lewis and Berry (1988:36), Africa's relative geologic stability has allowed many geologic processes to proceed further in Africa than in the younger continents. For example, in most of the middle, temperate latitudes, much of the soil is of recent origin, often derived from glacial activities. In most of Africa, however, the soils are of ancient origin and have been subject to intensive leaching of nutrients over long periods of time. As a result, African soils tend to lack fertility. This geologic fact means that Africa is actually more vulnerable to human activity than other continents in terms of deforestation, desertification, and soil erosion.

In terms of geographic location, over 75 percent of Africa lies between the tropics, and much of the land beyond the tropics is extremely dry. This land includes the Sahara Desert, which covers most of northern and northwestern Africa, and the Kalahari Desert, which covers large portions of southwestern Africa. About 90 percent of the continent is classified as having tropical climates. This means that the average annual temperatures are relatively high over most of the land. The exceptions to this are the northern and southern edges of the continent, which have a Mediterranean type of climate, and areas of high elevation such as the Kenya highlands, which have relatively cooler temperatures. With most of Africa being tropical, the major factor that distinguishes seasons is precipitation, i.e., wet and dry seasons. (See Chapter 2 for additional analysis of the geography of Africa, especially Maps 2.1 and 2.2.)

Over the centuries, humans have adapted their lives and existence to their environment. Certainly this was the case in Africa. The continent is believed to be the first human habitat, with discoveries of remains of the earliest humans both at Olduvai Gorge in northeastern Tanzania—approximately 1.75 million years old—and at several sites near Lake Turkana in northern Kenya and southern Ethiopia—approximately 2–4 million years old (Obenga, 1981:73). Most relevant to the study of the African environment in the contemporary period is the shift in human activity from foraging to domesticated food production, which is closely linked to the beginnings of African metallurgy (Austen, 1987:9). However, historical evidence as to what precisely happened in this shift from "savagery to culture" is still lacking and is open to much debate (Austen, 1987:10–16). Domesticated food production has been associated with the increase in population, a more predictable existence, and the establishment of communities. Historians have suggested that by the nineteenth century, Africans had long been organized into large numbers of communities. With the possible exception of a few small groups, such as San (in the Kalahari) and Twa (in the Zairean/Congo rainforest), the economies of true subsistence had largely disappeared (Lewis and Berry, 1988). Probably the most important thing to note is that humans evolved to conform to their environment and that for the greater part of their existence on earth have constantly been molded by that environment. It seems that over a long period of time, the key to survival was not resistance to change but meeting change with change (or adjustment); otherwise, the human race would not have survived.

The coming of colonialism in Africa significantly changed the nature of existing local or "community" economies that often had complex economic systems to deal with food and other crop production, handicrafts, and trade. For the most part, the economies were localized in specific regions. As Virginia DeLancey notes in Chapter 5, one fundamental change that was initiated during the colonial period and persists today was the creation of a new trading system due to the demand for African raw materials such as palm oil, rubber, ivory, and copper. This, in turn, created tremendous pressure on the African environment to respond to these new and increasing demands. To get a better picture of the overall pressure on the environment in Africa during the colonial and postcolonial periods, this chapter should be read in conjunction with Chapters 5 and 7.

■ CONTEMPORARY PROBLEMS OF THE AFRICAN ENVIRONMENT

□ Deforestation

Deforestation occurs when trees are cut down to provide firewood (a primary energy source) and timber, and to free up space for more crop cultivation or grazing land. Lester Brown has argued that

> a sustainable society will differ from the one we now know in several respects. Population size will more or less be stationary, energy will be used more efficiently, and the economy will be fueled largely with renewable sources of energy. (Brown, 1981:247)

Looking at the African environment with regard to maintaining the critical balance between existing forests and human activity, the continent is moving very quickly toward unsustainability. Much of the deforestation—like much other environmental degradation—is the result of large numbers of individuals engaging in decisions that are privately rational but collectively destructive (Bojo et al., 1990).

Human activity in Africa, like elsewhere, has altered the landscape of the earth. Forest clearing is one such activity. Deforestation in the tropics has accelerated dramatically in the years since World War II, but estimates of the area covered by tropical forests and rates of deforestation vary widely, mainly because countries use different measures and definitions of "forest" (Silver with DeFries, 1990:117). In spite of problems of measurement, a UNEP study (1990) reveals that globally speaking, just three countries—Brazil, Indonesia, and Zaire—contain a major share of the world's tropical

Growing land scarcity in Africa is leading to deforestation, soil erosion, and desertification as farmers clear forests or overuse the land in an effort to feed themselves.

Commercial logging, as in Gabon, is one factor leading to a rapid loss of forests, including rainforests, in Africa as elsewhere in the developing world.

forests. The study focused on two basic forest types. The first, closed tropical rainforests, have a relatively tight canopy of mostly broad-leafed evergreen trees sustained by 256 inches or more of annual rainfall. The second, open tropical forests, have a canopy that is not continuous but covers more than 10 percent of the ground. When both types are considered, Brazil contains 26.5 percent of the world total, Zaire 9.2 percent, and Indonesia 6.1 percent.[2]

The UNEP study noted that, globally, closed forests are being destroyed at a rate of about 0.6 percent annually. At this rate, closed forests may disappear in Africa within another 100 years. However, in terms of country variation, the problem seems even more serious. In some countries, such as Zaire, deforestation rates are as low as 0.2 percent a year, but in Côte d'Ivoire they reach 7 percent. Closed forests are thus expected to disappear altogether within twenty-five years in Africa unless effective steps are taken to conserve them. Perhaps the worst case is represented by Madagascar, which in the past few decades has lost more than four-fifths of its rainforest to land clearing (Wells, 1989:162). The following discussion is an examination of specific human actions as they relate to deforestation.

In Africa about 90 percent of the population uses fuelwood (firewood) for cooking. Measured in oil equivalent units, the amount is roughly 1.5 tons of oil per family per year (Anderson, 1987:7; Armstrong and Garry, 1984). These figures by themselves are not astonishing if the continent could devise a system of restoring the stock of trees that are cut down. But, according to Anderson,

> the current annual rate of consumption is estimated to exceed the mean annual incremental growth (MAI) . . . of local tree stocks and forest reserves by the following (rounded) amounts: in Senegal −35 percent (a slight surplus), in the Sahelian countries 30 percent, in Sudan 70 percent, in northern Nigeria 75 percent, in Ethiopia 150 percent, and in Niger 200 percent. (Anderson, 1987:7)

As fuelwood consumption increases, so does the disappearance of forests. It is generally acknowledged that with the rapid increase in the number of people on the continent and higher rates of urbanization, the need for fuelwood as a source of energy will continue to grow. In fact, urbanization seems to have a direct effect on the loss of forests in Africa, because the spread of deforestation is most noticeable near urban areas. According to Anderson (1987:8), the growth of towns and cities brings about increased demands for fuelwood and charcoal and accounts for much of the decline in tree stocks in the surrounding countryside, often for a radius of 80–160 kilometers or more.

Forest clearing to obtain fuelwood is indeed a major problem; however, fuelwood leads to the degradation of open forests only and plays little part in the destruction of closed forests. The major cause of deforestation in

Africa is the clearing of forests for purposes of crop cultivation—the need
to expand agricultural land (UNEP, 1990). This problem is also tied to the
increase in the number of people. Yet, the UNEP report cautions against generalizations that may not hold:

> Blame should not be laid at the door of shifting agriculture itself. Small
> strips of forest can be cleared, burnt, planted and left to return to natural
> forest again, provided the fallow period is long enough. [But] in many
> places it no longer is. The reasons for this are complicated. Often, as pro-
> ductive, cultivable land becomes scarce, small-scale farmers are pushed
> into more marginal areas, and shifting agriculturalists onto fragile upland
> forest areas unable to support their practices. *Fallow periods are then
> shortened as yields fall and populations increase.* It is estimated that shift-
> ing agriculture now accounts for 70 percent of deforestation in Africa.
> (UNEP, 1990:3; emphasis added)

But the larger point still holds: shifting cultivation is an important agent of
deforestation. Shifting cultivation is a practice in which subsistence farmers
clear and burn a plot of land in the forest, then grow crops for one or a few
years before repeating the cycle. This age-old method of subsistence agriculture recycles nutrients to the soil and maintains productivity without fertilizers, provided the fallow period is long enough to regenerate the forest
growth. But, with increasing population and pressure on the land, in many
places the fallow period is cut short. Eventually, the soil becomes unproductive, crops no longer flourish, and the trees do not grow back. It is important to remember that once forests are cleared for agriculture, grazing, or
logging, there is no guarantee that the trees can grow back. This is the
dilemma that many African countries face. Pierre Pradervand, who spent
several years traveling through Africa in a quest to understand the dynamics
of change on the continent, summarized the deforestation problem as follows:

> By far the most important cause [of deforestation] is the opening up of new
> land for agriculture. The most striking characteristic of deforestation that
> emerged in my discussions with the farmers was the speed at which it is
> taking place. In less than a generation they have seen their wooded envi-
> ronment literally disappear. There does not appear to be another major area
> of the world where such a transformation has been as rapid and severe.
> (Pradervand, 1989:37–38)

But perhaps more important than the cause of deforestation is its effect
on the quality of life for rural dwellers—about 75 percent of the population
in most African countries. In terms of subsistence, rural dwellers depend on
forests and trees for a long list of essential products: fuelwood, fodder, fruit,
nuts, dyes, medicines, and building materials. Fuelwood and fodder alone
are in many societies two of the most essential ingredients for survival;

without them, rural life would degenerate quickly into a mere struggle for existence (UNEP, 1990). Indeed, in some places this has already come to pass (Timberlake, 1986). Perhaps even more important, many rural families depend on tree products for income. Collecting, processing, and selling forest products are often the only ways by which rural women can obtain cash income. In the past, these activities have been called "minor forest industries." But in no sense are they minor. For example, in Egypt's Fayoum province, 48 percent of women work in "minor" forest industries. My own research in Mara region in northeastern Tanzania revealed that in at least 50 percent of the households surveyed, one member of the household was involved in activities related to the forest industry. It is obvious that when forests are depleted, rural families must survive without either the products on which they depend or the incomes they need.

Thus, for this reason and many others, the present forest situation in Africa is a matter of serious concern. Gunnar Poulsen (1990:4) of UNEP outlined the problem in a report to all African governments. In the report he noted the rapid loss of natural forest resources in Africa, including both flora and fauna. Reforestation efforts compensated for no more than 3.5 percent of the forests being destroyed (although this varies by country), and "forest plantations" did not compensate for the loss of biodiversity.

□ Desertification

Deforestation in Africa has also been attributed to structural adjustment programs, now ubiquitous on the continent. Here I will give the example of Ghana to illustrate the problem. Since the early 1980s, Ghana has been subject to SAPs as dictated by the International Monetary Fund and the World Bank. Besides other initiatives, SAPs have promoted the export of timber, Ghana's third most important export commodity. A variety of sources (Development GAP, 1993) have shown that major overseas aid and credit packages have been arranged with foreign exchange provided to timber companies to enable them to purchase new materials and equipment. As a result, from 1983 to 1988, timber exports increased from $16 million to $99 million.

But such a quick-fix solution to Ghana's need for foreign exchange earnings has contributed to the loss of Ghana's already depleted forest resources. Between 1981 and 1985, the annual rate of deforestation was 1.3 percent, and current estimates are as high as 2 percent. Ghana's tropical forest area is now just 25 percent of its original size. According to the Development GAP,

> The impact of deforestation is widespread, affecting the livelihoods of local people, disrupting important environmental functions and severely

> disturbing the biological integrity of the original ecosystem. . . . Widespread deforestation is leading to regional climatic change, soil erosion and large-scale desertification. (Development GAP, 1993:25)

The study concludes that since 75 percent of Ghanaians depend on wild game to supplement their diet, stripping the forest has led to a sharp increase in malnutrition and disease. For women, the food, fuel, and medicines they harvest from the forest provide critical resources, especially in the face of decreased food production, lower wages, and other economic shocks that threaten household food security.

Forests are part of a complex and delicate ecosystem. When the balance in the ecosystem is altered through human activities such as the cutting down of forests, a chain reaction occurs leading to the deterioration of other parts of the ecosystem. The problem of increased desertification in Africa has been associated with increased deforestation. As Eckholm and Brown have noted, "While 'desertification' has become something of a catch-all word, the problems usually covered by this term involve ecological changes that sap land of its ability to sustain agriculture and human habitation" (Eckholm and Brown, 1977:7).

Timberlake (1986) argues that "desertification" more accurately describes the conversion of productive land into wasteland by human mismanagement: "Crops are overcultivated; rangelands are overgrazed; forests are cut; irrigation projects turn good cropland into salty, barren fields" (Timberlake, 1986:59). In this chapter, I use Timberlake's concept of "desertification."

In Africa the declining ratio of mean annual incremental growth of local tree stocks has led to the decreased ability of land to sustain agriculture and human habitation. As with many environmental issues, it is difficult to have an accurate figure on how fast the deserts are spreading in Africa. However, in 1972, the United States Agency for International Development estimated that in the years since World War II, 650,000 square kilometers of land once suitable for agriculture or intensive grazing had been forfeited to the Sahara in its southern fringe (Eckholm and Brown, 1977:9). More recent estimates suggest that the problem has become worse. According to new estimates, the continent as a whole is losing an average of 36,000 square kilometers to the desert every year. In 1980 alone, 200,000 square kilometers of arable land were lost (Nnoli, 1990; Skoupy, 1988). The situation seems particularly serious in the Sahel zone.[3] But more countries are increasingly being affected. Notable among the affected areas are Niger, Mali, Burkina Faso, Mauritania, northern Nigeria, northern Ghana, Senegal, The Gambia, Chad, Sudan, and Egypt. From this list, it is obvious that desertification has become a major environmental concern in Africa.

To fully comprehend the nature of desertification in Africa, it is important to discuss the problem in a historical and geological context. We noted

Desertification threatens many areas of Africa, especially the Sahel.

earlier that geologically Africa is an old continent. This makes the continent more susceptible to natural processes such as soil erosion. It also makes the soil less fertile, with a diminished "carrying capacity" (ability to sustain human activity). There is, of course, a complex relationship between population and natural/environmental carrying capacity and between population distribution and desertification. The principal point is that, generally speaking, Africa's environment has always been fragile, at least in the last few thousand years (Lewis and Berry, 1988). The argument is usually presented as follows.

In terms of population settlement, Africa seems, at first glance, a vast and empty continent. But on closer inspection, it appears that many countries in Africa are becoming very crowded. Africa has been described as "underpopulated" because its population density is relatively low. Compared with most of Asia, or even Central America, Africa seems uncrowded. Population density, however, is just one side of the population–natural resources balance; land productivity is the other. About 80 percent of the continent cannot be considered arable. Half the potentially arable soils are lateritic and thus unsuited for permanent field crop agriculture. Of the land that is arable, only 7 percent has naturally rich alluvial soils (Revell, 1976; Lewis and Berry, 1988). Skoupy (1988:30) points out that arid and semi-arid regions constitute more than 50 percent of tropical Africa and support more than 35 percent of its population. The drylands of tropical Africa extend over twenty-four countries divided in the following way:

- Largely desert countries with more than 66 percent arid areas: Botswana, Cape Verde, Chad, Djibouti, Kenya, Mali, Mauritania, Niger, Somalia
- Countries with over 30 percent arid and semi-arid areas: Burkina Faso, Ethiopia, The Gambia, Mozambique, Senegal, Sudan, Tanzania, Zambia, Zimbabwe
- Countries with below 30 percent arid and semi-arid areas: Angola, Benin, Cameroon, Madagascar, Nigeria, Uganda[4]

It should be obvious that much of Africa's drier land can support only economically marginal, land-extensive uses, such as nomadic pastoralism, or at best only one meager grain crop per year. Thus, there are frequently good reasons why vast, unsettled areas have remained so. It was not by chance that they were left until last. Many regions that are unsettled today are empty precisely because they cannot support sustained settlement.[5]

Using products of modern science and technology such as fertilizer and irrigation may be one way to save the land from the encroaching desert. Certainly, an increase in food production using modern scientific methods would go a long way toward resolving the population problem. However, there is evidence that doing that would only increase environmental degradation. Tillman (1981) argues that modern technological inputs such as irrigation could improve yields. But this could be achieved only at great financial expense and with high environmental costs and public health risks. As real energy costs rise, so do the costs of irrigated agriculture, which depends on electricity or liquid fuel for pumping, and often upon such energy-intensive inputs as fertilizer and biocides—which create environmental hazards of their own.[6] Weir and Schapiro point to this kind of environmental degradation not just in Africa but throughout the Third World:

> Dozens of pesticides too dangerous for unrestricted use in the United States are shipped to underdeveloped countries. There, lack of regulation, illiteracy, and repressive working conditions can turn even a "safe" pesticide into a deadly weapon. According to the World Health Organization, someone in the underdeveloped countries is poisoned by pesticides *every minute*. (Weir and Schapiro, 1981:3)

It would seem, therefore, that continuing desertification makes countries in Africa use pesticides and fertilizers that in the long run are dangerous both to the environment and the population. Furthermore, excessive irrigation in dry climates often leads to salinization or alkalinization of cropland, so that much of the available water must eventually be used to flush away salts rather than to irrigate crops.

Finally, the issue of desertification has to be related to the problem of drought, as the two actually go together, the latter preceding the former. Of

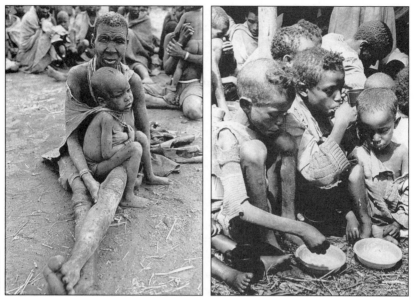

Photos: World Bank

Scenes of human suffering like these are becoming commonplace in Africa as drought and famine force millions of Africans to seek food aid.

course, drought may be a result of either natural decline in rainfall or a change in climatic patterns caused by the clearing away of forests (Eckholm and Brown, 1977). In any case, Gordon Wells (1989:148–192), using earth photographs taken by NASA satellites over the years, presents a devastating picture of the Sahel countries as they have progressively become desert as a result of drought conditions. As is generally known, from 1968 to the present, rainfall in the western Sahel (i.e., central Chad, coastal Senegal, and Mauritania) has been below the historical mean recorded from 1931 to 1960. Naturally, the environmental repercussion of the long drought is that it has destroyed the ability of the region to sustain its population. Wells (1989:163–164) gives an equally compelling description of the effects of drought on the environment where Chad, Niger, Nigeria, and Cameroon meet on Lake Chad. In June 1966, Wells reports, satellite photographs from the *Gemini 9* mission showed Lake Chad to be about 22,000 square kilometers; in the lake were numerous islands. A flourishing economy based on fishing and cereal production existed in the lake area, and villages were located on the islands. By the summer of 1985, these cultural patterns had collapsed due to the evaporation of the lake. Photographs taken by orbiting cameras in space indicated the lake had shrunk to only 2,500 square kilometers, although rains in January 1986 increased this to 5,000 square kilometers. Water levels were so low that irrigation projects at the center of regional development plans failed. Thousands of farmers have been forced to leave their land and raise crops or cattle along the receding lake shoreline. Such are the devastating effects of drought on desertification.

☐ Soil Erosion and Degradation

Soil erosion, like desertification, is tied in large measure to the problem of deforestation, reflecting the complex interdependence in the ecosystem. As Silver and DeFries (1990:120) have noted, forests are an important part of the earth system. On a local scale, trees protect the soil from rain and wind that would otherwise wash or blow it away. These two authors further note that despite the image of luxuriant growth in tropical forests, most of the soils that support that growth are remarkably unproductive. This is the case in Africa. High temperatures and rainfall throughout the year encourage leaching of nutrients from the soil, so that few nutrients remain except for those held by the plants themselves.

This naturally calls for better management of topsoils, which includes the need to reduce the clearing of forests. The twin processes of deforestation and soil erosion, especially in tropical Africa, have led to an increased concern to slow down the process. This concern is made more urgent by the nature of Africa's geologic formation, especially its (old) age and its geographic location in the tropics (Lewis and Berry, 1988:iii), which makes the continent more vulnerable to soil erosion. Richard Wagner provides a concise summary of why the cutting down of tropical forests has more serious consequences for the soil than would be the case in temperate rainforests:

> In a temperate rain forest, most of the minerals made available by decomposition of organic litter or disintegration of the parent rock are quickly absorbed by plant roots and incorporated into the vegetation. If you were to stand in an oak-hickory forest in midsummer you would find several inches of slowly rotting leaves covering the rich topsoil, itself black with incorporated humus. Conversely a tropical rain forest has such a continuing high rate of organic litter decomposition that no mineral pool has time to accumulate. Directly beneath the most recently fallen debris is a heavy, clay-containing, mineral soil. As a result of this tie-up of all available minerals in the standing vegetation, the cycling of minerals is rapid and direct. As soon as a leaf falls, it is decomposed and its minerals are absorbed by plant roots and channeled into the growth of another leaf. So tight is this cycling process that those few ions not absorbed by plant roots but leached through the soil into the water table, and then out of the system, are replaced by ions picked up by the tree roots from the slowly disintegrating bedrock below.
>
> When tropical forest is cut, minerals are suddenly released faster than crop plants or the remaining trees are able to use them. They leach out of the system and fertility drops sharply. If the disturbance covers only a few acres, weeds and short-lived successional species quickly invade the area, shield the soil, and begin to restore the balanced mineral cycle. But when

very large areas are cleared, this kind of recovery may be impossible. The lateritic nature of the soil also becomes part of the problem. When the forest is cleared, the heavily leached sesquioxides are exposed to high temperatures, and they bake into pavement-hard laterite. Once formed, laterite is almost impossible to break up and areas that once supported lush forest quickly become scrubland at best, supporting only shrubs or stunted trees. (Wagner, 1971:52–53)

Although there are many negative consequences associated with soil erosion, such as the loss of fertility, soil erosion itself is a natural process. As Silver and DeFries (1990) note, without it deltas would not form as soil erodes from the land and travels as sediment through streams and rivers. But the soil exposed in a deforested site generally accelerates the natural process, so much so that some dams in many parts of the tropics have filled with sediment far more rapidly than expected. Indeed, this process could be speeded as high as 100 times above normal. Naturally, the loss of fertility leads to serious land degradation. Because of the connection between deforestation—which is a human activity—and soil erosion, Blaikie and Brookfield (1987:1) have argued that land deforestation should by definition be a social problem, given the fact that purely environmental processes such as leaching and erosion occur with or without human interference. However, for these processes to be described as "degradation" implies social criteria that relate land to its actual or possible uses.

This seems to have been the case in Ethiopia, a country that has suffered the combined effects of drought, famine, and, more important, soil erosion. According to one source, Ethiopia now loses an estimated 1 billion tons of topsoil per year (Timberlake, 1986:129). The loss results from overcultivation and lack of forests to provide the natural protection when heavy rains come. In tropical Africa, most rainfall is concentrated in short fierce storms over a few months only. A good example of this concentration perhaps can be gleaned from comparing London (generally known for its rainy and damp weather) and Sokoto in northern Nigeria. Sokoto actually gets 100 millimeters more rain than London, but it falls only in the months of July, August, and September, while in London, the rain is spread throughout most of the year (Timberlake, 1986:66).

The Sokoto/London comparison is important if we are to comprehend the seriousness of soil erosion in many African countries. To return to the case of Ethiopia: as the topsoil is constantly eroded by rain, the process of cultivation itself becomes almost an impossible task. Timberlake tells a dramatic story of this tragedy:

> The people of highland Ethiopia felt the destructive impact of rain on overused soil during one week in May 1984. I was in Wollo Region [in the northeast] then during the third year of drought, and there were suddenly about four days of unseasonal, unexpected, heavy rainfall.
> Throughout the region, farmers harnessed up weak oxen and began to

sow wheat seeds they had left. But Wollo today is a moonscape of treeless hills and valleys. All the land that an ox can climb or a man stand upon has been cultivated. *Farmers even suspend themselves by ropes to sow hillsides too steep to stand on.*

The rains of May 1984 bounced off this compacted, vegetationless watershed soil. The water ran quickly off in flashfloods, carrying away soil and precious seeds towards the lowland deserts to the east, or towards the tide basin to the west. After a night of rain, I looked out from a hilltop to see massive erosion, hills looking as if they had been dynamited, mud and rocks from the fields of hill farmers strewn over the fields of valley farmers. (Timberlake, 1986:21–22; emphasis added)

Obviously, the results of this erosion are devastating in terms of soil fertility. The resulting unproductivity of the land has contributed to the decline in Ethiopian agriculture (Dejene, 1987).

Ethiopia perhaps represents the extreme case of the problem of soil erosion, which is exacerbated by the fact that Ethiopia is mostly a hilly country, which makes it more susceptible to floods in the event of torrential rains. But by no means is Ethiopia unique. Timberlake cites Tanzania, Mozambique, and other countries that have also faced similar problems, although on a relatively smaller scale. Stocking (1987:56–57) has documented soil erosion in various African countries and discusses the way soil erosion can be measured. He states that tree root exposure and pedestal development can be used to measure soil erosion. Using the fact that many trees and bushes can be dated, it is possible, by measuring the difference in height between the present surface and the old ground surface, to calculate a mean rate of erosion per year. Using this method, Stocking reports that for the Shinyanga region of Tanzania (south of Lake Victoria), "it was found that over the preceding twenty years the mean erosion rate was 22.4 tons/ha/year; between twenty and thirty years ago it was 10.5 tons/ha/year; and between thirty and ninety years ago it was only 1.4 tons/ha/year" (Stocking, 1987:57). The Shinyanga region in Tanzania is a relatively flat area, which suggests that soil erosion is not confined to hilly areas.

The fundamental problem associated with soil erosion and/or degradation is the reduced future carrying capacity of the land. Declining land fertility leads to declining yields, which in turn exacerbate the population problem. For example, during the periods 1969–1971 and 1977–1979, average annual yields of maize, millet, wheat, and cotton declined for the continent as a whole. Yields of sorghum, groundnuts, and pulses were lower in 1977–1979 than in 1961–1963 (World Bank, 1981). More recent experiences suggest that declining yields per acre often indicate either that more marginal land is coming into production or that fertility of the land is declining through overuse (World Bank, 1989). Most likely it is the combination of both.

■ DEVELOPMENT AND THE ENVIRONMENT

In Chapter 5 on economic development, Virginia DeLancey discusses the problems African governments face in their quest to improve the material conditions of their respective societies. In this chapter, I wish to point to some examples where economic development strategies have negatively affected the environment. The first example is that of cash crops, which are crucial as a source of foreign (hard) currency. The second example relates to the oil industry.

The production of cash crops has been the primary engine for the generation of foreign exchange in most African countries. When the economies of Africa began a backward slide in the 1970s, the World Bank (1981:6–7) advised African countries to continue producing and improving cash crops such as coffee, cotton, tea, and sugar. In many instances, cash crop production has led to misguided government policies that lead to environmental deterioration while yielding few benefits economically. Timberlake analyzes these conflicting goals African countries in general face and makes reference to the specific case of Sudan:

> To describe Africa's crisis as "environmental" may sound odd. . . . What have environmental concerns to do with the fact that in 1985 the entire Hadendawa people of north-eastern Sudan faced extinction due to starvation and dispersal? The Sudanese government, with the help of [foreign aid], has put vast sugar and cotton plantations on its best land along the Nile. It has ignored rapidly falling yields from smallholder farming in the 1970s. It seems not to have noticed that the land—the "environment"—upon which eight out of every [ten] Sudanese depend for their livelihoods is slowly perishing due to over-use and misuse. It invested little in dryland regions where people like the Hadendawa live. So when drought came, these pastoralists and peasants had no irrigated settlements in which to take temporary refuge, no government agencies to buy their livestock, no sources of drought-resistant sorghum seeds ready for planting when the rains resumed. *But neither have the government's investments in cash crops produced money to pay the nation's way through the drought.* The result is starvation and debt: Sudan's external debt in 1985 was estimated at $9 billion. President Nimeiri, overthrown in April 1985, has paid a personal price for leading Sudan to environmental bankruptcy. (Timberlake, 1986:9–10; emphasis added)

The political, economic, and environmental tragedy in Sudan continues. The Swar al Dahab regime, which succeeded Nimeiri's, never made things better. In turn, it was overthrown by the regime of Brigadier Omar Bashir, which so far has shown little in the way of reforming the system. If anything, the Bashir regime has become more authoritarian as it tries to cope under structural adjustment.

Deterioration of the environment in Africa is not confined to cash crop production. The example of the oil industry in Nigeria is presented here to show how widespread the problem is. In one of the rare studies of the ecological results of the oil industry in Nigeria, Eboe Hutchful (1985) notes the complexities involved in developing an oil industry. Oil revenues generated by the mining and selling of oil naturally have increased the capabilities of the Nigerian state, making it possible to finance much-needed development projects. But Hutchful comments that these same processes have generated growing regional inequalities, impoverishment, underemployment, and degradation of the Nigerian environment (Hutchful, 1985:113). Specifically, Hutchful shows that oil-industry activities—exploration, production, refining, and transportation—have caused widespread social and ecological disturbance. These include explosions from seismic surveys; pollution from pipeline leaks, blowouts, drilling fluids, and refinery effluents; as well as land alienation and widespread disruption of the natural terrain from construction of oil-related industrial infrastructure and installations. The areas that have been most affected are the oil-producing areas in three states: Rivers, Bendel, and Cross River (Hutchful, 1985:113–115).

Blowout of rigs is always a risk that oil drilling and exploration carry. Blowouts usually lead to major oil spills such as the one that occurred at the so-called Funiwa-5 location in eastern Nigeria. On January 17, 1980, the Funiwa well, located about 5 miles offshore in the Niger Delta, blew out during operation. Subsequent to the blowout, it took several days for the operating company and the Nigerian authorities to acknowledge the accident and the resulting oil spill, which could not be immediately contained. Although no full account of the accident or its effects ever came to light, the environmental consequences were serious, especially in the ecologically delicate Niger Delta. Hutchful attributes inaction on the part of the government to the enormous influence that foreign oil companies have on the industry. He argues that

> the problem of oil pollution in Nigeria has been exacerbated by the absence of effective regulations and the predatory attitudes of the oil companies. Clearly, as long as the [major oil companies] can maximize the availability of [economic] surplus from oil, the Nigerian state has had little interest in regulating their activities, particularly where such controls may threaten the expansion of production. After many years of widespread exploration and production activities, Nigeria still does not possess a comprehensive or coherent set of anti-pollution legislation. Existing legislation is scattered through a number of statutes limited to specific types of pollution and environment and lacking the backing of detailed regulations. The tendency is to leave considerable discretionary power in the hands of enforcement agencies and corresponding opportunity for the oil companies to evade regulations. (Hutchful, 1985:118)

Hutchful neglected to mention that discretionary power in the hands of bureaucrats also leads to corruption, because offending companies can always buy off their transgressions.

In more recent times, the environmental problems caused by the oil industry in Nigeria have resulted in political conflict between the Nigerian government and the foreign oil companies on the one hand, and the Ogoni people of Rivers state on the other. The Movement for the Survival of Ogoni People (MOSOP), under the leadership of Ken Saro-Wiwa, was established as a vehicle not only for demanding autonomy from the Nigerian state, but also for protesting the environmental hazards caused by the oil spillage and gas flaring that accompany it. The environmental hazards have led to the Ogoni people being net importers of food because of damage to farmland, whereas in years past, the Ogoni had been net food exporters. The crisis of the Ogoni led to the execution of Ken Saro-Wiwa and eight others by the Nigerian government in late 1995 on charges that most of the world saw as trumped up (Osaghae, 1995).

In conclusion, the two examples from Sudan and Nigeria make the important point that what passes as economic development may have serious environmental consequences that may take years, if not generations, to rectify.

■ **OTHER ISSUES OF ENVIRONMENTAL CONCERN**

Detailed discussions of specific environmental issues cannot be undertaken in a general survey such as this one. Neither can all issues be covered. However, it is important to note that we do recognize the shortcomings of this exercise. The issues not discussed in this chapter include the trade in and dumping of toxic waste in Africa, which has increasingly become a concern. A major problem in this area, however, is lack of data, as most of the trade and dumping is conducted "underground," especially with the increase in restrictions in toxic waste dumping in the developed countries.[7] The acceptance of foreign toxic waste by African countries is based in part on the attraction of the hard currency foreign companies are willing to pay—hard currency for which many African countries are desperate. Unfortunately, the harm that is done to the people whose areas become dumping sites gets little, if any, attention.

An example of the increasing awareness of the problem of toxic waste dumping by African countries occurred during the 1988 annual conference of the Economic Community of West African States in Lomé, Togo (Schissel, 1988:47–49). At the conference, it became clear that at least ten African states had signed or were negotiating waste disposal contracts. ECOWAS leaders agreed to make it a criminal offense to facilitate the dumping of dangerous waste and urged developed countries to tighten their regulation of such products. However, it was obvious even at the conference that there was divergence of opinion regarding the problem. On the one hand, countries such as Benin, having accepted foreign currency from European exporters of toxic waste, were less than enthusiastic about too tight a regulatory regime. Countries such as Guinea-Bissau, on the other hand, were willing to reconsider their position once the potential dangers of importing toxic waste had been made clear. One of the potential dump sites in Guinea-Bissau (Farim, in northern Guinea-Bissau) was close to a fishing and agricultural project funded by the European Economic Community and threatened to pollute the entire region. As Schissel (1988:48) relates from one source, you could not have picked a worse spot than Farim because the soil is extremely porous and marshy and it rains a lot, too, so the drums of waste would have quickly leaked their contents into the water table. Of course, this would have had disastrous consequences for drinking water. This particular case for Guinea-Bissau had a happy ending because the authorities canceled the deal, but nobody knows how many more deals are consummated in Africa without the public knowing.

The other issue not discussed in this chapter that nonetheless warrants mention is wildlife conservation. The issue of wildlife is important because of two interrelated reasons. First, wildlife forms part of the tourist industry, which is important as a source of foreign exchange for many African countries and therefore important for economic development. For example, tourism is already the biggest earner of foreign exchange in Kenya, where 700,000 visitors spent $400 million in 1988 and $510 million in 1994 (Kenya Ministry of Finance, 1995). Tourism based on wildlife viewing could be as valuable in other countries, such as Zimbabwe, Botswana, and Tanzania.

Second, although wildlife is important as a source of foreign exchange, there is controversy regarding the killing of different kinds of wildlife, principally for their skin (e.g., leopards), their ivory (elephants), or their horns (rhinos). In the case of elephants, Kenya perhaps represents the extreme case where, until 1990, the elephant population faced the danger of extinction from poachers. Kenya's elephant population dropped from 165,000 to 16,000 in twenty years (Dickey, 1990:42). In January 1990, the African elephant was placed on Appendix I of the Convention on International Trade in Endangered Species (CITES) after eight years in which their numbers were halved on the continent (*Economist,* 1991:16). The problem in Kenya seems to have been arrested because of the aggressive intervention of the former director of wildlife, Dr. Richard Leakey, who sought to enforce tough laws against poachers, who can be shot on sight.

But the problem of elephant population is not viewed the same way in countries such as Zimbabwe, Botswana, and South Africa. In the last few years, Zimbabwe's elephant population has actually grown. With other southern African states, Zimbabwe has set up an ivory trading association, arguing that it needs to sell tusks from culled herds to pay for conservation.

Protecting elephants from poaching, for example, costs $200 per square kilometer per year (*Economist,* 1991:16). Another argument advanced by Zimbabwe is that the government is taking care to institute policies regulating the cropping of elephants, without which there would be an excess of elephants and other wildlife competing for grazing and agricultural land with the human population. For Zimbabwe and other southern African states, the problem is one of management of existing resources. The question is what kind of scheme would be optimal in ensuring a balance between conservation and human needs (Hill, 1990:14–22). At the moment, Zimbabwe is campaigning to have elephants downgraded to Appendix II of CITES where regulated trade is allowed. The next meeting of CITES is planned for 1997 in Zimbabwe, and the country plans to use the forum to vigorously campaign for its position (*Herald,* Harare, March 5, 1995:4). The Zimbabwe government conducted a wildlife census in August 1995 and found that there had been a tremendous increase in the elephant population (*Herald,* Harare, August 15, 1995:1). Thus, it would seem that differences in approaches to conservation in various African countries are a result of a combination of several factors, including population density. This is an indication that the debate on conservation in Africa will continue to rage for a long time to come.

In some African countries, such as Zimbabwe, elephant populations are not endangered by poachers. This causes resentment of international policies that ban the ivory trade.

■ CONCLUSIONS

Studying the environment calls for a comprehensive approach that looks at the many-sided aspects of the problem. Our examination of the relationship among deforestation, desertification, and soil erosion certainly makes this point clear. Central to this comprehensive approach, however, is the role of humankind in the use of natural resources and the effects of human activity on the environment. In Africa, human activity can be said to be directed at two related objectives: economic development and human survival. In the last two decades, the attainment of both objectives has become increasingly questionable as economic development has eluded many African countries and as human survival at a very low level has become the order of the day (Danaher, 1994).

Yet, there are many things that African governments can do to alleviate the problem. From an institutional level, my studies at UNEP reveal that no African country has comprehensive national legislation and administrative machinery in the environmental field. (See also UNEP, 1987; Hutchful, 1985:118.) Much of these countries' legislation on the environment is scattered in different areas of concern, such as legislation covering water safety or wildlife preservation (Kabeberi, 1988). Unless legislation similar to the United States' Environmental Protection Act (1970) is passed in these countries, the governments' efforts at protecting the environment will continue to be hampered. But, we also have to be aware that the Environmental Protection Act in the United States has not been the answer to all problems. Nonetheless, similar legislation in African countries would be a good start.

In the final analysis, protecting the environment is about protecting human beings. In the contemporary period, human beings live in defined political units. This means that protecting the environment must be a political act by the political authorities, who must make policy choices on economic development strategy, legislation, and so on. Unless this fact is recognized, African countries may not be able to arrest the degradation of their environment anytime soon.

■ NOTES

1. The concept of "sustainable development" (SD) has now been popularized in discussions about the environment. In many documents, however, it is not clear how the term is defined. Such is the case in a recent study by the World Bank, *Toward Environmentally Sustainable Development in Sub-Saharan Africa: A World Bank Agenda,* August 1995. Belghis Badri (1994:2), a Sudanese scholar, writes:

> My understanding of sustainable development, as an African scholar, is that it is not a holistic, non-divisible concept. Rather, I can conceive of it as an amalgamation of several indicators that have developed at various stages since the 1960s. . . . To elaborate, our

indicators of sustainable development can be explained in terms of social development, economic development, environmental development, political development, intellectual development, women's development and international development.

The problem with Badri's formulation is that almost anything goes under her definition of SD. It should be noted that the generally accepted definition of SD is that of the World Commission on Environment and Development (WCED) (1987), which defined SD as "development that meets the needs of the present without compromising the ability of future generations to meet their own needs."

2. The UNEP study is also discussed in Silver with DeFries (1990).

3. Countries that are generally referred to as forming the Sahel region are Mauritania, Senegal, Mali, Burkina Faso, Niger, and Chad.

4. To get a broader perspective on the drylands problem, note that the drylands in Africa, including hyperarid desert, constitute 1,959 million hectares, or 65 percent of the continent and about one-third of the world's drylands. One-third of these African drylands are hyperarid deserts (672 million hectares), which are uninhabited except in oases. The remaining two-thirds, or 1,278 million hectares, comprise arid, semi-arid, and dry subhumid areas (Darkoh, 1994).

5. Timberlake (1986:39) provides an interesting comparative discussion of this issue. He states: "Whether or not Africa is over-populated, most of it is certainly not *densely* populated. The average population density of Sub-Saharan Africa is only 16 per square kilometer, much less in rural areas. This compares to 100/sq km in China, and 225/sq km in India."

6. For environmental hazards created by the use of fertilizer in the United States, see Weir and Schapiro (1981). The evidence relating to fertilizer pollution in Africa is very sketchy. For a U.S. public policy pronouncement on the export and effect of industrial pollutants, see Ives (1985).

7. The Panos Institute (1990) reports that at least six African countries—Nigeria, Guinea, South Africa, Congo, Guinea-Bissau, and Sierra Leone—have either received toxic waste from outside or were considering receiving it. See also Salamone (1989) and "The Global Poison Trade" (1988).

■ BIBLIOGRAPHY

Anderson, Dennis. 1987. *The Economics of Afforestation: A Case Study in Africa.* Baltimore: Johns Hopkins University Press (for the World Bank).

Armstrong, A., and M. Garry. 1984. "The Poor Woman's Energy Crisis." *African Review* 11:81–86.

Austen, Ralph A. 1987. *African Economic History: Internal Development and External Dependency.* London: James Currey.

Badri, Belghis. 1994. "Sustainable Development: An Analytical Framework for Agenda 21." In United Nations Non-Governmental Liaison Service (NGLS), *Voices from Africa,* no. 5, *Sustainable Development.* Geneva and New York: NGLS.

Berntsen, Thorbjorn. 1995. "Challenging Traditional Growth." *Our Planet* 7, 1:11–12.

Blaikie, Piers, and Harold Brookfield. 1987. "Defining and Debating the Problem." Pp. 1–26 in Piers Blaikie and Harold Brookfield (eds.). *Land Degradation and Society.* New York: Methuen.

Bojo, Jan, et al. 1990. *Environment and Development: An Economic Approach.* Boston: Kluwer Academic Publishers.

Brown, Lester R. 1981. *Building a Sustainable Society.* New York: W. W. Norton.
Caldwell, Lynton Keith. 1984. *International Environmental Policy: Emergence and Dimensions.* Durham, NC: Duke University Press.
Cole, N. H. Ayodele. 1986. "Environmental Problems and Policies in Africa." Pp. 31–52 in *Environment and Development: Opportunities in Africa and the Middle East.* Conference summary of the World Environment Center, September 25–27, 1985. Nairobi: UNEP.
Danaher, Kevin, ed. 1994. *50 Years Is Enough: The Case Against the World Bank and the International Monetary Fund.* Boston: South End Press.
Darkoh, M. B. K. 1994. "The Deterioration of the Environment in Africa's Drylands and River Basins." *Desertification Control Bulletin* no. 24:35–41.
Dejene, Alemneh. 1987. *Peasants, Agrarian Socialism, and Rural Development in Ethiopia.* Boulder: Westview Press.
Development Group for Alternative Policies (Development GAP). 1993. *The Other Side of the Story: The Real Impact of World Bank and IMF Structural Adjustment Programs.* Washington, DC.
Dickey, Christopher. 1990. "The End of the Ivory Trail?" *Newsweek* (April 16):42.
Dixon, John A., et al. 1988. *Economic Analysis of the Environmental Impacts of Development Projects.* London: Earthscan.
Eckholm, Erik, and Lester R. Brown. 1977. *Spreading Deserts: The Hand of Man.* Washington, DC: Worldwatch Institute.
Economist (London). 1989. April 29:18.
———. 1991. March 2:16.
"The Global Poison Trade." 1988. *Newsweek* (November 7):66–68.
Herald, Harare. Various issues.
Hill, Kevin. 1990. "Zimbabwe's Wildlife Conservation Regime: State-Society Relations and Policy Implementation in a Comparative Perspective." Paper presented at the 33d annual meeting of the African Studies Association, Baltimore, November 1–4.
Hutchful, Eboe. 1985. "Oil Companies and Environmental Pollution in Nigeria." Pp. 113–140 in Claude Ake (ed.). *Political Economy of Nigeria.* London: Longman.
Ives, Jane H. 1985. *The Export of Hazard: Transnational Corporations and Environmental Control Issues.* Boston: Routledge and Kegan Paul.
Kabeberi, Janet W. 1988. "Environmental Law in Kenya." Unpublished manuscript, Nairobi University Faculty of Law.
Kenya Ministry of Finance. 1995. *Kenya Economic Survey 1994.* Nairobi.
Leonard, H. Jeffrey (ed.). 1985. *Divesting Nature's Capital: The Political Economy of Environmental Abuse in the Third World.* New York: Holmes and Meier.
Lewis, L. A., and L. Berry. 1988. *African Environments and Resources.* Boston: Unwin Hyman.
Nnoli, Okwudiba. 1990. "Desertification, Refugees and Regional Conflict in West Africa." *Disasters: The Journal of Disaster Studies and Management* 14:132–139.
Nyang'oro, Julius E. 1989. *The State and Capitalist Development in Africa: Declining Political Economies.* New York: Praeger.
Obenga, T. 1981. "Sources and Specific Techniques Used in African History: General Outline." Pp. 72–85 in J. Ki-Zerbo (ed.). *UNESCO General History of Africa 1: Methodology and African Prehistory.* Berkeley: University of California Press.
Osaghae, Eghosa E. 1995. "The Ogoni Uprising: Oil Politics, Minority Agitation and the Future of the Nigerian State." *African Affairs* 94: 325–344.
Panos Institute. 1990. "The Next Link in the Dumping Chain." Pp. 32–33 in *We*

Speak for Ourselves: Social Justice, Race and Environment. Washington, DC: Panos Institute.

"Paper Mill to Close." 1989. *Durham Morning Herald* (January 5):B3.

Pirages, Dennis. 1978. *Global Ecopolitics.* North Scituate, MA: Duxbury Press.

Poulsen, Gunnar. 1990. *Report to the Third Meeting of the Committee of Forests and Woodlands (COFAW) of the African Ministerial Conference on the Environment.* Nairobi: UNEP.

Pradervand, Pierre. 1989. *Listening to Africa: Developing Africa from the Grassroots.* New York: Praeger.

Revell, Roger. 1976. "The Resources Available for Agriculture." *Scientific American* 235 (September):165–178.

Salamone, Salvatore. 1989. "The End of the Ivory Trail?" *Newsweek* (April 16):42.

Schissel, Howard. 1988. "The Deadly Trade: Toxic Waste Dumping in Africa." *Africa Report* 33 (September–October):47–49.

Silver, Cheryl Simon, with Ruth S. DeFries. 1990. *One Earth, One Future: Our Changing Global Environment.* Washington, DC: National Academy Press.

Skoupy, Jiri. 1988. "Developing Rangeland Resources in African Drylands." *UNEP Desertification Control Bulletin* 17:29–40.

Stebbing, E. P. 1935. "The Encroaching Sahara: The Threat to the West African Colonies." *Geographical Journal* 85:508–524.

Stocking, Mike. 1987. "Measuring Land Degradation." Pp. 49–63 in Piers Blaikie and Harold Brookfield (eds.). *Land Degradation and Society.* New York: Methuen.

Tillman, R. E. 1981. "Environmental Guidelines for Irrigation." Washington, DC: U.S. Agency for International Development.

Timberlake, Lloyd. 1986. *Africa in Crisis: The Causes, the Cures of Environmental Bankruptcy.* Washington, DC: Earthscan.

"Troubled Water: The Mississippi River Faces All of the Nation's Environmental Problems. How We Deal with Them Will Decide Its Future—and Ours." 1990. *Newsweek* (April 16):66–80.

United Nations Environmental Program (UNEP). 1987. *New Directions in Environmental Legislation and Administration, Particularly in Developing Countries.* Nairobi: UNEP.

———. 1990. *The Disappearing Forests.* UNEP Environmental Brief No. 3. Nairobi: UNEP.

Wagner, Richard. 1971. *Environment and Man.* New York: W. W. Norton.

Weir, David, and Mark Schapiro. 1981. *Circle of Poison: Pesticides and People in a Hungry World.* San Francisco: Institute for Food and Development Policy.

Wells, Gordon. 1989. "Observing Earth's Environment from Space." Pp. 148–192 in Laurie Friday and Ronald Laskey (eds.). *The Fragile Environment. The Darwin College Lectures.* Cambridge: Cambridge University Press.

World Bank. 1981. *Accelerated Development in Sub-Saharan Africa: An Agenda for Action.* Washington, DC: World Bank.

———. 1989. *Sub-Saharan Africa: From Crisis to Sustainable Growth: A Long-Term Perspective Study.* Washington, DC: World Bank.

———. 1995. *Toward Environmentally Sustainable Development in Sub-Saharan Africa: A World Bank Agenda.* Washington, DC: World Bank.

World Commission on Environment and Development (WCED). 1987. *Our Common Future.* New York: Oxford University Press.

▪ 9 ▪

Family and Kinship

Brian Siegel

"Don't be fooled," advised a senior Zambian bureaucrat. "Here in Africa, the family is first. This will never change." I was on my way to study the labor strategies of Copperbelt market gardeners, and I had told him my plans to consult the local officials charged with "developing" the "static rural masses." One should not, he advised, accept such programs at face value, for government offices and officials would never inspire the same loyalties as those of family ties.

The significance of such ties was dramatically illustrated in 1983, when 1.3 million migrant workers from Ghana—nearly one-tenth of all Ghanaians—were suddenly deported from Nigeria. Things looked bad, for severe drought had only worsened the chronic crisis that is the Ghanaian economy. Western relief agencies drew up plans for emergency camps to feed and house the deportees. Yet, this particular crisis soon evaporated, for within two weeks the Ghanaian deportees had all disappeared back into their families at home (Harden, 1990:6).

Still, those who honor their family obligations may do so out of a mixed sense of cynicism, dread, and guilt. Consider the Ghanaian sociologist Kwasi Oduro. With his mother's support, he became the first university graduate in his family. In spite of his enviable teaching job in Accra, his government salary cannot properly support his wife and five children. Yet, he shares his three-bedroom home with eleven home-village cousins (his classificatory brothers and sisters) and, during his rare visits home, cannot refuse his mother's, mother's sister's, and sister's desperate requests for cash. "I want out of the extended family trap," he says, "and when my mother dies I don't think I'll go back to the village anymore" (Harden, 1990:94).

Family ties are sometimes strained, and Africans do not always honor the ideals of family loyalty. Yet, it is important to note that such cultural ideals are as common to African societies as those of personal autonomy are in our own.

■ COMPARING MARRIAGE AND FAMILY FORMS

Families take different forms and are invested with different meanings. Whereas we in the United States typically conceive of family as conjugal, or nuclear, that composed of a married couple and their children, Africans generally use the term to denote the extended family, several generations of relatives living at home and away.

Still other aspects of the African family are best understood in terms of the broad historical contrast Jack Goody (1976) draws between Eurasian and black African societies. The preindustrial societies of Europe and Asia were generally based on labor-intensive regimes of plow and/or irrigation agriculture. Here, where permanent and heritable land-ownership was the primary index of wealth and status, marriage was wrapped up in property considerations. Polygamy (except in Muslim societies) was prohibited, premarital sex was discouraged, and parents used whatever property they held—the son's heritable estate or daughter's dowry—to ensure that their children maintained their social position by marrying within their own (or a higher-ranking) class or caste. Such considerations often delayed the age of marriage, and they prevented some—the elderly bachelors or spinsters from poor but honorable families—from ever marrying at all. In this respect, idealized celibacy, monasteries, and convents were peculiar to Eurasian societies.

Black African societies were very different, for most were based on labor-saving forms of slash-and-burn horticulture (or hoe-farming), in which crops are grown in the ash beds left after cut and dried trees and brush are burned. Thus, garden and even village sites are shifted as the old, unproductive gardens are abandoned. As Africa was generally marked by poor soils and low population densities, land was relatively abundant, and wealth and status were not measured in terms of necessarily impermanent land-use rights, but in control over the laborers needed to work the land. African societies had rulers, subjects, and slaves, but few had landlords, tenants, or serfs. This general lack of class or caste distinctions also meant that marriage patterns were relatively open, for even chiefs and kings, by marrying outside their own lineages or clans, had to marry commoners.

Accordingly, Africans still view marriage as a means for begetting children rather than a strategy for maximizing landed estates and class positions. There is no tradition of idealized celibacy, and many societies take a relatively casual view of premarital sex. Infertility and infant mortality are terrible personal tragedies, for children are desired and loved. Children are also the markers of adult status and are essential for becoming an immortal (i.e., remembered) ancestor; therefore, all normal adults expect to marry—and not just once, but often several times. This is obviously true of men, for all African societies permit polygyny (the practice of having more than one

wife), but women also participate in the common pattern of early marriage, divorce(s), and remarriage.

Let me offer a personal example of African ideas about marriage and children. My first child was conceived within days of my wife's arrival in Zambia. No sooner did the hospital confirm her pregnancy than I took her out to meet my Lamba village hosts. Evenings there are spent chatting around a fire, but one night she was just too exhausted to participate. Although it is Lamba custom not to tempt fate by discussing the yet unborn, I thought it better to tell our hosts about her condition than have them think her unsociably "proud."

Our conversation took a revealing turn. They wanted to know all about us, beginning with our ages and our previous children, living or dead. Since we had none, they suggested that she married me after her first marriage proved childless, a common ground for divorce. I certainly seemed to be fertile, so they then asked about my other wives and children. No, I insisted, though we were both in our late twenties, neither of us had been married before, and we had chosen to remain childless through a lengthy courtship and nearly three years of marriage.

My friends were surprised. They had just been lamenting Zambia's rising cost of living, so I explained that life in the United States was so expensive that we often delay marriage and children until we can afford them. Now these Baptist villagers were upset. What had money to do with marriage and children? They were our purpose here on earth. They had always heard we *Basungu* (whites) were a money-minded people, but they had never imagined us to be so perverted as to reduce marriage and childbearing to monetary calculations!

Goody (1976) is right. African ideas of marriage and family are, in these respects, very different from our own.

■ UNILINEAL DESCENT AND DESCENT GROUPS

Families take different forms, and kinship or family ties can be computed in different ways. Most North Americans are raised in one nuclear family, then, after marriage, begin another. We also have extended families, which may assemble for relatives' birthdays, weddings, and funerals. But we rarely live with them, for our custom is that of neolocal (literally, "new place") postmarital residence.

In fact, we all have more or less distant kin whom we barely know. And even those we do know, like our paternal and maternal cousins, are not necessarily related to each other. This is because we have a bilateral kinship system and trace family ties through the males and females on both our mother's and father's sides of the family. Bilateral descent gives us the largest kinship network of any descent system ever invented. But it makes it difficult to keep track of our kin. And this, together with neolocality, makes it nearly impossible to use kinship in structuring our social order.

The African notion of "family," by contrast, typically refers to the extended family system. Not only do members of an African extended family often live together, but they find it relatively easy to keep track of their kin. This is because the vast majority of African peoples have unilineal ("one line") descent systems that trace kinship through just one sex—either patrilineally, through a line of fathers, or matrilineally, through a line of mothers. With unilineal descent, Africans create still larger familistic groups, the unilineal descent groups called the lineage and clan. The difference between the two is largely one of size and genealogical depth. While the members of a given lineage can spell out their precise genealogical links, the members of a clan—which is usually composed of many constituent lineages—only know that they are somehow related. Such descent groups are so large and encompassing that they conveniently structure the organization of social life.

The point should be stressed here that while lineage members can specify their genealogical links, these are representations of sociological ancestry and do not always constitute objective historical or biological facts. Until the advent of writing, elders were free to interpret and edit their genealogical knowledge, and there is, over time, a common tendency for the smaller, less prolific lineage segments or lineage dependents, like the descendants of domestic slaves, to be assigned a suitable ancestor and be incorporated into its dominant segments. Wilson (1979:53–55), for example, tells how, from the sixteenth through eighteenth centuries, European and Muslim shipwreck victims along the southeastern African coast were absorbed into the neighboring chiefdoms' descent groups. And Lan (1985) tells how, during the 1971–1980 liberation struggle in northeastern Zimbabwe, Robert Mugabe's ZANU guerrillas established identities as the symbolic "grandchildren" of the local Shona's ancient chiefs.

The patrilineal Nuer of southern Sudan, as described by Evans-Pritchard (1940), inspired generations of anthropologists to study the genealogical charter of African social life. According to Evans-Pritchard (1950:368), any Nuer "can establish kinship of some kind—real, assumed, by analogy, mythological, or just fictitious—with everybody he comes into contact with during this lifetime and throughout the length and breadth of Nuerland . . . for all social obligation of a personal kind is defined in terms of kinship." Their patrilineal social structure is more accurately understood as an idealized model of the society (Gough, 1971; Mair, 1974:124, 133–134; Southall, 1986). In short, kinship is less a "God's truth" account of objective historical fact than an ideological framework, or plausible sociological fiction, for the ordering of social life (Moore, 1969; Karp, 1978; Vansina, 1980).

In theory, then, every individual is born into a conceptually immortal descent group that includes the living, the dead (ancestors), and the yet unborn. Like the corporations in our own society, a lineage or clan transcends the lifetimes of its individual members and controls property rights to such things as land and herds, leadership positions, and spiritual powers. As each lineage or clan is a giant extended family, its members must marry outside their own descent group. Thus, marriage more closely resembles an alliance of two preexisting families than the creation of a new one. And, like family, lineage or clan members have a collective obligation to assist one another, especially when it comes to settling disputes or paying compensation for each other's mistakes.

A final characteristic of the unilineal extended family is its lumping of different kin together under the same kinship term. Take parents, for example. The term "father" almost always includes your father's brothers, and the term "mother" includes your mother's sisters. The children of all these "mothers" and "fathers" (half of your cousins) are your "brothers" and "sisters"; and among most African peoples their children are your "children" too. While you cannot have sex with or marry your "brothers" and "sisters" (i.e., father's brothers' and mother's sisters' children), your "aunt's" (father's sisters') and "uncle's" (mother's brothers') children are fair game because they do not belong to either parent's descent group. In fact, these "cousins" (the other half of your cousins) are often your preferred marriage partners.

This may sound awfully confusing, but it does not entail any confusion over biological parentage. Such classificatory kinship terms merely reflect the elegant simplicity of unilineal descent and tell individuals how they are expected to relate to one another. My Lamba friends were just as baffled by our indiscriminate lumping of aunts, uncles, and cousins, and wondered how we managed to tell them all apart.

■ **AFRICAN DESCENT
AND RESIDENCE PATTERNS**

Patriliny, or descent through males, is the most common descent system in Africa and throughout the world. It is strongly associated with the pastoral (herding) peoples of the savannas of western and eastern Africa—like the Fulani (Fulbe) peoples (stretching from Senegambia to the Central African Republic), the Nuer (southern Sudan), and the Maasai (western Kenya and Tanzania). But it is also common to a wide variety of horticultural peoples— like the stateless Tiv (east-central Nigeria) and Gikuyu (central Kenya), and the state-level Yoruba (southwestern Nigeria) and Ganda (Uganda). All of these, like the vast majority of patrilineal peoples, practice patrilocality, in which, after marriage, the bride leaves home to live with or near her husband's family.

Descent was formerly regarded as a primary social fact, but Murdock (1949) persuaded most anthropologists that descent systems result from the composition of cooperative work groups and consequent patterns of post-marital residence. More recent research has broadened the notion of cooperative work to include warfare and trade with subsistence activities, for a key predictor of residence is whether a people have a history of internal or external warfare (Ember and Ember, 1971; Divale, 1974). Where a people has a history of internal warfare—intercommunity raiding between people speaking the same language—patrilocality and patriliny seem to result from the clear advantage of keeping a defensive core of related fathers, brothers, and sons living together in one place. Where, on the other hand, warfare was purely external, or between different peoples, patrilocality and patriliny seem to result from males' close cooperation in managing common land or cattle estates.

In patrilineal societies, the children born to a marriage legitimized by bridewealth or bride service (see "Marital Alliances" below) are members of their father's patrilineage or patriclan. Since descent is traced through fathers, a man and his brother, their children, and their sons' children are all members of the same descent group. Women are too, but a sister's or daughter's children will belong to their fathers' groups. Children do recognize kinship links with their mother's patrilineal relatives and often enjoy especially close ties with their mother's brother, but such matrilateral (literally, "mother's side") links are of secondary importance in the formal scheme of things. Yoruba women, for example, enjoy the same patrilineal inheritance rights as their brothers. But where the heritable resources—such as houses, cocoa lands, titles, or political offices—are in scarce supply, the patrilineal principles of inheritance tend to favor direct male descendants over sisters' children (Eades, 1980:52, 55–56, 60, 98; Lloyd, 1965:570).

Under patriliny, the lines of descent and authority converge in the person of one's father or husband. A wife, at the time of her marriage, exchanges the authority of her father for that of her husband, and in many patrilineal societies, especially in southern Africa, a wife is gradually absorbed into her husband's patrilineal descent group. Children typically view their father as an emotionally distant disciplinarian, for whatever affection they may feel toward one another is compromised by the respect and obedience they owe him as the immediate representative of their lineage or clan.

Matriliny, on the other hand, is largely confined to a few pockets in or near the coastal forests of western Africa (e.g., the Asante and other Akan peoples in Ghana), and to the broad "matrilineal belt" that stretches across the wooded savannas of south-central Africa, from Zaire and Angola to Tanzania and Mozambique (e.g., the Lamba and Bemba of Zambia). Here, where warfare was largely external, or where hunting or trading took men away for prolonged periods, and where most of the hoeing and weeding is performed by female work groups, the residence and descent patterns reflect the advantage of keeping a cooperative and related core of mothers, sisters, and daughters living together in one place (Ember and Ember, 1971; Divale, 1974).

Most such societies have either matrilocal or avunculocal residence. Under matrilocality, the groom leaves his family to live with or near his wife's matrikin, while under avunculocality the couple lives with or near the husband's mother's brother (*avunculus* in Latin) and the husband's matrikin. These two residence patterns can exist in the same society. A Lamba marriage, for example, is supposed to begin with an extended period of matrilocal bride service. Then, several years and children later, after proving his ability to care for his wife and children, the Lamba husband requests permission to remove them to his mother's brother's village. Should his wife's family refuse him, he can either "lump it" or terminate the marriage.

In matrilineal societies, a person is born into his mother's matrilineage or matriclan regardless of her marital status or the payment of bridewealth. Descent is traced through mothers. Thus, a woman and her sister, their children, and their daughters' children all belong to the same descent group. Men do too, but a brother's or son's children invariably belong to their own mothers' groups. While children in matrilineal societies recognize some affiliation with their father's matrikin and often enjoy warm ties with their father, such patrilateral ("father's side") links are of secondary importance when it comes to the inheritance of property, titles, or political office. For in these societies, one is supposed to inherit such resources from the mother's brother, the matrilineal authority figure, rather than one's father, as is the case in patrilineal societies.

Matriliny is not matriarchy (rule by women), for the formal positions of authority in a matrilineal descent group are usually held by either brothers or mother's brothers. Neither is it a mirror image of patriliny, for here the lines of descent and authority are split, and the husband's authority over his wife and children is strictly limited. A man may be the authority figure for his sister and her children, but his own wife and children fall under the authority of his brother-in-law. Matrilocal or avunculocal residence only complicates the issue, for a brother, his sister, and her sons and daughters may all live in different villages. The resulting tensions are, from the male's perspective, known as the "matrilineal dilemma."

The "war between the sexes" is a daily reality in such societies, and it is one in which women—at least those who are mothers—have a decided advantage. A mother's interests are narrowly focused upon the rights of her children, while the father's are divided between two rival groups—that of his wife and children, on the one hand, and that of his sister and sister's children on the other. While a married brother must try to balance these competing demands, his wife and sister need only be good mothers. Mothers can and do exploit men's divided interests to their own and their children's advantage. Whatever men in a matrilineal society may say about the inherent weakness and inferiority of women, they find it very difficult to control their wives and sisters (Beidelman, 1986:17–22). It is little wonder then, at least in eastern and central Africa, that marriage ties are notoriously more brittle in matrilineal than in patrilineal societies.

Anthropologists have devoted a lot of print to the question of matriliny's future and whether or not it restricts economic enterprise. As Mary Douglas (1969) notes, it seems to perform well under conditions of open opportunities and unrestricted resources. In southern Ghana, for example, the matrilineal cocoa-farming migrants from the Asante and other Akan peoples enjoy a distinct advantage over those from patrilineal societies, for they alone are able to form cooperative, descent-based "companies" for buying and recruiting labor—at least so long as their wives and poorer relatives can expect to receive their own farms for their efforts (Hill, 1963, 1986:134–138; Okali, 1983).

But matriliny's conflicting loyalties and diffuse authority relations are not well suited to conditions of interpersonal competition and restricted resources. Among the matrilocal and matrilineal Chewa-speaking people of southeastern Malawi (of mixed Nyanja and Lomwe origins), custom (perhaps reinforced by the present scarcity of land) denies most men access to their matrilineages' lands, and the land disputes between sisters in a given village have led to a wider recognition of the lowly, immigrant "sons-in-law" as nuclear family heads (Peters, 1994). Matriliny does not guarantee female solidarity. But since it generates "a political economy that minimizes male control of power and resources" (Poewe, 1979:115), most discussions of its future tend to assume a male perspective.

It is not surprising that Karla Poewe learned that male and female entrepreneurs have different attitudes toward matriliny. The Luapula River valley, along Zaire's southeastern border with Zambia, has long hosted the long-distance trade in fish and crops and is famous for a long tradition of wealthy entrepreneurs. The large fish- or crop-trading businessman in Zambia's Luapula province has little use for his matrikin's claims for support. Like the opportunistic "therapeutic Muslim" converts described in David Parkin's (1972) study of Kenya's Giriama cocoa entrepreneurs, he becomes a Jehovah's Witness or Seventh-Day Adventist and uses their ideology of the patriarchal nuclear family to distance himself from such claims. While such men see matrilineal claims as an economic threat, the large Luapula businesswoman feels threatened by the marital claims of her husband and his matrikin. She avoids the churches her husband prefers. Through multiple divorce and refusal of the levirate (the inheritance of a deceased man's widow by his brother), she seeks to distance herself from the claims of her husband and his family and to preserve her wealth for her children's and brothers' benefit (Poewe, 1980).

In the present century—due to the historical impact of the slave trade, Islam or Christian mission teachings, labor migration, cash cropping, and other forms of enterprise—many matrilineal peoples have adopted some of the customs of neighboring patrilineal peoples (Phiri, 1983; Colson, 1961). Chewa men in both Zambia and Malawi, for example, have adopted the bridewealth customs of the neighboring Ngoni to obtain permanent custody of their children. And, with the consequent emergence of patrilocal residence, village headmanships often pass from fathers to their children, rather than to a sister's children (Phiri, 1983; Skjønsberg, 1989).

Although a similar pattern exists among Lamba villagers, it is most obvious among the cash-cropping Lamba farmers, who abandoned the "noise" (quarrels) of village life to establish their own patrilocal extended family farms. They and their sons consider the custom of matrilineal inheritance to be fundamentally wrong, for how can a man enlist his wife's and children's help in building a family farm if it will eventually pass to his sister's children? Many have adjusted their descent lines accordingly. In one such case, a farmer's sons and grandchildren deny being members of their mothers' clans, but, instead, claim to be members of their father's and paternal grandfather's (matrilineal) clan (Siegel, 1984:180–188).

Such a change in inheritance does not necessarily weaken the matrilineal system (Colson, 1980; Peters, 1994). Few people are able to refuse the means of advancement potentially available through matrikin assistance or inheritance, and the same people who resent the claims made by their matrikin show no hesitation when it comes to pursuing identical claims of their own (Colson, 1980; Poewe, 1980). "The security associated with the extended matrilineal kinship network is thus still significant"—especially, but not only, for the poor—and "matrilineal descent is highly adaptive, especially under conditions where one needs access to a diversity of support" (Colson, 1980:372–373).

Johan Pottier (1988) has documented a parallel trend among the patrilocal and patrilineal Mambwe, who straddle the Zambia-Tanzania border between Lakes Tanganyika and Malawi. As described by William Watson (1958), the Mambwe became a classic example of a people who prospered during the flow of migrant laborers to the Copperbelt mines. The neighboring Bemba suffered from the loss of male labor migrants because, being matrilocal and matrilineal, their villages lacked a core of related males (Richards, 1939, 1940). But Mambwe men were permanently attached to their heritable land and cattle estates at home. So the younger men, while away, could entrust their wives, children, and garden labor to older patrikin.

But the 1970s collapse of the Zambian copper industry forced many Mambwe back upon increasingly scarce lands. Divorced or widowed Mambwe women have always left their children with their husbands' kin and returned to their fathers' villages. But now, to obtain secure land rights and cooperative female labor for their cash crop gardens, they remain in

their natal villages even after remarrying. Thus, many villages include a core
of matrilocal but patrilineally related women, each with a mother or daughter living in a Tanzanian border village. Such mother-daughter links are now
a valuable resource, for they serve to establish family partnerships in the
extralegal Zambia-Tanzania border trade. Here, where population pressure
effectively precludes further agricultural intensification, it is ironic that the
welfare of so many patrilineal Mambwe depends upon family ties traced
through women (Pottier, 1988).

Finally, a handful of peoples in western and south-central Africa practice dual (or double unilineal) descent. They have both patri- and matrilineal descent groups, though each serves a different purpose. Among the Yakö
of southeastern Nigeria, rights to garden lands are defined patrilineally,
whereas inheritance rights in movable property are transmitted matrilineally.
The basic difference between double and single unilineal descent systems is
that under dual descent, the kinship rights and obligations are split between
two different descent groups, each with divergent interests in the same individual. Analogous descent group rivalries also occur in single unilineal societies, as when, in a patrilineal society, a mother's brother's patrilineage takes
the part of their sister's son in a dispute with the members of his patrilineage. But here the rivalries are between descent groups of the same sex.

■ MARITAL ALLIANCES AND TRANSACTIONS

In Africa, marriage is not so much a union between two individuals as
an alliance between two extended families and descent groups (Sudarkasa,
1980). In some respects, the personal identities of the married couple are
less important than the alliance they represent. African marriages are most
commonly marked by the exchange of bridewealth, formerly (and mislead-
ingly) called "bride price," in which the bride's group accepts livestock or
other movable property in compensation for the loss of their daughter's
labor and fertility. In most such societies, bridewealth is essential for legit-
imizing a marriage and its children.

This is rarely paid in full or all at once, for the bride's group maintains
some leverage over their in-laws by keeping the groom and his kin in their
debt. Bridewealth expenses vary with the number of marriageable men and
women, herd sizes, and the opportunities for earning cash, so they reflect the
laws of supply and demand. Yet, if the immigrant Shona farmers in Zambia
are any example, the men and women involved in such transactions do not
regard bridewealth as the calculated buying and selling of wives but as symbolic tokens of women's value (Siegel, 1984:223–229).

Where bridewealth involves a substantial amount of property, older men
can use their greater wealth to monopolize the supply of younger, marriage-

Bridewealth and polygyny reflect the vital productive contributions of women to the family. Women kin often work together in the fields and share other work as well.

able women and, by contributing to their bridewealth, to gain influence over their junior kinsmen wanting to get married. Such influence is always resented, but this is especially true when, instead of helping his adult sons, a man uses his wealth to accumulate additional young wives for himself. This kind of selfishness, however, has its own risks, because such a situation can turn ugly and divisive should the father discover that his young wife is romantically involved with one of his sons.

Bridewealth can also operate to strengthen marriage ties. The cruel, abusive husband might forfeit his bridewealth and alienate his kinsmen if his wife should leave him. The same is true for the wife, because, unless she has sound reasons for deserting her husband, her kinsmen must refund their shares of her bridewealth. Since both groups have a vested interest in perpetuating a given marriage, high bridewealth payments are associated with low divorce rates. It was precisely this realization that forced the Christian missionaries in Botswana to abandon their opposition to the "heathen" custom of "bride price" (Schapera, 1940:74–76).

In still other African societies, marriage is marked by the custom of bride service. This is particularly true where the tsetse fly (and sleeping sickness) prevents the accumulation of livestock. Here the groom, like the biblical Jacob, offers his parents-in-law his labor instead of property. From the male's perspective, this has several disadvantages over bridewealth.

First, it requires the husband to accept a subordinate position in his wife's village. Since his labor is his own, he has no relatives to defend his interests, while his wife can rely upon her family's support in any dispute. Such marriages are more unstable, and the husband forfeits his investment should the marriage end. It is little wonder, then, that those societies that emphasize bridewealth exchange regard bride service as an inferior, "poor man's" alternative.

Two other customs reflect the alliance aspect of marriage: the levirate and the sororate. Given both the desire for children and the distinctly complementary roles of men and women in the sexual division of labor, marriage is essential to an active and productive life. Should one spouse die, the marital alliance provides the other partner with a replacement. Under the levirate, a man assumes the responsibility for his dead brother's widow and children, while under the sororate, a woman takes the place of her dead or barren sister. These replacements need not be actual biological brothers or sisters; rather, they might easily include those cousins who, according to African systems of (unilineal) descent, are considered "brothers" or "sisters" of the unfortunate spouse.

African peoples enforce these duties with differing intensity. They are undoubtedly burdensome when custom compels a person to perpetuate a marital alliance against his or her will. But this is equally true when a Christian church, in forbidding polygamy, forces a respectably married deacon or elder to leave his church for honoring his customary obligations to his dead brother's widow. Most peoples, however, permit greater personal choice in honoring these obligations. Elderly widows and widowers are often tired of marriage and prefer to live with a married son or daughter. In most respects, the levirate and sororate provide a valued security net for widows and widowers.

■ FAMILY TIES AND SOCIAL ORDER

Family ties are more than a curious feature of African social life, for they also play an important role in political relations and the maintenance of social order. This is particularly true in traditionally stateless societies—those decentralized political orders without a bureaucratic hierarchy and coercive authority, as Thomas O'Toole discusses in Chapter 3—but the same general features also operate in traditional state-level societies. People everywhere are socialized to learn the boundaries of expected and acceptable behavior and to share some concern for what others might think of them. While gossip and slander, ridicule and shame, and the fear of other negative sanctions are common mechanisms of social control in all societies, they are particularly potent ones in politically decentralized societies, where the political, economic, and religious aspects of social life are all wrapped up around family ties.

The Lugbara, for example, are a traditionally stateless horticultural people in northwestern Uganda. As described by Middleton (1960), the Lugbara live in dispersed, patrilocal, and patrilineal extended family clusters of some twelve to sixty members. Each extended family cluster is under the direction of a single male elder, the senior representative of a local lineage segment. His dependents treat him with a respectful mixture of affection, obedience, and fear, for, as the custodian of their ancestors' shrines, he has direct access to the guardians of customary morality. While it is the ancestors who punish their sinful descendants with sickness and misfortune, it is the family elder who brings such troublemakers to their attention; therefore, lineage elders— when supported by the ancestors, mystical curses, or special knowledge of medicines—can use the threat of misfortune to exercise some control over their juniors (see Saitoti, 1986:82, 92, 141–143, and Bohannan, 1965:539–543, on the Maasai and Tiv, respectively).

But misfortunes strike the just and unjust alike, and the fear of such sanctions tends to backfire where people believe that the same troubles can be credited to jealous, antisocial witches. The Lugbara family cluster goes through a predictable cycle of internal growth, conflict, and fragmentation as, over time, its elder finds it increasingly difficult to reconcile his dependents' competing needs for land. As discontented factions form around the elder's rivals, the suspicion grows that his witchcraft is the cause of their chronic misfortunes and quarrels. Here, as among the matrilineal peoples of central Africa (see Marwick, 1965; Turner, 1957), witchcraft accusations are the standard device used by rival, would-be leaders to split away and establish their own settlements elsewhere. When based on the fear of misfortune, such patriarchal authority often contains the seeds of its own destruction (Middleton, 1960).

Perhaps the most famous example of the political role of familistic ties is Evans-Pritchard's (1940) classic account of the Nuer and their segmentary lineage organization. Like the Tiv, who share a similar political organization (Bohannan, 1965:523–525, 531–533), these fiercely independent cattle pastoralists in southern Sudan are stateless people, and political relations within and between each of over a dozen Nuer tribes can best be described as an "ordered anarchy" (Evans-Pritchard, 1940:5–6). The tribe was the largest sovereign and peacemaking group, which merely means that fellow tribesmen should not raid each other's cattle and that they should pay compensation for intratribal injuries or killings. Members of different tribes, on the other hand, may raid each other's cattle, but they should avoid destroying granaries or killing women and children. No such rules apply where foreigners are concerned.

Nuer political relations are modeled on the ideology of patrilineal descent. As each tribe has its dominant clan, the Nuer speak of their villages, districts, and still larger tribal sections as the localized segments of the dominant clan. Each segment in this genealogical pyramid corresponds to a similar territorial section of the tribe. These genealogical relations are most important in pursuing disputes, for most Nuer disputes are settled through the threat of force. The parties to a common dispute each recruit as many supporters as they possibly can, and it is the genealogical distance between them that determines whom they can call upon for support.

In general, more closely related lineage segments are supposed to unite against more distantly related ones. But as differing disputes involve different levels of genealogical distance, the rivals in one dispute will be allies in another. Two neighboring villages, for example, will set aside their quarrels when a new one pits a member of their district against someone from another. Should these districts belong to different tribes, their quarrel will pit one tribe against another. Ultimately, all Nuer tribes will unite against a common foreign enemy. And, Kelly (1985) argues, it was the organizational effectiveness of these dominant clan genealogies that enabled the nineteenth-century Nuer to cut and occupy a 35,000-square-mile swath through the territory of their Dinka neighbors.

Such situationally determined alliances are only temporary, however. Once the common threat is removed, each alliance dissolves into its mutually antagonistic segments. A political system based on the segmentary lineage organization is one of balanced opposition, a constantly fluctuating equilibrium between the fission and fusion of lineage segments. There is order in this apparent anarchy, and it is organized and expressed through the plausible sociological fiction of the dominant clan's patrilineal genealogy.

A third example of the political role of familistic ties comes from Elizabeth Colson's (1953) elegant analysis of crosscutting social ties among the Plateau Tonga in southern Zambia. The Tonga are matrilineal and patrilocal, but every person is considered a member of both his or her mother's and father's matrilineal descent groups. Ever in search of good land and cooperative neighbors, these cattle-keeping plow farmers settle wherever they choose. As a result, the residents of any given village, and of the seven to eight villages in a given neighborhood, are likely to represent most of the Tonga's twelve dispersed matrilineal clans. Neighbors are bound by ties of kinship, marriage, and friendship, as well as by cattle loans and the exchange of labor. One's sense of community has less to do with kinship than with residents' cooperative interdependence.

One day, at a neighborhood beer drink, a man from the Eland clan quarreled with and struck a Lion clan man, putting him into a coma. The victim died some days later, and his assailant was arrested and eventually tried and imprisoned for manslaughter. As Colson (1953) describes it, the Eland clan elders had long anticipated such problems from this quarrelsome troublemaker. They had previously enlisted him in the wartime army and, disappointed in his safe return, had supposedly tried to finish him off with a witchcraft-induced illness. But the Lion clansmen were not satisfied with his imprisonment and, according to Tonga custom, held the Elands collectively responsible for their kinsman's death. In precolonial times, the Lions would have taken revenge against the Elands, thereby precipitating a blood feud.

Though the Elands acknowledged their blood debt, they lacked any way of telling this to the Lions. Following their kinsman's death, the Lions not only cut off all relations with their Eland villagers and neighbors but also began threatening the Eland wives married to Lion clansmen. Everyone with Lion or Eland spouses was also affected, and the fear of a blood feud soon infected relations throughout the neighborhood.

This placed a special strain on the victim's village headman. He not only had Lion and Eland clan wives and children, but his father was the murderer's village headman. As such, he became the spokesman for all the neighbors with similarly divided loyalties. Working through his father and his Lion and Eland brothers-in-law, he got the Lions to accept the Elands' promise of cattle compensation. Although tensions eased, the Elands delayed their promised payments until the son of an Eland husband and Lion wife fell sick and died. The diviner determined that the victim's angry spirit had caused the death and would continue to afflict his relatives until the Elands paid their debt.

Here the diviner, as the mouthpiece of public opinion, forced the Elands to honor their pledge. But public opinion was shaped by the neighborhood's dense network of crosscutting social ties. Many individuals—Lions, Elands, and others—had divided loyalties and interests in this dispute, and it was these same individuals who pressured for a settlement. This illustrates that when people of different descent groups must marry, live among, and cooperate with one another, their crosscutting ties—together with the pervasive fear of feud (Colson, 1974:42–43)—constitute an important mechanism for the maintenance of social order (Colson, 1953; Gluckman, 1955).

Family ties also play an important, if not always central, role in the political organization of traditional state-level societies. This is probably best illustrated by the Yoruba city-states in southwestern Nigeria. The Yoruba, the largest of sub-Saharan Africa's ethnic groups, might best be described as urban peasants, for while most men are cash-cropping farmers, their permanent homes are in large and densely settled towns (Bascom, 1955). "The Yoruba have lived in towns as long as they can remember and despise their townless and kingless neighbors" (Lloyd, 1965:554).

Among the more populous, northern Yoruba, these towns consist of a central palace and marketplace surrounded by compound wards, each consisting of a series of linked, rectangular courtyards that house the members of the compound's patrilocal and patrilineal extended family. Some rooms in the old-style courtyards are now often leased to strangers, and some have been razed and replaced by mazes of individual bungalows and two-story houses; nevertheless, the compound's land remains corporate lineage prop-

erty. Although such a compound is no longer a single structural entity, it "is
certainly still a social unit with a strong sense of its unity and cohension displayed at the regular meeting in the house of its head," or lineage elder
(Lloyd, 1974:115). Such elders from the town's prominent lineage compounds also inherit their lineages' titled chieftainships and serve on the
town's council of senior chiefs.

The precolonial government of the Yoruba city-state was a constitutional monarchy, one based upon the balanced opposition of its reclusive,
sacred king and his council of senior chiefs. The kingship rotated among the
rival houses of the royal lineage, and the king was appointed by his council
of senior chiefs. In theory, the government was invested in this council, and
the king was supposed to accept the decisions of those who had selected him
to rule. Just as an unpopular senior chief could be removed by the members
of his lineage, the senior chiefs could depose the king by requesting that he
take his life. The king had no coercive power over his senior chiefs, but he
did have the sacred right to rule, and he could influence the senior chiefs
either by playing them off against each other or by rallying his people's support against the will of their own chiefs (Lloyd, 1965:567–572). Here,
among the Yoruba, residence, titles, and political organization were all regulated by the principles of patrilineal descent.

In other traditional African states, such as Buganda (in southern
Uganda), kinship became secondary to contractual, patron-client ties.
Although the Ganda have chiefs of their exogamous (i.e., out-marrying)
patriclans and clan segments, such descent groups are not strongly localized
corporate units, and their chiefs now serve as the managing directors of
ancestral burial grounds, a kind of headquarters for their widely dispersed
relatives. As the proverb says, "A man goes to live where he finds people of
his own sort," and these do not usually include close kin. "The Ganda atti-
tude seems to be that kinship is a good thing—but you can have too much
of it" (Southwold, 1965:102).

Originally, the king of Buganda (a position abolished in 1966) was the
most prominent of these hereditary, descent-group chiefs. Over the centuries, the kings gained the right to confirm their successors to office and, by
creating a new category of appointed bureaucrats with nonheritable titles
and estates, established an unusually centralized state under "a despotic
monarch who could remove areas from descent-group control and put in
charge of them personal appointees of his own choosing" (Fallers,
1964:172). As these "king's men" recruited their own clients as loyal assis-
tants, Ganda society became dominated by the custom of regularly changing
residence and patrons in the search for better prospects (Southwold,
1965:102; 1971:50). Clientship, rather than kinship, became the avenue of
social mobility.

Kinship in general is valued, because scattered, distant kinfolk offer a
wider choice of places to live. And where tenuous kinship links cannot be

traced, they are readily and regularly created by adopting strangers into other clans (Obbo, 1979). Although even unrelated neighbors are regarded and addressed as relatives (Obbo, 1980:115), precise kinship ties are considered an irrelevant embarrassment. The Ganda prefer to use personal names when referring to relatives outside the nuclear family, and as much as eighty years ago they had an imperfect command of such rarely used kinship terms (Southwold, 1971:50–51). Social life is dominated by clientship and the linkage of residential and social mobility. "'Friendship is stronger than kinship,' the Ganda say—though they add that kinship lasts longer" (Southwold, 1965:103).

■ CONTEMPORARY TRENDS

The Ganda's increasing emphasis on clientship as compared to kinship relations is also found in the traditional Hausa-Fulani city-states of northern Nigeria (Smith, 1965:134–135) and among the Hausa traders in the Yoruba

Although African societies are changing, the role of families in passing on valuable skills to their children remains important. In urban Zambia, a self-employed father is teaching his young son to make charcoal burners.

towns to the southwest (Cohen, 1969). It certainly resembles the progression
from family-based status and politics to the contractual relations and territorial political organization envisioned by the nineteenth-century lawyer-
anthropologists and social evolutionists Sir Henry Maine (*Ancient Law,*
1861) and Lewis Henry Morgan (*Ancient Society,* 1877). Yet, it is surely
mistaken to think, as they did, that social change follows an inevitable and
unilinear sequence and, accordingly, that African peoples are bound to arrive
at Western patterns of family and kinship organization. To be sure, they are
subject to the same political and economic forces that continue to shape our
own society. But in adapting to these challenges, Africans reinterpret their
own family and kinship patterns, and their disparate and often contradictory
adaptations will reflect a distinctly African blend of the old and new
(Epstein, 1981:191–194).

One of the greatest challenges to confront African peoples has been the
penetration of the world economic system; the strains and conflicts generated by this intrusive change have themselves generated further change. A
good example of this is the response of the Tswana (of Botswana) to the
migrant labor system of central and southern Africa. From 1820 to 1880,
first the Ndebele and then the Boers raided the Tswana for their cattle, grain,
land, and labor. The protests of the British missionaries had little effect until
Cecil Rhodes's British South Africa Company, concerned that the Boers
might deny it access to the rumored mineral wealth farther north, joined
their petitions for the creation of the Bechuanaland Protectorate in 1885.
When the Rand goldfields were discovered in 1886, a cash hut tax and labor
recruitment monopolies were established among the overcrowded and
impoverished Tswana to supply cheap, subsistence-level labor to the South
African gold and diamond mines.

Today, as described by Hoyt Alverson (1978) and Marianne Alverson
(1987), 90 percent of the Tswana males in the Gaborone countryside have
participated in the migrant labor system, while 60 percent of the males in
their twenties are away at work at any time—mostly in the South African
mines. Though the Tswana are cattle-keeping plow farmers, only 25 to 30
percent of the households in this area have both land and cattle needed for
farming, and rural productivity clearly suffers from rural poverty and the
shortage of able-bodied males. So the men go off to work—first, because
their wage remittances supply the only source of cash and consumer staples
for most rural households and, second, because their savings provide them
the bridewealth they need to marry. The women left behind do gain greater
personal freedom during their husbands' prolonged absences, but this comes
at the expense of greater domestic responsibilities and anxiety for their husbands' return.

But the migrant labor system fosters economic individualism that
threatens all kinds of Tswana family ties. The old ancestral cult, which once
supported extended family loyalties, was largely dead by the late 1920s

(Schapera, 1928). Even the nuclear family is threatened, for "children are less dependent upon parents and less mindful of filial obligations; the social importance of producing children has diminished; husbands are not so dependent upon their wives; and the family is less intimately connected with other social groupings" (Schapera, 1940:320). Youths seek to escape the grinding drudgery of life at home, and most fathers' estates are so small that the threat of disinheritance provides them little leverage over their increasingly autonomous sons. Sons are well aware that they can earn their own bridewealth and consumer goods by working in the mines. Once there, however, they begin to question the obligation to assist their parents and other relatives, who, they feel, envy their meager material success. Many become lost to the towns and never return. The older ones who eventually do go back resent, in turn, the autonomy demanded by their own children and other youths. And so the cycle repeats itself (Alverson, 1978; Schapera, 1940).

Migrant labor or cash cropping presumes a monetized economy, and this entails economic individualism and the commoditization of social relations. In general, those with limited access to money—like women—are the losers. Bridewealth is a good example, because, inasmuch as the supply of marriageable women is relatively fixed, the monetization of bridewealth payments often leads to rapid inflation of bridewealth costs (see, for example, Bohannan, 1959).

The switch from bridewealth paid in cattle to that paid in cash has had particularly devastating effects upon women among Zulu, Swazi, and other patrilineal peoples of southern Africa (Ngubane, 1987). Here the monetization of bridewealth has transformed it from a cooperative alliance between two extended families into a purely private transaction between the bride's husband and her father, for they alone are involved in calculating—and giving and receiving—her monetary value as a commodity. As such, neither the bride's nor the groom's extended family has much of a stake in the success of such a marriage. And since the cash transaction eliminates most of the former marriage ceremonies, the bride and her mother are denied not only the ceremonial cattle they once received but also the capital assets, the social and economic security, and the ritual power they represented. But the transformation to monetized bridewealth has also stimulated an increased demand for traditional healers and medicines and for new spiritual cults among women seeking to reverse their situation (Ngubane, 1987).

Reports concerning the death of the extended family are, to paraphrase Mark Twain, both exaggerated and premature. It is often claimed, for example, that the extended family system is an obstacle to economic development and that the obligatory diversion of scarce resources to assist less fortunate relatives is not only wasteful but discourages entrepreneurship and capital accumulation. One can—and Africans do—debate the wastefulness of assisting every needy relative. And while they take pride in this extended family safety net, it does not always work. In times of crisis, orphans, the elderly, and hungry poor must instead depend upon the mercy of formal welfare or relief institutions (Iliffe, 1987:212–213, 245–250).

Still, the economic criticisms of the African extended family system are only half-truths. Much of the assistance given to relatives goes to "the genuinely poor and needy, for whom the state provides no support," whereas the assistance given to finance relatives' schooling surely benefits the entire society. And where wealth and generosity are the traditional path to prestige, as in West Africa, such familial expectations can sometimes be a stimulus rather than a hindrance to entrepreneurship and economic development (Lloyd, 1969:90–92).

There is little doubt that the strain of extended family obligations is most strongly felt by the urban and educated African elite, since they often constitute the first and most important resource—both for food and lodging and personal contacts—for the school-leavers seeking work in town. "The average young Yoruba uses his kin-based network," particularly his close, well-to-do relatives, "with [the] expectation that this is the best way to secure not only a job but also a particular kind of job." Such hospitality is, however, both a financial and emotional drain, and it tends to wear thin over time. "In several cases, senior civil servants who had grown tired of the demands made on them, had rented slum accommodation for their younger brothers and nephews" (Gutkind, 1977:253; also Iliffe, 1987:172, 180–181). By the same token, unemployed relatives resent being put to work as house servants for their wealthier kin, so they eventually construct their own job-seeking networks and strike out on their own.

It is important to note here that the strength of family ties and obligations varies among different African peoples. Yoruba and Luo (Kenya) job seekers rely upon their urban relatives for assistance, while the Ibo tend to rely upon unrelated homeboys from their village improvement associations (Gutkind, 1977). The Luo migrants to Nairobi are famous for the strong patrilineal organization that links urban and rural kin (Parkin, 1978). But ethnicity is just one of the social identities that determine the strength of kinship ties between town and country. In East London, South Africa, for example, the "Red" (i.e., "traditional") Xhosa migrants remain encapsulated within their patrilineal networks of homeboy ties, while the "School" (i.e, urban, mission-educated) Xhosa are largely lost to their rural kin; but they are characterized by broader social networks composed of like-minded friends and selected maternal and paternal relatives (Mayer, 1971; Pauw, 1972).

African elites are generally tied to their rural kin. Most, however begrudgingly, send some money home—at least to the parents or other kin who reared them. The elite may, depending upon their relatives' needs, the state of the national economy, and the cost of urban life, entrust their children to their parents' care back home. Others provide school fees and

The extended family is a vital safety net during times of crisis. But in Ethiopia, many people have been forced to rely on relief organizations during recent droughts and civil war, because aid from kin was unavailable.

lodging for their own or for favorite classificatory brothers or sisters and put up relatives visiting the hospital or market. The gifts of food these visitors bring can be a welcome supplement to the household diet. Elite wives have a particular investment in maintaining these extended family ties because not only might they recruit a relative to provide childcare when they are away at work, but such ties also offer an insurance against the risk of divorce. And elite men must certainly maintain their family ties if they intend to retire among their relatives at home (Oppong, 1981).

The government bureaucrats in Jacobson's (1973) study of the Mbala elite are an exception that proves the rule. These "itinerant townsmen" are likely to be transferred many times in their careers and, at the expense of their poorer, rural relatives, to invest their energies in cultivating a wide network of similarly privileged friends of friends. Because they intend to retire in or around Uganda's urban centers, they can afford to neglect their relatives' annoying requests for aid and even manage to "forget" their kinship ties to lower-class relatives. This is not, he notes, the general pattern elsewhere in Africa (Jacobson, 1973:57–58, 131–137).

Yet, such family ties often place a real emotional strain on African elite marriages, particularly between the wife and her in-laws. The partners to such marriages are often from different ethnic groups, and the husband's kin may, if they disapprove of his wife's background, do everything to sabotage the marriage (e.g., Schuster, 1979:128–129). In turn, the wife may object when her lower-class in-laws insist on their customary rights to coresidence, property, and financial maintenance. Such couples may attempt to whittle down their extended family obligations in an attempt to realize the Euro-American model of the closed and cooperative nuclear family couple. But old customs die hard, and this is an elusive goal for the first-generation African elite who have little previous experience of geographical and social mobility. Such adjustments, as Oppong (1981) shows, are far easier for the rare second- and third-generation members of the African elite.

Another problem confronting elite couples are the children from previous marriages or affairs. Among the elite and subelite couples in Lusaka, the general "'rule' is that the man's wishes are paramount" (Schuster, 1979:108). Because household size is a measure of a man's personal prestige, his previous children are reclaimed from their natural mother, while the wife farms hers out to her maternal kin (Schuster, 1989:107–108, 129–130). A similar pattern seems to prevail among the African elite who live in Kampala, Nairobi, Dar es Salaam, and abroad (Obbo, 1987).

Given the cultural emphasis on childbearing, the elite woman courting a particular man must prove she will make a chaste and faithful wife and also demonstrate her fertility. She thus uses pregnancy as a tool—whether it be to lure a man from his older wife, to try to hang on to a man, or to nudge one into marriage. If she fails, she is stuck with an "outside" child who may well resurface, some six to seventeen years later, at the father's home. Given the fierce competition for elite men and her limited hold on her husband, the elite wife has little choice but to ignore her husband's extramarital affairs; instead, she perpetuates the mythical distinction between "good" and "bad" women by focusing her anger on rival female "home wreckers" (Obbo, 1987; Schuster, 1979).

The institution of polygyny persists among the African elite. The Nigerian elite disapprove of traditional "public" polygyny as a "lesser" form of marriage practiced only by "bush" Africans. Nonetheless, according to Karanja (1987), the vast majority of elite men practice "private" polygyny with "outside" wives. Female undergraduates refuse to date their male counterparts. They prefer an "outside" marriage with "a 'mature' man, who will 'set them up nicely' immediately after graduation, rather than insisting upon entering a first marriage with a 'struggling' fellow [student]" (Karanja, 1987:256). While this preference sets up intense conflicts with the male students, it is only the older "sugar daddies" who can provide these future elite women with a rented flat, monthly pocket money, children's allowances, a car, and all-expense-paid shopping trips to the Euro-American capitals.

The overwhelming majority of elite Nigerian women fiercely disapprove of these relationships, but they are unable to prevent them. Their husbands, however, enjoy the benefits and prestige from their peers. They defend such arrangements as a return to African tradition while retaining the semblance of monogamy for public consumption. As in Schuster's (1979) study, men and women entertain very different conceptions of what marriage entails. Although these different conceptions generate considerable tension between husbands and wives, the men continue to do just as they please (Karanja, 1987). As I once heard an African elite male tell a class of outraged female graduate students in the United States, "Africa is still a man's world," a point well documented by April Gordon in Chapter 10.

■ CONCLUSIONS

African family and kinship systems seem to be headed in varied and apparently contradictory directions. The competition for land and other scarce economic resources often seems to work against matrilineal descent. Yet it persists, and one finds an increasing trend toward female-headed households and the cultivation of matrilateral kin among even the most decidedly patrilineal peoples. Although the penetration of the world economic system has fostered economic individualism, the narrowing of kinship relations, and greater selectivity of relatives included in personal networks, the same individuals try to maintain, and even create, a wide network of real and fictive kin on whom they can rely for support and assistance.

While the specific patterns of African marriage and family forms continue to change, we see the new forms take on old meanings, and old forms invested with new ones. Whatever happens, African marriage and family forms will remain distinctly African. They will never be pale imitations of our own.

■ BIBLIOGRAPHY

Alverson, Hoyt. 1978. *Mind in the Heart of Darkness: Value and Self-Identity Among the Tswana of Southern Africa.* New Haven: Yale University Press.
Alverson, Marianne. 1987. *Under African Sun.* Chicago: University of Chicago Press.
Bascom, William. 1955. "Urbanization Among the Yoruba." *American Journal of Sociology* 60:446–454. Reprinted in Simon and Phoebe Ottenberg (eds). *Cultures and Societies of Africa.* New York: Random House, 1960. Pp. 255–267.
Beidelman, T. O. 1986. *Moral Imagination in Kaguru Modes of Thought.* Bloomington: Indiana University Press.
Bohannan, Paul. 1959. "The Impact of Money on an African Subsistence Economy." *Journal of Economic History* 19:491–503. Reprinted in George Dalton (ed.). *Tribal and Peasant Economies.* Garden City, NY: Natural History Press, 1967. Pp. 123–135.
———. 1965. "The Tiv of Nigeria." Pp. 515–546 in James L. Gibbs, Jr. (ed.). *Peoples of Africa.* New York: Holt, Rinehart and Winston.
Cohen, Abner. 1969. *Custom and Politics in Urban Africa: A Study of Hausa Migrants in Yoruba Towns.* Berkeley: University of California Press.
Colson, Elizabeth. 1953. "Social Control and Vengeance in Plateau Tonga Society." *Africa* 23:199–211. Reprinted in Elliot P. Skinner (ed.). *Peoples and Cultures of Africa.* Garden City, NY: Doubleday/Natural History Press, 1973. Pp. 397–415.
———. 1961. "The Plateau Tonga." Pp. 36–95 in David M. Schneider and Kathleen K. Gough (eds.). *Matrilineal Kinship.* Los Angeles: University of California Press.
———. 1974. *Tradition and Contract.* Chicago: Aldine Press.
———. 1980. "The Resilience of Matrilineality: Gwembe and Plateau Tonga Adaptations." Pp. 359–374 in Linda S. Cordell and Stephen Beckerman (eds.). *The Versatility of Kinship.* New York: Academic Press.
Divale, William T. 1974. "Migration, External Warfare, and Matrilocal Residence." *Behavior Science Research* 9:75–133.
Douglas, Mary. 1969. "Is Matriliny Doomed in Africa?" Pp. 123–137 in Mary Douglas and Phyllis M. Kaberry (eds.). *Man in Africa.* London: Tavistock.
Eades, Jeremy S. 1980. *The Yoruba Today.* Cambridge: Cambridge University Press.
Ember, Melvin, and Carol R. Ember. 1971. "The Conditions Favoring Matrilocal Versus Patrilocal Residence." *American Anthropologist* 73:571–594.
Epstein, Arnold L. 1981. *Urbanization and Kinship: The Domestic Domain on the Copperbelt of Zambia, 1950–1956.* New York: Academic Press.
Evans-Pritchard, E. E. 1940. *The Nuer: A Description of the Modes of Livelihood and Political Institutions of a Nilotic People.* Oxford: Clarendon Press.
———. 1950. "Kinship and the Local Community Among the Nuer." Pp. 360–391 in A. R. Radcliffe-Brown and Daryll Forde (eds.). *African Systems of Kinship and Marriage.* London: Oxford University Press.

Fallers, Lloyd A. 1964. "Social Stratification in Traditional Buganda." Pp. 151–209 in Lloyd A. Fallers. *Inequality: Social Stratification Reconsidered.* Chicago: University of Chicago Press, 1973.

Gluckman, Max. 1955. "The Peace in the Feud." Pp. 1–26 in Max Gluckman. *Custom and Conflict in Africa.* Oxford: Basil Blackwell.

Goody, Jack. 1976. *Production and Reproduction: A Comparative Study of the Domestic Domain.* Cambridge: Cambridge University Press.

Gough, Kathleen. 1971. "Nuer Kinship: A Re-examination." Pp. 79–121 in T. O. Beidelman (ed.). *The Translation of Culture.* London: Tavistock.

Gutkind, Peter. 1977. "Social Organization of the Unemployed in Lagos and Nairobi." Pp. 251–262 in Peter C. W. Gutkind and Peter Waterman (eds.). *African Social Studies.* New York: Monthly Review Press.

Harden, Blaine. 1990. *Africa: Dispatches from a Fragile Continent.* New York: W. W. Norton.

Hill, Polly. 1963. *The Migrant Cocoa-Farmers of Southern Ghana: A Study in Rural Capitalism.* Cambridge: Cambridge University Press.

———. 1986. *Development Economics on Trial: The Anthropological Case for a Prosecution.* Cambridge: Cambridge University Press.

Iliffe, John. 1987. *The African Poor: A History.* Cambridge: Cambridge University Press.

Jacobson, David. 1973. *Itinerant Townsmen: Friendship and Social Order in Urban Uganda.* Menlo Park, CA: Cummings.

Karanja, Wambui Wa. 1987. "'Outside Wives' and 'Inside Wives' in Nigeria: A Case Study of Changing Perceptions in Marriage." Pp. 247–261 in David Parkin and David Nyamwaya (eds.). *Transformations of African Marriage.* Manchester: Manchester University Press.

Karp, Ivan. 1978. "New Guinea Models in the African Savannah." *Africa* 48:1–16.

Kelly, Raymond C. 1985. *The Nuer Conquest: The Structure and Development of an Expansionist System.* Ann Arbor: University of Michigan Press.

Lan, David. 1985. *Guns and Rain: Guerrillas and Spirit Mediums in Zimbabwe.* London: James Currey; Berkeley: University of California Press.

Lloyd, Peter C. 1965. "The Yoruba of Nigeria." Pp. 549–582 in James L. Gibbs, Jr. (ed.). *Peoples of Africa.* New York: Holt, Rinehart and Winston.

———. 1969. *Africa in Social Change.* Baltimore: Penguin.

———. 1974. *Power and Independence: Urban Africans' Perception of Social Inequality.* London: Routledge and Kegan Paul.

Mair, Lucy. 1974. *African Societies.* Cambridge: Cambridge University Press.

Marwick, M. G. 1965. *Sorcery in Its Social Setting.* Manchester: Manchester University Press.

Mayer, Philip. 1971. *Townsmen or Tribesmen: Conservativism and the Process of Urbanization in a South African City.* Cape Town: Oxford University Press.

Middleton, John. 1960. *Lugbara Religion.* London: Oxford University Press.

Moore, Sally Falk. 1969. "Descent and Legal Position." Pp. 374–400 in Laura Nader (ed.). *Law in Culture and Society.* Chicago: Aldine Press.

Murdock, George Peter. 1949. *Social Structure.* New York: Macmillan.

Ngubane, Harriet. 1987. "The Consequences for Women of Marriage Payments in a Society with Patrilineal Descent." Pp. 173–182 in David Parkin and David Nyamwaya (eds.). *Transformations of African Marriage.* Manchester: Manchester University Press.

Obbo, Christine. 1979. "Village Strangers in Buganda Society." Pp. 227–241 in William A. Shack and Elliot P. Skinner (eds.). *Strangers in African Societies.* Berkeley: University of California Press.

————. 1980. *African Women: Their Struggle for Economic Independence.* London: Zed.

————. 1987. "The Old and the New in East African Elite Marriages." Pp. 263–280 in David Parkin and David Nyamwaya (eds.). *Transformations of African Marriage.* Manchester: Manchester University Press.

Okali, Christine. 1983. *Cocoa and Kinship in Ghana: The Matrilineal Akan of Ghana.* London: Routledge and Kegan Paul.

Oppong, Christine. 1981. *Middle Class African Marriage: A Family Study of Ghanaian Senior Civil Servants.* London: Allen and Unwin.

Parkin, David. 1972. *Palms, Wine, and Witnesses: Public Spirit and Private Gain in an African Farming Community.* Prospect Heights, IL: Waveland Press.

————. 1978. *The Cultural Definition of Political Response: Lineal Destiny Among the Luo.* New York and London: Academic Press.

Pauw, B. A. 1972. *The Second Generation: A Study of the Family Among Urbanized Bantu in East London.* Cape Town: Oxford University Press.

Peters, Pauline E. 1994. "Revisiting Matriliny: Land and Gender in Southern Malawi." Paper presented at the 1994 African Studies Association meetings, Toronto, Ontario, November 1994.

Phiri, Kings M. 1983. "Some Changes in the Matrilineal Family System Among the Chewa of Malawi Since the Nineteenth Century." *Journal of African History* 24:241–256.

Poewe, Karla O. 1979. "Women, Horticulture, and Society in Sub-Saharan Africa: Some Comments." *American Anthropologist* 81:115–117.

————. 1980. "Matrilineal Ideology: The Economic Activities of Women in Luapula, Zambia." Pp. 333–357 in Linda S. Cordell and Stephen Beckerman (eds.). *The Versatility of Kinship.* New York: Academic Press.

Pottier, Johan. 1988. *Migrants No More: Settlement and Survival in Mambwe Villages, Zambia.* Bloomington: Indiana University Press.

Richards, Audrey. 1939. *Land, Labour and Diet in Northern Rhodesia.* London: Oxford University Press.

————. 1940. *Bemba Marriage and Present Economic Conditions.* Rhodes-Livingstone Paper No. 4. Livingstone, Zambia: Rhodes-Livingstone Institute.

Saitoti, Tepilit Ole. 1986. *The Worlds of a Maasai Warrior: An Autobiography.* Berkeley: University of California Press.

Schapera, Isaac. 1928. "Economic Changes in South African Native Life." *Africa* 1:170–188. Reprinted in George Dalton (ed.). *Tribal and Peasant Economies.* Garden City, NY: Natural History Press, 1967. Pp. 136–154.

————. 1940. *Married Life in an African Tribe.* Harmondsworth, England: Penguin, 1971.

Schuster, Ilsa M. G. 1979. *New Women of Lusaka.* Palo Alto: Mayfield.

Siegel, Brian. 1984. *Farms or Gardens: Ethnicity and Enterprise on the Rural Zambian Copperbelt.* Ann Arbor: University Microfilms International.

Skjønsberg, Else. 1989. *Change in an African Village: Kefa Speaks.* West Hartford, CT: Kumarian Press.

Smith, Michael G. 1965. "The Hausa of Northern Nigeria." Pp. 121–155 in James L. Gibbs, Jr. (ed.). *Peoples of Africa.* New York: Holt, Rinehart and Winston.

Southall, Aidan. 1986. "The Illusion of Nath [Nuer] Agnation." *Ethnology* 25:1–20.

Southwold, Martin. 1965. "The Ganda of Uganda." Pp. 83–118 in James L. Gibbs, Jr. (ed.). *Peoples of Africa.* New York: Holt, Rinehart and Winston.

————. 1971. "Meanings of Kinship." Pp. 35–56 in Rodney Needham (ed.). *Rethinking Kinship and Marriage.* London: Tavistock.

Sudarkasa, Niara. 1980. "African and Afro-American Family Structure." *The Black Scholar* 11:37–60.

Turner, V. W. 1957. *Schism and Continuity in an African Society.* Manchester: Manchester University Press.

Vansina, Jan. 1980. "Lignage, idéologie et histoire en Afrique équatoriale." *Enquêtes et documents d'histoire africaine* 4: 133–155.

Watson, William. 1958. *Tribal Cohesion in a Money Economy.* Manchester: Manchester University Press.

Wilson, Monica. 1979. "Strangers in Africa: Reflections on Nyakyusa, Nguni, and Sotho Evidence." Pp. 51–66 in William A. Shack and Elliot P. Skinner (eds.). *Strangers in African Societies.* Los Angeles: University of California Press.

▪ 10 ▪

Women and Development
April A. Gordon

Since Ester Boserup's (1970) pioneering work on women and development in the Third World, studies continue to confirm her findings that women are not equal beneficiaries with men of the fruits of so-called modernization and development. Studies of women in Africa are consistent in showing that although there have been some gains for women, such as greater educational parity with men or official declarations professing support for gender equality, overall the prospects for women are ominous in many areas. As in other parts of the world, African women have neither the political, legal, educational, nor economic opportunities of their male counterparts. Men in Africa overwhelmingly dominate the institutions of society and have used their positions more often than not to further the control and advantages men have in both the public and domestic arenas.

In discussing the conditions peculiar to Africa that affect women's status and roles, several general factors must be kept in focus. One is that the overall economic and political problems of Africa make life difficult for most African men as well as women. Inequality, oppression, poverty, and lack of opportunity are widespread societal concerns. Nonetheless, women as a group suffer more and have access to fewer resources and opportunities than men do. We must also note that African societies and gender roles are highly diverse; this makes efforts at generalization somewhat tentative and not applicable to every society. Also important is that class as well as gender influences the status and opportunities of individual women. That is, girls born to more elite families will typically have the opportunity to acquire a good education and prestigious career, although they are unlikely to achieve great political or economic power on their own. However, they are prime candidates for marriage to the African men who do wield power and influence. This contrasts dramatically with the modest or nonexistent prospects their peasant or working-class sisters have. The results are that although women as a group suffer from inequality, the interests and perspectives of elite women often diverge from those of poorer women. Last, the forms gender inequality take in Africa reflect indigenous, precolonial, and European influences. European expansion into Africa during the colonial period both undermined sources of status and autonomy that women had and strengthened elements of indigenous male dominance or "patriarchy." At the same time, Western gender ideology and practices that promote male dominance and female dependency have been superimposed on Africa. Since independence, Africa's male leaders have continued to add laminations to the patriarchal structures they inherited from their colonizers, often so with the support of Western international investors and donors whose "development" assistance mostly goes to men.

As the following discussion shows, the culmination of precolonial, colonial, and postindependence history is the prospect that women in general will continue to lose ground economically, politically, and socially unless concerted efforts are made by women themselves, African governments, and the international community to ensure that the fruits of development are extended equally to women and men.

■ WOMEN IN PRECOLONIAL AFRICA

Sub-Saharan Africa is a diverse continent whose precolonial history and culture may never be accurately known, since little of it was written down; so it is with considerable caution that we attempt to generalize about gender roles (or anything else) today or in the past. The accuracy of reports on precolonial times must also be questioned, since much of it was filtered through the cultural biases and perceptions of European males during the period of slavery or colonialism. Referring to the British, but applicable to other Europeans as well, Hammond and Jablow (1970:197) conclude that "four centuries of writing about Africa have produced a literature which describes not Africa but the British response to it. . . . As in a morality play, the British and the Africans are the exemplars of civilization and savagery, respectively." Depictions of women as dominated, servile beasts of burden is an example of the kinds of distortions that have resulted from European ethnocentrism in dealing with African cultures. Moreover, since the 1500s, beginning with the Atlantic slave trade, African societies were increasingly distorted by contact with Europeans. Even before most Africans ever saw a white man, the impact of slavery was felt in all parts of the continent. Population movements, wars, disease, loss of productive labor power, and a breakdown of familiar social institutions altered indigenous social patterns (Cutrufelli, 1983:14–16).

Despite problems of the reliability of data, some patterns of gender relationships were prevalent, if not universal, in Africa before the period of European penetration. Politically, for instance, African women in most societies have been influential political actors in informal ways, if not through formal political roles. Women varied from being highly subordinated "legal minors" under the control of their menfolk among groups like the Tswana and Shona in southern Africa to holding positions as chiefs among the Mende and Serbro of Sierra Leone and "headmen" among the Tonga of Zambia. In some societies women even had formal roles in male councils. The figure of the queen mother in many societies of western Africa was very influential, and it was she who selected the king. Women warriors fought for the *fon* (king) of Dahomey, and powerful warrior queens led their people in battle. Notable examples are Queen Amina of Hausaland, who ruled in the fifteenth and sixteenth centuries, and Nzinga of Angola, who led the earliest and most effective resistance against the Portuguese (Parpart, 1988:208–210).

In addition to such important formal roles as these, women's organizations existed that acted as parallel authority structures to those of males. These included women's courts, market authorities, secret societies, and age-grade institutions (Staudt, 1987:195; Parpart, 1988:208–210). Most generally, parallel authority structures allowed men and women to exercise authority over their own sex and activities. These organizations reflected the sexual division of labor and the different spheres of activity for men and women. There was also recognition that men could best make decisions about men's affairs as could women about their own concerns. One example of parallel male-female organizations was societies that conferred honorific titles upon accomplished members of the community. Both titled men and women had a great deal of prestige and exercised considerable influence. The *ekwe* title, associated with the goddess Idemili, is a case in point. This title is taken by high-status Ibo women of Nigeria, and the most powerful of these women, the *agba ekwe,* reputedly was the most powerful political figure among her people (Amadiume, 1987). In some cases, goddess-focused religions provided a basis for women to control major religio-political functions through societies dedicated to the goddess. Ambrose Moyo, in Chapter 11, points out other religious leadership roles held by women as well as men, such as shaman, diviner, and spirit medium.

Even though women did have these positions of influence and power, males typically had more formal authority positions than females, so a degree of male dominance existed. For most women, power was (and still is) exercised indirectly and informally as sisters, mothers, and wives within the extended family system and was closely associated with women's economic power. Where women had rights to land, animals, labor, and the products of their own or others' labor, their status was higher than if such resources were under male control. Enhancing women's position was the critical role they played in the sexual division of labor within their households. Women were producers: they grew most of the family's food, tended animals, and made tools and other articles used by the family. They cooked, helped construct

Photo: World Bank

African women play vital economic roles as well as being mothers. This Zambian woman in her maize field exemplifies both roles.

residences and other buildings, hauled wood, and so on. In many cases, women also sold their surplus in local markets, thus dominating these commercial activities and demonstrating their business acumen. Women were also reproducers in societies where children were wealth, old age security, and the guarantors that one would be venerated as an ancestor after death and not forgotten. (See, again, Moyo's chapter on religion, in which he discusses the significance of ancestors.) These vital roles were normally translated into high status for women and more autonomy than was typical for women in most regions of the world.

Other manifestations of this relative autonomy and high status of women are seen in marriage customs. Bridewealth, typical in Africa, is a custom that requires a transfer of goods and services from the male's family to that of the bride or to the bride herself. Bridewealth is not to be equated with "selling" daughters. Rather, it indicates the high value attached to women in African society; families must be compensated for the loss of their daughters and the wealth she will bring to her husband's family. Bridewealth not only adds to the prospective bride's sense of her own worth but also provides material benefits for her family. In fact, women often work together both to arrange suitable marriages and to maximize the bridewealth. Traditionally, African women do not take their husband's name when they marry, thus retaining their own identity with respect to their family of origin. Once married, a woman has the right to leave a husband who mistreats her or one with whom she no longer chooses to live. Certain factors, however, discourage this: her family might have to return the bridewealth, or, in patrilineal families, the woman might have to leave her children with her husband and his family. But, unlike in many cultures, a divorced or widowed African woman usually has little difficulty attracting a new spouse, again a tribute to the importance of women and their vital contributions to family and community. (For more on bridewealth and family systems, see Chapter 9.)

Polygyny, a man's right to have more than one wife, has been widely accepted in Africa. Often misunderstood by Europeans as a sign of women's low status, polygyny is more accurately indicative of the centrality of women to the economic well-being of the family. Since family labor was the primary means of accumulating wealth, acquiring women was necessary to family prosperity. By having more than one wife, the family gained not only her productive contributions but also more children. Women in the family also benefited from the greater prosperity of their households. Additional wives helped each other with tasks, provided companionship (often lacking with husbands), and gave pregnant, nursing, or older women a needed respite from the sexual demands of their husbands.

■ EUROPEAN PENETRATION:
THE COLONIAL LEGACY

By the time outright colonial domination of Africa began in the 1800s, some loss of autonomy for African women may have already occurred. A major reason is that the disease, warfare, and dislocations slavery introduced in earlier centuries put more pressure on women to reproduce and perform maternal functions in order to offset population losses that were occurring (Cutrufelli, 1983:2). Control over women's productive activities in the family may also have intensified.

The record is much clearer on the impact of colonialism. African societies were forceably integrated into the expanding global capitalist economy dominated by the European powers. To extract the mineral and commodity wealth of Africa and to ensure a cheap labor supply, radical changes were imposed. The commercialization of agriculture through the introduction of cash crops altered the customary gender division of labor in ways mostly disadvantageous to women. Men were taught to grow new cash crops such as cocoa and coffee for export, while women continued to grow food crops for the family and local consumption. Men were forced into the wage economy to work in the mines, on the plantations, or in town; most women remained in the rural areas, often assuming the responsibilities their absent menfolk could no longer perform. Schooling and the teaching of new skills were made available primarily to males. All in all, although both men and women were exploited within the colonial economy, men gained some access to important resources such as money, skills, land, and education less available to women.

Men also gained political advantages as customary sources of female power were ignored or undermined. Europeans imposed their own prejudices about the proper authority of men over women by dealing only with male leaders. All-male "native authorities" were created in many areas to allow some local government, based on frequently arguable "traditional" or "customary" laws. Tradition was usually interpreted in ways that favored men's control over women, allowing men to gain at women's expense (see Chanock, 1982). For example, as men were provided new commercial opportunities in cash crop agriculture, they began to assert their customary rights to land and the labor of wives in order to accumulate income for themselves; they were not obligated to share this money with their wives. In some cases, this resulted in great wealth for some enterprising men. For instance, among the Beti in Cameroon, some men married many women in order to get virtually free labor from them on their cash crop farms. By custom, women had to help their husbands for little compensation even though these farms were now commercial ventures bearing little similarity to the subsistence family farms of the past (Guyer, 1984). In the Zambian Copperbelt, wives were required to perform their customary domestic services for their husbands in town, although they were unable to claim any share of their husband's income. Unable to get jobs of their own, women often had to support themselves by selling sex, food, homebrew, or domestic services to other men (Langley, 1983:94–95). Not only were women economically responsible for themselves, but the burden of providing for children also fell mostly on women—another matter of custom from precolonial times.

At the same time as their responsibilities were growing, women's rights to land were undermined. Often, the most or the best land was given to the men for cash crops, and there were growing pressures to deprive women of their inheritance rights to land in favor of males in the family (Cutrufelli, 1983:64–69). One of the most damaging colonial land policies for women involved efforts to introduce private ownership of land. In Kenya in the 1950s, the Swynnerton Act was to provide deeds to male heads of households, replacing the African land tenure system that ensured everyone's access to land (Davison, 1988:164–165). Such policies have continued in the postcolonial period. They pose a major threat to the economic well-being of women, since land is the crucial resource for survival among the large numbers of Africans who are small farmers.

Colonial officials and male elders often worked together to get better control of women. Frequently, European officials did not want women in the towns; they wanted only the labor of African men. Therefore, many restrictions were placed on the movement of women (Cutrufelli 1983:22–26). Zambia (then Northern Rhodesia) is a good example of colonial regulation of migratory labor in southern Africa. Rural tribal authorities were given the right to prevent unmarried women and children from moving to the towns, and urban authorities had the power to send those who defied such restrictions back to the villages. Some women did marry or cohabit with men in the towns, but they had no access to wage labor until late in the colonial period (Hansen, 1987:11–13).

Among pastoralists, the introduction of new property and commercial relations also eroded the status of women. Among the Tugen of Kenya and other groups, for instance, women's rights to cattle and the status they once derived from the vital tasks they performed were undermined as men asserted their right to ownership of animals and other property. Ownership rights were redefined in Western commercial terms. This now meant that men, not women, could make decisions and profit from the sale or acquisition of family property. Women themselves became another form of property to be controlled as they lost effective control over their own labor. They had to work for their husbands in order to survive, because they had no rights to own wealth-producing property of their own. Compounding her economic vulnerability, a woman, if divorced, had no right to the wealth she helped her husband acquire through her labor (Kettel, 1986). (See Lovett, 1989, for a good general discussion of gender and the colonial state.)

■ THE POSTINDEPENDENCE PERIOD: DEPENDENCY AND INEQUALITY OF WOMEN

In many ways, the problems of women since independence are a continuation of policies and forces set in motion during the colonial period. Although African gender relations were transformed during the colonial period to further European economic and political exploitation of Africa, such distorted and patently unfair practices often continue to be justified by appeals to "African tradition." Despite women's contributions to the struggle for independence and rhetoric in favor of equality for all, the new African states and social institutions are largely Africanized replicas of their colonial predecessors. Advantages men had gained in access to education, jobs, and property enabled them to gain control of most of the wealth, jobs, and leadership positions in newly independent African countries.

Male dominance has been enhanced as many of Africa's new Westernized elites, both male and female, have modeled their own gender roles on those of their Western tutors. These roles are, in turn, disseminated to the masses via education, the media, and many government and women's organizations (cf. Nweke, 1985; Obadina, 1985; Nzomo, 1989; Bujra, 1986). Rather than promoting equal political and economic rights and opportunities for women in their societies, women are often encouraged instead to pursue domesticity and economic subordination to a male who is "head of the family" (see Schuster, 1982). Male control of formal political power in Western-style political systems is widely portrayed as a natural extension of such male-dominated African institutions as chieftaincies and councils of elders. While this might appear to be consonant with previous gender roles of African societies in which men and women had distinctly different roles in the division of labor, current role expectations are operating in a very different economic and political environment. As in other parts of the world, access to money and other economic resources (e.g., land, businesses, wage jobs, credit) are vital to survival, social mobility, and status.

However, while housewives in the West have a measure of legal protection to compensate for their economic dependency on their husbands, economically dependent women in Africa typically do not have guaranteed rights to their husband's income or property, nor do their children should the husband die or the marriage end in divorce. Moreover, male political power is no longer exercised primarily through families and local organizations in which women have leverage in the decisionmaking process. Power is now exercised through the state and bureaucratic institutions whose centralization of power and control of resources are vastly greater than those of the typical decentralized political institutions of the past. In Chapter 4, Donald Gordon discusses how important access to state power and patron-client relationships are in Africa. If women have few positions in the new institutions of power and men are allowed to make the decisions, women face the risk of being politically, economically, and socially marginalized and their interests neglected within their societies.

The minority of Africans who would challenge pervasive male dominance face a double obstacle. Not only must they contend with the structures in their societies that perpetuate existing gender inequality, but the foreign "development establishment" that African nations depend upon for assistance is imbued with many of the same biases against women. Western corporations, lending institutions, governments, and development agencies are all male-dominated institutions from male-dominated societies. Gender inequality has been such an inherent feature of Western culture that the discriminatory effect of seemingly "neutral" policies inevitably occurs. Sometimes it has simply been assumed that men would be the leaders and the beneficiaries of aid and training. In other cases, projects and development assistance that favor men are justified by the resistance of Africans and their cultures to providing equity for women. For example, extension services are often given only to men because they are "heads of households," and they might resist resources being given to their wives. Regardless of the assumptions made, the net results are usually the same: women lose access to the resources necessary to improve their lives and often the lives of their children.

With the above general perspectives in mind, three topics will be looked at in more depth: (1) women in the economy, (2) women and politics, and (3) prospects for women.

■ **WOMEN IN THE ECONOMY**

Most women and men in sub-Saharan Africa are still employed in agriculture—66 percent according to the World Bank (1989:8). On average, women are 46 percent of the agricultural labor force (Gladwin and McMillan, 1989:348) and produce 70 percent of the staple food (World Bank, 1989:103). But labor force statistics underrate the amount of work most women perform. Women work in the fields an average of 1,000 hours per year and spend an additional three to four hours a day preparing food, cooking, and collecting firewood and water. While their husbands also farm in many cases, during the long slack season men reportedly spend most of the day drinking or visiting friends and relatives (Faruqee and Gulhati, 1983:36–37). Women commonly complain about the inequitable division of labor, that women work while men sit around and tell them what to do, or that women must carry heavy loads (water, wood, children) while the man carries nothing. They also complain that men do not support their families

Preparing food and fetching water are among the many time-consuming jobs performed daily by women.

Women also grow most of the food in Africa.

but spend their money on drink, other women, or goods for themselves. Many men even try to claim for themselves money the woman earns herself (Staudt, 1987:206–207). Although the husband may use his income (including that derived from his wife's labor on his farm) to pay off family debts, pay taxes, buy medicine, and offer gifts to his wife, men often spend more on bikes, watches, and radios for themselves. By contrast, women use most of their income for the household and their children (Blumberg, 1995:6–11; Weekes-Vagliani, 1985:105–106).

Most women farmers get little help to ease their burdens. As Virginia DeLancey points out in her chapter on African economies, only a small share of investment has gone to rural development in most African countries, and investments that are made go primarily for cash crops, mechanization, extension services, and resettlement projects that mostly help men. More and more women are managing the family farm alone as men turn to other forms of employment. Because farms are increasingly likely to be registered to the husband as the sole owner, women are often ineligible for most farm aid available only to farmers with legal title to their land (World Bank, 1989:103). Even worse, without legal title to the farm, a woman stands to lose everything should her husband die or divorce her.

Not surprisingly, women as well as men are seeking new employment opportunities in the towns. But here too women often find their opportuni-

ties circumscribed. One reason is that women are not given the same education or training opportunities as men. The gap between schooling for males
and females remains wide: 81 girls are in primary school for every 100 boys;
in secondary school the ratio of girls per 100 boys drops to 72 (World Bank,
1995:219). While there are educated women in good jobs and professions,
most wage jobs for women are in jobs that, in the West, are typically held by
women: as nurses, teachers, clerks, and secretaries. But even these jobs are
hard to get, and most women find work in the informal (nonwage) sector
selling foodstuffs, homebrew, or services (including prostitution) as they did
during the colonial period. In much of West Africa, women still dominate
local markets for food. In general, commerce has been a major means for
women to get ahead, despite the hostility such successful and independent
women often arouse (Vellenga, 1986). In countries like Zaire, husbands
have the legal right to take over their wives' business assets in the "interests
of the household." Women cannot even open a bank account without their
husbands' permission, and they find it difficult to get commercial credit
(MacGaffey, 1986).

Only in the past decade or so have Western development agencies come
to realize how their efforts have often hampered rather than helped African
women. They erroneously thought that if men were better off, women and
general family welfare would improve as well. Instead, it is now recognized
that women's economic opportunities and income more often declined while
their workload increased. Examples include Bernal's (1988) study in northern Sudan and Carney's (1988) study in The Gambia; both studies found that
irrigation schemes frequently result in men gaining control of, if not always
title to, land and production decisions at women's expense. Resettlement
schemes also tend to give male farmers land, subsidies, and credit, as in
Cameroon (Goheen, 1988) and Zimbabwe (Pankhurst and Jacobs, 1988),
although women are required to work on these farms, continue to grow food
for their families, and perform other domestic chores such as cooking and
childcare. It is not unusual for men to take the income from the farm or other
earnings and spend it on beer, women, or goods for themselves. In the
Zimbabwe study, several women reported how the state marketing board
paid their husbands for their cash crops, and how the men then decided how
much to give their wives. If women complained about the lack of money,
they were beaten. Some women resorted to selling their sexual services to
other men to get additional money for household expenses.

To help address these inequities, women in development (WID) initiatives have been given more attention since the 1970s. For example, to
address the inequities in U.S. development aid, the Percy Amendment
passed by Congress has required a "women's impact statement" in every
USAID project in developing countries. USAID now stresses that improving the education and status of women is a key element in its objectives of
promoting "sustainable development" in Africa (Green, 1994). The UN,

European donor agencies, and most major foundations have developed or expanded women's programs as well (Newland, 1991:124). The World Bank in its publications (e.g., 1989:103–104; 1990) stresses the need to redress the neglect of women's education, health, training, and access to productive resources. In 1987, a Women in Development Division was created, and in 1989, a coordinator for women in development was included in the Bank's four regional complexes, including Africa. More than one-third of all the Bank's 1989 operations in Africa reportedly included actions specifically addressed to women (World Bank, 1990:10). Nonetheless, the gap between men and women in growing, and only a small proportion of development assistance is directly targeting or benefiting women (Russo et al., 1989; Goetz, 1991).

■ WOMEN AND POLITICS

Since independence, women have been excluded from most of the important political positions in African states. For instance, there have been no women heads of state, and as of the mid-1980s, women held only 6 percent of the legislative positions in Africa. In only a few states—e.g., Rwanda, Cameroon, Malawi, and Senegal—were over 10 percent of legislative positions filled by women. At cabinet-level or equivalent positions, only 2 percent were held by women; in half of Africa's states, there were no women at all in cabinet-level positions. Women were only somewhat better represented at local levels of government (Parpart, 1988:8–9). A recent study of twenty-seven countries by the Economic Commission for Africa shows that women's political participation at the national level has not increased significantly; less than 8 percent of such offices are held by women. The highest percentage of women in parliament is found in South Africa, where women hold one-fourth of the seats in the new House of Assembly (Morna, 1995:58). Ruling Africa has been largely a male preserve, and the state has been more responsive to the interests of men than of women.

Africa's male political leaders rarely speak out against the culture of male dominance, most believing that gender arrangements are "natural" or "traditional" and must not change. Daniel arap Moi, president of Kenya, exemplifies this view. When Kenyan women at the International Conference on Women in Nairobi in 1985 recommended that women be more equitably represented in parliament, Moi responded that "God made man the head of the family," and "challenging that was tantamount to criticizing God" (in Staudt, 1987:50). Given such views, it is not surprising that as of September 1987, 51 percent of African governments had not signed the UN Forward-Looking Strategies accord agreed upon at the Nairobi conference (versus 42 percent of governments in the rest of the world). Many of those who have signed have no serious intention or program of action to promote women's equality and end sex discrimination as stipulated in the accord, according to Longwe (1990:4, 16).

Women have not passively accepted the economic and political disadvantages they face. Formal and informal women's associations have flourished in the postindependence period. Many grassroots self-help groups have been formed, often by poor, peasant women who are so frequently neglected by government or development agencies. These groups provide vital economic assistance, such as credit for farming or business ventures, or other forms of mutual assistance to members (e.g., childcare, piped water). They have their roots in precolonial women's groups where women worked together and provided each other assistance within the extended family network or in age-based groups (Enabulele, 1985; Safilios-Rothschild, 1990). For many women, groups are the only way they can get power or the resources they need because husbands have no power over the group as they do over women as wives. Group solidarity also builds women's self-confidence, and many women feel their efforts have improved their lives and the welfare of their families and communities (Kabira and Nzioki, 1993:62–64, 73).

Some women's groups reflect Western colonial influences. During colonialism, many African women's groups were created and modeled on Western "ladies associations." They supported various social welfare activities in the community (such as literacy campaigns) or held classes on such homemaking activities as cooking and sewing for women. Typically dominated by middle-class and elite African women, these groups, since independence, have been active in promoting such causes as nation-building ("good citizenship") and in making many useful social welfare contributions: promoting health campaigns, environmental cleanups, and female education; providing daycare for working mothers; and assisting orphans and the handicapped (Enabulele, 1985).

After the 1975 International Women's Year, international organizations began to promote women's groups in the hope of improving women's economic, political, and social positions. Women's groups were used to implement small-scale, income-earning "women's projects," such as commercial handicrafts production. Isolated from mainstream development efforts, however, these projects were rarely successful. Women got neither the training nor the political influence to alter women's disadvantaged position (Safilios-Rothschild, 1990:102).

There are other problems limiting the effectiveness of women's groups in advancing the status of women. Some of these problems reflect women's lack of education, management training, or capital. Insufficient linkages between organizations is another problem. Social welfare work performed by women has the disadvantage of putting additional burdens on women's time. While this may help community development, it does not usually earn women themselves commensurate tangible rewards. A good example of this was a water and soil conservation program in rural Kitui in Kenya. Women did most of the work in the project, which involved strenuous activities such as terracing the land and planting trees, but they were given fewer project resources in the way of training, cash, or decisionmaking power than the small minority of men in the project (Safilios-Rothschild, 1990:103–104).

Perhaps the greatest problem is that most women and women's groups do not challenge the fundamental gender roles that subordinate them to males and that extol the sexual division of labor that gives wealth and power primarily to men. This is partly because most national women's organizations are controlled by more educated, middle-class women who by and large accept a Western "housewife" view of "a woman's place." They can more often afford to imitate the Western housewife role as invented by the West, that is, the woman who manages the domestic arena (home and children) and who is to varying degrees financially dependent on a male breadwinner for money. Their interests and perspectives often diverge widely from the masses of less-educated women who must earn their own incomes to survive as well as take care of the home and children, yet who find that discrimination and inequality too often frustrate their efforts. Rather than offend the male ruling establishment, women's groups tend to be antifeminist and promote their own interests in securing more access to their husband's income, seeking more advantageous marriage and divorce laws, and promoting education in the domestic arts or beauty and fashion. Such groups are sometimes insensitive to or unresponsive to poor rural and urban women and their needs (Bujra, 1986; Staudt, 1987; Kabira and Nzioki, 1993).

Despite their shortcomings, women's organizations are growing in number and importance as African women struggle for more rights, opportunities, and economic resources. Some have achieved notable success in promoting greater political and economic empowerment for women. In Kenya's 1992 elections, a record six women were elected to parliament, largely due to the efforts of the National Committee on the Status of Women (NCSW). NCSW's agenda is to increase women's political participation and officeholding, eliminate all discriminatory laws against women, mainstream gender issues in political party documents and programs, and sensitize both men and women to issues of gender equity (Nzomo and Kibwana, 1993). In war-torn Mozambique, the almost all-female, 11,000-member General Union of Cooperatives (UGC) has attained remarkable economic success. The union has built 210 farm cooperatives that supply the capital city of Maputo with most of its fruit and vegetables. Recent privatization reforms have allowed the co-op to assist its members to acquire land titles, expand their economic activities, and open their own bank accounts for the first time. Co-op women are breaking gender stereotypes by learning new skills for such nontraditional jobs as electrician and mason. These and other accomplishments have increased both the number and status of UGC members and leaders (Lima, 1994). Other women's groups are confronting such serious social issues as sexual harassment, domestic violence, female circumcision, and abortion rights (Ampofo, 1993; Tripp, 1991:28–29; TAMWA, 1993).

Growing local and international pressure to include women in development planning has helped to some extent to raise African men's and women's consciousness that neglecting women and discriminating against them is hurting the entire development effort. One response has been for many African governments (e.g., in Cameroon, The Gambia, Kenya, Lesotho, and Zimbabwe) to create special women's bureaus in the government to deal with women's issues and, as in Kenya, to coordinate all women's programs in the country. The problem is that these bureaus are not given much power or funding, and as government organs they cannot be highly critical of government policies or push for radical change (Nzomo, 1989). Another approach to expanding women's political participation in government, as in Tanzania, is to set aside a guaranteed proportion of seats in the legislature for women (Meena, 1989:31). There are also some verbal commitments to provide more resources for women.

As already mentioned, as of 1987 most African governments had not signed the UN Forward-Looking Strategies accord on women's rights (Longwe, 1990), and as Morna (1994) reports, only thirty-three of fifty-three African governments have signed the 1979 Convention on the Elimination of all Forms of Discrimination Against Women. At the regional level, SADCC (now SADC) delegates, at their 1991 annual conference, issued a statement advocating equal access for women to land, credit, education, and services, along with the elimination of all legal, social, and economic barriers (Scott, 1995:82–85). The problem is that despite such public pronouncements, governments are often unwilling or unable to carry through with the far-reaching reforms that would be needed to make practice in compliance with egalitarian sentiments.

This does not mean that no real reforms have been made. For instance, countries such as Côte d'Ivoire, Kenya, and Ethiopia give women the right to inherit and own property. In Côte d'Ivoire, polygyny and bridewealth are now forbidden (World Bank, 1986:40). In Islamic Senegal, women can no longer legally be married without their consent, men cannot take additional wives without their first wife's consent, and men can no longer repudiate (divorce) their wives unless a judge grants the divorce (Sow, 1989:34–35). Since 1985, Ghana's Intestate Succession and Property Laws require that all customary marriage and family property be registered and distinction made between self-acquired and family property. If a man dies intestate (without a will), his wife and children now get three-quarters of his property; one-quarter goes to his matrikin. Previously among Ghana's matrilineal ethnic groups, most of a man's estate could be taken by his mother's side of the family, leaving his wife and children with little or nothing (Dei, 1994:132–133). Kenya's 1994–1996 national economic program calls for joint family decisionmaking on land use and an equal distribution of economic benefits between spouses. The attorney general has set up a task force to review all laws affecting the status of women (Munyakho, 1994:8–9).

Such changes do suggest that in some countries efforts to improve women's rights and opportunities are being made. The rate and extent of change are highly variable across the continent, however, and there is often considerable resistance to reforms that would undermine "traditional" male dominance over the household or the sexual division of labor that relegates most domestic and childrearing tasks to women. Moreover, legal rights can result in little improvement in women's lives if access to education, health and reproductive services, training, and productive resources are not made more available as well.

■ PROSPECTS FOR AFRICAN WOMEN

I began this chapter by expressing concern for the future of the majority of Africa's women. Although having an education and/or affluent parents improves women's opportunities, the vast majority are limited by both economic underdevelopment and sex discrimination. Consequently, most women will, for the foreseeable future, continue to have a very difficult existence as subsistence farmers. It is becoming recognized, however, that raising agricultural production in Africa will require helping these women farm; this means giving them title to or control of land in their own names as well as providing agricultural training and extension services, credit, better technology, and so on (see World Bank, 1989; Palmer, 1991).

But what about other women? Most women who live in the towns and burgeoning cities of Africa have ambitions for nonagricultural jobs and upward mobility. The evidence suggests that most of these women will, as is true of their male counterparts, continue to find meager remuneration from what is called the "informal sector" of microbusinesses specializing in services, crafts, repairs, and petty manufacturing and trade (cf. Robertson, 1995; Vuorela, 1992; Freeman, 1993). The informal sector, if given the support rather than hostility or indifference of government, could be the fertile ground for the expansion of indigenous African entrepreneurial activity and economic growth. The informal sector has already been the launching ground for successful African businesswomen in such areas as trading, food processing, and real estate (cf. Tripp, 1992; Nelson, 1988; MacGaffey, 1986). If African governments removed legal barriers for women entrepreneurs and obstacles to their acquiring credit and technology, thus allowing women to compete, traditional female qualities such as hard work, thrift,

Women's contributions to national development and their need for economic assistance, such as better tools and agricultural extension services, are receiving greater attention in many African countries.

and skills in commerce could conceivably promote a large, female, small- to medium-business class.

Although some women by choice or necessity are depending on their own businesses or jobs for survival or personal advancement, many socially mobile women who rationally assess the limited opportunities for women pursue either marriage or an informal sexual relationship with men to get ahead. This is the same strategy most women throughout the world are compelled to "choose" as long as economic and political resources are monopolized by men. Access to the resources of men can provide women with greater economic rewards than trying to earn an independent income in a sex-biased labor market (cf. Nelson, 1988; Dinan, 1983).

The dilemma of Africa's women who are trying to survive or get ahead in male-dominated societies is eloquently addressed by two of Africa's best-known male novelists, Chinua Achebe (Nigeria) and Ngugi wa Thiong'o (Kenya). (See Chapter 12 for more on these two writers and on women writers who are critical of African societies' treatment of women.) While perhaps overstating the case to some extent, their accounts suggest that opportunities for most women are limited to being subordinate wives, "sugar girls," or mistresses (i.e., the "ready-to-yield") to well-to-do men. By the same token, elite men gain status from the number of women they have.

In Achebe's *Anthills of the Savannah,* Beatrice, an educated career woman in a government ministry, had to overcome the socialization of her family, who discouraged her ambition and pressured her to be "feminine"— that is, a pleasing and compliant decoration (wife) for some elite man. Beatrice's feminism contrasts with the sexism of her male newspaper-editor friend, Ikem, a champion of the oppressed who nonetheless treats women primarily as sex objects not to be taken seriously.

Even more biting than Achebe, Ngugi denounces throughout his satirical novel *Devil on the Cross* Africa's subordination and denigration of women. While focusing generally on the venality and corruption of Kenya's postindependence elites, he castigates men for their treatment of women. Africa's "bosses," who control the economic opportunities of women, exact a high price for the jobs, homes, and material security they can either provide or withhold from women. Wariinga, the heroine of the story, is a victim of the system. A promising student, Wariinga is seduced by her father's boss with the help of her own father, who essentially sells his daughter in exchange for his own job advancement. Enticed by the boss's car, gifts, and flattery, Wariinga becomes his mistress until she becomes pregnant and he abandons her. Eventually she becomes a secretary, a woman's job that pays low wages and earns women little respect. Women in such jobs are also subjected to the sexual demands of their bosses and have little recourse except submitting or losing their hard-to-get jobs. As Wariinga laments, "Except for the lucky few, most of us can get jobs or keep them only by allowing the likes of Boss Kihara to paw our thighs" (Ngugi, 1982:206).

Marriage would seem a more permanent and happy arrangement for women. But this may not be so if women have, as is often the case, no legal rights to their husband's income for themselves or their children. Also, wives often must submit to the indignity of their husbands having "sugar girls," mistresses, or additional, often younger, wives. Divorce or widowhood may leave an ex-wife with little or no financial security or may cost her her children.

Even if legal reforms make the economic situation of wives more secure, and even if the dependent housewife role many Westernized Africans admire becomes more widespread, the overall advantage of this role is another issue. As both Achebe and Ngugi see it, the Western housewife role in Africa would further marginalize women from the economic and political life of their societies and reduce affluent women to an existence of superfluity and little purpose beyond conspicuous consumption—all under the guise of "modernization."

In *Devil on the Cross,* at the "devil's feast" the women of wealthy Kenyan men are provided with entertainment reflecting their significance in African development:

> I would like to remind the women here, whether they are wives, mistresses, or girlfriends, that after the competition there will be a fashion parade, a chance for you to show off your jewellery, your gold, diamonds, silver,

rubies, tanzanites, pearls. We must develop our culture, and you know very well that it is the way that women dress and the kind of jewellery they wear that indicates the heights a culture has reached. So . . . have ready your necklaces, earrings, rings and brooches, so that we can impress our foreign guests and show them that we too are on the way to modern civilization. (Ngugi, 1982:125)

In a similar vein, Achebe, through the character Ikem, discusses the "woman on a pedestal," once extolled in the West as the ideal domesticated woman. After recounting the original oppression of women in society and myth, Ikem concludes that becoming men's dependents is just a more enlightened form of oppression of women.

> So the idea came to Man to turn his spouse into the very Mother of God, to pick her up from right under his foot where she'd been since Creation and carry her reverently to a nice, corner pedestal. Up there, her feet completely off the ground she will be just as irrelevant to the practical decisions of running the world as she was in her bad old days. The only difference is that now Man will suffer no guilt feelings; he can sit back and congratulate himself on his generosity and gentlemanliness. (Achebe, 1988:89)

As elsewhere in the world, it is unclear what African women's long-term role in development will be or how development (whatever that turns out to be) will alter women's roles. Much will depend on the external environment: the changing global economy and its effects on the division of labor, investments, credit, and development assistance in Africa. Political pressure on multinational corporations, governments, lenders, and international donors by men and women dedicated to sexual equality will be vital to ensure that women's interests are not neglected. Within Africa itself, independent and representative women's organizations, from peasant cooperatives and credit associations to large nationwide groups, need to be supported and expanded. Nonsexist education and training for women and men as well as equal access to jobs, property, and leadership positions must be provided. Finally, women's full humanity and citizenship must be legally acknowledged and vigorously protected.

Given Africa's critical economic and political problems, it appears increasingly obvious that suppressing the talents and skills of women to protect men's privileges is an enormous waste of human resources that Africa—with its vast potential—can no longer afford.

BIBLIOGRAPHY

Achebe, Chinua. 1988. *Anthills of the Savannah*. New York: Anchor.
Amadiume, Ifi. 1987. *Male Daughters, Female Husbands: Gender and Sex in an African Society*. London: Zed.

Ampofo, Akosua Adomako. 1993. "Controlling and Punishing Women in Ghana." *Review of African Political Economy* 56 (March): 102–111.

Bernal, Victoria. 1988. "Losing Ground—Women and Agriculture on Sudan's Irrigated Schemes: Lessons from a Blue Nile Village." Pp. 131–156 in Jean Davison (ed.). *Agriculture, Women, and Land: The African Experience.* Boulder: Westview Press.

Blumberg, Rae Lesser. 1995. "Introduction: Engendering Wealth and Well-Being in an Era of Economic Transformation." Pp. 1–14 in Rae Lesser Blumberg, Cathy A. Rakowski, Irene Tinker, and Michael Monteon (eds.). *Engendering Wealth and Well-Being: Empowerment for Global Change.* Boulder: Westview Press.

Boserup, Ester. 1970. *Women's Role in Economic Development.* London: Allen and Unwin.

Bujra, Jane B. 1986. "Urging Women to Redouble Their Efforts: Class, Gender, and Capitalist Transformation in Africa." Pp. 117–140 in Claire Robertson and Iris Berger (eds.). *Women and Class in Africa.* New York: Africana.

Carney, Judith A. 1988. "Struggles Over Land and Crops in an Irrigated Rice Scheme: The Gambia." Pp. 59–78 in Jean Davison (ed.). *Agriculture, Women, and Land: The African Experience.* Boulder: Westview Press.

Chanock, Martin. 1982. "Making Customary Law: Men, Women, and Courts in Colonial Northern Rhodesia." Pp. 53–67 in Margaret Jean Hay and Marcia Wright (eds.). *African Women and the Law: Historical Perspectives.* Boston University Papers on Africa 7.

Cutrufelli, Maria R. 1983. *Women of Africa: Roots of Oppression.* London: Zed.

Davison, Jean. 1988. "Who Owns What? Land Registration and Tensions in Gender Relations of Production in Kenya." Pp. 157–176 in Jean Davison (ed.). *Agriculture, Women, and Land: The African Experience.* Boulder: Westview Press.

Dei, George J. Sefa. 1994. "The Women of a Ghanaian Village: A Study of Social Change." *African Studies Review* 37 (September):121–145.

Dinan, Carmel. 1983. "Sugar Daddies and Gold-Diggers: The White Collar Single Women in Accra." Pp. 344–366 in Christine Oppong (ed.). *Female and Male in West Africa.* London: Allen and Unwin.

Enabulele, Arlene Bene. 1985. "The Role of Women's Associations in Nigeria's Development: Social Welfare Perspective." Pp. 187–194 in *Women in Nigeria Today.* London: Zed.

Faruqee, Rashid, and Ravi Gulhati. 1983. *Rapid Population Growth in Sub-Saharan Africa: Issues and Policies.* No. 559. Washington, DC: World Bank.

Freeman, Donald. 1993. "Survival Strategy or Business Training Ground? The Significance of Urban Agriculture for the Advancement of Women in African Cities." *African Studies Review* 36 (December):1–22.

Gladwin, Christine H., and Della McMillan. 1989. "Is a Turnaround in Africa Possible Without Helping African Women to Farm?" *Economic Development and Cultural Change* 37 (January):345–369.

Goetz, Anne Marie. 1991. "Feminism and the Claim to Know: Contradictions in Feminist Approaches to Women in Development." Pp. 133–157 in Chandra Talpode Mohanty, Ann Russo, and Lourdes Beneria (eds.). *Third World Women and the Politics of Feminism.* Bloomington: Indiana University Press.

Goheen, Miriam. 1988. "Land and the Household Economy: Women Farmers of the Grassfields Today." Pp. 90–105 in Jean Davison (ed.). *Agriculture, Women, and Land: The African Experience.* Boulder: Westview Press.

Green, Cynthia P. (ed.). 1994. *Sustainable Development: Population and the Environment.* Washington, DC: USAID.

Guyer, Jane I. 1984. *Family and Farm in Southern Cameroon.* Boston: Boston University, African Studies Center.

Hammond, Dorothy, and Alta Jablow. 1970. *The Africa That Never Was.* New York: Twayne Publishers.

Hansen, Karen T. 1987. "Urban Women and Work in Africa: A Zambian Case." *TransAfrica Forum* 4 (Spring):9–24.

Kabira, Wanjiku M., and Elizabeth A. Nzioki. 1993. *Celebrating Women's Resistance: A Case Study of Women's Group Movement in Kenya.* Nairobi: African Women's Perspective.

Kettel, Bonnie. 1986. "The Commoditization of Women in Tugen (Kenya) Social Organization." Pp. 47–61 in Claire Robertson and Iris Berger (eds.). *Women and Class in Africa.* New York: Africana.

Langley, Philip. 1983. "A Preliminary Approach to Women and Development. Getting a Few Facts Right." Pp. 79–100 in Gerard M. Ssenkoloto (ed.). *The Roles of Women in the Process of Development.* Douala, Cameroon: Pan African Institute for Development.

Lima, Teresa. 1994. "Women's Co-ops Spur Mozambican Farmers Union." *African Farmer* (April):16–17.

Longwe, Sara H. 1990. *From Welfare to Empowerment: The Situation of Women in Development in Africa: A Post UN Women's Decade Update and Future Directions.* Working Paper No. 204 (March). Lusaka: Zambia Association for Research and Development.

Lovett, Margot. 1989. "Gender Relations, Class Formation, and the Colonial State in Africa." Pp. 23–46 in Jane L. Parpart and Kathleen A. Staudt (eds.). *Women and the State in Africa.* Boulder: Lynne Rienner Publishers.

MacGaffey, Janet. 1986. "Women and Class Formation in a Dependent Economy." Pp. 161–177 in Claire Robertson and Iris Berger (eds.). *Women and Class in Africa.* New York: Africana.

Meena, Ruth. 1989. "Crisis and Structural Adjustment: Tanzanian Women's Politics." *Issue: A Journal of Opinion* 17, 2 (Summer):29–31.

Morna, Colleen Lowe. 1994. "African Women Caught Between New Laws and Social Traditions." *Christian Science Monitor* (December 19):7.

———. 1995. "Plus ça Change." *African Report* 40 (January-February):55–59.

Munyakho, Dorothy. 1994. "Kenyan Women Press for Land Rights." *African Farmer* (April):8–9.

Nelson, Nici. 1988. "How Women and Men Get By: The Sexual Division of Labor in the Informal Sector of a Nairobi Squatter Settlement." Pp. 183–203 in Josef Gugler (ed.). *The Urbanization of the Third World.* New York: Oxford University Press.

Newland, Kathleen. 1991. "From Transnational Relationships to International Relations: Women in Development and the International Decade for Women." Pp. 122–132 in Rebecca Grant and Kathleen Newland (eds.). *Gender and International Relations.* Bloomington: Indiana University Press.

Ngugi wa Thiong'o. 1982. *Devil on the Cross.* London: Heinemann.

Nweke, Therese. 1985. "The Role of Women in Nigerian Society: The Media." Pp. 201–207 in *Women in Nigeria Today.* London: Zed.

Nzomo, Maria. 1989. "The Impact of the Women's Decade on Policies, Programs and Empowerment of Women in Kenya." *Issue: A Journal of Opinion* 17, 2 (Summer):9–17.

Nzomo, Maria, and Kivutha Kibwana (eds.). 1993. *Women's Initiatives in Kenya's Democratization.* Nairobi: The National Committee on the Status of Women.

Obadina, Elizabeth. 1985. "How Relevant Is the Western Women's Liberation Movement for Nigeria?" Pp. 138–142 in *Women in Nigeria Today.* London: Zed.

Palmer, Ingrid. 1991. *Gender and Population in the Adjustment of African Economies: Planning for Change.* Geneva: International Labour Organisation.

Pankhurst, Donna, and Susie Jacobs. 1988. "Land Tenure, Gender Relations, and Agricultural Production: The Case of Zimbabwe's Peasantry." Pp. 202–227 in Jean Davison (ed.). *Agriculture, Women, and Land: The African Experience.* Boulder: Westview Press.

Parpart, Jane L. 1988. "Women and the State in Africa." Pp. 208–230 in Donald Rothchild and Naomi Chazan (eds.). *The Precarious Balance: State and Society in Africa.* Boulder: Westview Press.

Robertson, Claire. 1995. "Trade, Gender, and Poverty in the Nairobi Area: Women's Strategies for Survival and Independence in the 1980s." Pp. 68–87 in Rae Lesser Blumberg, Cathy A. Rakowski, Irene Tinker, and Michael Monteon (eds.). *Engendering Wealth and Well-Being: Empowerment for Global Change.* Boulder: Westview Press.

Russo, Ann. 1991. "We Cannot Live Without Our Lives." Pp. 297–313 in Chandra Talpode Mohanty, Ann Russo, and Lourdes Beneria (eds.). *Third World Women and the Politics of Feminism.* Bloomington: Indiana University Press.

Russo, Sandra, Jennifer Bremer-Fox, Susan Poats, and Lawrence Graig. 1989. *Gender Issues in Agriculture and Natural Resource Management.* Washington, DC: WID/AID.

Safilios-Rothschild, Constantina. 1990. "Women's Groups: An Underutilized Grassroots Institution." Pp. 102–108 in *The Long-Term Perspective Study of Sub-Saharan Africa.* Vol. 3. Washington, DC: World Bank.

Schuster, Ilsa M. G. 1982. "Marginal Lives: Conflict and Contradiction in the Position of Female Traders in Lusaka, Zambia." Pp. 105–126 in Edna G. Bay (ed.). *Women and Work in Africa.* Boulder: Westview Press.

Scott, Catherine V. 1995. *Gender and Development: Rethinking Modernization and Dependency Theory.* Boulder: Lynne Rienner.

Sow, Fatou. 1989. "Senegal: The Decade and Its Consequences." *Issue: A Journal of Opinion* 17, 2:32–36.

Staudt, Kathleen. 1987. "Women's Politics, the State, and Capitalist Transformation in Africa." Pp. 193–208 in Irving L. Markovitz (ed.). *Studies in Power and Class in Africa.* New York: Oxford University Press.

TAMWA (Tanzanian Media Women's Association). 1993. "Violence Against Women in Tanzania." *Review of African Political Economy* 56:111–116.

Tripp, Aili Marie. 1991. "Women and Democratization in Africa: Reflections on the Tanzanian Case." Paper presented at the meeting of the African Studies Association, St. Louis, Missouri, November 23–26.

———. 1992. "The Impact of Crisis and Economic Reform on Women in Urban Tanzania." Pp. 159–180 in Lourdes Beneria and Shelley Feldman (eds.). *Unequal Burden: Economic Crises, Persistent Poverty and Women's Work.* Boulder: Westview Press.

Vellenga, Dorothy D. 1986. "Matriliny, Patriliny, and Class Formation Among Women Cocoa Farmers in Two Rural Areas of Ghana." Pp. 62–77 in Claire Robertson and Iris Berger (eds.). *Women and Class in Africa.* New York: Africana.

Vuorela, Ulla. 1992. "The Informal Sector, Social Reproduction, and the Impact of the Economic Crisis on Women." Pp. 109–123 in Horace Campbell and Howard Stein (eds.). *Tanzania and the IMF: The Dynamics of Liberalization.* Boulder: Westview Press.

Weekes-Vagliani, Winifred. 1985. "Women, Food, and Rural Development." Pp.

104–110 in Tore Rose (ed.). *Crisis and Recovery in Sub-Saharan Africa.* Paris: Organization for Economic Cooperation and Development.

World Bank. 1986. *Population Growth and Policies in Sub-Saharan Africa.* Washington, DC: World Bank.

———. 1989. *Sub-Saharan Africa: From Crisis to Sustainable Growth: A Long-Term Perspective Study.* Washington, DC: World Bank.

———. 1990. *Women in Development: A Progress Report on the World Bank Initiative.* Washington, DC: World Bank.

———. 1995. *World Development Report.* New York: Oxford University Press.

▪ 11 ▪

Religion in Africa

Ambrose Moyo

The importance of religion in any attempt to understand African life in all its social, economic, and political aspects cannot be overemphasized. Mbiti's (1969:1) observation that African people are "notoriously religious," consciously or unconsciously, is still true of a large majority of people, urban or rural, educated or less educated. Even those who claim to be atheist, agnostic, or antireligion, of whom there is a growing number, often have no option but to participate in extended family activities, some of which require the invocation of supernatural powers. Religion permeates all aspects of African traditional societies. It is a way of life in which the whole community is involved, and as such it is identical with life itself. Even antireligious persons still have to be involved in the lives of their religious communities, because in terms of African thought, life can be meaningful only in community, not in isolation.

Because of the size of the African continent and the great diversity of religious traditions, with variations even within the same tradition, it would be an impossible task to cover the subject of this chapter in one volume, let alone in one chapter of a book. Consequently, this chapter is a survey of the following three principal religious traditions on the continent: (1) the African indigenous religious beliefs and practices that, for lack of a better term, have been called in Africa scholarship African Traditional Religions (Idowu, 1971); (2) Christianity, including its expressions in the African indigenous Christian movements; and (3) Islam. There are other religious traditions practiced on the continent, such as Hinduism, Buddhism, Judaism, and Baha'i, but they are practiced by small minorities that include few indigenous African people (Barrett, 1982:782).

The study of the Christian and Islamic traditions poses no insurmountable difficulties with regard to our sources of information. Both have their sacred books, namely the Old and New Testaments for Christianity, and the Quran for Islam. The founders of these two traditions, their primary sources, and their geographical origins remain the same for all the adherents of these faiths regardless of the different interpretations. African Traditional Religions have no sacred books, their beginnings cannot be pinpointed, and each of the many traditions is practiced by one African group with no reference whatsoever to the religion practiced by other groups. Each African group exists as a complete social, economic, religious, and political entity with no missionary designs. With the many basic, common elements, there are also some differences in religious beliefs and practices that speak against generalizations. As unrelated and independent as African groups may appear, they nonetheless share some of the same basic religious beliefs and practices. These common, basic features suggest a common background or origin and lead to African Traditional Religions being treated as a single religious tradition, just as Christianity and Islam have many denominations or sects within themselves but continue to be treated as single entities.

However, since this chapter is only a survey and an introduction to African religions, the need is to concentrate on the basic, common elements and point out some of the significant differences as we go along.

Perhaps a question may be raised concerning our sources of information on African Traditional Religions since there are no sacred scriptures or clearly defined and documented dogmas. Indeed, many studies have recently appeared on different aspects of African Traditional Religions, but hardly any of them speak from the tradition they present. They are primar-

Many African societies have used masks to represent ancestors and other spiritual figures. These dancers are Dogon of Mali.

ily the works of sociologists, anthropologists, and theologians, many of whom have had little or no experience of these religions as their own faith. Consequently, the African arts, paintings, sculptures, music and dance, myths and rituals, archaeological findings, and oral tradition become extremely important as sources of information. We begin our survey with African Traditional Religions, and the examples used will be drawn from the sub-Saharan region.

■ AFRICAN TRADITIONAL RELIGIONS

Although African Traditional Religions have no sacred books or definitive creeds upon which to base any analysis of these religions, from the sources referred to above, the following religious phenomena seem to be basic and common to most of them: (a) belief in a supreme being, (b) belief in spirits/divinities, (c) belief in life after death, (d) religious personnel and sacred places, and (e) witchcraft and magic practices. This section of the survey will focus on these aspects of African Traditional Religions.

□ Belief in the Supreme Being

The African perception of the universe is centered on the belief in a supreme being who is the creator and sustainer of the universe. God, as far as the African traditionalist is concerned, is the ground of all being. Humanity is inseparably bound together with all of God's creation since they both derive their lives from God, the source of all life. This strong belief in God appears to be universal in traditional societies. The question to be asked is: How is this God perceived?

Names in African societies tell a whole story about the family—its history, relationships, hopes, and aspirations. African societies have so much to tell about God as they relate to him; hence, each society has many names for the Supreme Being. These names are expressions of the different forms in which God relates to creation. In other words, God in African traditional thought can only be known in the different relationships as expressed in God's names. For example, among my people in Zimbabwe, God is *Musikavanhu* (creator of humankind) / *Musiki/uMdali* (creator), which affirms that God is the originator of all there is. But *Musikavanhu* goes beyond the idea of Creator to the notion of the parenthood of God. Hence, God is also designated *Mudzimu Mukuru* (the Great Ancestor). As parent, God is also the sustainer of creation. God's creativity is continuous and is celebrated with every new birth, and each rite of passage is an expression of gratitude to God for having sustained the individual and the community that far. These names also affirm the belief in the continuous creativity of God.

Similarly, in the names *Chidziva Chepo* or *Dzinaguru,* God is perceived as the giver and the source of water. Each time it rains, God is sustaining creation in a visible way. This explains, in ceremonies relating to drought, why people appeal directly to God. So also the name *Samasimba* (owner of power/almighty) affirms God not only as the most powerful being but also as the source and owner of all power.

The African traditionalist does not perceive God as some supreme being in merely speculative terms. African thought in general is not given to speculation. That which is real has to be experienced in real-life situations, directly or indirectly. God can, therefore, be real only insofar as God has been experienced in concrete life situations in his different relationships with people and the rest of creation. In other words, African traditional thought cannot conceive of God in abstract terms as some being who exists as an idea mysteriously related to this world—distant, unconcerned, uninterested in what goes on here below. African thought can express itself only in concrete and practical terms. Consequently, Africans' view of God can arise only out of concrete and practical relationships as he meets their needs. In that way, they experience God's love and power (see McVeigh, 1974; Mbiti, 1970).

In terms of African thought, there can be only one Supreme Being. Interestingly enough, before the encounter with Christianity, some African societies already had some concept of the Trinity. This seems to have been the case in some African societies, as demonstrated by Twesigye (1987:93) in his research into his people's traditional religions in southern and western Uganda. In an interview with an old traditionalist, Mr. Antyeri Bintukwanga, Twesigye uncovered the following information:

> Before the Europeans came to Uganda and before the white Christian missionaries came to our land of Enkole or your homeland of Kigezi, we had our own religion and we knew God well. We knew God so well that the missionaries added to us little. . . . We even knew God to be some kind of externally existing triplets: *Nyamuhanga* being the first one and being also the creator of everything, *Kazooba Nyamuhanga* being his second brother who gives light to all human beings so that they should not stumble either on the path or even in their lives. . . . *Kazooba's* light penetrates the hearts of people and God sees the contents of the human hearts by *Kazooba's* eternal light. . . . The third brother in the group is *Rugaba Rwa Nyamuhanga,* who takes what *Nyamuhanga* has created and gives it to the people as he wishes. . . . You see! We had it all before the missionaries came, and all they did teach us was that *Nyamuhanga* is God the Father, *Kazooba* Jesus Christ his son and not his brother as we thought, and that *Rugaba* as the divine giver is the Holy Spirit. (Twesigye, 1987:93)

In traditional societies, God is believed to be eternal, loving, and just, the creator and sustainer of the universe. God's existence is simply taken for granted, hence the absence of arguments for or against the existence of God.

Atheism is foreign to African thought. The most widely used name for God among my people is *Mwari,* which means literally "the one who is."

A question often raised is whether God is actually worshiped in African Traditional Religions. Some Western observers have concluded that African people do not worship God but rather have no religion at all, are animists, or worship ancestor spirits or many gods. This issue will be examined in conjunction with the discussion on ancestors and lesser divinities in the next section.

□ **Belief in Divinities and Spirits**

The Supreme Being is believed to be surrounded by a host of supernatural or spiritual powers of different types and functions. Their nature, number, and functions vary from region to region, and they may be either male or female, just as God in many African traditions is perceived as being both male and female. The numerous divinities, called *orisha* among the Yoruba in Nigeria or *bosom* among the Akan of Ghana (and sometimes referred to as "lesser divinities" in order not to confuse them with the Supreme Being), are found in most western African traditions but generally not in eastern and southern African traditions. These *orisha* are subordinate to the Supreme Being. They are believed to be servants or messengers of *Olodumare* (God). God has assigned to each one of them specific areas of responsibility. For example, the divinity *Orun-mila* is responsible for all forms of knowledge, and he is therefore associated with divination and the oracle at Ile-Ife in Nigeria. The *orisha* are believed either to have emanated from the Supreme Being or to be deified human beings. Some of the divinities are associated with the sky, earth, stars, moon, trees, mountains, rivers, and other natural elements (see Idowu, 1962).

Perhaps more universal among African traditionalists is the belief in ancestor spirits, called *vadzimu* among the Shona people of Zimbabwe or *amadhozi* among the Zulu/Ndebele traditions. These are spirits of the deceased mothers and fathers who are recognized in a special ceremony, held usually a year after they have died. This ceremony is called *umbuyiso* (the bringing-home ceremony) in Zulu/Ndebele or *kurova guva* by the Zezuru. From that moment, the deceased person becomes an active "living dead" member of the community and is empowered to function as a guardian spirit and to mediate with God and other ancestors on behalf of his or her descendants. Among my own people, it is to these spirits that most prayers and sacrifices are made, but often the prayers are concluded by instructing the ancestors to take the prayers and offerings to *Musikavanhu* (creator of humankind) or *Nyadenga* (the owner of the sky/heavens).

The significance of ancestors among Africans has led to the common misconception that these spirits are worshiped. Traditionalists will categorically deny that they worship their ancestor spirits but rather worship God through them. Ancestor spirits are departed elders. African peoples in general have a very high respect for elders. If, for example, one has grievously wronged his or her parents, it would be utterly disrespectful and unacceptable to go directly and ask for forgiveness. One would have to go through some respectable elderly person to whom one would give some token of repentance to take to the parent. Similarly, when a young man and his fiancée decide to get married, the prospective father-in-law will have to be approached by the young man's parents through a carefully chosen and respectable mediator. In the same spirit, one cannot approach a chief or king directly but must have his or her case taken to the chief through a subchief. Even more so, God—the transcendent, the greatest and most powerful being, the Great Ancestor and creator of all—must be approached through intermediaries. The ancestor spirits are believed to be closest to both their living descendants and to the Supreme Being and are thus most qualified to function as intermediaries.

Ancestor spirits are not the objects of worship. They are guardian spirits and intermediaries. They are believed to be responsible to God for all their actions. As family elders they must be respected, and if not, they too, just like the living elders, can get angry and demand that they be appeased. Quite often, the name of the Supreme Being is not mentioned in petitions; still, it is believed that God is the ultimate recipient of all prayer and sacrifices. Although not worshiped, the ancestors in some traditions are closely associated with the Supreme Being, so much so that it becomes difficult to determine in some of the prayers whether the address is to God or to the ancestor. Take, for example, the following prayer of the Shilluk, who rarely address God directly. Nyikang is the founding ancestor of the Shilluk.

> There is no one above you, O God (Juok). You became the grandfather of Nyikang; it is you Nyikang who walk with God, you became the grandfather of man. If famine comes, is it not given by you? . . . We praise you who are God. Protect us, we are in your hands, and protect us, save me. You and Nyikang, you are the ones who created. . . . The cow for sacrifice is here for you, and the blood will go to God and you. (Parrinder, 1969:69)

One of my Shona informants told me that, as far as the Shona are concerned, God and the ancestors are one; an address to one is an address to the other. This means that even if at times one does not hear the name of God mentioned, it does not mean the people do not worship God. God and ancestors are closely associated and work very closely with each other. For example, they believe that children are a gift of *Mwari* (God) and the *vadzimu* (ancestors). So frequently one will hear the people say *kana Mwari nevadzimu vachida* ("if God and the ancestors are willing"). When faced with misfortune, one will say: *Ko Mwari wati ndaita sei?* ("What crime does God accuse me of?"), or they will say *mudzimu yafuratira* ("the ancestors have turned their backs"; i.e, on the individual or family, hence the misfortune) (Moyo, 1987).

There are different categories of ancestor spirits. There are family ancestors, family being understood in its extended sense. These have responsibility over the members of their families only, and it is only to them that the members can bring their petitions, never to the ancestors of other families. Then there are ancestors whose responsibilities extend over the whole tribe and not just over their own immediate families. These relate to the founders of the tribe and are represented by the royal house. These play an active role in matters that affect the entire community or tribe, such as drought or some epidemic. They are called *Mhondoros* (lion spirits) among the Shona people.

Most significantly, ancestor spirits serve as intermediaries. However, there are times when most of the African peoples will pray and make sacrifices to God directly. When, for example, one is in critical danger—face-to-face with some man-eating animal, or when thunder and lightning strike, or drowning—then one would approach God directly.

□ Belief in Life After Death

Death is believed to have come into the world as an intrusion. Human beings were originally meant to live forever through rejuvenation or some form of resurrection. So, most African peoples have myths that intend to explain the origin of death. There are, for example, some myths that depict death as having come in because some mischievous animal cut the rope or removed the ladder linking heaven, the abode of the Supreme Being, and earth, the abode of humankind. Such a rope or ladder allowed people to ascend to and descend from heaven for rejuvenation. Other myths see death as punishment from God for human disobedience. God and human beings lived together until a tragic event that led to the intervention of death, which then separated God and people.

Despite the loss of the original state of bliss and the intervention of death, it is generally believed that there is still life beyond the grave, that life may take several forms. In some traditions, the dead may be reincarnated in the form of an animal such as a lion, a rabbit, or a snake. In that form one cannot be killed, and if reborn as a lion, one can protect one's descendants from the danger of other animals. Or the person may be reincarnated in one of his or her descendants. In general, people believe there is a world of the ancestors, and when one dies, one goes on a long journey to get to that world. The world of the ancestors is conceived of in terms of this world; hence, people are buried with some of their utensils and implements. That world is also thought of as overlapping with this world, and ancestors are believed to be a part of the community of the living. The terms "living dead" or the "shades" are approximately accurate English renderings of those invisible members of the community (see Mbiti, 1969; Berglund, 1976).

That there is life after death is also affirmed in the belief that a dead person can return to punish those who have wronged him or her while still alive. One of the most feared spirits among the Shona is the *ngozi,* a vengeful spirit that will kill members of the family of the person who wronged the individual while still alive until payment or retribution has been made.

In general, people believe they are surrounded by a cloud of ancestors with whom they must share everything they have, including their joys and frustrations. Their expectation of the hereafter is thought of in terms of what people already know and have experienced. People know there is a future life because they interact with their departed ancestors through spirit mediums.

□ Religious Leadership and Sacred Places

There are different types of religious leaders in African Traditional Religions. These can be either male or female. Where the tradition has regular shrines for specific deities, there will be some resident cultic officials. At the shrine at Matongeni in Zimbabwe, for example, the priestly community is made up of both males and females, with roles clearly defined. The Yoruba and the Akan have regular cultic officials presiding at the shrines of their divinities. They offer sacrifices and petitions on behalf of their clients. Among most of the Bantu-speaking peoples, heads of families also carry out priestly functions on matters that relate to their families.

Another category of religious leadership, perhaps the most powerful, is that of spirit mediums. These are individual members of the family or clan through whom the spirit of an ancestor communicates with its descendants. They can be either male or female, but most are female. Among these are family spirit mediums and the tribal or territorial spirit mediums such as Mbuya (grandmother) Nehanda in Zimbabwe. The territorial spirits wield a great deal of power, and, to use the example of Zimbabwe, they played a very significant political role in mobilizing people in their struggles for liberation from colonialism. The first war of liberation in Zimbabwe (then Southern Rhodesia) was led by Mbuya Nehanda, a spirit medium who was eventually hanged by the colonial regime. During the time of the second war of liberation, her mediums as well as other spirit mediums worked very closely with the freedom fighters by mobilizing the people and sanctioning the war. The freedom fighters, most of whom claimed to be Marxist-Leninist, soon discovered that they could not wage a successful war without the support of the spirit mediums (Ranger, 1985:175–222; Lan, 1985). Thus, the mediums have political as well as religious roles to play. Through these mediums, people discern the will of the ancestors, get an explanation for the causes of whatever calamities they may be enduring, or obtain advice on what the family or the tribe should do in order to avert similar danger. Mediums are highly respected members of the community from whom people seek advice of any nature.

The other important category of religious leaders is that of the diviner. Again, diviners may be either male or female. Communication with the spirit world is vital for African Traditional Religions. Through divination, people are able to communicate with their ancestral spirits and the divinities. These are consulted in the event of some misfortune, sickness, death, or calamity. They communicate with the spirit world to determine the cause of the problem and to seek possible solutions. There are different methods of divining, using, for example, palm nuts, bones, a bowl of water, wooden dice carved with animals and reptiles, sea shells, or pieces of ivory. Divination would normally be conducted at some location such as a hut set aside for that purpose. In Yorubaland, Ifa divination centered at Ile-Ife is the most famous. The system is very elaborate and uses palm nuts (Awulalu, 1979; Bascom, 1969).

Finally, since religion permeates all aspects of life, the kings and the chiefs also carry out some leadership roles. Where the whole nation or tribe is involved, it is the responsibility of the head of the community to take the necessary action to consult the national or territorial spirits. It is also their duty to ensure that all the religious functions and observances are carried out by the responsible authorities.

With regard to sacred places, reference has already been made to shrines that serve particular divinities such as those among the Yoruba of Nigeria or the Akan of Ghana. Among the Zulus of South Africa, there is a room in each homestead with an elevated portion (*umsamu*) where rituals to the ancestor spirits are performed. The cattle kraal is also associated with ancestors and is therefore an important place for ritual action. Sacred mountains and caves are almost universal among African peoples. They are often associated with ancestors or any of the divinities. Religious officials will ascend these mountains or go into those caves only on special occasions. Such mountains are also often associated with the abode of the Supreme Being. In Zimbabwe, there are several such mountains that serve as venues for prayer and sacrifice, particularly in connection with prayers for rain in cases of severe drought.

☐ Witchcraft and Magic

To complete our study of the African Traditional Religions, it is also necessary to look at the negative forces in these religious traditions. African traditionalists believe that God is the source of all power, which he shares with other beings. The power of the divinities and ancestors, or that derived from medicine, is primarily viewed as positive power to be used for constructive purposes. However, that same power can also be used for destructive purposes, in which case it becomes evil power. Witches and sorcerers represent those elements within African societies that use power for the purpose of destroying life. (In general, witches are female and sorcerers are male.)

Witchcraft beliefs are widespread in Africa. It is generally believed that witches can fly by night, can become invisible, delight in eating human flesh, and use familiar animals such as hyenas or baboons as their means of transport. Witches are believed to be wicked and malicious human beings whose intention is simply to kill, which they do by poisoning or cursing their victims. Witches, sorcerers, and angry ancestor spirits are usually identified as the major causes of misfortune or death in a family.

Magic has two aspects: to protect or to harm. On the one hand, it is used to protect the members of the family, as well as their homestead, cattle, and other property, from witches and other enemies of the family or the individual. On the other hand, magic can also be used through spells and curses to harm or to kill. Beliefs related to magic and witchcraft clearly belong to the category of superstition. They represent ways in which people try to explain the causes of misfortune or social disorders. Misfortune, sickness, or death may also be explained as an expression of one's ancestors' displeasure regarding the behavior of their descendants (see Evans-Pritchard, 1937).

In conclusion, it must be stated that African Traditional Religions continue to influence the lives of many people today, including some of the highly educated as well as many African Christians and Muslims. It must also be pointed out that African religions are not static. Contacts with Christian and Islamic traditions have brought about transformations and syncretism in all three. As Bohannan and Curtin (1988:206–207) have remarked, "There is an amazingly close overlap between the basic ideas of Islam and Christianity, and of the African religions. Neither Islam nor Christianity is foreign in its essence to African religions"; the reverse is also true. Although Christianity and Islam have added distinct elements to African religions, each has been and continues to be adapted to and shaped by Africa's indigenous religious heritage, as will be shown in the following sections.

■ CHRISTIANITY IN AFRICA

Christianity is one of the oldest religions in Africa, and since the 1800s, the number of Christians and Christian churches has expanded rapidly. According to Barrett (1982:8), the total number of Christians in 1985 was estimated to be close to 250 million. By this estimate, Christianity is now the largest religion in sub-Saharan Africa. Growth is most noticeable in the African Independent Churches, denominations or churches that separated from the European-dominated churches. Since so much has been written on Christianity as a religion, it is not necessary for our purpose to deal with its beliefs, so I will focus instead on the historical development of the religion on the African continent. Special attention will be paid to those aspects that give African Christianity its own identity.

☐ Early Christianity in North Africa and Ethiopia

Christianity in Egypt dates back to the first century. According to the ancient historian Eusebius, writing about A.D. 311, the Christian church in Egypt was founded by St. Mark, author of the second Gospel and a companion of Paul, a tradition still maintained by the Coptic (Egyptian) church. By the end of the first century, Christianity had penetrated into rural Egypt and had become the religion of the majority of the people. Egypt has one of the oldest Christian churches, surpassed perhaps only by Rome in terms of longevity of tradition and continuity in the same locality (King, 1971:1). Recent discoveries of some Christian and non-Christian documents at the Nag Hammadi caves in Egypt show that quite early in the history of Christianity, Egypt had become a center for many different and even conflicting Christian groups and a center for theological reflection and debate (Robinson, 1982). The city of Alexandria was the home of outstanding theologians such as Origen, Cyprian, Clement of Alexandria, and others, whose writings on the different aspects of the Christian faith have influenced the church throughout the ages. The great "heretic" Arius (died A.D. 336), originally from Libya, provoked a controversy that rocked the church for several decades when he taught that Christ was only a human being. The controversy produced two creeds, namely, the Nicene and the Athanasian creeds, which are used together with the Apostles' Creed as definitive statements of the Christian faith throughout Christendom. The two creeds were formulated at the two great councils of Nicaea in A.D. 325 and of Alexandria in A.D. 362. The Athanasian Creed was named after Athanasius, the bishop of Alexandria, who championed the case against Arius.

The recent discoveries from Nag Hammadi show that Egyptian Christians were very open-minded as they searched for an African Christian identity, welcoming and accommodating new ideas in their search for indigenous expressions of their Christian faith. For instance, in its search for an authentic Christian life devoid of all fleshly desires and serving God through a life of self-denial, prayer, and worship, Egypt was the mother of monasticism. The many caves and the nearby desert provided most ideal locations for ascetic pursuits. Christianity continued to be a vibrant religious tradition until Egypt was conquered by the Muslims during the seventh century. Christianity has survived, although it has been reduced to a religion of a small minority (Robinson, 1982).

Moving south of Egypt, Christianity came to Ethiopia fairly early. The apostle Philip is reported in the Acts of the Apostles to have baptized an Ethiopian eunuch, who returned to his home country to share his newfound faith with his people. Independent evidence dates the coming of Christianity to Ethiopia to the fourth century. With the conversion of the emperor, church and state became united. The Ethiopian Orthodox church, which is one of the most thoroughly African churches in its ethos (Oduyoye, 1986:30), has continued to the present and has maintained close links with the Coptic church.

In "Roman Africa," which comprised the present-day countries of Tunisia, Morocco, and Algeria, Christianity is known to have had a strong following as early as the second century. It produced influential theological thinkers and writers such as Tertullian of Carthage, who was the first person to use the word "Trinity" in his description of the Godhead, and St. Augustine, the bishop of Hippo, whose ideas on such issues as grace, original sin, and the kingdom of God shaped both Western Catholicism and the Protestant Reformation. This church did not survive the Arab conquests, and this area today is almost totally Islamic.

□ Christianity South of the Sahara

There is no evidence of attempts by the African churches described above to take Christianity south of the Sahara. The earliest such efforts to Christianize the rest of Africa were those of the Portuguese missionaries of the Jesuit and Dominican orders in the fifteenth century who followed Portuguese traders traveling around the coast of Africa on their way to the East, often going into the hinterland of Africa to trade in gold and ivory. In western Africa, Roman Catholic missionaries established Christian communities in the Congo and Angola beginning in 1490, but these disintegrated after two centuries, in part because of the slave trade. Missionary work was also started in southern Africa at Sofala (Mozambique). It was from there that Father Gonzalo da Silveira led a group of Portuguese Jesuit missionaries in 1560 to the people of the vast empire of Mwanamutapa in what is now Zimbabwe. On his way to the capital of the empire, he claims to have baptized 450 persons among the Tonga people. His mission, however, ended with his execution by the emperor, whom he had converted and baptized Christian. This was apparently the result of pressure from the emperor's Arab Muslim trading partners, who feared Christian missionaries would open the door for Portuguese traders to threaten their monopoly. Subsequent Portuguese missionary efforts to the empire by both the Jesuits and the Dominicans were also unsuccessful. Their missionary efforts in eastern Africa suffered a similar fate.

Many Christian churches, such as this cathedral in Bangui, Central African Republic, were built by missionaries during the colonial period.

A new phase in the evangelization of Africa was introduced by the rise of the antislavery movement in Europe and the United States in the early nineteenth century. The result was that the British decided to send freed slaves to Sierra Leone, while the Americans sent their freed slaves to Liberia. In both cases, the freed people who had become Christians in their captivity spread Christianity to their fellow black people. Famous among these was Samuel Adjai Crowther, who was missionary to his own people in Nigeria and later became the first African Anglican bishop. The evangelical movement culminated in a missionary scramble for Africa that involved all major denominations in Europe and North America. Famous characters in this process included David Livingstone and Robert Moffat. Many Africans were also involved in these missionary efforts after their conversions, crossing borders in the company of white missionaries or by themselves. As a result of the efforts of such people, Christianity was firmly established in most of Africa by the beginning of the twentieth century (see Sanneh, 1983).

☐ The Rise of New African Christian Denominations

The nineteenth-century missionary activities in Africa were a resounding success, in which almost all major Christian denominations were involved. These activities were facilitated by the support and protection that missionaries received from colonial administrators. Indeed, the Christianization of Africa went hand in hand with its colonization. The missionaries arrived in most countries before the colonialists and learned the language of the local people. They helped the colonialists negotiate and draft the agreements that cheated African chiefs out of their land and its resources. To African nationalists, missionaries appeared to have collaborated with the forces of imperialism. In what is now a famous aphorism, the role of Christian missionaries in the colonization of Africa was once described by Kenyan nationalist leader (and Kenya's first president) Jomo Kenyatta: "When the missionaries came the Africans had the land and the Christians had the Bible. They taught us to pray with our eyes closed. When we opened them they had the land and we had the Bible" (in Mazrui, 1986:149–150). (See the discussions in Chapters 3 and 4 for more information on colonialism.)

The Christian church, despite its dubious association with colonialism, has continued to expand, but it is now taking on new, distinctly African forms. Some of these indigenous Christian denominations are radically different in their polity, doctrines, and general ethos from their Western parent churches. These new denominations or churches have often been labeled "African Independent Churches" or, negatively, "sects," but they should be viewed more accurately as authentic African expressions of the Christian faith.

The first of these new denominations appeared in western and southern Africa; thereafter, others emerged in eastern and central Africa. Researchers have traced the beginnings of these movements back to a Congolese woman named Donna Beatrice, who as early as 1700 claimed to have been possessed by the spirit of St. Anthony. Giving up all her belongings to the poor, she proclaimed a message of the coming judgment of God. She proclaimed that Christ and his apostles were black and that they lived in São Salvador (present-day Angola). For the first time, we have a cry from Black Africa for an indigenous Christ, an expression of a "deep yearning," "the yearning for a Christ who would identify with the despised African" (Daneel 1987:46). The basic question Beatrice raised and that many of the new African Christian churches have been asking is: "How could the white Christ of the Portuguese images, the Christ of the exploiters—how could he ever help the suffering African, pining for liberty?" (Daneel, 1987:46).

By the 1960s, there were at least 6,000 new denominations or African indigenous churches spread throughout most of Africa, including Islamic Africa (Barrett, 1968:18–36). The reasons for the emergence of the new phenomenon of African Christianity have been many and varied. Some of them began as revival movements within the historical churches and had no intention of breaking away. A good example of this is the Kimbanguist church in Zaire, which was started by Simon Kimbangu, a great healer and prophet.

Since his activities were not acceptable to the missionary church, he was arrested shortly after the start of his ministry and tried for subversive activities by the Belgian government. He was sentenced to death, but the sentence was later commuted to life imprisonment; he died in 1951. Today, the Kimbanguist church, officially known as the Eglise de Jésus Christ par le Prophète Simon Kimbangu (the Church of Jesus Christ according to the Prophet Simon Kimbangu), is one of the largest of the new denominations, with followers not only in Zaire but also in other countries in central Africa such as Zambia (see Mazrui, 1986:152–156).

The reasons for the emergence of other African Independent Churches have been discussed extensively (see, for example, Fashole-Luke et al., 1978; Hastings, 1976; Daneel, 1987; Barrett, 1982) and need not detain us here for too long. I shall just highlight some of the major reasons as summarized by Daneel (1987:68–101). First, the African Christians did not find much of an African ethos in the missionary-founded churches. They wanted churches in which they could express their Christian faith in African symbols and images, churches where they could feel at home, so to speak. Christianity as proclaimed by the missionaries was for them not comprehensive enough to meet their spiritual needs; hence, many people even today secretly continue to participate in African traditional rituals. There was no serious attempt on the part of the historical churches to understand African traditional spirituality and culture. Instead, many traditional beliefs and practices were simply labeled "heathen" or "superstitious" and were thus forbidden.

Second, as far as the Africans were concerned, the missionaries and the colonialists were birds of a feather. After all, they shared a common worldview and a common racist perception of the African. The missionaries tolerated and even practiced racial discrimination to the extent of providing separate entries and sections in sanctuaries, and "by so doing [the church] preached against itself and violated human rights" (Plangger, 1988:446). Such contradictions in what people heard missionaries preach and what they practiced contributed significantly to the formation of some of the independent churches.

Third, with the translation of the Bible into African languages, African Christians could now read and interpret the Bible for themselves. They soon discovered, for example, that biblical paragons of faith such as Abraham and David were polygamists. They also found out that the Fifth Commandment demands that parents be honored and that it is the only commandment that comes with a promise, namely, "that your days may be long on earth." For African peoples the "parents" include the ancestor spirits. The translation of the Bible into African languages is thus one of the major contributions by the missionaries to the development of indigenous African Christian spirituality and to the development of African Christian theologies. In the African independent churches, the Bible plays a central role, and in some of the churches, one service may have as many as five or six sermons, all of which are biblically based. The tendency in these churches is to be fundamentalistic in interpretating the Bible.

Fourth, indigenous churches are a response to the refusal or slowness on the part of missionaries to relinquish church leadership to the indigenous people; to the missionaries' discouragement of practices such as faith healing, prophecy, and speaking in tongues (all of which were practiced in the early church); and, finally, to missionaries' disapproval of polygamy, ancestor veneration, witches, and traditional medicine. Some indigenous churches headed by women are a reaction to the male dominance found in Western Christian churches and in African society in general. (See the discussion of male dominance in Africa before and after European expansion in Chapter 10.) For example, spirit possession cults in eastern Africa are dominated by women. They are considered to be the female counterpart of male veneration of lineage ancestors. Again, folk Catholicism in Zimbabwe is a largely feminine popular religion, with an emphasis on devotion to the Virgin Mary, mother of Jesus (Ranger, 1986:42, 52, 58).

Finally, Africans also began to search for forms of Christianity that would relate to if not redress their political and economic powerlessness under colonialism and now under frequently repressive African states that have done little to improve the lives of the poor masses. In white-ruled South Africa, independent churches were both a refuge from economic, political, and racial domination by whites and a source of resistance to racist government policies. An example is the Church of the Children of Israel founded by Enoch Mgijima. In 1921, the congregation refused to move from land that the white government had designated for whites only. South African troops opened fire, killing 163 defenseless people and wounding 129 others (Davidson, 1989:26).

Most of these religions are not overtly political. They seek to deal with the evils of the world by religious means, their grievances voiced in religious terms. A South African independent church member expressed the importance of religion to many of the poor forced to live under apartheid:

> The members of our Churches are the poorest of the poor. . . . We are what they call the working class. . . . Our people, therefore, know what it means to be oppressed, exploited and crushed. . . . But we also know that God does not approve of this evil and that racial discrimination and oppression is rejected by the Bible. And so what do our people do about it? They join political organizations or trade unions and take part in the struggle for liberation. . . . Politics is not a Church matter. . . . People meet together in our Churches to pray and to worship and to experience the healing of the Spirit. . . . The "Churches of the People" and the political organizations of the people have different roles to play. (Ranger, 1986:20–21)

Because of the variety of factors that led to the emergence of the new denominations, the spiritualities of those denominations take different forms (see Daneel, 1987:43–67). There are basically three types. First, there is what has been called the Ethiopian-type churches. These are essentially protest movements that broke way from the white-dominated missionary churches that tended to align themselves with the oppressive colonial regimes. They identified themselves with the aspirations of oppressed black people and sought to give theological expression and spiritual support to the struggle for liberation. The references to Ethiopia in texts such as Psalm 68:31 were, as observed by Daneel (1987:38), "interpreted as a sign that the oppressed Black people have a specially appointed place in God's plan of salvation." The Ethiopian-type churches are found mainly in southern and eastern Africa, with the majority of them originating toward the end of the nineteenth century and the beginning of the twentieth century. They tend to maintain the same doctrine and church polity as the church from which they broke away, and they even use the same hymnbooks; but they have African leaders. They are nonprophetic movements and do not place a great deal of emphasis on the Holy Spirit and all the extraordinary activities assigned to the Holy Spirit in the other new denominations.

The second kind of new denomination is the spirit-type churches. These are often referred to as Zionist churches because the name Zion often appears in the self-designations of these movements. They are prophetic in character and place a great deal of emphasis on the work of the Holy Spirit, who manifests herself in speaking in tongues, healing, prophecy, dreams, and visions and who helps to identify witches and cast out evil spirits. Their worship services include drums and dancing. They are more concerned with the practical benefits that religion can provide in this world than with other-world salvation. At the same time, they forbid their members to have anything to do with traditional African religion (Morrison, Mitchell, and Paden, 1989:76). Zionist churches include the Aladura or "praying" churches in Nigeria and the Harris churches in Côte d'Ivoire. The Zionist churches appeal to those who are more aggrieved by the destruction of African socio-cultural norms than by political and economic injustice (Ranger, 1986:3).

The third type was called the "messianic churches" in the early studies of these movements. The special focus in this movement is on the leader, who has prophetic powers and often appears to be a messianic figure occupying a special place between his followers and God. The heavily debated question among researchers has been whether Jesus' position has been replaced by a black messiah in the person of the leader of the movement. Scholars such as Sundkler, Beyerhaus, Martin, and Oosthuizen have argued that the leader does assume the place of Christ and serves as the mediator with God on behalf of the followers (see Daneel, 1987:180–195). However, Sundkler and Martin have come to the conclusion that the so-called black messiahs, such as Simon Kimbangu, were not perceived as messianic figures by their followers. In the movements they founded, "there is no conscious attempt to minimize the revelation of Jesus. Sermons and testimonies underline that Jesus is the Ultimate Authority and Final Judge" (Sundkler, 1976; Daneel, 1987:188). Daneel's research into movements of a similar character in Zimbabwe, such as Mutendi's Zion Christian Church and Johane Maranke's Vapostori, also confirmed that their leaders were not perceived as black messiahs (Daneel, 1987:190).

The new denominations represent a serious attempt to Africanize the Christian faith by responding concretely to the needs and aspirations of the African people. These movements take the African's worldview seriously; for instance, if salvation is to be real, it must include liberation from evil spirits, sickness, and disease. For it to be meaningful and relevant, Christianity must offer protection against black magic, sorcery, and witchcraft, all of which are issues of vital concern to African societies. Except for the Ethiopian-type churches, the other movements are uncompromisingly against participation in the traditional rites and substitute specifically Christian rites to fill the vacuum. The prophet who is inspired by the Holy Spirit, for example, takes the place and assumes the functions of the traditional diviners and spirit mediums; requests for rain are now made directly to God through the mediation of Christian leaders rather than through the tribal spirits mediated by traditional leaders.

In conclusion, it must be pointed out that Christianity has had a significant political impact on contemporary Africa. Wherever the missionaries went, they built schools, where a large majority of the present generation of African leaders were educated (see Mazrui, 1986:285–286). These institutions helped create an awareness among oppressed black people that before God they were of equal value with their oppressors, and this inspired many to rise up in defense of their freedom or to liberate themselves. The education black people received from mission schools gave them a sense of pride and value that the colonial regimes in countries like Zimbabwe, Zambia, Kenya, Malawi, and South Africa, to mention only a few, were not interested in creating. Despite their close cooperation with colonial agencies, many of the missionaries often stood up for some of the rights of black people. In independent Africa, Christian churches have been advocates of social justice and critics of corrupt and repressive regimes, not only in South Africa but in black-ruled states as well (cf. Lungu, 1986; "Churches," 1995). As mentioned in Chapter 4, church groups are among those actively supporting democratization.

■ ISLAM IN AFRICA

The third principal religion in Africa is Islam. The total number of Muslims in sub-Saharan Africa was estimated at approximately 215 million in 1985 (Barrett, 1982:782). While Muslims can be found in every African country, they are concentrated in areas bordering the Sahara Desert. Islam, which means "submission to God," was founded in the seventh century in Arabia by the Prophet Muhammad. Influenced by Judaism and Christianity, Islam established monotheism and a scripturally based religion first among Arab tribesmen around the towns of Mecca and Medina. Allah (God) revealed to Muhammad how he wanted his followers to live and structure their communities. This revelation is found in the Quran and is believed to be the literal word of God. Muslim Arabs, like Jews, believe they are descendants of Abraham, and they respect the Old Testament and the Prophets. Muslims also revere the New Testament and regard Jesus as a prophet. Muhammad, however, is the last and greatest of the Prophets, and the Quran is God's supreme revelation. Unlike Judaism, both Christianity and Islam are missionary religions; as such they have been the major contenders for the religious allegiance of Africans. Rather than discussing the faith and doctrine of Islam, this study will focus on the historical development of the tradition in Africa and its distinctively African features.

□ The Spread of Islam: The First Wave

Soon after the death of Muhammad in A.D. 632, his followers embarked on wars of conquest, first among Arabs and then non-Arab peoples in north-

Photo: Donald L. Gordon

Mosques, with their tall minarets, can be found throughout Africa. This one is in central Nairobi, Kenya.

ern Africa and elsewhere. Most of Egypt was taken over by the Muslims by 640. By then, Egypt's rulers supported the Byzantine Orthodox church, while many Egyptians were Coptic Christians who did not accept the Orthodox church's teachings or authority. Many welcomed Arab rule as less oppressive than they had experienced under the Byzantines. The Arabs established themselves initially as a ruling and powerful minority, but Christians were treated as "protected people" (*dhimmi*) who were allowed to practice their faith and regulate their affairs through their own leaders. Still, Christians were second-class citizens required to pay a special tax (*jizya*) in lieu of military service. Nonetheless, educated Christians often held prominent positions in the new Muslim state. Conversion to Islam was gradual. There was some localized persecution and pressure to convert, but most did so for other reasons, e.g., attraction to Islamic tenets, commercial advantage, and desire to avoid the *jizya* and second-class status. By the end of the eleventh century, Christianity in Egypt had become a minority religion (Mostyn, 1988:190).

After Egypt, the Arabs moved on to Roman northern Africa, where they defeated the Christians, who were primarily based in the towns, and the Berbers, who had remained untouched by Christianity in the rural areas. Trimingham observes that

> the North African Church died rather than was eliminated by Islam, since it never rooted itself in the life of the country. Although considerations such as the prestige of Islam derived from its position as the religion of the ruling minority and the special taxation imposed on Christians encouraged change, the primary reasons for their rapid conversion were the less obvious ones deriving from weaknesses within the Christian communities. Among these were Christianity's failure to claim the Berber soul and its bitter sectarian divisions. (Trimingham, 1962:18)

The conversion of the pagan Berbers of northern Africa was a slow process. After their initial military conquests, the Arabs located in the towns. They gradually intermarried with the Berbers, who became increasingly Islamized and Arabized. Many Berbers were incorporated into Arab armies. This period of conquest and gradual Islamization of northern Africa is reported by the great Arab historian Ibn Khaldun:

> After the formation of the Islamic community the Arabs burst out to propagate their religion among other nations. Their armies penetrated into the Maghrib and captured all its cantonments and cities. They endured a great deal in their struggles with the Berbers who, as Abu Yazid has told us, apostatized twelve times before Islam gained a firm hold over them. (Trimingham, 1962:18)

Whereas Islam spread to northern Africa in the aftermath of conquest, the spread of Islam south of the Sahara was primarily the result of peaceful, informal missionary efforts by Arabized Berber merchants who traded manufactured goods from the Mediterranean lands in exchange for raw materials such as gold, ivory, gum, and slaves. They followed the established trade routes, many of which had existed long before the rise of Islam. Wherever they went, Muslims established commercial and religious centers near the capital cities. The Nile River provided access to Nubia, Ethiopia, and Sudan. From Sudan, some of the traders went across to western Africa. The introduction of the camel also made it possible to cross the desert from northern Africa and establish contacts with western and central Africa (Voll, 1982:80; Lewis, 1980:15–16).

Muslim communities were established fairly early in several states in western Africa. In Ghana, for example, King (1971:18) reports that already by 1076, there was an established Muslim center with several mosques almost competing with each other. By the fifteenth and sixteenth centuries, Islam was the religion of the rulers and elites of many large African states such as the Songhai empire (Voll, 1982:14). (See Map 2.4.) Islam appealed to African elites for several reasons. One was its association with Arab-Muslim civilization and its cosmopolitanism. Islam was also very compatible with or at least tolerant of African religious and cultural practices such as ancestor veneration, polygamy, circumcision, magic, and beliefs in spirits and other divinities. In fact, most African believers were barely Islamized, perhaps observing the Five Pillars of the faith—belief in one God and that Muhammad is his prophet, alms (*zakat*) for the needy, prayer five times a day, fasting during the month of Ramadan, and pilgrimage (*haj*) to Mecca—but often ignoring elements of the *shari'a* (Muslim law) or other Islamic practices (e.g., veiling women), which they found incompatible with local custom (Lewis, 1980:33–34, 60–62; Callaway and Creevey, 1994).

In eastern Africa, Islam was spread by Persian and Arab merchants beginning in the late seventh century. These merchants established coastal trading towns with local Africans all the way down to southern Africa. Through intermarriage and commercial contacts, a unique Swahili language and culture developed. There was little movement of traders or Islam into the interior until the late tenth century, however, because there were few centralized kingdoms to attract them (Lewis, 1980:7). (See Chapter 3 for additional information on this period.)

Islamic civilization contributed much to Africa's own cultural development. Islam is a way of life (*dar al Islam*) affecting all spheres of human activity. It emphasizes literacy and scholarship, traditions that Islam promoted in previously nonliterate African societies. Islam's stress on the community of believers (*umma*) demands the subordination of regional and tribal loyalties that often separated Africans and impeded the growth of larger political units. Islamic law (*shari'a*) as the framework for community life along with Islamic Arab administrative and political structures provided models for Africa's state-builders and gave built-in religious legitimacy to the claims of rulers over the ruled (see Mazrui, 1986:136–137; Davidson, 1991:28–29; Lewis, 1980:37).

☐ The Spread of Islam:
The Second Wave

By the eighteenth century in western Africa, Islamic consciousness was spreading from the upper classes to the masses. This new wave of Islamization was being carried by African Muslims through militant mass movements under the religious banner of jihad (holy war). The desire of pious Muslim leaders such as Uthman dan Fodio in northern Nigeria (early nineteenth century) was for social, moral, and political reform. The imposition of more rigorously Islamic theocratic states on lax African believers and non-Islamic peoples was the goal. Jihad thus became a religious justification for wars of conquest and political centralization (Mazrui, 1986:184–185; Voll, 1982:80–81).

The new wave of Islamization was not solely the result of militant movements. Various Sufi (mystical) religious orders or brotherhoods (*tariqas*) dedicated to a more faithful adherence to Islam were at work. One of the earlier ones (sixteenth century) was the Qadiriyya, introduced to the great Muslim center of learning Timbuktu by an Arab *shaikh* (leader) (Lewis, 1980:18–19). In the nineteenth century, the Tijaniyya from Fez, Morocco, gained many followers. The Qadiriyya greatly influenced Uthman dan Fodio, one of the foremost jihad leaders (Voll, 1982:80–81). (Again, see Chapter 3.)

Sufi brotherhoods under the inspiration of their religious leaders (*marabouts*) were able to mobilize large numbers of people for political and economic as well as purely religious ends. Among these ends was resistance to European imperialism in the nineteenth century. Using the ideas of jihad and the brotherhood of all believers, Muslims were able to organize resistance on a wider scale than African political units or ethnicity would allow (Mazrui, 1986:284). In Senegal, the Mourides transformed jihad into economic enterprise as *marabouts* organized their followers to produce peanuts on brotherhood land. Even today, the Mourides are a major political and economic force in Senegal. They attract many followers for practical reasons but also because of their liberalism in enforcing Islamic law (Voll, 1982:249–250).

In eastern Africa, Mahdism galvanized mass religio-political opposition to European imperialism in the Sudan. The *Mahdi* in Islam is a messianic figure sent by God to save the believers during times of crisis. The Mahdi Muhammad Ahmed and his followers defeated the British at Khartoum in 1885, although the Mahdist forces were eventually defeated (Mazrui, 1986:151–152).

European colonialism and missionary Christianity did not halt the spread of Islam in Africa. In western Africa, colonial rulers made peace with Muslim leaders by protecting their conservative rule over their people and prohibiting Christian proselytizing or mission schools in Muslim areas (Voll, 1982:247). Muslims won many new converts for a variety of reasons. The racism and segregation policies of the Europeans contrasted sharply with the Muslim belief in the equality of believers. Also, in many cases, Muslim army officers under the British and the French treated Africans kindly, dealing with their grievances. They were tolerant in helping fellow Africans adjust African customary law to Islamic law (Zakaria, 1988:203). Indirectly, colonialism promoted Islamic expansion through the introduction of improved communications and rapid social change (Voll, 1982:245). Islam proved able to adjust and change as well as to meet new needs and conditions.

□ Islam Since Independence

Islamic organizations and practices have undergone remarkable changes in order to cope with Western influences, including Christianity. In some cases the process has involved accommodation and new interpretations of Islam. In other instances, Christianity and Westernization are seen as enemies of Islam and failed experiments, unable to solve Africa's many problems. Such views have spawned a growing number of fundamentalist movements.

Initially after independence, conservative nineteenth-century organizations either died out or transformed themselves. In Sudan, the followers of the Mahdi formed a modern political party that competed in national elections. In Nigeria, also, conservative and reformist Muslims formed political parties, partly in competition with Christians in non-Muslim sections of the country. Few of these political parties, however, were explicitly Islamic. The Mourides of Senegal reorganized and assumed modern economic and political roles to maintain their influence (Voll, 1982:145–250).

The spirit of jihad and forced conversion were largely replaced by a respect for religious pluralism. This was undoubtedly a result of the long history of mutual accommodation between African Traditional Religions and Islam in the past as well as contact with Christianity. In most sub-Saharan African states, Muslims are a minority or, at least, not the only religious community, a fact that tends to reinforce Muslim support for secular states. Muslim leaders readily accepted non-Muslim leaders such as Léopold Senghor (a Catholic), who was president of Senegal for many years. Pluralism is also promoted by the fact that family and ethnic loyalties still take precedence over religious ties for most Africans (Zakaria, 1988:204–205). (See Chapter 9 for more on the centrality of the family in Africa.)

For the masses of Muslim Africans, African traditional beliefs and practices have continued, although with some adaptations to conform to similar practices in Islam. In writing about the Wolof of Senegal, Mbiti concluded:

> In spite of the impact of Islam, there is still a much deeper layer of pagan belief and observances. . . . Men and women are loaded with amulets, round the waist, neck, arms, legs, both for protection against all sorts of possible evil, and to help them achieve certain desires. Most frequently these contain a paper on which a religious teacher has written a passage from the Koran, or a diagram from a book on Arabic mysticism, which is then enveloped in paper, glued down and covered with leather, but sometimes they enclose a piece of bone or wood, a powder, or an animal claw. (Mbiti, 1969:245)

These are basically African elements, not Islamic, and are practiced by most African groups.

A survey of African indigenous Islamic communities in other parts of Africa also reveals the persistence of African-based practices. Ancestor veneration, the wearing of amulets to ward off misfortune and to protect cattle and homesteads, and beliefs in magic, witchcraft, and sorcery have continued with little discouragement. New elements include the use of charms. Also, as Mbiti (1969:249) observed, "In addition to treating human complaints, the medicine men perform exorcisms, sometimes using Koranic quotations as magical formulae."

African Muslims, as well as African Christians, are seeking to redefine or modify their religion and religious identity in response to modern needs and problems. For many Muslims, this means finding a way to incorporate more orthodox Islamic practices and beliefs into those of their pre-Islamic African religious and cultural heritage. Moreover, many African Muslims are seeking new religious responses to meet the political, economic, and social problems they are facing. This has led some Muslims to seek a fundamentalist reaffirmation of Islam, often influenced by fundamentalist movements in North Africa and even Iran (cf. Hunwick, 1995; Ilesanmi, 1995; Voll, 1982:250, 337; Brenner, 1993).

Adapting to contemporary concerns, Sufi brotherhoods have been at the forefront in providing new ways to find accommodation between the demands of Islam and popular aspirations, both religious and secular. One such movement is Hamallism, a branch of the Tijaniyya. Hamallism is a social and religious reform movement that stresses the full equality of all people and the liberation of women. It opposes the materialism and corruption of conservative Islamic leaders. Before independence, Hamallists opposed those Muslim leaders who cooperated with French colonialism. Hamallism influenced political leaders like Modibo Keita, former president of Mali, and Diori Hamani, former president of Niger (Voll, 1982:254.). On the other hand, anti-Sufi movements such as the Izala in Nigeria and Niger (Movement for Suppressing Innovations and Restoring the Sunna) have attracted many from the urban merchant class with their opposition to *marabouts* and emphasis on individualism and putting wealth into investments (Grégoire, 1993).

In Sudan, Islamic fundamentalists have gained dominant influence over the government. Their efforts to impose the *shari'a* (Islamic law) on the entire country, including the non-Muslim south, have led to an ongoing civil war since 1983 (O'Fahey, 1993). They have virtually obliterated previous nonsectarian, modernist Islamic movements such as the Republican Brothers, founded by M. M. Taha. The Brothers sought a reform of Islam in light of modern realities, including advocating the equality of men and women. Taha was executed in 1985 for "heresy" (Al-Karsani, 1993).

Elsewhere, and similar to the new Christian churches that are searching for a more African Christianity, some Muslims are promoting controversial new forms of Africanized Islam. In East and West Africa, the Ahmadiyya movement (originally from India) owes its modest success to its vigorous missionary efforts. The Ahmadiyya translated the Quran into Swahili and other local languages (the first to do so), since most African Muslims do not know Arabic. The Ahmadiyya have stirred up much opposition among more orthodox believers by claiming that Muhammad was not the last prophet. For some Africans, this has led to hope for an African prophet to succeed Muhammad. In Nigeria one such prophet was Mahammadu Marwa. Marwa was killed along with 100 other people when his followers sparked a violent confrontation with police in the city of Kano in 1980. Also controversial, the Mourides of Senegal have come to revere the town of Touba, where the brotherhood originated, as a site of pilgrimage rivaling Mecca in importance (Mazrui, 1986:151–152).

There remain alarming and growing underlying tensions among more moderate Muslims, Christians, and a growing number of Muslim fundamentalists who would prefer a more theocratic social and political order. Religious conflict continues to devastate Sudan. In Kenya, fundamentalists are challenging both expanding Christianity and secularization (Sperling, 1993). Occasional conflicts over the *shari'a* continue to break out in Nigeria, and tensions between the Muslim north and Christian south have led to violence that threatens national unity (Hunwick, 1995; Ilesanmi, 1995). All of this has led some observers to fear that, as another divisive element, fundamentalist Islam in Africa may undermine the fragile democratic gains that have been made in many countries (DeCalo, 1994).

■ CONCLUSIONS

Although it is not possible to do justice to so broad a topic as African religions within the space of a chapter, this survey has, I hope, illustrated the

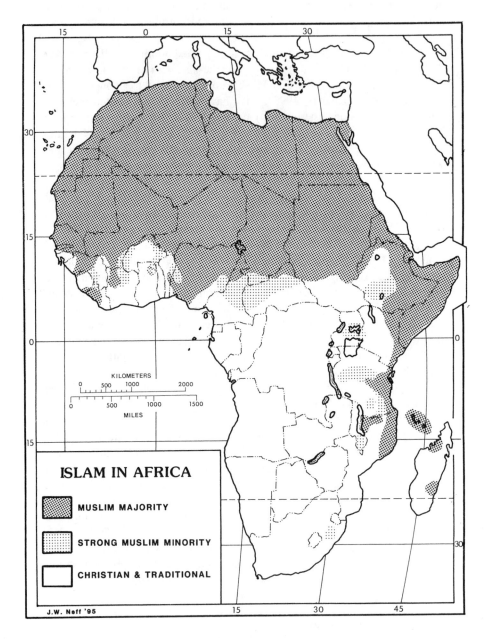

ISLAM IN AFRICA

MUSLIM MAJORITY

STRONG MUSLIM MINORITY

CHRISTIAN & TRADITIONAL

J.W. Neff '95

Map 11.1

breadth of the continent's religious traditions. African Traditional Religions and Islam have generally been able to accommodate each other, but there are some strong voices within the Muslim community that are becoming more critical of the less than rigorous practices of African Islam. African Christian churches, on the other hand, have been openly negative toward African Traditional Religions, but at the same time have found ways of adapting some of their rituals and beliefs so that the African Christian has felt at home in the new indigenous denominations. The combined efforts of the early missionary and colonial powers to destroy African cultures and religions have led to a crisis of identity that, ironically, has promoted the continued practice of African Traditional Religions as a major aspect of African cultures.

Bohannan and Curtin (1988:206) predict that African Traditional Religions will dwindle with development and industrialization. Indeed, conversions to Christianity and Islam are growing steadily. This prediction, however, presupposes that the current economic and political crises of Africa improve and that rural dwellers and the poor in general become situated more securely in the network of relationships and activities we call "modern." Even though African Traditional Religions may dwindle as Africans affiliate with branches of the world's two major religions, Christianity and Islam, Africans will continue to preserve in their new faiths elements of the old, as they have always done.

People will embrace religions they feel speak to their experience and their need for identity and meaning, religions that promise some kind of justice and redress of their existential problems. Bishop Patrick Kalilombe's address to the second general assembly of the Ecumenical Association of African Theologians (in 1984) sums up well the relationship between Africans' current spiritual and existential needs. He also suggests the revolutionary potential of an emancipatory religion that enables people to change themselves and the world.

> People at the grassroots react in the face of a growing sense of powerlessness and exploitation. The preponderant reaction is that of people everywhere who . . . become convinced that indeed they are . . . powerless, ignorant, or out of touch with the mainstream of history. They develop reflexes of inferiority. . . . They try to insulate themselves in a little world of their own. Sometimes they take refuge in some type of religious cults, or other distracting hobbies. . . . It becomes difficult for them to analyze events and realities soberly. . . . And yet it is the people at the grassroots that have the potential for meaningful change.
>
> Grassroots theologizing is a project of empowerment . . . potentially a revolutionary and explosive enterprise, capable of unleashing power among those who have hitherto been powerless. . . . People begin to think for themselves in a critical way. . . . Change is likely to be revolutionary because the reflection is done in the light of God's Word which is a fearful double-edged sword that judges the desires and thoughts of people's hearts. (Ranger, 1986:53)

The question in Africa, as well as in many other areas of the world, is whether emancipatory religions rather than religions of intolerance and repression are embraced as people seek to meet their worldly and spiritual needs.

■ **BIBLIOGRAPHY**

Al-Karsani, Awad Al-Sid. 1993. "Beyond Sufism: The Case of Millennial Islam in Sudan." Pp. 135–153 in Louis Brenner (ed.). *Muslim Identity and Social Change in Sub-Saharan Africa*. Bloomington: Indiana University Press.

Awulalu, J. Omosade. 1979. *Yoruba Beliefs and Sacrificial Rites*. Burnt Mill, Harlow (Essex), England: Longman.

Barrett, David B. 1968. *Schism and Renewal in Africa*. Nairobi: Oxford University Press.

———. 1982. *World Christian Encyclopedia: A Comparative Survey of Churches and Religions in the Modern World 1900–2000*. Nairobi: Oxford University Press.

Bascom, William. 1969. *Ifa Divination: Communication Between Gods and Men in West Africa*. Bloomington: Indiana University Press.

Berglund, Axel-Ivar. 1976. *Zulu Thought Patterns and Symbolism*. London: C. Hurst.

Bohannan, Paul, and Philip Curtin. 1988. *Africa and Africans*. Prospect Heights, IL: Waveland Press.

Brenner, Louis (ed.). 1993. *Muslim Identity and Social Change in Sub-Saharan Africa*. Bloomington: Indiana University Press.

Calloway, Barbara, and Lucy Creevey. 1994. *Islam: Women, Religion, and Politics in West Africa*. Boulder: Lynne Rienner Publishers.

"Churches Seek 'Critical Distance.'" 1995. *Christian Century* 112 (April 19):416.

Daneel, M. L. 1987. *The Quest for Belonging: Introduction to a Study of African Independent Churches*. Gweru, Zimbabwe: Mambo.

Davidson, Basil. 1989. *Modern Africa: A Social and Political History*. London: Longman.

———. 1991. *African Civilization Revisited*. Trenton, NJ: Africa World Press.

DeCalo, Samuel. 1994. "The Future of Participatory Democracy in Africa." *Futures* 26 (November):987–992.

Evans-Pritchard, E. E. 1937. *Witchcraft, Oracles and Magic Among the Azande*. Oxford: Clarendon Press.

Fashole-Luke, G., R. Gray, A. Hastings, and G. Tasie (eds.). 1978. *Christianity in Independent Africa*. London: Rex Collins.

Grégoire, Emmanuel. 1993. "Islam and the Identity of Merchants in Maradi (Niger)." Pp. 106–115 in Louis Brenner (ed.). *Muslim Identity and Social Change in Sub-Saharan Africa*. Bloomington: Indiana University Press.

Hastings, Adrian. 1976. *African Christianity*. New York: Seabury.

Hunwick, John O. 1995. *Religion and National Integration in Africa: Islam, Christianity, and Politics in the Sudan and Nigeria*. Evanston, IL: Northwestern University Press.

Idowu, E. B. 1962. *Olodumare: God in Yoruba Belief*. Ikeja, Nigeria: Longman.

———. 1971. *African Traditional Religion: A Definition*. Maryknoll, NY: Orbis.

Ilesanmi, Simeon O. 1995. "Recent Theories of Religion and Politics in Nigeria." *Journal of Church and State* 37 (Spring):309–327.

King, Noel. 1971. *Christian and Moslem in Africa.* New York: Harper and Row.

Lan, David. 1985. *Guns and Rains: Guerrilla and Spirit Mediums in Zimbabwe.* Harare: Zimbabwe Publishing House.

Lewis, I. M. 1980. *Islam in Tropical Africa.* Bloomington: Indiana University Press.

Lungu, Gatian F. 1986. "The Church, Labour and the Press in Zambia: The Role of Critical Observers in a One-Party State." *African Affairs* 85 (July):385–410.

Mazrui, Ali A. 1986. *The Africans: A Triple Heritage.* London: BBC Publications.

Mbiti, John S. 1969. *African Religions and Philosophy.* New York: Praeger.

———. 1970. *African Concepts of God.* New York: Praeger.

McVeigh, Malcolm J. 1974. *God in Africa: Conceptions of God in African Traditional Religion and Christianity.* Cape Cod, MA: Claude Stark.

Morrison, Donald G., Robert C. Mitchell, and John N. Paden. 1989. *Understanding Black Africa.* New York: Irvington Publishers.

Mostyn, Trevor. 1988. *The Cambridge Encyclopedia of the Middle East and North Africa.* New York: Cambridge University Press.

Moyo, Ambrose. 1987. "Religion and Politics in Zimbabwe." In Kirsten Holst Peterson (ed.). *Religion, Development and African Identity.* Uppsala: Scandinavian Institute of African Studies.

Oduyoye, Mercy. 1986. *Hearing and Knowing: Theological Reflections on Christianity in Africa.* Maryknoll, NY: Orbis.

O'Fahey, R. S. 1993. "Islamic Hegemonies in the Sudan: Sufism, Mahdism, and Islamism." Pp. 21–35 in Louis Brenner (ed.). *Muslim Identity and Social Change in Sub-Saharan Africa.* Bloomington: Indiana University Press.

Parrinder, Geoffrey. 1969. *Religion in Africa.* New York: Praeger.

Plangger, Albert. 1988. "Human Rights: A Motive for Mission." Pp. 441–459 in Carl F. Hallencreutz and Ambrose Moyo (eds.). *Church and State in Zimbabwe.* Gweru, Zimbabwe: Mambo.

Ranger, T. O. 1985. *Peasant Consciousness and Guerrilla War in Zimbabwe: A Comparative Study.* London: James Currey.

———. 1986. "Religious Movements and Politics in Sub-Saharan Africa." *African Studies Review* 29:1–70.

Robinson, James M. 1982. *The Nag Hammadi Library.* New York: Harper and Row.

Sanneh, Lamen. 1983. *Christianity in West Africa: The Religious Impact.* Maryknoll, NY: Orbis.

Sperling, David C. 1993. "Rural Madrasas of the Southern Kenya Coast, 1971–92." Pp. 198–209 in Louis Brenner (ed.). *Muslim Identity and Social Change in Sub-Saharan Africa.* Bloomington: Indiana Unversity Press.

Sundkler, Bengt. 1976. *Zulu Zion and Some Swazi Zionists.* Oxford: Oxford University Press.

Trimingham, J. S. 1962. *A History of Islam in West Africa.* London: Oxford University Press.

Twesigye, Emmanuel K. 1987. *Common Ground: Christianity, African Religion and Philosophy.* New York: Peter Lang.

Voll, John Obert. 1982. *Islam: Continuity and Change in the Modern World.* Boulder: Westview Press.

Zakaria, Rafiq. 1988. *The Struggle Within Islam.* London: Penguin.

▪ 12 ▪

African Literature

George Joseph

Since 1986, three inhabitants of the continent of Africa have received the Nobel Prize in literature: Naguib Mahfouz (Egypt), Nadine Gordimer (South Africa), and Wole Soyinka (Nigeria). These three Africans, however, belong to three different literatures. The work of Mahfouz, who writes in Arabic, belongs to Arabo-Islamic literature, a literature from a cultural space that stretches from Morocco along the Mediterranean across North Africa into the Middle East and beyond. Nadine Gordimer's fiction, written in English, belongs to the settler tradition of South Africa, which in its themes and techniques is representative of a body of literature written by European colonizers of Africa and their descendants. Wole Soyinka, who also writes in English, combines indigenous African traditions with those of European literature. He represents a tradition that took its impetus from African attempts to tell a story about Africa different from the one told in European colonial literature. The tradition to which Soyinka belongs extends over a geographical space that stretches from just south of the Sahara to the tip of southern Africa. The main subject of this chapter will be the indigenous African tradition represented by Wole Soyinka.[1]

Even within this single tradition, there are several different literatures throughout a vast area south of the Sahara Desert. Most accessible to U.S. students are the national literatures written in European languages from countries such as Senegal, Ghana, Nigeria, Cameroon, Kenya, and South Africa, but these literatures are only the tip of a very large iceberg. Not only are there written literatures in African languages, such as Hausa, Swahili, Zulu, Wolof, and Bambara, but there are also as many oral traditions as there are peoples. A chapter of this sort can give only the broadest of outlines.

The concept of "literature" most of us hold is of European origin. Typically, literature implies "written letters," but oral traditions in Africa are full-fledged literary traditions regardless of the means of their transmission. I shall use the term "oral literature" to emphasize the links between oral and written literature, while paying careful attention to the specificity of oral traditions.

303

"Literature" can also imply an artistic use of words for the sake of art alone. Without denying the important role of aesthetics in Africa, we should keep in mind that, traditionally, Africans do not radically separate art from teaching. Rather than write or sing for beauty in itself, African writers, taking their cue from oral literature, use beauty to help communicate important truths and information to society. Indeed, an object is considered beautiful because of the truths it reveals and the communities it helps to build. As someone once said, for an African mask to be beautiful, one must believe in the being for which it stands. The emphasis in this chapter, however, will not be history, ethics, religion, or philosophy but rather the recognized verbal art forms through which the truths of such material are communicated.

■ AFRICAN ORAL LITERATURE

It is impossible to give a full account of contemporary African authors' debt to oral traditions, not only because much work remains to be done by scholars but also because even a brief account of what is already known is beyond the scope of this chapter. Yet, this debt is widely recognized, and current investigations reveal it to be always greater than previously suspected, even in the case of authors who write in a European language that has few if any visible "Africanisms." In this section of the chapter, I will introduce aspects of African oral literature with which a reader of written African literature should have some familiarity. These include (1) the status, preservation, and transmission of oral literature in African societies and (2) the genres that have so far been identified.

☐ The Status and Transmission of Oral Literature in African Society

Although folklore is defined as traditional customs or tales preserved orally among a people, the status of African oral literature is different from that of the folklore of a people with writing. Folklore in countries such as Italy, France, or England stands as popular literature in opposition to the written productions of an elite and indeed may be influenced by the latter. African oral literature, on the other hand, represents the aspirations of an entire people and ranges from sublime religious ideals to everyday practical advice.

The constants of African oral traditions are transmitted in a variety of ways. In some societies, such as the Dogon (Mali), whom Marcel Griaule studied, any elder who takes the time can learn oral traditions. At the other extreme is the case of the Wolof (Senegal) *griot,* who belongs to a hereditary caste attached to a noble family. The *griot* learns the traditions by heart from his or her father (there are women *griots,* but with a different store of

The Wolof griot *Yoro M'Baye*

knowledge) from the time he or she can speak. This information is considered a sacred trust. In precolonial times, a mistake about a family's lineage could mean a *griot's* life. Since there are a variety of terms to describe the person charged with the oral tradition throughout Africa, we shall use the term "bard" to refer to all of them. Whatever the mode of transmission, it is the elders who are repositories of the treasures of oral tradition, so that it is said, "Every time an old one dies, a library burns down."

Yet, despite careful protection and transmission of the constants of oral traditions, any oral form such as an epic, myth, tale, or praise song can actually be different every time it is performed. (Exceptions would be priestly incantations and prayers, as will be seen below.) A bard will modify his or her material according to the circumstances of the performance. For example, a story will be made less violent if it is performed for a woman. Certain types of information are withheld from foreigners and uninitiated members of a group, while other types of information are communicated only in certain social situations such as initiation rites or other important ceremonies. Stories and myths may always be modified to accommodate recent events, and there are always changes to give pleasure to the audience of the moment. Because a work will change according to these and other such circumstances, it would seem that a bard learns the skeletal structure of a story, myth, epic, or poem and fleshes it out according to fixed formulas that are dictated by the situation. As a result, a researcher will find that a poem, such as an epic, that he or she has recorded will be very different on returning to record it at another time or sending someone else to record it. Furthermore, the written text of an oral performance is a pale reflection of its original, which may have been chanted, sung, or combined with elements of dance and ritual. A true reproduction of a work of oral literature would have to be a videotaped performance, but even this record creates a false impression of fixed works.

Although the function of oral literature is to provide entertainment and preserve the history, wisdom, and religious beliefs of a society, oral literature takes various forms. The fluidity of the tradition must be kept in mind when reading the following discussion of its relatively fixed characteristics. It should also be kept in mind (1) that the following classification cannot take into account African terms or verbal forms, (2) that our vision of oral literature reflects what researchers have happened to record and informants are willing to give, and (3) that a strict purity of genres is a Western concept. Just as African civilizations tend to be pluralistic in philosophy and religion (they accept the possibility of many versions of truth instead of one), the forms in which they find expression mix poetry and prose, words, dance, and ritual.

□ Genres of African Oral Literature

Prose Tales

Prose in the African oral tradition is that which tends toward ordinary speech as opposed to chanting or singing, although it may contain elements of the latter. Its principal form on record is the tale, which contains elements of myth, legend, and history. Tales, which are generally performed at night by adults, may include mime, dance, and song; may mix animals, humans, and divine beings; and may exist in related groups or cycles, such as the cycle of the hare or the tortoise or the hyena. There is not the same distinction between human, animal, and divine as in Western cultures, since there is a totemic link between humans and animals, both of whom are manifestations of the divine force that pervades the world. In fact, animals often stand in for specific persons, so as not to embarrass the latter or their descendants.

The most widespread theme in this literature is that of the trickster-hero, who recalls the Yoruba (Nigeria) god Eshu-Elegba. (The theme should not be taken to mean that Africans are immoral, since all societies tell tales where cunning overcomes power or advantage.) The trickster may be either a person or an animal. The trickster stands in opposition to the normal order of things. Rather than follow the rules of a society, he gets by on his own cleverness, often against far more powerful opponents. The most common animals in the trickster tradition are the hare (ancestor of the African American Br'er Rabbit in the tales of Uncle Remus), the hyena, the spider, and the tortoise. An example of such a trickster tale is one in which a tortoise challenges both an elephant and a hippopotamus to a tug-of-war and then positions them on opposite sides of a mountain so that they will be tugging against each other. After the resulting stalemate, the two animals gain a new respect for the tortoise.

Tales serve many other functions: they can explain a behavior, such as that of a hen scratching the earth; or a geographical detail, such as the two hills called *les mamelles* outside Dakar, Senegal. The tale pertaining to the latter, by the way, upholds the moral order. The *mamelles* are actually the humps of a hunchbacked wicked woman. One of the humps is her own. Fairies transfer the other hump to her from the back of a kinder woman.

Other tales pose a problem rather than give a clear moral lesson. For example, which of three brothers is the most responsible for saving their father: the first, who magically saw that their father in a distant land was ill; the second, who magically transported the three brothers to their father's side; or the third, who healed their father once they were there?

Tales can also explain the founding of a dynasty, the origins of a people, or the behavior of a god. In these latter cases, tales touch on elements of myth (sacred tales that shape belief) and legend (the stories of heroes and dynasties). Yet, since such elements do not make the tales recognized as authoritative sources of history and religious belief, one must assert that myth and legend in prose form do not have the status of more ceremonial religious poems and formal chanted epics. In other words, tales may use elements from myths and legends without necessarily being the source of those myths and legends.

Myths

Myth may be defined as a "story or a complex of story elements taken as expressing . . . certain deep-lying aspects of human and transhuman existence" (Wheelwright, 1965:538). Most of the prose narrative myths that we have—such as the great Dogon cosmogonic myth that explains how the universe spirals out from a single seed—were collected in conversations between a field researcher and native informant. While the content of such myths is doubtlessly authentic as far as it goes, we do not necessarily know it in the fullness and in the form that an initiated Dogon audience would accept as sacred and authoritative. Further research may reveal such texts, but it is possible that a developed formal narrative myth constituting the foundation of belief in the sacred will never be revealed to the uninitiated.

Poetry

Poetry in oral literature is distinguished from normal speech by the sustained rhythm and modulation of the voice. It ranges from formal epic chants to informal melodic songs.

Narrative epic. Usually a chanted formulaic narrative that takes several days to perform, the epic tells historical legends dealing with conquerors and founders of dynasty. Epics such as the *Ozidi* epic of the Ijo of southern Nigeria or the *Mwindo* epic of the Myanga people of eastern Zaire involve the entire community in dramatic festivities of music, dance, and poetry. Others, such as the famous *Sundiata* of Mali, may be chanted from beginning to end by a single bard. Sundiata, the legendary founder of Mali, is a shamanistic hero descended from a woman whose totem animal is the magical buffalo of Do. Although he is lame in his early childhood, when he finally walks he has superhuman strength so that he can uproot trees. He is, nevertheless, driven into exile by his brother, and only after a series of magical exploits that reveal his virtue as well as his strength does he return home to reign over the new empire of Mali. An epic of this sort is a source of history and social relations between families. For example, the coronation scene contains a list of the families who are allied to Sundiata and his descendants.

Occupational poetry. There are various forms of lyric poetry that accompany all aspects of life. Occupational poetry consists of poetry that belongs to a group exercising a trade such as farming, fishing, or hunting. For example, the Yoruba *ijala* are songs sung by hunters under the inspiration of the god Ogun of the Yoruba pantheon. They deal with a wide range of subject matter, including human ethics and relations, family lineages, distinguished individuals, mythology, animals, and plants. These are speech-like songs chanted at gatherings for Ogun. Occupational poetry, such as songs of Ewe fishermen and farmers, also includes poems sung during work, not just to relieve drudgery (as do work songs) but also to recall religious functions pertaining to the calling of a group.

Cult poetry. Cult poetry is sung during rituals for the divinities and as an aid in the practice of medicine. It is also used for incantations and as a tool for divination. This poetry, which either invokes or celebrates the forces of nature, contains the most conservative texts of oral literature, since its validity depends on an exact repetition or precise verbal formulas. The human word in this poetry is more than just a sound. It is a powerful act that controls forces of the universe. It is the human word, for example, that calls the force of a divinity to live in a wooden statue or mask.

Cultic chants consist of an enumeration of the characteristics and accomplishments of a divine being and an invocation for help. Consider, for example, this Tanzanian prayer to Ruwa, or God, that accompanies the sacrifice of a bull:

> We know you Ruwa, Chief, Preserver.
> He who united the bush and the plain.
> You, Ruwa, Chief, the elephant indeed,
> He who burst forth men that they lived. . . .
> Chief, receive this bull of your name,
> Heal him to whom you gave it and his children.
> (Mapanje and White, 1983:119)

Praise songs. As cultic chants are to divinities, praise songs can be to rulers and other important men and women. Although praise songs serve many functions, such as preserving family history or historical values, their words are believed to empower a warrior about to go into battle by recalling the forces of that warrior's ancestors of whom he is the living representative. Because of their belief in the empowerment of the word, Wolof rulers are known to have gone into battle with encroaching French invaders against overwhelming odds.

The basic units of praise songs are (1) epithets that refer to a town, animal, or other object or event associated with a person or thing praised and (2) the proper name of a person. The latter can be expanded into a genealogy that outlines a whole family history. For example, in the praise song for the Wolof princess Semu of western Africa, instead of naming an important Wolof ruler, the *griot* lists four of his horses and the battlefields on which they died. In this song, a person's forename is usually followed by his or her mother's and father's names. But one can skip one or the other and proceed along either the paternal or the maternal line. Thus, in the song for Semu, the latter is referred to either as Semu Ganka Yaasin Mbaru (Ganka Yaasin being the father and Mbaru a remote paternal ancestor) or Semu Coro Wende (Coro Wende being the mother; see Joseph, 1979).

The following are praise names of the great Zulu chieftain Shaka from the southern tip of the continent:

> He is Shaka, the unshakeable,
> Thunderer-while-sitting, son of Menzi.
> He is the bird that preys on other birds,
> The battle-axe that excels over other battle-axes.
> He is the long-strided pursuer, son of Ndaba,
> Who pursued the sun and the moon.
> He is the great hubbub like the rocks of Nkandla
> Where elephants take shelter
> When the heavens frown . . .[2]

There are many other genres of oral literature that are too numerous to mention. Among them are a wealth of love songs, work songs, and children's songs, as well as the epigrams, proverbs, and riddles that sprinkle African speech. As the Ibo of Nigeria say, "Proverbs are the palm oil with which words are eaten." An example of a riddle is the phrase "a house in which one does not turn around"; the answer is "a grave." There are yet other forms that incorporate acting and dialogue. For example, while a group of Wolof women are pounding millet, one will give the signal and the others will fall into a patterned conversation that follows the preordained plan of a kind of play.[3]

■ WRITTEN LITERATURE
IN AFRICAN LANGUAGES

Originating not in indigenous oral literature but in the missionary efforts of Islam and Christianity, written literature bore an uneasy relationship to oral traditions. (See Ambrose Moyo's chapter on religion for additional insights into the relationship among African religions, Christianity, and Islam.) African literatures under Islamic influence, such as Wolof, Swahili, and Hausa, were originally written in Arabic script and reflect the spirituality of the Quran—a spirituality sometimes at odds with traditional African cultures. Hausa secular verses in Arabic, for example, worked against sacred praise poetry, which should sing only of the Prophet Muhammad.

Literatures in such languages as Sesuto, Xhosa, Zulu, and Yoruba stand in the shadow of translations of the Bible and books such as John Bunyan's *Pilgrim's Progress*. Early works such as Thomas Mfolo's 1906 *Travelers of the East* came out on missionary printing presses. Yet, as Christianized writers became interested in indigenous oral traditions, they encountered the hostility of their missionary patrons. Thus, works like Mfolo's *Chaka* (Shaka), which is about the famous Zulu hero, did not appear in print until 1925, seventeen years after it was written.

The tension between Euro-Christianity and African traditions is also apparent in the Yoruba novels of the Nigerian chief Fagunwa. In works such as *The Forest of a Thousand Daemons,* Fagunwa, nourished by memories of his grandfather's court and a deep knowledge of Yoruba mythology, evokes a traditional world upon which he imposes references to a Christian God.

Patterns of latent opposition to Islamization or Christianization have given way to outright resistance to colonization in contemporary African writing in African languages. Writers such as Ngugi wa Thiong'o in Kenya and Ousmane Sembene and Cheikh Anta Diop in Senegal call for a literature in African languages as an essential step in "decolonizing the mind." According to Ngugi wa Thiong'o, it is only "revitalized African languages . . . which will be best placed to give to and receive from the wealth of our common [African and world] culture on an equal basis" (Ngugi, 1990:981). Elsewhere, Ngugi eloquently states the rationale for writing in one's native language:

> In writing one should hear all the whisperings, all the shouting, all the crying, all the loving and all the hating of the many voices in the past, and those voices will never speak to a writer in a foreign language. For us Kenyan writers, we can no longer avoid the question, whose language or history will our literature draw upon. (Zell, Bundy, and Coulon, 1983:434)

Cheikh Anta Diop and Ngugi wa Thiong'o see the African writer's situation very much like that of the English or French writer of the Renaissance in the face of Latin cultural imperialism. Just as Renaissance writers had to forge national languages while borrowing from all cultures, so the African writer must encompass the entire range of expression. In Senegal, for example, nationalists are translating major works of literature, arts, and sciences into Wolof. A writer such as the Senegalese Cheikh N'Dao has written his more recent works in Wolof first, before translating them into French, to give freer rein to his creative genius. Ousmane Sembene increasingly resorts to films in Wolof in order to reach his Senegalese audience. Mazisi Kunene from South Africa writes in Zulu before he translates into English. He has written *Zulu Poems* (1970) and two epics, *Emperor Shaka the Great* (1979) and *Anthem for the Decades* (1981). Although literatures in European languages such as French, English, and Portuguese remain important for the time being, movements such as those in Senegal and South Africa will inevitably change the map of African literature as the production of works in African languages increases.

■ AFRICAN LITERATURE IN EUROPEAN LANGUAGES

The following sections on written African literature in European languages deal with two main themes: (1) the African literary response to European accounts about Africa and (2) the shift in the postcolonial era from responding to European literature to addressing problems of the new African nations. Much of the rest of the chapter is also devoted to naming African authors and works to provide a starting point for newcomers to this literature.

Written African literature in European languages was born in reaction to European colonial writings intended to explain Africa to other Europeans. The Europeans claimed a privileged, objective knowledge about Africa based on extended study, short voyages, or prolonged residence. Some, such as South Africa's Nadine Gordimer and J. M. Coetzee, consider Africa to be their home. European writings take many forms, including novels such as Joseph Conrad's *Heart of Darkness* (1902), travelogues such as André Gide's *Voyage to the Congo* (1927), and reports to various commercial companies intending to set up operations on the continent. Colonial newspapers

are also an important source of European views. Much of this writing paints
Africa in terms of extremes. Africans are represented either as noble savages
in a picturesque exotic setting or as primitive wild beings suffering from disease, devoid of spiritual and moral qualities, and in need of the civilizing
benefits of European colonialism.

Although individual authors have varying positions, they tend to
smooth over differences in order to "invent" the concept of Africa as a place
with cultural constants. Even distinguished colonial ethnographers such as
Frobenius and Delafosse or intellectuals such as the anticolonialist Gide
remain "Eurocentric" (i.e., they "see" Africa through European cultural
biases). They benefit from colonial power, which domesticated the continent
for European travel, and, in turn, often use their knowledge and insights to
further colonial power. For example, Placide Tempels's *Bantu Philosophy*
studies the religion of black Africans in order to facilitate conversion by
Catholic missionaries. The French general Faidherbe wrote distinguished
studies of the Wolof (Senegal) with the intention of infiltrating them and
subjecting them to French domination.

□ **African Literature in French**

Negritude Poetry and Pan-Africanism
as a Response to Colonial Literature

After isolated works such as Bakary Diallo's *Force Bonté,* which sang
the praises of the French colonizers, African literature in French came into

its own as an alternate voice to European colonial literature in the late 1940s with the founding of the journal *Présence africaine* (1947). Other important works were the publication of Léopold Sédar Senghor's collection of poetry entitled *Chants d'ombre* (1945) and his *Anthologie de la nouvelle poésie nègre et malagache* (1948), which included poems by other African and Afro-Caribbean writers. Senghor's poetry—which also includes *Hosties noires* (1948), *Chants pour Naëtt* (1949), *Ethiopiques* (1956), *Nocturnes* (1961), *Elégie des alizés* (1969), and *Lettres d'hivernage* (1973)—embodies the tenets of the Negritude movement, which was born in the 1930s.[4] At that time, students from francophone African countries and African American writers in exile in Paris discovered their African roots in the context of pan-Africanism.

Pan-Africanism, which ultimately harks back to the late eighteenth-century effort to return African slaves to the newly created state of Liberia, was forged in a series of congresses held in London, Paris, Brussels, Manchester, Lisbon, and New York between 1900 and 1945. Some of its distinguished early founders included E. W. Blyden and W. E. B. Du Bois. Writings inspired by the pan-African movement continue the European quest for global constants of an African culture and are often inspired by the work of European ethnographers. But, instead of a privileged European narrator, pan-African writings call into question European objectivity by substituting narrators and main characters whose privileged position of authority comes from their identity as Africans. According to "Black Orpheus," Jean-Paul Sartre's preface to Senghor's anthology, such writing turns the tables so that it is the European who is the object of the African's objectifying gaze instead of the other way around. Yet, as we shall see, the meaning of the term "Negritude" depends on the worldview of the author.

Negritude defines an African way of being in the world that is antithetical to that of the European. This definition recalls European thinking according to which the European is "intellectual, inventive, violent, steel-hard, and asexual"; by contrast, the African is "emotional, uninventive, at peace with nature, humane, and oversexed" (Owomoyela, 1979:39). But Senghor gives new value to characteristics traditionally attributed to Africans so that "uninventiveness" is attributed to "peace with nature," and what puritanical Europeans consider as "oversexed" is seen as a healthy sensuality. Senghor attempts to give his verse "swing and dance in the rhythms of his native Serer" (Beier, Knappert, and Moser, 1974:141). An example of Senghor's verse is the famous "Black Woman," which establishes a canon of black beauty:

> Naked woman, dark woman
> Firm-fleshed ripe fruit, sombre raptures of black wine, mouth
> making, lyrical my mouth.

Negritude, with its insistence on working out a definition of African cultural identity, made particular sense in the context of the assimilationist poli-cies of French colonialism, which were designed to make Africans culturally into black French people. For some proponents of Negritude, however, the return to cultural roots is not to be confused with cultural isolationism. Although poetry such as Senghor's paints an idealistic picture of African tra-ditions, it owes much to Europe. One sees the influence of the poetry of Paul Claudel and St. John Perse. Jean-Paul Sartre's preface to Senghor's anthol-ogy, with its emphasis on ways of being and on the gaze of the black under-ling, places the anthology squarely under the aegis of existentialism. Poems in the anthology such as those of Aimé Césaire reflect the influence of sur-realism and Marxism.

Thus, a mixed identity of voice is inherent in Negritude—and, indeed, the entire tradition of written African literature that is the subject of this chapter. As Alioune Diop, the founder of *Présence africaine* (1947), says:

> Neither white nor yellow nor black, incapable of returning entirely to the traditions of our origins or to assimilate ourselves to Europe, we have the impression of constituting a new race of mental mulattoes but a race that has never been revealed in its originality and had hardly ever been aware of it.[5]

The Negritude poets work out their cultural ambiguity in differing ways. Senghor does not attempt to return to a pure state of Africanness but to give new value to traditions and ways of being African in a world in which Africa and Europe are "joined by the navel" (Owomoyela, 1979:41). Senghor has also written essays on various cultural and political subjects; the best known are the three volumes entitled *Liberté I, II* and *III*.

Other poets, such as Birago Diop (*Leurres et lueurs,* 1967) and David Diop, reject assimilation. David Diop's poetry is particularly forceful:

> My poor brother in the silk-faced dinner jacket
> Squealing murmuring and strutting in condescending drawing rooms
> We pity you. (Quoted in Owomoyela, 1979:45)

The Congolese poet Tchicaya U Tamsi is of a younger generation. Although his poetry inherits its surrealism through Aimé Césaire, it is more private and Christian than Césaire's. Tchicaya U Tamsi's collections of poems include *Le Mauvais Sang* (1955; *Bad Blood*), *Feu de brousse* (1957; *Brush Fire,* 1964), *Triche-coeur* (1960; *A Game of Cheat Heart*), *Epitomé* (1962), *Le Ventre* (1964; *The Belly*), and *La Veste d'intérieur* (1977). U Tamsi's greater freedom is typical of the second generation of African writers.

Owing to the establishment of African literature as a fact by their pre-decessors, later generations are able to pursue more independent approaches that do not deal directly with issues of assimilation. Such is the case in the poetry of Zairiah V. Y. Mudimbe, whose *Déchirures* (1971) is a collection of love verse.

Fiction from Colonialism to Independence

Like the Negritude poets, the novelists of the 1950s and 1960s established a point of view that is culturally mixed. Camara Laye represents the beauty and harmony of traditional African culture but also the painful necessity of change. His *L'Enfant noir* (1953; *Dark Child*) is the autobiography of a young man who has made the decision to study in Paris and who laments the loss of a traditional childhood. Yet, for Laye, assimilation should work both ways, as we see in his second novel, *Le Regard du roi* (1954; *Radiance of the King*), where the European Clarence is obliged to learn the ways of his African hosts. Laye's third novel, *Dramouss* (1966; *A Dream of Africa*) warns of the dangers of assimilation without respect for African cultural roots. The novel is an account of the author's return home after six years in Paris. The harmonious traditional society of his childhood is now replaced by a society of violence.

Cheikh Hamidou Kane's philosophical novel *Aventure ambiguë* (1961; *Ambiguous Adventure*) is a more troubling account of assimilation. A family that embodies the essence of traditional African royalty decides to risk sending one of its sons, Samba Diallo, to school in Europe so that he may help his society open up to European technology. The experiment fails, however, when Samba, unable to hold the two cultures together, commits suicide.

Two postcolonial novels by V. Y. Mudimbe also portray the impossibility of holding two cultures together. In *Entre les eaux: Dieu, un prêtre, la révolution* (1973), a priest, Pierre Landu, fails in his attempt to adapt Catholicism and Marxism for what J. Ngate calls an "anti-colonial and ideal view of justice" (Ngate, 1988:13); whereas in *L'Ecart* (1979), Nara goes mad because of his inability to choose between the West and Africa in either love or intellectual activity.

The novels of two francophone Cameroonian novelists, Ferdinand Oyono and Mongo Beti, embody an aesthetic of politically committed realism at odds with the gentler approach of novels such as *L'Enfant noir*. The works of these novelists present a frankly pessimistic view of cultural assimilation in tones of satiric irony that imply a scathing critique of the French colonial civilizing mission. Oyono's tragicomic novels *Une Vie de boy* (1956; *Boy*) and *Le Vieux Nègre et la médaille* (1956; *The Old Man and the Medal*) represent heroes who come to the painful awareness that colonialism and its masters are a sham and that assimilation means humiliation, exploitation, and, in the case of Toundi in *Boy*, death.

Mongo Beti also portrays the failure of the colonial system in his novels. *Le Pauvre Christ de Bomba* (1956; *Poor Christ of Bomba*), *Mission ter-*

minée (1957; *Mission to Kala*), and *Le Roi miraculé* (1958; *King Lazarus*) satirize the work of Christian missionaries and French schools. Mongo Beti's later novels, written after independence, will be discussed below.

Oyono and Beti's colonial novels, however, stand in the movement of Negritude as part of the opposition. They represent authentic African voices, but voices that explode not only the myths of the European civilizing mission but also the ethnographic constructions of Africa on which so much of the Negritude movement is based. The satiric realism of Oyono and Beti has been called pessimistic. Although politically committed to the struggle against colonialism, it portrays contemporary Africans as lost and acculturated with no hope for the future because of the disastrous policies of the colonial masters.

Two novels of the 1960s stand as a transition between colonial Negritude fiction and later postcolonial fiction, which deals with problems of African society with little or no reference to Europeans.

Yambo Ouologuem's *Devoir de violence* (1966; *Bound to Violence*) attacks the ethnographically inspired myths of a harmonious precolonial African culture with a representation of the African past as a series of violent episodes. It presents an even more negative view of the African past than do the ironic Oyono and Beti.

Ahmadou Kourouma's 1968 *Soleils des indépendances* (*Suns of Independence*), features a deposed African prince who attempts to adjust to conditions in a modern African state. What is striking about this novel is its pluralism. Here there is no authoritative voice or privileged perspective, African or otherwise. Rather, events can be partially, but not entirely, explained by various mutually exclusive perspectives provided by Islamic, European, or traditional African spiritual traditions. The language of the novel, which Africanizes French with expressions drawn from the author's native Mandingo, is probably the most original in African francophone fiction.

Ousmane Sembene and the Afro-Asiatic Movement

Like pan-African writers, those inspired by Afro-Asianism also replace the European perspective with an African one. These writers assume the role of conscience of their people. Respectful of African traditions but rejecting the Negritude aesthetic altogether, writers in the Afro-Asiatic movement seek to mobilize their people against European colonial domination through a call to Marxist-inspired political struggle rather than a return to cultural purity. Afro-Asianism, which crystallized at the conference of Bandung, Indonesia, in 1955, marks a coming together of the African struggles for independence with forces generated by (1) movements of Arab and Asian nationalism, (2) the support of the Soviet Union for colonized peoples against Western imperialism, and (3) the newfound independence of China, India, Egypt, and Indonesia.

Ousmane Sembene embodies the Afro-Asiatic aesthetic in both literature and film.[6] His most important novel is the classic *Les Bouts de bois de Dieu* (1960; *God's Bits of Wood*), which is the story of the successful 1947 Dakar-Niger railroad strike against the French during the colonial period. The author's role as conscience of his people, holding up the way of liberation, is clear in an author's note that precedes the novel:

> The men and women who, from the tenth of October, 1947, to the nine-teenth of March, 1948, took part in this struggle for a better way of life owe nothing to anyone: neither to any "civilizing mission" nor to any parliament or parliamentarian. Their example was not in vain. Since then, Africa has made progress.[7]

Other works include the autobiographical *Docker noir* (1956) about the author's experiences as a dock worker in Marseille, *Oh pays, mon beau peuple* (1957), *Voltaïque* (1962; *Tribal Scars and Other Stories*), *L'Harmattan* (1964), *Le Mandat et Véhi Ciosane* (1969; *The Money Order with White Genesis*), *Xala* (1973), and *Le Dernier de l'empire* (1981).

Although *God's Bits of Wood* was successful in Europe, Sembene was dissatisfied because he was unable to reach his own people. Thus, he took advantage of an offer from the Moscow Film School to learn cinema. His first film was *Borom saret,* which tells the story of the driver of a donkey-drawn taxi cart. From that point on, Sembene, the father of African cinema, has converted many of his short stories into films in which he uses native Senegalese languages instead of or along with French. The subsequent work of Ousmane Sembene spans the entire gamut of African filmmaking—primarily a phenomenon that emerged in former French colonies in Africa—and will be used to represent African cinema in this chapter. His *Emitaï* (1971) and *Camp de Thiaroye* (1988) describe colonialist abuses during and immediately after World War II. *La Noire de . . .* (1965; *Black Girl*) recounts the travails of a maid who is so mistreated by her French master and mistress that she commits suicide.

Other films explore issues in the precolonial past—not to reestablish cultural purity, however, but to make a point about present domination. Sembene's film *Ceddo* (1977) is a study of African resistance to conversion to Islam. This film and *Camp de Thiaroye* are politically so explosive that they have been either banned or edited by censors in Senegal.

Films such as *Mandabi* (winner of a prize at the Venice Film Festival) and *Xala* (1974) are socialist-realist denunciations of abuses in postcolonial Senegalese society. *Xala*—the title means temporary sexual impotence in Wolof—attacks the political economic and cultural impotence of the

Senegalese black bourgeoisie. This shift from an emphasis on answering
European accounts about Africa to a concern to identify problems and issues
in contemporary independent Africa is also characteristic of fiction written
after French African colonies achieved independence in the early 1960s.

Postcolonial Fiction in French

Postcolonial fiction explores many different directions. Postcolonial
"novels of disillusion" attack the abuses of postcolonial African states: dictatorship, corruption, and misery. This fiction is less clearly didactic in
nature. It neither embodies a clear-cut ideology nor does it present authoritative visions of the African past—although the influence of African tradition remains present in many subtle ways. Postcolonial fiction, rather,
explores reality in order to open new possibilities. This stance was already
prepared by the colonial novels of Beti, Oyono, and Kourouma and is
embodied in Mongo Beti's later novels: *Perpétue ou l'habitude du malheur*
(1974; *Perpetua and the Habit of Unhappiness*), *Remember Ruben* (1974),
and *La Ruine presque cocasse d'un polichinelle.* Another writer in this vein
is Sony Labou Tansi, whose novels include *La Vie et demie* (1979), and
L'Etat honteux (1981). More recent fiction abandons political agenda altogether for either a variety of inner adventures, such as Ibrahima Ly's *La
Toile d'araignée,* or a portrait of the decadence of Senegalese society, as in
Abasse Ndione's *Vie en spirale.*

Women's writing is an important phenomenon in Africa. Much of it cor-
rects the vision of Africa in men's writing just as African men's writing corrected European accounts of Africa. Women's writing draws back from
authoritative positions as it seeks a new language. For example, Mariama
Bâ's *Une si longue lettre* (1979; *So Long a Letter*) portrays a woman caught
between the rhetoric of the traditional Senegalese family and that of a modern Europeanized feminism as she struggles, first to create her marriage and
then to survive it when it turns unexpectedly polygynous. In this first-per-
son narrative, no voice, including the narrator's own, suffices to explain
events with authority. There is, for example, no explicit call for monogamy.
Bâ's second novel, *Le Chant écarlate* (1981), is similar; it explores the problems encountered by a Frenchwoman in her marriage to a Senegalese man.

Aminata Maïga Ka's two novellas, *La Voie du salut* and *Miroir de la vie*
(1985), also present women whose lives diverge from their ways of thinking. Although largely third-person narratives, these pieces taken together
artfully reproduce in French the ways of thinking and speaking characteristic of various classes of people. Aminata Maïga Ka's characters typically fail
to cope with the realities that overwhelm them. They turn to suicide and
alcohol. Such failures are brought about not only by external events but also
by the rhetorics of class, honor, and family in which the characters are
trapped. Like the novels of Mariama Bâ, these novellas open up new per-

spectives brought about by women's voices but leave readers to draw their own conclusions.

The most prolific of Senegalese women writers is Aminata Sow Fall, who writes in a more pluralistic vein. Her novels include *Le Revenant* (1976), *La Grève des battus ou les déchets humains* (1979), and *L'Appel des arènes* (1982). These novels not only elaborate a woman's language but also explore the contradictions and blind spots of male discourse. For example, Aminata Sow Fall's most recent novel, *L'Ex-père de la nation* (1987), explores the self-deceptive rhetoric of the male narrator, who is a deposed African head of state in prison thinking back over the events of his rise and fall. What seems at first a language of pretension turns out to be a rhetoric of light, transparency, and cleanliness that ironically blinds the narrator to the machinations of power going on inside and outside the presidential palace. Aminata Sow Fall artfully reproduces the various French dialects characteristic of different classes of society.

Theater in French

Theater in French has not been a very successful genre in Africa. The formal setting of theaters contrasts sharply with the setting of the popular village square where much West African oral literature takes place. The strongest Negritude playwright is Martinique's Aimé Césaire, whose plays *La Tragédie du roi Christophe* (*Emperor Jones*) and *Une Saison au Congo* are distinguished by a highly original use of French. Another playwright from the early period is Cheikh N'dao, whose *Exil d'Albouri* dramatizes a moment from the traditional African past.

More recently, however, the African stage has been distinguished by the works of Sony Labou Tansi (*Conscience de tracteur,* 1979; and *La Parenthèse de sang,* 1981) and Werewere-Liking (*La Puissance de UM,* 1979; and *Une Nouvelle Terre,* 1980). Werewere-Liking's *Orphée d'Afric/Orphée d'Afrique* is a mixed genre, a novel followed by a play.

☐ African Literature in Portuguese

Before going on to African literature in English, a word is in order about lusophone (Portuguese) African literature. Poets such as the first president of Angola, Agostinho Neto, the Angolan José Craveirinha, and the Cape Verdean Baltasar Lopes write in the tradition of pan-Africanism. The works of these writers and others are known to English speakers primarily from Mário de Andrade's *Antologia de poesia negra de espressão portuguesa* (1958). Fiction writers include José Luandino Vieira (*Luuanda,* 1963; and *A Vida verdadeira de Domingos Xavier,* 1961; *The Real Life of Domingos Xavier*) and Luís Bernard Honwana (*Nós natanis a cão tinhoso,* 1964; *We Killed Mangy Dog and Other Stories*).

☐ African Literature in English

African writers in English tend to be more independent than those in French because they often came to English culture by choice while secure in their African cultural roots. The British did not have a unified policy of "cultural imperialism" (imposing their own culture) as did the French. Thus, African writers in English have been more interested in experimenting as artists of the written word than in asserting their identity as "African." For example, the best-known Nigerian writer, Wole Soyinka, has said in reference to Negritude, "A tiger does not proclaim his tigritude, he pounces." He goes on to say that what one should expect from poetry is "an intrinsic poetic quality, not a mere name-dropping" (quoted in Zell, Bundy, and Coulon, 1983:491).

As a result, African literature in English has rich traditions in the novel, poetry, and drama. Unlike French, where most writers tend to write in one genre alone, African writers in English practice several genres. The phenomenon is so rich and diverse that it does not yield to so neat a periodization as does French African literature, since novelists of the earlier English African generations already were writing social criticism of African life of the kind common in the third period of French African literature.

Nigerian Fiction

Aside from scattered beginnings in the eighteenth and nineteenth centuries (Olaudah Equiano and Phillis Wheatley), Nigerian literature in English took its impulse from two sources. One is the popular tradition of Onitsha novels (named after the market where they were sold) that began in the 1940s. The second is the educational infrastructure provided by the founding of the University College of Ibadan in 1948. Now called the University of Ibadan, this institution had more autonomous policies than later French universities, so that African writers could teach there and establish a closer relationship between African culture and writing in English than could writers who used French.

The best-known and most prolific writer to come out of the Onitsha tradition is Cyprian Ekwensi. Although a man of considerable education, Ekwensi writes popular novels such as *People of the City* (1954), *Jagua Nana* (1961), *Divided We Stand* (1980), and *Motherless Baby* (a novella). He has also written several children's books. Ekwensi's novels feature people from various walks of life but often deal with such issues as prostitution, urban lowlife, and political violence.

The major Nigerian novelist of this early generation is Chinua Achebe, who has also written poetry (*Beware Soul Brothers and Other Poems,* 1972), short stories (*Girls at War and Other Stories,* 1972), and various children's stories. Achebe is a writer from the more learned tradition of Nigerian writing, having completed his studies at the University College of Ibadan in 1953. His great cycle of novels written between 1958 and 1966 spans a period of Nigerian history from the onset of colonialism to the eve of the civil war sparked by the attempt of Biafra to secede from the country in the 1960s.

Like French writers, Achebe—whose statements on the role of the writer in Africa have been published in a collection entitled *Morning Yet on Creation Day* (1975)—originally began to write in order to correct European writings on Africa. He said in a Bill Moyers interview that in college, while reading Conrad's *Heart of Darkness,* he realized that he was not the white hero but "one of the natives jumping up and down on the beach." It was then that he knew that it was time to write another story. Elsewhere he says, "I would be quite satisfied if my novels (especially ones I set in the past) did no more than teach my readers that their past—with all its imperfection— was not one long night of savagery from which the first Europeans acting on God's behalf delivered them" (Zell, Bundy, and Coulon, 1983:345).

Accordingly, Achebe's first novel, *Things Fall Apart* (1958), is the story of the tragedy that the arrival of Christianity and the onset of colonialism represent for the village of Umuofia. Thus, the novel frequently leaves the main character, Okonkwo, in the background in order to give rich descriptions of the traditional village life that is disrupted by the arrival of the Europeans. Achebe alludes to the great life cycles implied in planting and harvesting, getting married and dying, and passing the various ceremonial stages of social promotion.

Achebe's third novel, *Arrow of God* (1964), is set in the 1950s but also deals with the conflict between traditional and modern values. It is the story of the backfire of the project of a village priest named Ezeulu, who sends his son Oduche to the mission school to learn the white man's secrets: Oduche converts to Christianity and kills the sacred python of Ezeulu's traditional African religion.

Achebe's first and third novels recall the literature of Negritude because of their emphasis on African tradition. His second and fourth novels, which deal with conflicts and tensions in modern Nigeria, prefigure novels of contemporary African literature. *No Longer at Ease* (1960) is the story of Okonkwo's grandson, who has difficulties adapting to Nigerian society after he returns from school in England. He falls in love with an outcast woman and succumbs to bribes that ultimately ruin his career. *A Man of the People* (1964) is a satire on the government of Nigeria. The end of the novel, which evokes a military coup, foreshadows the onset of the 1967 Nigerian civil war against secessionist Biafra.

After a period of more than twenty years, Achebe published another novel, *Anthills of the Savannah,* in 1987. This novel describes the power plays and corruption of contemporary African society from the perspective of several narrators, including the president of the country, two of his school friends, and their girlfriends. This kaleidoscopic vision leaves the reader to draw conclusions as to the whys and wherefores of the plot.

Achebe is a master of the English language and draws heavily on classical European as well as Ibo and Yoruba cultures. For example, the title of *Things Fall Apart* is derived from W. B. Yeats's "The Second Coming." The stately English of Achebe's early novels is colored with Ibo-inspired proverbs, whereas in *Anthills of the Savannah,* he reproduces modern spoken Nigerian English, including "pidgin," used by the less educated.

A much more extreme experimentation with English is evident in the works of the non-Ibo novelists Amos Tutuola—whose novels, such as *The Palm-Wine Drinkard* (1952), use speech patterns of the Yoruba language— and Gabriel Okara, who reproduces patterns of his native Ijo syntax in his novels, such as *The Voice.*

Like their French-speaking counterparts, women novelists in Nigeria have been productive, writing in voices different from those of male authors. Flora Nwapa is the first published woman novelist in Africa. Her *Efuru* (1966) and *Idu* (1969) describe the difficulties women encounter as they come to terms with their expected social roles as wives and mothers. Her *Never Again* (1976) is a description of an episode in the Nigerian civil war from a woman's perspective. Flora Nwapa has also published collections of short stories such as *This Is Lagos and Other Stories* (1971) and *Wives at War and Other Stories* (1980). She has founded a publishing house that has published her novel *One Is Enough* (1981) and children's stories, which she hopes will be read by children the world over.

Another major Nigerian woman novelist is Buchi Emecheta, who has been hailed as having given a realistic and complex alternative to the one-sided picture of African women found in male fiction. A sociologist who obtained her training while a single parent supporting five children, Emecheta got her start writing a regular column recording her observations of London society for the *New Statesman.* Her first two novels, the autobiographical *In the Ditch* (1972) and *Second Class Citizen* (1974), detail difficulties of African women in England, whereas *The Bride Price* (1976), *The Slave Girl* (1977), and *Joys of Motherhood* (1979) deal with the difficulties encountered by women as they marry, bear children, or find themselves tools for the ambitions of their male relatives. Other novels deal with the civil war (*Destination Biafra*) and problems in contemporary Nigerian society (*Naira Power* and *The Double Yoke*).

Emecheta is a powerful writer whose images are metaphors for deep female experience as well as literal descriptions of traditional African supernatural forces. For example, in *Joys of Motherhood,* the experience of the main character, Nnu Ego, is often explained in terms of water imagery that recalls that she is accursed by her *chi,* a water deity.

Nigerian Poetry and Theater

Two main forces behind Nigerian literature are the Mbari Club—which is not only a meeting place for writers and artists but also a publishing outlet—and the literary journal *Black Orpheus,* which has published the work of many Nigerian poets in its pages.

Christopher Okigbo (*Heavensgate,* 1962, and *Limits,* 1964) is a poet originally published by Mbari. A posthumous collection entitled *Labyrinths with Paths of Thunder* (1971) came out in London after Okigbo's life was cut short in the civil war. Okigbo, who considered himself a reincarnation of his maternal grandfather—a priest of Idoto—draws on a good background in Western culture as well as the cultures of Nigeria. He has said that his poetic sequence *Heavensgate, Limits,* and *Distances* is "like telling the beads of a rosary; except that the beads are neither stone nor agate but globules of anguish strung together on memory" (Zell, Bundy, and Coulon, 1983:448). An example of his cultural eclecticism is *Heavensgate,* which is written as an Easter sequence conceived as a Catholic mass offered to Mother Idoto.

In his 1965 verse collection, *A Reed in the Tide,* John Pepper Clark, a playwright as well as a poet, calls himself a "mulatto—not in flesh but in mind" (Zell, Bundy, and Coulon, 1983:367). His other verse includes *Poems,* brought out by Mbari in 1962, and *Casualties* (1968).

Clark is also a playwright of distinction whose plays include *Song of a Goat* (1962), *The Masquerade,* and *The Raft.* His *Ozidi* (1966) is based on an Ijo saga. He subsequently published a book-length edition (*The Ozidi Saga,* 1977), which in the oral tradition takes seven days to perform.

Wole Soyinka, who won the 1986 Nobel Prize in literature, is the most prominent writer in Nigeria. He is perhaps the best contemporary dramatic poet in English, as well as a distinguished novelist, essayist, and playwright.

Soyinka's first verse was published in *Black Orpheus.* His first collection, *Idanre, and Other Poems* (1967), includes the long poem "Idanre," which was written for the Commonwealth Arts Festival of 1965. "Idanre" is a creation myth of Ogun, the Yoruba god of iron, who, with his aspects of creation and destruction, represents human dualism and is for Soyinka the "symbol figure" of his society. Other collections include *A Shuttle in the Crypt* (1971), written during Soyinka's civil war imprisonment, and *Ogun Abibman* (1976), which is a tribute to the African struggle for liberation.

Soyinka's first novel, *The Interpreters* (1965), is the story of a group of university-educated friends who attempt to interpret their role in Nigerian society. The novel has an extremely dense texture of language that recalls James Joyce. *Season of Anomy* (1973) incorporates the myth of Orpheus and Eurydice as it tells the quest of Ofeyi for his abducted mistress, Iriyise, the cocoa princess. The novel is a political allegory of the social ills of modern

Nigeria that mixes reality and fantasy, African ritual nature myths, and European archetypes. Soyinka's *Ake: The Years of Childhood* (1981) is an autobiography of his first twelve years.

Soyinka is best known for his more than twenty plays, which use themes concerning African culture and politics as well as the confrontation between Europe and Africa to explore universal constants of the human mind and metaphysical problems of good and evil. Soyinka sets out his views on writing in a collection of essays entitled *Myth, Literature and the African World* (1976). In this work, one of his goals is to establish parallels between a classical Yoruba worldview and the Greek tradition in European literature. His essay "The Fourth Stage" is on the Yoruba concept of tragedy, whereas in "Drama and the African World View," he affirms that the differences of European and African drama result from two different world visions:

> Westerners have a compartmentalizing habit of thought which selects aspects of human emotion and even scientific observations and "turns them into separatist myths." African creativity, on the other hand, results from "a cohesive understanding of irreducible truths." (Zell, Bundy, and Coulon, 1983:52)

Soyinka is a brilliant satirist. In a lighter vein are his early *Lion and the Jewel* (1959), which mockingly chronicles the competition between a polygynous, lecherous village chief and a Europeanized schoolteacher for the hand of a village beauty, and *The Trials of Brother Jero* (1963), which satirizes the syncretistic Christian cults of Nigeria.

Other plays written for important occasions unflinchingly attack popular conceptions. *A Dance of the Forests,* performed to celebrate Nigerian independence in October 1960, criticizes "the myth of the glorious African past, rejecting the Negritude concept that the revival of African culture must be inspired by the African cultural heritage alone" (Beier, Knappert, and Moser, 1974:142). *Kongi's Harvest,* written for the 1966 World Festival of Negro Arts in Dakar, relentlessly satirizes African dictatorships. *The Road* (1965), performed at the Commonwealth Arts Festival (1965), is one of the fullest expressions of Soyinka's tragic view of life.

Works such as the satirical sketches gathered in *Before the Blackout* (1971) and *Madmen and Specialists* (1971) use theater of the absurd techniques to attack the civil war. *Madmen and Specialists,* however, uses the events of the civil war as a context to consider the problem of evil, whereas Soyinka's *Bacchae of Euripides* (1973) combines elements of the Greek play with allusions to public executions on Bar Beach in Lagos during the civil war to conduct a ritualistic exploration of the human mind.

Death and the King's Horseman (1975) is based on historical events in which a district officer prevented the Elesin Oba from committing suicide to follow his king into death. According to Soyinka,

The confrontation in the play is largely metaphysical, contained in the human vehicle which is Elesin and the universe of the Yoruba mind—the world of the living, the dead and the unborn, and the numinous passage which links all: transition. (Zell, Bundy, and Coulon, 1983:489)

(Soyinka, by the way, served as editor of the distinguished cultural and political magazine *Transition* [*Ch'indaba*], which he is now in the process of reviving.)

Soyinka's *Opera Wonyosi* (1981) draws on Brecht's *Threepenny Opera* and John Gay's *Beggar's Opera* to satirize contemporary Nigerian life. According to Robert MacDowell, Soyinka

makes use of fascinating devices in his own expressionistic plays; dancing, singing, miming, speeches in verse, flashbacks (sometimes covering eons of time), and characters from the spirit world. He employs techniques familiar at Nigerian festivals, and utilizes any poetic methods which enforce the emotional and intellectual impact of his dramas; in short he has no slavish attachment to the merely naturalistic level of presentation. (Zell, Bundy, and Coulon 1983:490)

Soyinka is a committed writer but one who has a high conception of his art. At the 1967 African-Scandinavian Writers Conference in Stockholm, he criticized foreign publishers who create reputations for insignificant authors and the African author whom he characterizes as "the most celebrated skin of inconsequence to obscure the true flesh of the African dilemma" (Zell, Bundy, and Coulon 1983:491). He goes on to say that such a writer

was content to turn his eye backwards in time and prospect in archaic fields for forgotten gems which would dazzle and distract the present. But never inwards, never truly into the present. . . . The artist has always functioned in African society as the record of the mores and experience of his society and as the voice of vision in his own time. It is time for him to respond to this essence of himself. (Zell, Bundy, and Coulon 1983:491–492)

Other Nigerian and West African Authors

Nigerian authors of the second generation who deserve mention are poets Tanure Ojaide, Odia Ofeimun, Niyi Osundare, and Harry Garuba; the dramatists Femi Osofisan, Ola Rotimi, and Tess Onwueme; and the novelists Kole Omotoso and Festus Iyayi. There is also now a third generation, which includes the poets Afam Akeh, Uche Nduka, Esiaba Irobi, Kemi Atanda-Ilori, and Catherine Acholonu as well as the novelist Wale Okediran.

Nigerian literature dominates West African anglophone writing, but some other notable writers are the Gambian poet Lenri Peters and the Ghanaians Kofi Awooner (poet), Efua Sutherland (playwright), Ami Ata Aidoo (playwright and novelist), and Ayi Kwei Armah (novelist).

East Africa

East African writing in English has not developed into as full a tradition as West African writing in English. Important writers from East Africa include the Kenyan short story writer Grace Ogot, who incorporates tribal laws and wisdom in her works; the Ugandan poet Okot p'Bitek; and the Somalian novelist and playwright Nruddin Farah.

The major East African literary figure to date is Ngugi wa Thiong'o (formerly James Ngugi), whose novels *Weep Not Child* (1964), *The River Between* (1965), and *A Grain of Wheat* (1967) parallel Achebe's novels in Nigeria in that they trace the history of Kenya from the arrival of the British to modern times. According to Andrew Gurr,

> They start with the alienation of Gikuyu land and end with the alienation of the social and individual psyche of the colonised. The first [novel] begins at a time when the Gikuyu have their land, and the colonial presence is little more than one of missionaries and mission schools, a force which divides the people but does not yet dispossess them. In the second novel they are the dispossessed, tenant farmers, landless laborers or fighters seeking to regain the land which is home. In the third novel the white colonial landlords are going, leaving behind them the traumatised victims of the struggle and the new black landlords who threaten to perpetuate the system of alienation which colonialism set up. (Zell, Bundy, and Coulon, 1983:432)

Ngugi's *Petals of Blood* (1977) is a picture of corruption in modern-day Kenya with flashbacks to the fight for independence. According to Christopher Ricks, the book

> begins with a fire—arson?—in which there are killed three prominent, corrupt figures of the new Kenya. It ends with our knowing exactly what happened and why. But its journey, which has at its heart an actual journey taken by the drought-stricken people of the village of Ilmorog in order to beg for help from the city-world of its MP and of the national conscience, takes it back through all the sufferings of the fight for national freedom. (Zell, Bundy, and Coulon, 1983:433)

Devil on the Cross (1982) was originally written in Kikuyu on leaves of lavatory paper while the author was in prison for a year but under no charges. The novel centers on the heroine Wariinga, who is "fired for refusing to sleep with her boss, and evicted from her shanty for refusing to pay exorbitant rent" (Zell, Bundy, and Coulon, 1983:190).

Ngugi is one of the most powerful writers in Africa today and one of the leading proponents of writing in African languages. His production also includes several plays (*This Time Tomorrow,* 1957; *The Black Hermit,* 1968; *The Rebels,* 1970; *Wound in the Heart,* 1970; and *I Will Marry When I Want,*

1982) originally performed in Kikuyu, short stories (*Secret Lives and Other Stories*, 1975), and critical essays (*Homecoming: Essays on African and Caribbean Literature, Culture and Politics*, 1972; *Writers in Politics, Essays*, 1981; and *Detainees: A Writer's Prison Diary*, 1981).

South Africa

Just as West and East African writers in European languages began to write in an effort to tell a story about Africa that had been left untold in European colonial writing, nonwhite South African writers in English, who have been excluded by the white community, tell a story that would otherwise remain smothered by apartheid. Rather than delve into the African past, these writers denounce the nefarious effects they suffer from apartheid in the present. The earliest novelist is Peter Abrahams, whose novels include *Mine Boy*, 1946; *Song of the City*, 1945; *Path of Thunder*, 1948; *Wild Conquest*, 1950; *A Wreath for Udomo*, 1965; and his memoirs, *Tell Freedom*, 1954. Todd Matshikiza, Ezekiel Mphahlele, Richard Rive, Alex La Guma, and Can Themba have all published short stories in magazines such as the famous *Drum*. Ezekiel (Es'kia) Mphahlele's *Down Second Avenue* (1959) is an example of autobiographies written by South African writers to denounce the oppression of the white regime.

Nonwhite writers in South Africa have worked against enormous odds, including not only the inaccessibility of education but also censorship, prison, and exile. Two of the strongest prose writers are Richard Rive and Alex La Guma. Richard Rive's *Emergency* (1964), for example, tells the story of the state of emergency declared by the South African government after the Sharpeville massacre. Like most others, Rive is an urban South African who eschews the pastoralism of Negritude in favor of urban themes: "life in the slums, the consequences of overt protest and the ironies of racial prejudice and color snobbery" (Zell, Bundy, and Coulon, 1983:472). According to Bernth Lindfors, Rive's style is "characterized by strong rhythms, daring images, brisk dialogue and leitmotifs (recurring words, phrases, images) which function as unifying devices within stories" (Zell, Bundy, and Coulon, 1983:472).

Alex La Guma is also a writer who concerns himself with life in the city, prison, and town. The short story "A Walk in the Night" (1962) tells of Michael Adonis, a "coloured" boy who is fired from his job and ultimately becomes a fatality of police brutality. His *And a Threefold Cord* (1964) is a novel about life in a ghetto bordering Cape Town. Other novels include *The Stone Country* (1967), which tells of life in South African jails; *In the Fog of the Season's End* (1972), which deals with political activism; and *Time of the Butcherbird* (1979), which recounts the forced resettlement of whole communities to other townships. La Guma's style, according to Lindfors, is "characterized by graphic description, careful evocation of atmosphere and mood, fusion of pathos and humor, colorful dialogue and occasional surprise endings" (Zell, Bundy, and Coulon, 1983:402).

Unlike these urbanized writers, Bessie Head has settled in rural Botswana. She has published three novels that make up a kind of trilogy: *When Rain Clouds Gather* (1969), *Maru* (1971), and *A Question of Power* (1974). Of Bessie Head's style Arthur Ravenscroft states:

> In *A Question of Power* we are taken nightmarishly into the central character's process of mental breakdown, through lurid cascades of hallucination and a pathological blurring of the frontiers between insanity and any kind of normalcy. (Zell, Bundy, and Coulon, 1983:390)

Bessie Head's interest in tradition is reflected in her *Serowe: The Village of the Rainwind* (1981), which is a series of interviews conducted among the villagers of Serowe.

South African poets include Dennis Brutus, Keorapetse Kgositsile, Mazisi and Daniel Kunene, and Mongane Wally Serote. All of these poets have been forced to live in exile. Kgositsile has become well known in African American circles. His *Spirits Unchained* (1969) fuses the experience of African Americans with that of South Africans. His *My Name Is Afrika* (1971) is an angry denunciation of institutional hypocrisy. Other collections include *The Present Is a Dangerous Place to Live* (1974) and *Places and Bloodstains* (1976). Dennis Brutus is perhaps the best known of these poets. Beginning with *Sirens, Knuckles and Boots* (1963), he has steadily published his poetry in the face of greatest adversity. His *Letters to Martha* (1968) are poems written to his sister-in-law in the form of letters, to elude the censor's interdict against his poetry. In *Poems from Algiers* (1970) Brutus questions his right as an exile to speak as an African voice. In *Simple Lust* (1973) and *Strains* (1975), he deals with the cruelty of apartheid and the difficulties of exile. Yet, according to S. C. Nolutshungu, "Brutus is dignified, self-controlled, almost urbane even when the pain is at its worst" (quoted in Zell, Bundy, and Coulon, 1983:207). In this, he is like many South African writers who rise above adversity and oppression to preserve their humanity and sense of beauty.

■ CONCLUSIONS

African literature is full of threatened promise. For the time being, oral traditions manage to survive despite serious interruptions in time-honored modes of transmission. The children of *griots* go to modern schools before their training in oral traditions is complete. Elsewhere, the attraction to modern life turns attention away from traditions conserving the past.

Written African literature will continue to turn—as it already has—away from a primarily European audience to an African one. As colonialism has receded in time, and problems of the postindependence period have commanded attention, local issues rather than proving an "African" identity to the European world have grown in importance. In addressing these concerns, African writers are incorporating fragile oral traditions into their work to make them accessible to an audience more at ease with oral than with written communication. The choice of language is also changing as writers communicate more often in African languages.

Because of the political and economic instability in Africa discussed throughout this book, African writers have faced and continue to face very real threats of prison, exile, and death. Moreover, writers must make their way through the labyrinth of the Western-dominated publishing market. Despite such obstacles, writers are developing distinct national literatures in both European and African languages. It is already possible to speak of full-blown Nigerian, Senegalese, Cameroonian, and Ghanaian literatures. Other literatures not mentioned in this chapter, such as Zairian and Tanzanian, will also increasingly make their mark. If all goes well, the reader of the twenty-first century will find a rich and highly diverse situation in which the term "African literature" will be as vague a generalization as "European literature" or "Asian literature."

■ NOTES

I would like to thank Emmanuel Obiechina and Ousmane Sene for so kindly reading earlier versions of this chapter, and Wlodzimierz Borejsza-Wysocki for his help in obtaining the photograph of printed African works.

1. This tradition corresponds to what Janheinz Jahn (1966) calls "Neo-African literature."

2. Tr. Ezekiel Mphahlele, as cited in Beier, Knappert, and Moser, 1974: 140.

3. Anthropologist Judith T. Irvine has graciously shared this information with me.

4. Selections from Senghor's poetry have been translated into English as follows: *Léopold Sédar Senghor: Selected Poems* (1964) and *Léopold Sédar Senghor: Prose and Poetry* (1965; both translated by John Reed and Clive Wake), *Selected Poems/Poésies choisies* (tr. Craig Williamson, 1976), and *Selected Poems of Léopold Sédar Senghor* (tr. Abiola Irele, 1977.)

5. *Présence africaine* 1 (November-December 1947), p. 8. Quoted in Mouralis, 421. My translation.

6. Although the reverse appears in some works, the true order of the author's name is Ousmane Sembene. The reversal in many francophone authors' names is due to the fact that in the French schools, the roll was called last name first.

7. Sembene Ousmane, *God's Bits of Wood,* tr. Francis Price (1961) (London: Heinemann, 1983), page facing p. 1.

■ BIBLIOGRAPHY

☐ Bibliographies and Readers' Guides

Arnold, Stephen H., and Milan V. Dimić. 1985. *African Literature Studies: The Present State/L'Etat présent.* Washington, DC: Three Continents Press.
Berrian, Brenda. 1989. *Bibliography of African Women Writers and Journalists.* Washington, DC: Three Continents Press.
Herdeck, Donald E. (ed.). 1973. *African Authors: A Companion to Black African Writing.* Vol. 1: 1300–1973. Washington, DC: Black Orpheus Press.
Jahn, Janheinz. 1965. *A Bibliography of Neo-African Literature: From Africa, America and the Caribbean.* New York: Praeger.
Jahn, Janheinz, and C. P. Dressler. 1971. *Bibliography of Creative African Writing.* Nendeln, Liechtenstein: Kraus-Thomson.
Jahn, Janheinz, Ulla Schild, and Almut Nordmann (eds.). 1972. *Who's Who in African Literature: Biographies, Works and Commentaries.* Tübingen, Germany: Horst Erdmann Verlag.
Zell, Hans M., Carol Bundy, and Virginia Coulon. 1983. *A New Reader's Guide to African Literature.* New York: Africana.

☐ Oral Literatures

Beier, Ulli. 1966. *The Origin of Life and Death: A Collection of Creation Myths from Africa.* London: HEB.
———. 1970. *Yoruba Poetry: An Anthology of Traditional Poems.* London: Cambridge University Press.
———. 1980. *Yoruba Myths.* Cambridge: Cambridge University Press.
Finnegan, Ruth. 1970. *Oral Literature in Africa.* Oxford: Oxford University Press.
Frobenius, Leo. 1937. *African Genesis.* New York: Stackpole Sons.
Griaule, Marcel. 1948. *Conversations with Ogotemmeli.* London: Oxford University Press.
Herskovits, Melville J., and Frances S. 1958. *Dahomean Narrative.* Evanston: Northwestern University Press.
Joseph, George. 1979. "The Wolof Oral Praise Song for Semu Coro Wende." *Research in African Literatures* 10:145–178.
Mapanje, Jack, and Landeg White. 1983. *Oral Poetry from Africa: An Anthology.*
Oxford Library of African Literature volumes:
   Evans-Pritchard, E. E. (ed.). 1967. *The Zande Trickster.*
   Johnston, H. A. S. 1966. *A Selection of Hausa Stories.*
   Mbiti, John S. (ed.). 1966. *Akamba Stories.*
   Whiteley, W. H. 1964. *A Selection of African Prose.* Vol. 1. Traditional Oral Texts.

☐ Written African Literatures in African Languages

Gérard, Albert. 1971. *Four African Literatures: Xhosa, Sotho, Zulu, Amharic.* Berkeley: University of California Press.
———. 1980. *African Language Literatures: An Introduction to the Literary History of Sub-Saharan Africa.* Washington, DC: Three Continents Press.

☐ Modern Literatures in European Languages—Criticism

Achebe, Chinua. 1975. *Morning Yet on Creation Day: Essays.* London: HEB.

Awoonor, Kofi. 1975. *The Breast of the Earth: A Survey of the History, Culture, and Literature of Africa South of the Sahara.* Garden City, NY: Anchor Press/Doubleday.

Beier, Ulli. 1967. *An Introduction to African Literature: An Anthology of Critical Writing.* Evanston: Northwestern University Press.

Beier, Ulli, Jan Knappert, and Gerald Moser. 1974. "African Arts." *Encyclopaedia Britannica: Macropaedia, Knowledge in Depth.* Vol. 13: 139–145.

Blair, Dorothy S. 1976. *African Literature in French: A History of Creative Writing in French from West and Equatorial Africa.* Cambridge: Cambridge University Press.

Brench, A. C. 1967. *The Novelists' Inheritance in French Africa: Writers from Senegal to Cameroon.* London: Oxford University Press.

Burness, Donald. 1989. *Fire: Six Writers from Angola, Mozambique, and Cape Verde.* Washington, DC: Three Continents Press.

Burton, Samuel H., and C. J. H. Chacksfield. 1979. *African Poetry in English.* London: Macmillan.

Cartey, Wilfred. 1969. *Whispers from a Continent.* New York: Random House.

Chinweizu, Onwuchekwa Jemie, and Ihechukwu Madubuike. 1980. *Toward the Decolonization of African Literature. Vol. 1: African Fiction and Poetry and Their Critics.* Enugu, Nigeria: Fourth Dimension.

Clark, John Pepper. 1971. *The Example of Shakespeare.* London: Longman.

Cook, David. 1977. *African Literature: A Critical View.* London: Longman.

Cornevin, Robert. 1976. *Littératures d'Afrique noire de langue française.* Paris: Presses Universitaires de France.

Dathorne, Oskar R. 1974. *The Black Mind.* Minneapolis: University of Minnesota Press.

———. 1975. *African Literature in the Twentieth Century.* Minneapolis: University of Minnesota Press.

Diop, Cheikh Anta. 1974. *The African Origin of Civilization: Myth or Reality.* Edited and translated by Mercer Cook. New York: Lawrence Hill.

———. 1987. *Precolonial Black Africa.* Translated by Harold Salemson. New York: Lawrence Hill.

Echuero, Michael J. C. 1977. *Poets, Prophets and Professors.* Ibadan, Nigeria: Ibadan University Press.

Egejuru, Phanuel A. 1978. *Black Writers, White Audience: A Critical Approach to African Literature.* Hicksville, NY: Exposition Press.

———. 1980. *Towards African Literary Independence: A Dialogue with Contemporary African Writers.* Westview, CT: Greenwood Press.

Erickson, John D. 1979. *Nommo: African Fiction in French South of the Sahara.* York, SC: French Literature Publishing.

Gakwandi, Shatto Arthur. 1977. *The Novel and Contemporary Experience in Africa.* London: HEB.

Gérard, Albert. 1986. *European-Language Writing in Sub-Saharan Africa.* Budapest: Akademiai Kiado.

Githae-Mugop, Micere. 1978. *Visions of Africa.* Nairobi: Kenya Literature Bureau.

Gleason, Judith. 1965. *This Africa: Novels by West Africans in English and French.* Evanston: Northwestern University Press.

Gordimer, Nadine. 1973. *The Black Interpreters: Notes on African Writing.* Johannesburg: Ravan Press.

Graham-White, Anthony. 1975. *The Drama of Black Africa.* New York: Samuel French.

Gray, Stephen. 1979. *Southern African Literature: An Introduction.* New York: Harper and Row.

Hale, T. A., and R. O. Priebe (eds.). 1977. *The Teaching of African Literature: Selected Working Papers from the African Literature Association.* Austin: African Literature Association, University of Texas Press.

Harrow, Kenneth. 1991. *Faces of Islam in African Literature.* Portsmouth, NH: Heinemann.

Irele, Abiola. 1990. *The African Experience in Literature and Ideology.* 1981. Bloomington: Indiana University Press.

Jahn, Janheinz. 1961. *Muntu: An Outline of the New African Culture.* New York: Grove Press.

———. 1966. *A History of Neo-African Literature.* London: Faber and Faber.

JanMohamed, Abdul. 1983. *Manichean Aesthetics: The Politics of Literature in Colonial Africa.* Amherst: University of Massachusetts Press.

Joseph, George. 1979. "The Wolof Oral Praise Song for Semu Coro Wende." *Research in African Literatures* 10:145–178.

Kennedy, J. Scott. 1973. *In Search of African Theatre.* New York: Charles Scribner's Sons.

Kern, Anita. 1980. *Women in West African Fiction.* Washington, DC: Three Continents Press.

Kesteloot, Lilyan. 1972. *Intellectual Origins of the African Revolution.* Translated by A. Mboukou. Washington, DC: Black Orpheus Press.

———. 1974. *Black Writers in French: A Literary History of Negritude.* Translated by E. C. Kennedy. Philadelphia: Temple University Press.

Killam, G. D. (ed.). 1972. *African Writers on African Writing.* London: HEB.

Klima, Vladimir. 1969. *Modern Nigerian Novels.* Prague: Oriental Institute.

Klima, Vladimir, Frantisek Ruzicka, and Petr Zima. 1976. *Black Africa: Literature and Language.* Prague: Academia Publishing House.

Larson, Charles R. 1972. *The Emergence of African Fiction.* Bloomington: Indiana University Press.

———. 1976. *The Novel in the Third World.* Washington, DC: Inscape.

Laurence, Margaret. 1968. *Long Drums and Cannons: Nigerian Dramatists and Novelists.* London: Macmillan.

Lindfors, Bernth (ed.). 1974. *Dem-say: Interviews with Eight Nigerian Writers.* Austin: University of Texas Press.

Lindfors, Bernth, Ian Munro, Richard Priebe, and Reinhard Sander (eds.). 1972. *Palaver: Interviews with Five African Writers in Texas.* Austin: University of Texas Press.

Madubuike, Ihechukwu. 1980. *The Senegalese Novel: A Sociological Study of the Impact of the Politics of Assimilation.* Washington, DC: Three Continents Press.

Moore, Gerald. 1969. *The Chosen Tongue: English Writing in the Tropical World.* London: Longman.

———. 1980. *Twelve African Writers.* Bloomington: Indiana University Press.

Mortimer, Mildred. 1990. *Journeys Through the French African Novel.* Portsmouth, NH: Heinemann.

Mouralis, Bernard. 1984. *Littérature et développement: Essai sur le statut, la fonction et la représentation de la littérature négro-africaine d'expression française.* Paris: Silex.

Moyers, Bill. 1988. "Chinua Achebe Videorecording." *Bill Moyers' World of Ideas.* Alexandria, VA: PBS Video.

Nazareth, Peter. 1972. *Literature and Society in Modern Africa: Essays on Literature.* Nairobi: East African Literature Bureau.

Neto, Agostinho. 1979. *On Literature and National Culture.* Luanda: Angolan Writers Union.

Ngate, Jonathan. 1988. *Francophone African Fiction: Reading a Literary Tradition.* Trenton, NJ: Africa World Press.

Ngugi wa Thiong'o. 1981. *Writers in Politics: Essays.* London: HEB.

———. 1986. *Decolonising the Mind: The Politics of Language in African Literature.* Portsmouth, NH: Heinemann.

———. 1990. "Return of the Native Tongue." *The Times Literary Supplement* No. 4,563 (September 14–20):972, 981.

Obiechina, Emmanuel. 1975. *Culture, Tradition and Society in the West African Novel.* New York: Cambridge University Press.

Olney, James. 1973. *Tell Me Africa: An Approach to African Literature.* Princeton: Princeton University Press.

Owomoyela, Oyekan. 1979. *African Literatures: An Introduction.* Waltham, MA: Crossroads Press.

Palmer, Eustace. 1972. *An Introduction to the African Novel.* London: HEB.

Peters, Jonathan. 1978. *A Dance of Masks: Senghor, Achebe, Soyinka.* Washington, DC: Three Continents Press.

Roscoe, Adrian. 1971. *Mother Is Gold: A Study in West African Literature.* London and New York: Cambridge University Press.

———. 1977. *Uhuru's Fire: African Literature East to South.* London and New York: Cambridge University Press.

Sartre, Jean-Paul. 1963. *Black Orpheus.* Translated by S. W. Allen. Paris: Présence africaine.

Soyinka, Wole. 1976. *Myth, Literature and the African World.* London: Cambridge University Press.

Taiwo, Oladele. 1976. *Culture and the Nigerian Novel.* London: Macmillan.

Traore, Bakary. 1972. *The Black African Theatre and Its Social Functions.* Translated by Dapo Adelugba. Ibadan, Nigeria: Ibadan University Press.

Wauthier, Claude. 1978. *The Literature and Thought of Modern Africa.* London: HEB.

Wheelwright, Philip. 1965. "Myth." P. 538 in *Princeton Encyclopedia of Poetry and Poetics.* Princeton: Princeton University Press.

■ 13 ■

South Africa

Patrick J. Furlong

South Africa demonstrates many of the same historical currents that are found elsewhere on the African continent. The area was populated by black Africans for millennia and was subject to similar dynamics of cultural change and migratory movements of peoples. Black Africans in South Africa also came into contact with expansionist European countries in search of trade, slaves, and conquest. South Africa was a rich area for European colonial exploitation because of its fertile soils, mineral wealth, and technologically less advanced people who could be subjugated and converted into cheap labor for the benefit of their foreign masters.

At the same time, South Africa is also something of an anomaly. Along with a few other colonized areas like Kenya, Southern Rhodesia (Zimbabwe), Algeria (in North Africa), and South-West Africa (Namibia), South Africa exemplifies a phenomenon known as "settler colonialism." In settler colonial areas, Europeans sought more than economic enrichment and political control. They settled in large numbers, taking the best land for themselves and displacing local people, who were relegated to menial labor or slaughtered if they resisted (Emmanuel, 1982:93–94).

Even among settler colonial states, however, South Africa is unique. Until the advent of black majority rule in 1994, it was the only white minority–dominated state left in Africa. It was also the oldest settler colony, with European settlement dating back to the mid-1600s. Consequently, many of the whites have lived in South Africa for generations and no longer see themselves as Europeans. Unlike more recent white settlers in other parts of Africa, many South Africans had more at stake in preserving their dominance since they had no mother country to which they could return. It was by exerting increasing and eventually almost total control over its black majority (and by fortuitously taking possession of great gold and diamond wealth) that white South Africans were able to develop the richest and most industrialized society in Africa. Under the now abolished system of

335

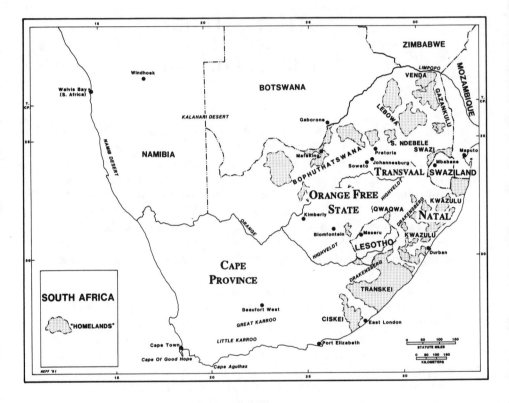

Map 13.1

(South Africa, 1991)

apartheid (apartness), South Africa was a society based on a rigid hierarchy of white racial privilege, on the one hand, and degradation and exploitation of nonwhites on the other.

South Africa is currently undergoing a dramatic transition, fraught with many potential problems. To understand what is happening and what the future may bring we must understand this land's complex and tortuous past. In this chapter, we will look first at South Africa before European contact, followed by the impact of Dutch settlers (later called Afrikaners) and British colonialism, the role of capitalism, and the development of apartheid. Finally, we will examine the dismantling of the apartheid state and the establishment of a "nonracial" South Africa.

■ THE PEOPLING OF SOUTH AFRICA

Contrary to a common white South African myth, the country was no empty land when Dutch settlers arrived in the seventeenth century (Thompson, 1985:199–201). The ancestors of the Khoisan-speaking, hunter-gatherer San people (sometimes known as Bushmen) preceded the whites by at least 30,000 years. Over time, some came to own cattle, probably obtained from iron-using Bantu speakers who crossed the Limpopo River into South Africa as early as the fourth century. The cattle-owning Khoisan were called "Khoi" (or, pejoratively, "Hottentots" by the Dutch) as distinct from the hunter-gatherer San (cf. Elphick, 1985:3–42; Wilson, 1969). (See Chapter 3 for more information on Khoisan- and Bantu-speaking peoples.) The Khoi alone may have numbered 200,000 in the seventeenth century, apart from several million Bantu-speaking mixed farmers in the lusher east. Two centuries later, the whites, in contrast, numbered just over 200,000 (Thompson, 1969:425; Wilson, 1969: 68).

If South Africa was not empty, neither were its inhabitants fixed ethnic "tribes." The Khoi might become hunter-gatherers in hard times; in times of plenty some San became clients of the Khoi or of Bantu speakers, and trade, marriage, or clientage led to a mixing of both peoples and languages (Elphick, 1985:17–18, 30–42, 62–67). After A.D. 1000, the Bantu pushed beyond the northern and eastern fringes of South Africa until, by the sixteenth century, they occupied most of what later became the Transvaal, Orange Free State, and Natal, along with Lesotho and much of the eastern and northern Cape. With superior iron technology they overwhelmed the San and Khoi, who often withdrew into the arid west or the most remote mountain areas (Maylam, 1986:1–9; Hall, 1987:1–45).

■ THE ROOTS OF RACIAL DISCRIMINATION:
THE DUTCH ERA

The first whites in South Africa were the Portuguese, who knew the coast as early as the fifteenth century; but they did not stay. The thrifty Dutch East India Company saw the Cape differently—as a halfway house to the Orient—and in 1652 sent Jan van Riebeeck to found a refreshment station there. Almost from the start it became a permanent settler colony. In the first few years the limited numbers of settlers forced the company to grant small plots to its retired officials in order to make the colony more viable. Only a trickle of additional white settlers arrived in an immigration scheme that ended early in the next century, but the nucleus of the Afrikaners already existed. "Afrikaner" was what the descendants of the original, mostly Dutch, but also French Huguenot and German settlers came to be called. Because of an unequal sex ratio, which improved only gradually, the men turned for brides or concubines to Khoi and especially slave women (at the Cape slaves were usually of Malagasy, East Indies Bengali, or Indonesian stock). Thus, the emerging Afrikaans language, a Dutch-based creole, was shaped as much by the mixed-race "coloured" descendants of whites, slaves, and Khoi servants as by the settlers themselves. Today it is spoken by 3 million white Afrikaners and as many coloureds (Elphick and Shell, 1989:184–242).

The increasing need for land and labor hastened the conquest of the Cape Town area by 1700 and led to the continued importation of slaves to supplement an allegedly inadequate work force. The best Khoi lands in the southwest were occupied by whites, and white disease and drink took their toll. Many Khoi escaped inland or sought service with white farmers. They did not disappear, as was once held, but their numbers dwindled dramatically. Those not incorporated into the coloureds moved east to become clients of the Bantu-speaking Xhosa people or north to live among runaway slaves, renegade whites, and other dispossessed Africans. Colonial guns and horses helped them terrorize other Africans in the northern Cape and Orange Free State, and they eventually created what were called "Korana" and "Griqua" states along the Orange River (Elphick, 1985; Legassick, 1989).

Just behind were the white nomadic cattle farmers, the *trekboers,* expanding the colony with each generation. By the 1770s, *trekboers* confronted the similarly seminomadic Xhosa people. Their encounters on the frontier were not always hostile; both sides traded goods as often as they stole cattle or defended themselves from raids. Some whites cohabited with Xhosa women, allied with one chief against another, or lived over the frontier among the Xhosa (Legassick, 1980).

It was not on the frontier but in the western Cape heartland that the racially divided, oppressive face of South Africa first appeared. While miscegenation with slave or Khoi women was common, the offspring usually joined the mother's society and status. Actual marriage with slaves was banned, although masters sometimes freed favored slaves in order to marry them. But as more white women arrived in the colony, racially mixed public unions dwindled in number. By then, however, Asian and African ancestry had already become part of the Afrikaner heritage. Despite their later claims to the contrary and efforts to maintain "racial purity," South African whites never were purely Caucasian (Elphick and Shell, 1989:194–204; Worden, 1985; Shell, 1994:322–324).

Nonetheless, a complex combination of a class- and racially based caste society was developing. Below the senior company officials and the few great landholders, who held many slaves, were the other whites. Next came the free or freed blacks, then Khoi servants, and finally the slaves. Control over the population, white and nonwhite, was maintained by the use of brutal punishments like mutilation, torture, and excruciating execution methods, such as impalement (Ross, 1980). Blacks and slaves, however, faced the most discrimination. Slaves had to carry a pass beyond their master's premises; blacks were subject to a curfew; and even free blacks lost the right to own property (Elphick and Shell, 1989:214–216).

■ THE ADVENT OF THE BRITISH FACTOR: A QUESTIONABLE LIBERALISM

Due to the harsh rule of the Dutch East India Company, with its maze of exploitative and monopolistic regulations, there was little settler resistance to British occupation of the Cape Colony in 1795 and again in 1806, after a brief Dutch interregnum from 1803. British rule meant free trade but no cessation of slavery. Even the 1807 abolition of the overseas slave trade by the British did not halt the flow of slaves into the Cape (Shell, 1994:146). And even when criticism of slavery developed in the 1820s, Cape "liberals" valued property rights in slaves more highly than abolition (Watson, 1990:5–6).

The British tried to assist the old "Cape Dutch" settlers with their labor problem, especially as slave prices rose rapidly after 1807. Slaves taken off ships by the navy were landed as "apprentices," and "apprenticing" soon included the Khoi and even Xhosa near the frontier. Apprentices differed from slaves only in the written contract establishing conditions of employment—which few could read. The issue of dispossessed Khoi was met by an 1809 law forcing free blacks to carry passes when not on their employer's property and by an 1812 law apprenticing Khoi servants' children until they reached adulthood.

The new order was not uniformly favorable to the Cape Dutch. By

1830, several thousand British colonists had arrived. Many settled near the eastern frontier, but they proved poor farmers and flocked to the towns, increasing competition for what limited commercial opportunities existed. These problems affected the Dutch most sharply; they were angered by English becoming the sole official language and by the British concern to preserve law and order even on the frontier, where farmers had long provided their own rough justice. Now servants could bring complaints against cruel masters, who had to record all punishments.

The Dutch were equally angered by British vacillation toward the Xhosa. (On Xhosa-settler relations, see Mostert, 1992, and Peires, 1982.) When the 1828 Ordinance No. 50 gave legal equality to free blacks, followed in 1833 by the abolition of slavery, many Boers (Dutch farmers) left the Cape. Perhaps a quarter of the Cape Dutch and their Khoi servants and ex-slaves moved in a "Great Trek" into lands seemingly occupied only thinly by the Griqua, Korana, and a few earlier *trekboers* (see Walker, 1960).

The land the trekkers thought empty was actually home to thousands of Africans on the run from Shaka, creator of the Zulu empire; from lesser expanding chiefdoms; and from raiders like the Korana. As these refugees invaded other populated areas, they set off further refugee waves of people fleeing their land to seek safety elsewhere. As a result, the Highveld became seemingly depopulated. The impetus for these disruptions is unclear, but it may have been related to pressures caused by drought, an expanding ivory trade, or the growing threat from slavers operating from Portuguese East Africa to the north and also from the Cape Colony (see Ballard, 1986; Wright and Hamilton, 1989; Omer-Cooper, 1993).

Using a revolutionary form of warfare, Shaka, chief of the Zulu clan, had completed earlier trends to centralize authority in Natal. He favored a short stabbing spear, a large shield, and close combat tactics based on precision drill and utter ruthlessness. His state gave his subjects a new sense of identity. All became "Zulu," much as refugees in the interior created new "nations," providing the basis for modern South African ethnic identities, which twentieth-century Nationalist politicians used to justify their "separate development" policy of "homelands" for each African "tribe." These ethnic groups included the Zulu, Mzilikazi's Ndebele (who later went to Zimbabwe), the Tsonga-Shangaan on the Transvaal-Mozambique border, the Swazi, and in the highest parts of the eastern plateau, the Basotho (formed primarily from widely assorted Sotho-speaking refugees) (see Omer-Cooper, 1966).

The trekkers thought the sad condition of the depopulated Highveld was permanent; today some of their descendants justify their occupation on that basis. In fact, as soon as near normalcy returned with the 1828 accession of Dingane, a Zulu king less effective than Shaka, many refugees came home. In the late 1830s, most trekkers moved into Natal, where they defeated Dingane while allying with his disaffected half-brother, Mpande. Placing

Mpande on the throne, they took control of the devastated land to the south, renaming it the Republic of Natalia. But the British could accept neither Boer (trekker) access to the coast nor the Boers' harsh policies toward the Xhosa's northern neighbors. By 1843, Britain had annexed Natal, and most trekkers had returned inland to join their cousins in forming several small republics (Ballard, 1989:119–125).

The Cape authorities grew worried about the potential for trouble posed by the trekkers, so in 1848 they annexed Transorangia (the land between the Orange and Vaal rivers), including the Transvaal. But London did not favor unnecessary entanglements beyond the already overly large and expensive Cape Colony and, between 1852 and 1854, opted for a cheaper policy of independence for the trekkers in the Transvaal and the Orange Free State (as independent Transorangia was now called). For a generation thereafter, the Boers were left to fight their African neighbors and squabble among themselves (see Galbraith, 1963).

Meanwhile, the Cape Colony gained greater internal autonomy. In 1872, the British allowed the Cape to have its own parliament complete with a prime minister. A theoretically nonracial vote permitted wealthier, more Westernized male Cape blacks to participate, and the several electoral districts with many coloured and African voters had a significant impact on Cape politics. The Dutch- and English-dominated political parties greedily courted black votes, even if the white members of parliament did little to deliver on their promises (Bickford-Smith, 1995:67–72).

Although limited, the civil freedoms of Cape blacks, especially voters, were vast compared to those of blacks farther north. In British Natal, only the few male Africans who proved they were sufficiently Westernized could be considered for voting rights. The large Indian community, imported in the 1860s to supplement "unreliable" Zulu labor, faced more explicit electoral discrimination. Along with attempts to curb trading and require passes similar to those forced on Natal Africans, an 1896 law kept Indians from voting (see Bhana and Brain, 1990:59–60).

In the Boer republics, the situation was still worse; Africans could still live on the lands of the white cattle-owning aristocracy, provided they used their agricultural talents to feed their new rulers. But pass laws controlled Africans' movements, African women and children were often enslaved, and white supremacy and segregation were constitutionally entrenched (Morton, 1994:173–181). The few Transvaal Indians fared as poorly as in Natal. In the Orange Free State, restrictions barred most Indians from working or residing there, a law repealed only in the 1980s (Bhana and Brain, 1990:96).

On the fringes of the Boer states, African kingdoms such as those of the mountain-dwelling Pedi and Venda struggled to survive, but invariably they were forced by the whites into the most desolate, remote parts—the future "reserves." To the south, Moshoeshoe (leader of the Basotho people), held out from his mountain stronghold against the Orange Free State Boers; in

1868, he reluctantly sought British protection. London had no great love for Moshoeshoe, but imminent Basotho collapse threatened a Boer presence behind the Africans along the Eastern Frontier. Britain, therefore, was forced into a special relationship with the Basotho that lasted until modern Lesotho gained its independence in 1966 (Thompson, 1975).

■ THE MINERAL REVOLUTION: CAPITALISM AND SEGREGATION

The African kingdoms were in disarray before the white advance, and with the discovery of diamonds in 1867, the interior became more valuable. Diggers swarmed around the confluence of the Orange, Vaal, and Harts rivers, territory claimed by the Boer republics, the Griqua, and the local Tswana people. The British simply annexed most of the area under the guise of protecting Griqua land claims. A decade later the Griqua lands were incorporated by the British into the Cape Colony (Thompson, 1971:253–257).

The rapid exhaustion of surface diggings meant that the rich diamond-bearing soil could be exploited only by expensive deep-level mining. Kimberley, the central site, was quickly dominated by a few large-scale capitalists. The greatest was Cecil Rhodes, who bought out his competitors and became the kingpin in the De Beers diamond empire. The Cape was suddenly wealthy; railways sprang up, and diggers rushed in to make their fortunes.

At first, the mines meant new opportunities for Africans. Cash wages allowed many to obtain guns, while independent African peasants prospered in the eastern Cape, taking advantage of the new market for produce. Others, including many whites, joined the wagon-transport business. But the white authorities soon disarmed the Africans, and railways displaced wagons. Black diggers disappeared quickly because of white pressure and limited funds. To keep prices high, Rhodes's De Beers diamond monopoly emerged. Mine owners ensured huge profits and maximum security by hiring a cheap, black male labor force from the rural areas and requiring them to live in fenced-off, single-sex compounds. Migrants' families remained in the rural areas, subsisting on their small farm plots (cf. Turrell, 1987; Worger, 1987).

Conditions deteriorated for rural blacks too as Cape peasants were squeezed off their land and out of the market by white farmers. Both white farmers and mining companies needed to increase the supply of cheap black labor (Bundy, 1988). In response, discriminatory laws and institutions spread across South Africa. Hut, poll, and head taxes were introduced in the rural areas and the residual African lands, or "reserves." Since payment was required in cash, many Africans were forced to seek employment under whites.

In the Cape, discrimination intensified as whites sought to increase their control over the many blacks incorporated into the colony as the frontier expanded eastward. Passes regulated Africans' movements more thoroughly than in the past. By 1910, urban Africans were segregated in "locations" for "hygienic" reasons (Swanson, 1977). Enfranchised Africans with traditional "tribal" land tenure lost the vote; then in 1892, income qualifications were raised, disenfranchising many additional Africans and coloureds alike (Bickford-Smith, 1995:69–70).

The mineral revolution had other results. South Africa was now too potentially wealthy for the British to ignore, but administrative expenses were a concern. A Cape-led settler federation with one "native policy" would lower administrative costs and end the customs barriers limiting the growth of an efficient modern economy. But only Natal, fearful of the Zulu, was truly interested in joining a federation. The Transvaal Boers were the major obstacle; if they could be subdued, the Cape and the Free State would surely oblige. In 1877, London annexed the financially ailing Transvaal under the guise of restoring order and destroying the Pedi threat in the northeast; British troops soon subdued the Pedi and, for good measure, the Zulu as well (cf. Delius, 1983; Edgerton, 1988).

Britain was if anything *too* successful. Now the Transvalers saw no need for British rule, which they overthrew in the first Anglo-Boer war (1880–1881). And without the Zulu threat, even Natal lost interest in federation (Giliomee, 1989:36–37).

Then in 1885, gold was discovered on a low ridge in the southern Transvaal, the Witwatersrand. The Transvaal now attracted far more British interest. Deep-level, capital-intensive (highly mechanized) mining was again required, centered on the sprawling new city of Johannesburg. Even more so than with diamonds, gold attracted foreign, especially British, capital. Because of the vast amount of gold available, this second phase of the mineral revolution had a greater impact than that induced by diamonds, but the same institutions for exploiting and regulating African labor were used and greatly expanded. Passes, hut and poll taxes, the single-sex compound system, and a wide, racially differentiated wage scale became the norm (Wheatcroft, 1987).

Diamond magnate Cecil Rhodes soon moved into gold, allying with the Afrikaner Bond, the Cape Dutch political party. In 1890, he became prime minister of the Cape Colony. A union of agriculture and mining interests had advantages: it allowed a united assault on the growing Cape black vote, limited intrawhite competition for labor, and presented a single face to London in Rhodes's campaign to expand toward the rumored goldfields beyond the Limpopo River. Rhodes had to advance around the Boer republics to the west. The southern Tswana people were annexed, while their northern cousins in Bechuanaland (the future Botswana) received British "protection." From 1890, Rhodes's British South Africa Company occupied the trans-Limpopo hinterland, now renamed Southern and Northern Rhodesia (cf. Davenport, 1966; Galbraith, 1974).

In addition, Rhodes and his colleagues increasingly resented Transvaal government policies that limited both their profits and their influence. Facing pressure from Rhodes and other British imperialists, London decided to annex the Transvaal once again. In late 1899, the British high commissioner presented an ultimatum requiring Transvaal president Paul Kruger to renounce all real sovereignty. Supported only by the Free State, the Transvaal attacked the British, thus starting the second Anglo-Boer war (1899–1902). Most Africans, hoping for an extension of the Cape franchise, supported the British by destroying isolated Boer homesteads and ambushing patrols. When conventional tactics failed to subdue the Boers, the British burned Boer farms and interned their families and black servants in racially segregated concentration camps, where thousands died of disease and malnutrition (cf. Pakenham, 1979; Warwick, 1983).

Afrikaner attitudes toward the English became deeply scarred, but when the Boers finally surrendered, their foes proved conciliatory. The Transvaal generals Louis Botha and Jan Smuts led the large Boer landholders who decided to collaborate with the new order. Both the Transvaal and Orange Free State were allowed internal self-government in 1907. Once again, federation among the republics was attempted. The all-white National Convention of 1908–1909 met to draw up a scheme for union. The Natal English and Cape liberals favored a loose federation, but the northerners wanted a unitary state with limited provincial powers and no extension of the Cape franchise to blacks in the interior. Despite black protests, most Cape delegates conceded these points, but salvaged the nonracial franchise for their province. Qualified Cape blacks could vote at all levels and stand for municipal or provincial office, but they could not sit in the Union parliament (Thompson, 1960).

The British Parliament refused to block this flawed constitution for a few thousand potential black voters in the northern colonies, and in 1909 it passed the Act of Union with the pious wish that one day whites would broaden their democracy. On May 31, 1910, the Union of South Africa was established. Despite losing the war, the settlers had triumphed, while the British flag still flew at little cost to London. The only real losers were the black majority. London could not see that a racially distorted version of the British Westminster system ill-suited so diverse a society. Without U.S.-style checks and balances, even the token multiracialism of the Cape had little chance to survive, and any expansion of liberties was impossible without a Bill of Rights or the principle of judicial review.

■ THE UNITED SETTLER STATE: THE INTENSIFICATION OF SEGREGATION

The new Union parliament was dominated by Louis Botha's South African Party, formed from the union of smaller Afrikaner parties. The main opposition party, the Unionists, represented English speakers wanting close ties to Britain. The government advocated white partnership in building a British-protected "nation." Both parties agreed not to tamper with the Cape franchise, but neither would broaden black civil liberties.

The small Labour Party, representing militant white workers who feared black competition for jobs, sought more extensive measures to limit black rights. It pressured parliament to pass the 1911 Mines and Works Act, barring blacks from skilled and semiskilled mine jobs. The devastating 1913 Natives Land Act followed, limiting African landownership to the "reserves"—just 6 percent of South Africa—and banning sharecropping and squatting on white farms. Only Cape voters were exempted. Thousands of Africans were evicted from their homes; only wage laborers working at minimal rates could remain. A vast reservoir of dispossessed black labor was now available—on the whites' terms (Keegan, 1988; Plaatje, 1982).

The chief author of this law, the Orange Free State general J. B. M. Hertzog, opposed both the Cape franchise for Africans and Botha's policy of reconciliation with the British. He led militant, large-scale Afrikaner farmers and poorer, mainly Afrikaner whites who were migrating to the towns. Hertzog appealed also to embittered Afrikaners excluded from the best positions in the government bureaucracy (Giliomee, 1989:48–49). In late 1913, he was expelled from the cabinet for his views; in 1914 he founded the National Party (NP), the precursor of the party that ruled South Africa from 1948 to 1994.

Just two years before, a different nationalism had encouraged African professionals led by the Reverend John Dube to form the South African Natives National Congress (SANNC) to oppose discrimination and push for greater political rights for Africans. The SANNC, from 1923 the African National Congress (ANC), made no real attempt to reach the masses and limited itself to the failed methods of deputations, petitions to expand the Cape franchise, and polite requests for rights due "civilized men" (cf. Walshe, 1970; Meli, 1989).

This strategy was used also by the coloured African Peoples' Organization of Dr. Abdurahman, a member of the Cape Provincial Council. Since 10 percent of the Cape electorate was coloured, white politicians, including Hertzog, did sometimes suggest expanding their freedoms (Lewis, 1987:64–118). Only the Indians, led by M. K. Gandhi, managed to secure some concessions by mass action. His "passive resistance" prevented more discriminatory measures similar to those applied to Africans, particularly curbs on freedom of movement, from being applied to Indians. However, mass action by his Natal Indian Congress was weakened by Gandhi's failure to combine with other oppressed groups and by his departure for India in 1914 (Swan, 1985).

Without a unified black political movement, whites could consolidate power. Black miners tried to organize, but they were brutally crushed, as were striking white miners. Justice minister Jan Smuts became known as the "friend" of capitalists because of his repression of labor militants of all races. When many Afrikaners rebelled in 1914 rather than support involvement in the First World War on the side of Britain, Smuts's firm response added to his notoriety as also the friend of the British. Hertzog reviled Smuts as a traitor, and the NP made large gains in the 1916 elections (cf. Hancock, 1962–1968; Garson, 1979).

After the war, Botha and Smuts achieved a reputation at the Versailles peace conference for supporting self-determination for oppressed nations, but such liberalism was not applied in South African–controlled areas. For instance, minor African revolts in the South African–mandated territory of South-West Africa (now Namibia) and in the eastern Cape were met with aerial bombs or machine guns. Then in 1922, when white gold miners revolted against a mine owners' policy of replacing whites with cheaper black workers, Smuts bombed the rebels in Johannesburg and hanged, jailed, or deported the ringleaders.

An outraged Labour Party was happy to arrange a pact with Smuts's political rival Hertzog, and Smuts was defeated in the 1924 elections. Hertzog became prime minister and set about strengthening Afrikaner power, increasing South African autonomy from Britain, and protecting white workers (Simons and Simons, 1983:271–299). In 1925, Afrikaans became an official language (replacing Dutch), Afrikaners were recruited for the civil service, and a new flag and anthem were used beside those of Britain. South Africa's status as an independent dominion under the British monarch (along with Canada, Australia, and New Zealand) was defined in several conferences and statutes between 1926 and 1934. White workers' interests were secured by a "civilized white labor" policy that replaced thousands of Africans in menial jobs in the government railways and similar occupations with poor whites. New parastatal (government-controlled) companies also were created (Yudelman, 1984:214–262).

In all these areas, Hertzog achieved a minor revolution, improving poor whites' conditions without unduly threatening the leading capitalists. His African policy was largely that of Smuts, embodied in the 1923 Natives Urban Areas Act, authorizing municipalities to adopt the strictly regulated system of locations and passes for urban African residents (Rich, 1978). Unsurprisingly, a 1927 law to prohibit extramarital intercourse between whites and Africans had broad bipartisan support (Furlong, 1994:59).

Only in one area of racial policy did Hertzog go far beyond Smuts, and that was the Cape nonracial vote, which Hertzog wanted to end. First, by granting white women the vote in 1930, and ending property and educational requirements for white voters in the Cape and Natal in 1931, he weakend black voting strength. Still lacking the two-thirds majority he needed to change the Cape African vote, Hertzog's NP merged with Smuts's followers in 1934 to form the United Party. Then, over anguished black protests, Cape

Africans were removed from the common voters' roll in 1936, made possible because Smuts no longer needed their votes.

An elaborate compromise salved white consciences: the size of the reserves was doubled and the advisory natives' Representative Council was created. Cape African voters would send three white members to the House of Assembly, and four white senators, representing Africans in all provinces for the first time, would also be elected (Simons and Simons, 1983:493–495).

But Hertzog did not comprehend the appeal to poorer Afrikaners of a more thoroughly exclusive, segregationist vision than even he had proposed. They did not understand his resistance to segregating also the coloureds from white economic and political life. They wondered why he did little to stop German Jewish refugees from taking precious jobs or why he did not send the Indians "back" to India. Above all, they did not understand why he sat next to Smuts, declaring himself satisfied with the constitutional position of the Union, or why he did not push for an Afrikaner-ruled republic.

In response to such sentiments, a former minister of the Afrikaner Dutch Reformed Church, Daniel Malan, led discontented NP elements into forming the Purified National Party (Stultz, 1974:23–39). Purified Nationalist intellectuals worked to mobilize Afrikaners on an unprecedented scale. Inspired by what many had seen or heard of changes under way in Nazi Germany, they proposed a revolution to end the threat of black "swamping" and English and Jewish capitalist domination. Through their secret, all-male organization, the Afrikaner Broederbond (Afrikaner Brotherhood), these intellectuals set up numerous front organizations to pursue their political objectives (cf. Serfontein, 1978; Bloomberg, 1989).

When in September 1939 Smuts convinced a narrow parliamentary majority to support Britain in the Second World War, most of Hertzog's followers joined the Purified Nationalists in opposition, forming the Reunited National Party the next year. Many Afrikaner nationalists actively worked to undermine the war effort, praying that Hitler's victories would bring them to power (Furlong, 1991:105–119).

In contrast, black South Africans wanted to believe Smuts's rhetoric of a war for democracy against the racist Hitler. Led by the ANC, many volunteered for military service, although Smuts refused to give them guns for fear of white reaction. More blacks came to the cities to work in manufacturing, which now boomed. Smuts declared that segregation had fallen on evil days and temporarily suspended the pass laws. For a while, it seemed an Allied victory might bring real changes.

Smuts's Afrikaner opponents were eager for changes of another sort. The Broederbond drew up an authoritarian draft constitution, and the "cultural" Ossewabrandwag (Ox-Wagon Guard, or OB) was transformed into a massive paramilitary and semifascist organization. Most of Malan's

Reunited Nationalists belonged to the OB, but its increasing extremism threatened the NP's leadership, and the OB went into decline (see Marx, 1994). Malan especially opposed the *Stormjaers* (Stormtroopers), the OB extreme right wing, who planted bombs and beat up soldiers; there was even a foiled attempt to assassinate Smuts and set up a puppet Nazi government.

Malan now turned against the far right, particularly as a Nazi victory became unlikely. In the 1943 election, Smuts's landslide victory overshadowed an ultimately more significant event: Malan trounced all his Afrikaner nationalist rivals, from the moderate Afrikaner Party followers of Hertzog (who had died in 1942) to the OB extremists. He was the unchallenged *volk* leader in the battle against Smuts himself (Stultz, 1974:83–91; Furlong, 1991:201–205).

The aging Smuts was oblivious to this. He alienated himself from blacks, reinstating the pass laws once he was no longer threatened; he brutally crushed a black miners' strike in 1946 and caved in to Natal English supporters in proposing curbs on Indians buying additional property. At the same time, his scare tactics, describing the Nationalists as "Malanazis," failed to restrain public anger at continued rationing after the war's end, at failure to provide jobs for demobilized soldiers whose places had been taken by black workers, or at the growing role of his liberal lieutenant, Jan Hofmeyr. Hofmeyr's influence was seen behind both Smuts's attempts to buy off the angry Indians with an offer of three white representatives in parliament and the government-appointed Fagan Commission, which recommended in early 1948 that the permanence of the urban black presence be accepted and freehold tenure be granted them (Furlong, 1991:235–239, 249–250; Paton, 1964).

In 1948, this smacked of "liberalism." So confident was Smuts about the 1948 election that he was unaware of his United Party's vulnerability and poor organization. All were surprised when Malan's National-Afrikaner Party coalition gained a five-seat majority. Malan could not effect all his proposals, such as nationalizing the mines, expelling the Indians, or creating a republic; but he did have the first all-Afrikaner Union cabinet (Stultz, 1974:147–159; Lipton, 1986:274–278).

■ **NATIONALIST RULE AND THE
CREATION OF THE APARTHEID STATE**

Having come to power with the slogan "Apartheid," Malan set about creating a more systematically segregated society than anything previously conceived. Some have argued that he was really acting in tandem with capitalist business interests to provide more thoroughgoing control over labor in order to maximize profits in the diversified and complex postwar economy (Johnstone, 1976). While this might be true, it is only part of the explanation for apartheid. In truth, Broederbond intellectuals had long toyed with elaborate schemes of racial social engineering. Now they could realize their dreams, particularly as the NP fell under the control of uncompromisingly segregationist leaders. Malan was moderate compared with his blunt successor, J. G. Strijdom, the advocate of *baasskap* (white boss-ship), or Dr. Hendrik Verwoerd, the coldly brilliant intellectual who succeeded Strijdom in 1958 and whose ties to the Broederbond were much closer than those of his predecessors (Serfontein, 1978:83–98). The apartheid regime had a very simple aim: to make South Africa safe for a small, relatively poor people new to the city and incapable without state assistance of surviving either English guile and business experience or black competition on an open labor market. The old mechanisms no longer seemed enough. A planned economy, a rigged political system, and a rigidly segregated society provided the desired recipe (Furlong, 1991:240; Lipton, 1986).

To this end, the remaining ties to Britain, symbolized by the Union Jack and the governor-general, were eliminated and replaced by a republic in 1961. The civil service and the military were purged of non-Nationalists; Namibian whites and those between eighteen and twenty-one were given the vote (they were reliable sources of further Nationalist support); and the Afrikaner Party was persuaded in 1951 to merge with the NP.

A fierce constitutional struggle was fought to remove the Cape coloured voters from the common roll. The token white representatives given in exchange were, like those granted the Africans in 1936, gradually dispensed with. When Africans insisted on electing Communist white representatives (under a 1950 law the latter had been ejected from parliament), the Communist Party was banned, and anyone suspected of "communism" (defined broadly enough to include many U.S. liberal Democrats) could be placed by ministerial decree under a five-year banning order, which amounted to house arrest (Davenport, 1987:361–381).

The paraphernalia of segregation hit coloureds much harder than before, while Africans' lives became particularly miserable. Marriage or sex between whites and nonwhites was banned, procedures for racially classifying (or later reclassifying) all citizens were devised, and residential segregation was rigidly enforced, resulting in mass removals, especially of coloureds and Indians. In 1953, public amenities were segregated under a law that explicitly stated that such facilities need not be equal.

The administration of the pass laws was centralized and made more comprehensive—African women and Cape voters were included for the first time. A vast panoply of legislation to control Africans' movements in "white" South Africa and African labor organizations followed. Universities were segregated and African mission schools were slowly strangled by Verwoerd's state-financed "Bantu education," intended to train Africans for menial tasks rather than commerce or the professions (cf. Posel, 1991; Kallaway, 1984).

Through all this, white political opposition was minimal. Small groups like the Liberal Party, founded in 1953, and the more conservative Progressive Party (1959) had little success. Even many whites who frowned at the extremism of new legislation felt it was painfully necessary to maintain law and order. They convinced themselves that the government was sincere in claiming that this "negative" phase of apartheid would be followed by the creation of "positive" institutions for blacks in their own areas.

Blacks stood aghast at the way things had gone from bad to worse. The ANC's old tactics had long been discredited by their ineffectiveness (Simons and Simons, 1983:353–385). Younger ANC members such as Nelson Mandela, Walter Sisulu, and Oliver Tambo realized mass organization was even more crucial now, and their ANC Youth League pushed the ANC toward mass involvement by adopting their Action Program in 1949 (Gerhart, 1978:45–84; Lodge, 1983:1–32).

Borrowing from the tactics of Gandhi and in alliance with similar movements among Indians, coloureds, and left-wing whites, the ANC (under Chief Albert Luthuli) now spearheaded the Congress Movement, using passive resistance on a grand scale. In 1955, the alliance drew up the Freedom Charter, a document demanding the creation of a nonracial democracy (Suttner and Cronin, 1986). The government retaliated massively; passive resistance was punished by flogging, and dozens of Congress Movement leaders were charged with treason. None of the charges stuck, but in the

The Sharpeville massacre resulted in sixty-nine deaths when South African forces fired on protesters demonstrating against the pass laws.

intervening five-year "Treason Trial," the ANC's unprecedented strength quickly dissipated (Lodge, 1983:33–200; Lazerson, 1994:161–195).

In 1958, frustrated and embittered by ANC failure to achieve meaningful change, some younger members under Robert Sobukwe broke away in protest against alleged ANC domination by white liberals and white and Indian Communists. In 1959, they founded the Pan-Africanist Congress (PAC) with the slogan "Africa for the Africans." To embarrass the ANC, which had advocated burning passes, the PAC announced a similar campaign a month earlier, in March 1960. The result was the Sharpeville (an African township south of Johannesburg) massacre, in which policemen fired on an advancing crowd intent on surrendering their passbooks (Gerhart, 1978:124–246; Lodge, 1983:201–230).

Unrest now broke out across the country. A state of emergency was declared, and in 1961 the ANC and PAC were banned. Both went underground and into exile; both also reluctantly chose the path of armed struggle since all nonviolent alternatives seemed exhausted. Nelson Mandela organized the ANC armed wing, Umkhonto we Sizwe (Spear of the Nation), but Mandela's capture and trial, along with those of other ANC and PAC leaders, seemed to have forced all active resistance underground by 1964 (Lodge, 1983:231–260; Mandela, 1994:258–261).

Verwoerd had a strategy to confuse international opinion, shocked by the government's brutality. In a cynical imitation of independence and self-government occurring elsewhere in Africa, "positive" apartheid was initiated by the government. Under the guise of "Separate Development," the reserves were encouraged to develop their own legislative assemblies, achieve internal autonomy, and eventually reach "independence." In this way, all Africans would ultimately become citizens of "homelands" but foreigners in South Africa, the land of their birth. On the other hand, white South Africans, (only 15 percent of the population) would achieve the old dream of a white man's country in 87 percent of the republic (Kenney, 1980). (Note the location of homelands on Map 13.1.)

The legislative mechanisms were enacted in 1959, and in 1963 the largest reserve, Transkei, "home" to most of the Xhosa-speakers, became the first self-governing homeland under its malleable chief minister, Kaiser Matanzima. Others followed. Although in every case there was intimidation of anti-independence groups and widespread corruption of homeland leaders and their cronies, by the early 1970s the policy was pursued with increasing determination. While the government poured vast (but in real terms hopelessly inadequate) sums of money into entities such as Bophuthatswana (composed of six separate segments) these new "countries" were never viable. While the small inner circles of blacks dominating the homelands grew wealthy, most residents were desperately poor, because few jobs were available and the land was often unsuitable for farming (Stultz, 1980; Butler, Rotberg, and Adams, 1977).

After Verwoerd's 1966 assassination in the assembly chamber by an allegedly deranged parliamentary messenger, his successor, B. J. Vorster, a former OB "general," not only realized much of this "grand apartheid" but actively pursued a policy of détente with neighboring black states. "John," as he liked to be called by his English-speaking golfing friends, tried to endear himself to all South African whites while presenting a firm but friendly face to his black neighbors. Yet, only one country, Malawi, was willing to swallow his blandishments wholeheartedly and accept Pretoria's money in exchange for diplomatic relations.

The rest of Africa, now predominantly independent of its former colonial masters, was more cautious. For beside the "benevolent" side of separate development was the iron fist inside the velvet glove. Vorster had already introduced detention without trial as Verwoerd's minister of police; he soon made it indefinite in duration (Foster, 1987). Political prisoners began to die mysteriously. Every remaining loophole in the web of earlier petty apartheid legislation was carefully closed, the pass laws were enforced even more strictly, and by the 1970s mass removals of rural Africans from "black spots" in white farming areas had become widespread. This was necessary to achieve a tidier homelands map and Verwoerd's projected 1977 date for turning back the African influx to "white South Africa." To realize this fantasy, blacks would be transported, voluntarily or otherwise, to the homelands, where farming was increasingly impossible because of overcrowding, soil erosion, inadequate technology, and the migration of so many adult men to South African cities in search of work (Platzky and Walker, 1985).

World opinion was beginning to turn against South Africa. One sign of this disapproval was an international ban on South African participation in international sporting events. Vorster's limited attempts to placate world opinion by taking a few token steps toward integration created a fierce white backlash. In 1969, Albert Hertzog, the late general's son, led the first significant split in the National Party right. His party never fared well at the polls, but it did prepare the ground, especially among Afrikaner blue-collar workers, for later far-right successes as the NP was belatedly forced to come to terms with a fast-changing southern Africa.

■ THE ATTEMPT TO MODERNIZE APARTHEID

Vorster could not escape some obvious truths. The 1970s saw an increasingly expensive guerrilla campaign in South African–occupied Namibia and the Portuguese revolution of 1974, which led to the granting of independence to Mozambique and Angola. These events were accompanied by the tightening stranglehold of sanctions and insurgency against South

Africa's last white ally, the rebel state Rhodesia. Soon there would be no more buffer states against the tide of black liberation.

Internally, economic and political problems were mounting. For one, arms and oil embargoes, plus the 1973 oil crisis, meant this was no booming decade like the previous one. Making things worse, black resistance to apartheid was increasing. In the factories, blacks were resorting to illegal strikes. In the universities, black students led by Steven Biko were forming "black consciousness" groups independent of the old white liberal organizations. In 1976, police reacted violently when Soweto schoolchildren demonstrated against compulsory education in Afrikaans, a new component of "Bantu education" (cf. Hirson, 1979; Woods, 1987). By the end of the year, as many as a thousand youthful protesters had been killed by the police.

The climate of escalating black resistance and violent white repression underscored for growing numbers of whites that change was needed. Big business especially wanted reforms to accommodate black frustration in order to make white capitalists competitive again and prevent revolution (Torchia, 1988). Realignment in the political arena was one response. The United Party collapsed, and its more liberal members fled to an enlarged Progressive Federal Party (PFP). By 1977, the more reform-minded PFP was the new official opposition party in parliament, dominated by the massive but stagnant NP.

The solution to the race problem suggested by the more liberal wing of the NP was simple: as many blacks as possible would be co-opted into the system as junior partners of a thereby strengthened NP-controlled state. The homelands would have to take those Africans who could not be accommodated. Those included in white South Africa would provide the skilled labor needed by a changing, increasingly mechanized economy. The old manual jobs were fewer now. Migratory labor could deal with those needs, but for the factories, well-trained workers with a stake in the system were needed. Capitalists had always borne the Nationalists' whites-only variety of socialism on sufferance. They preferred that black and white workers compete for jobs, thus lowering wages for both. In difficult times, expensive, poorly educated, and inefficient white workers could no longer be carried, even if they meant guaranteed NP votes. Besides, the white working class was shrinking under the weight of relative Afrikaner affluence, because so many had benefited from the selective socialism of Nationalist rule (Kenney, 1991:253–271; van der Berg, 1989).

Vorster made some moves in the desired direction, but new leadership was required to push major reforms. Fortuitously, a scandal over Vorster's alleged misuse of government funds led to the election in 1978 of Cape NP leader P. W. Botha as the new party chief and prime minister, replacing Vorster. As leader of the more enlightened wing of the NP, Botha's victory marked a stunning victory over the mainly conservative Transvalers, who had dominated the party leadership since Malan's retirement in 1954 (cf. Rees, 1980).

Botha did not waste time. He appointed a host of investigative commissions, a tried NP method of accustoming voters to major changes. African and nonracial trade unions were legalized, many public amenities were quietly integrated (mainly in the more liberal cities), and Africans were gradually allowed to own property in urban townships or even to do business in central commercial areas of towns. By 1985, even the old "sacred cows," the laws against interracial sex or marriage, had been repealed. The abolition of the pass laws followed in 1986. Henceforth, blacks who could find approved housing (of which there was precious little) would be permitted to work in the urban areas. Thus, big business would have its permanent work force with a stake in the system, organized in carefully regulated trade unions that could strike only after elaborate arbitration measures had failed. The homelands would meanwhile be encouraged by all means available to take independence (Kenney, 1991:290–307).

Yet, Botha's major contribution was his attempted resolution of a matter Vorster had always tried to paper over: how to fit the coloureds and Indians into the apartheid framework of government. His solution was a tricameral parliament, with one chamber for each group, in which all joint decisionmaking would be dominated by the largest chamber, the white assembly. To head this apparatus would be a powerful executive president, chosen by an NP-dominated electoral college. Each chamber would pass laws affecting its "own affairs," but in matters of common concern ("general affairs"), the consent of all three chambers was required. Where the other chambers disagreed with the assembly, an NP-dominated president's council would provide the convenient break to the deadlock (Lijphart, 1985; Omond, 1986:41–46).

It was easy to find participants in this exercise; those who had previously been involved in the defunct Coloured Representative Council and South African Indian Council (two largely advisory bodies invented a decade earlier to provide limited consultation with those communities) jumped at the opportunity. Even the coloured Labour Party, which had previously destroyed its representative council out of frustration with government intransigence, offered to give the new scheme five years to prove itself (Van der Ross, 1986:344–353; Du Pré, 1994:161–178). Yet, the great majority of the coloured and Indian communities, especially in urban areas, rejected the tricameral system, as did the outraged African population, excluded from even token participation in the central government. Even Gatsha Buthelezi, the conservative leader of the Zulu homeland, Kwazulu, and of the avowedly procapitalist Inkatha movement, scathingly condemned participation in so flawed an experiment (Maré and Hamilton, 1987:161).

Botha also found angry right-wing opposition to such power sharing within his own party, especially in the Transvaal. The hardliners, led by Transvaal NP leader Andries Treurnicht, left the party in 1982. Treurnicht's new, unabashedly white supremacist Conservative Party (CP) soon became the major far-right voice. Beyond the CP, many small groups, such as the neo-Nazi Afrikaner Resistance Movement, rapidly emerged (cf. Giliomee, 1982).

Although Botha's new constitution was passed in an all-white referendum, barely 20 percent of registered Indian voters and 30 percent of coloured ones bothered to participate in the elections for their new chambers in 1984. The boycott of these elections spawned a giant nonracial umbrella body, the United Democratic Front (UDF), drawing on hundreds of grass-roots organizations devoted to undoing the tricameral system and creating a South Africa based on the ANC Freedom Charter (cf. Barrell, 1984; Davies, O'Meara, and Dlamini, 1988).

Botha had even less success with his supplementary plan to buy off urban Africans with greater economic opportunities (through eliminating most remaining statutory job discrimination), basic amenities (such as the electrification of Soweto), and full-fledged municipalities. Although blacks were now allowed to vote in township municipal elections, turnout was pathetically low. By 1985, resistance to any participation in government-sponsored local political bodies had led to such widespread unrest in the townships that Botha proclaimed a state of emergency in many areas (Omond, 1986:51–52, 246–256). In the following year, this was extended to the whole country. Nonetheless, violence increased, and some suspected government informers were "necklaced" with burning tires around their necks by black militants. The ANC called from abroad for the townships to be rendered ungovernable and stepped up its sabotage actions. The security police arrested thousands. Among whites, there was growing resistance to military conscription, as draftees were for the first time sent to garrison the townships rather than the border (see Murray, 1987).

Meanwhile, corruption scandals and several coups and coup attempts in the homelands signaled the breakdown of the tribal homelands component of apartheid. Botha's reliance on his generals to create a new buffer zone by fomenting assassinations and civil wars in neighboring countries like Mozambique, Lesotho, Botswana, and Angola became too expensive—the army was needed at home, and international opposition was forcing a South African withdrawal from southern Angola and later from long-suffering Namibia (cf. Hanlon, 1986; Grundy, 1986).

While white, far-right death squads terrorized the townships, many blacks, tired of the violence and now able to pay higher rents, moved to the inner suburbs of cities like Johannesburg, where there were hundreds of empty apartments. It seemed as though the apparatus of apartheid was breaking down as crime figures shot up, the South African currency collapsed with the withdrawal of key foreign bank loans, and foreign economic sanctions bit ever deeper into the pockets of blacks and whites alike (cf. Yudelman, 1987; Lewis, 1990).

It was clear that Botha, trapped by his own history, was incapable of taking the next vital steps toward more fundamental reform. His South Africa was unrecognizable from that of Verwoerd, but the new black middle classes had not been bought off. Rather, they had, like all disenfranchised bourgeoisies, become even more vocal in demanding a central role in governing the society. At the same time, by the 1987 election, the far-right Conservative Party was strong enough to become the main opposition party, displacing the Progressives (van Vuuren et al., 1987). The National Party now enjoyed almost as much English as Afrikaner support, while it seemed that soon most Afrikaners would favor the CP.

The NP's "brown" junior partners, exasperated by Botha's refusal to end what remained of petty apartheid, threatened to expose the tricameral system as unworkable, while even Inkatha's chief Buthelezi refused to negotiate until Botha released all political prisoners and unbanned all anti-apartheid organizations. While the ANC's bombs became more frequent, the government's chief response was massive press censorship and an effective ban on the UDF and all major extraparliamentary groups. Big business had lost confidence in Botha's neo-apartheid; now, even within the NP there was growing talk of the need for new leadership and a new policy (see Davis, 1987).

■ DISMANTLING THE APARTHEID STATE

In 1989, Botha, suffering from the effects of a stroke, was forced out as party leader in favor of Transvaal NP leader F. W. de Klerk, a belated convert to a more enlightened approach. He showed a willingness to talk about an expanded form of power sharing. From prison, Nelson Mandela was quietly attempting to open negotiations between the NP and ANC (Mandela, 1994:501–545). Moreover, there were some signs in a new election held later that year that more than two-thirds of the whites would support de Klerk–style reform or the more avowedly liberal policies of the Democratic Party (the new white umbrella parliamentary group on the Nationalists' left). Botha, unwilling to support further reform, was forced by the NP parliamentary caucus to step down as president in favor of de Klerk (Thompson, 1990:241–242).

The new president was not entirely altruistic in pursuing a new direction. Regardless of what he did now, the deeply alienated Conservatives would never return to the NP fold, and the 1989 assembly election had consolidated the Conservatives' position in the Transvaal and Free State. Further CP electoral gains threatened the reform effort. The political chessboard had to be remade to preclude this, but that meant going much further toward majority rule than all the previous talk of power sharing. The dismal voter turnout for the two junior chambers of the tricameral parliament, even worse than in the previous election, merely confirmed that there could be no going back.

De Klerk, therefore, moved more boldly in February 1990, when he unbanned numerous organizations, including the ANC, PAC, and Communist Party. He declared his support for negotiations for a new constitution granting political rights to all but protecting the rights of minorities (meaning the whites), and freed Nelson Mandela, the long-imprisoned leader of the ANC, who alone appeared to have the stature to bring blacks together to negotiate with whites (Price, 1991).

The ANC-Communist alliance had little choice but to accept the new conditions; after several months of hesitation, it renounced the armed struggle and agreed to work toward negotiations. Communist regimes were collapsing in Eastern Europe, and the Soviet Union had too many problems to continue underwriting the expensive ANC campaign, while the harsh realities of politics suggested that the West was far more interested in helping Eastern Europe than in assisting black liberation. Nor could African countries be as helpful as before. Many old friends, such as Zambia's Kenneth Kaunda, faced angry citizens tired of economic devastation and corruption and demanding an end to one-party rule.

Nelson Mandela addresses well-wishers in New York City four months after his release from prison.

The positive features of reform were soon clear enough. Namibia achieved its long-delayed independence early in 1990, numerous near legendary exiled figures began to return to South Africa, and many of the corrupt homeland regimes were overthrown in popular revolts and replaced by administrations more sympathetic to the ANC (see Bank, 1994). In other cases, such as the Transkei, existing regimes threw their support to Mandela. Only Kwazulu (stronghold of Buthelezi's Inkatha movement) and "independent" Bophuthatswana remained aloof from the rush to embrace the ANC, although the government of Ciskei gradually distanced itself from the liberation movements.

Relatively peaceful protest marches became a standard occurrence in most towns, and there were repeated meetings between members of the government cabinet and the ANC leadership to settle on preliminary details such as the timing of the release of political prisoners, amnesty for exiles who had committed violent acts, and the creation of a climate conducive to negotiations for a new constitution.

In parliament, de Klerk took several steps to show his goodwill: for example, he repealed the Separate Amenities Act and set terms under which white state schools could, with the overwhelming support of parents, open up at least partly to black students. In 1991, de Klerk repealed the hated 1913 Lands Act, the Population Registration Act (prescribing race classification at birth), and the Group Areas Act, which in many cities was already almost a dead letter.

The NP took perhaps the most symbolic step of all when it opened its membership to all races. Polls suggested that a substantial nonwhite minority, especially among more conservative coloureds and Indians, would support the NP now that it professed support for capitalism and democracy. Not surprisingly, now that the NP had stolen most of the Democratic Party's policies, the latter lost support dramatically. At the same time, a strong conservative backlash, even in traditionally more "liberal" seats, suggested that de Klerk had to move rapidly to change the rules of elections or lose his majority in the assembly.

Right-wing whites spoke menacingly of resistance, even civil war, if de Klerk sold out to blacks as in Namibia. In some towns, blacks taking advantage of integrated public amenities were severely beaten by white extremists. Mysterious white death squads and agents provocateurs were rumored to be behind growing intrablack violence in the townships. There was evidence of elements in the government being behind at least some of this, particularly of police favoring conservative blacks, such as Zulu Inkatha members, against the ANC. As Inkatha tried to expand its membership into the Transvaal townships, the long-simmering and often bloody struggle between Inkatha and ANC-UDF supporters spread.

Superficially, intrablack conflict often seemed ethnically based or "tribal," since Inkatha was overwhelmingly Zulu and many ANC leaders were Xhosa, but the situation was much more complex. Many urban Zulu in particular were ANC supporters, and the struggle was as much between old and young or urban and rural as between different "tribes." Growing black unemployment, 40 percent or more in places like Soweto, sharpened old hostilities, themselves long encouraged by a government maintained by brute force and divide-and-rule tactics.

There had long been tension, for instance, between temporary migrants from the rural areas and the more permanent township residents. In addition, since 1976 the ANC and other liberation groups had placed the youth, often children of ten or twelve years, in the forefront of the struggle. Not yet dependent on white jobs and not yet beaten into submission, this generation had lost the traditional respect shown in African society to one's elders and had largely abandoned formal education for the sake of "liberation now" (see Love and Sederberg, 1990). With so many older leaders imprisoned or in exile, there often seemed no other option but to let the children lead the struggle. But the long-term effects of this policy were devastating. Older township residents, especially migratory workers from rural areas like Natal, had grown resentful of the insolence of many young "comrades" and their incessant demands for yet another boycott or strike or for just one more sacrifice for freedom.

On top of these considerations, there were serious ideological divides between the nonracial and broadly prosocial democratic ANC and its allies (united around the 1955 Freedom Charter) and the capitalist Inkatha, not to mention the militantly socialist and racially exclusive PAC or its counterpart, the black consciousness Azanian People's Organization (AZAPO) movement (see Hirschmann, 1990). Inkatha demanded an equal role in negotiations, which the ANC was reluctant to grant to a "homeland" organization, while the PAC (using the slogan "One Settler, One Bullet!") and AZAPO criticized the ANC for negotiating when the real issue, from their viewpoint, was transfer of power and land to the majority.

These divides were also reflected in the trade union movement. Inkatha had created its own union network, while AZAPO and the PAC were concentrated in the National African Confederation of Trade Unions (NACTU). The ANC and the Communists were allied with the giant worker arm of the now defunct UDF, the Congress of South African Trade Unions (COSATU) (Marx, 1989). COSATU was by no means synonymous with its two partners, however; it was suspicious that the ANC, dominated by an educated middle-class leadership, might easily ignore worker interests in negotiations, especially as Mandela seemed to drop demands for nationalizing key industries in favor of black empowerment within a primarily capitalist economy (see Nattrass, 1994).

In this political environment, township violence grew while police often seemed unwilling or unable to stop the bloodshed. Crimes committed by gangsters taking advantage of the power vacuum struck fear into white hearts and undermined what was left of the fabric of African social life.

At the same time, the ANC was having difficulty transforming itself

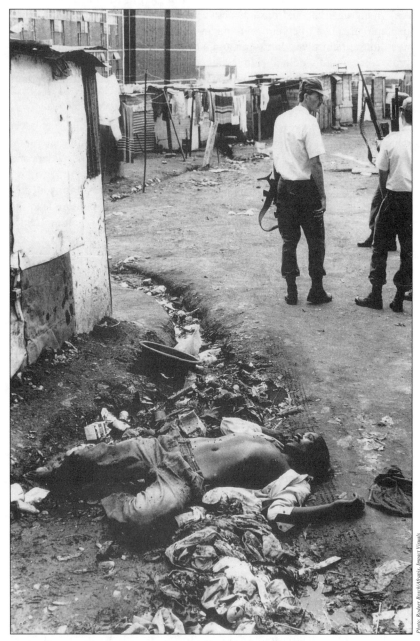

Photo: Rodger Bosch/Afrapix, Impact Visuals

As black and white leaders negotiated the end of white rule, mounting violence in South Africa's black townships threatened to derail the peace process.

from a secret liberation movement into a mass party. There was local criticism of the exiled leadership, and membership drives delivered only 150,000 members by November 1990. Frustrated ANC members sought to retain public attention by involving the community in mass action, especially a campaign to force remaining black city councillors out of office. But this merely added to the confusion in black areas, while ever more numerous strikes threatened to paralyze an already stricken economy.

■ **THE TORTUROUS ROAD**
TO A NEW SOUTH AFRICA

Meanwhile, negotiating the transition to majority rule progressed in fits and starts. Through much of 1991, the opposing sides could not get beyond talks about how to start negotiations. Eventually, rising violence and looming economic disaster forced them to agree to a multiparty preliminary conference. In practice, the Convention for a Democratic South Africa (CODESA), which met at last in December, was dominated by the NP and ANC, with Buthelezi's Inkatha (renamed the Inkatha Freedom Party or IFP) in distant third place (Strauss, 1993). By May, CODESA had fallen apart as it became clear that the ANC wanted a rapid transition to unfettered majoritarian rule, while the NP sought a protracted transition that would retain a key role for itself (Friedman, 1993:21–31).

Even private bilateral ANC-NP talks went nowhere as the ANC tried to bolster support among frustrated supporters by approving unprecedented mass action in the form of strikes, marches, and boycotts. A massacre of black township dwellers by masked gunmen in Boipatong, south of Johannesburg, led the ANC to suspend talks. The resulting effort to take mass action into the rural areas culminated in the shooting of dozens of ANC supporters by soldiers of the Ciskei homeland. This shook both sides into returning to the table in September, with the ANC and NP signing a Record of Understanding. The necessary concessions in turn convinced the IFP, right-wing whites, and conservative black leaders of Ciskei and Bophuthatswana that the NP was selling them out. Nonetheless, a revised CODESA-type multiparty forum was convened in April 1993.

Despite great tensions, especially after a right-winger assassinated Communist Party secretary-general Chris Hani, the government and ANC drew closer. The ANC's "sunset clause," allowing all major parties a five-year role in the cabinet after nonracial elections, and its acceptance of some powers for new provinces, helped here. Late in 1993, after much compromise on all sides, an interim constitution was unveiled, to be implemented after elections in April 1994.

For a while, continuing IFP hostility and right-wing white resistance

Voters in line at the polling station in Rosebank, April 27, 1994

threatened to derail the process. But Buthelezi and more moderate right-wingers, led by several retired Afrikaner generals, were persuaded to partic-ipate in the elections by two last-minute concessions: The Zulu king's role in the IFP's Natal stronghold would be honored and the possibility of creat-ing a *volkstaat* (Afrikaner region) was not ruled out. At the same time, Bophuthatswana, the last homeland holdout, was reincorporated into South Africa after a mass revolt against its unpopular rulers (Friedman and Atkinson, 1994; Kotzé and Greyling, 1994:33–36, 68–81, 220–227).

Against all expectations, the elections were peaceful. The ANC won 62 percent of the vote, including the great majority of African votes, and con-trol of seven of the nine newly created provinces. The NP trailed with 20 percent, and the IFP surprisingly got nearly 10 percent. The other parties did poorly, but proportional representation ensured many of them some repre-sentation in the new parliament. Still, the ANC was disappointed at the NP's winning control of the Western Cape provincial legislature (due to extensive support from the coloured majority there) and the IFP's victory in Kwazulu-Natal (Reynolds, 1994:182–220; Southall, 1994).

Nelson Mandela was duly sworn in as president, with de Klerk one of two deputy presidents in a "Government of National Unity," comprising the ANC, NP, and IFP. Communists, trade unionists, nationalists, Zulu conservatives, and longtime ANC activists sat together in parliament, as a new brightly colored flag was widely embraced as a symbol of this new "rainbow nation."

From the outset, daunting problems faced the new government: continued strikes, the slow return of foreign investors, massive unemployment, phenomenally high crime rates, rural Africans streaming into urban areas, and the ANC-IFP conflict in Kwazulu-Natal. Whites and coloureds feared affirmative action policies giving Africans priority for jobs, white bureaucrats feared losing their livelihood, white farmers feared losing their large properties to land redistribution, and old NP loyalists feared having past abuses uncovered by an impending Truth Commission. There was much friction over demarcating new nonracial local authorities. Nor was drawing up a final constitution strife-free. The ANC favored a strong central government, whereas the NP, IFP, and DP demanded more provincial autonomy. Some ANC leaders feared that the new provinces (many coinciding with concentrations of particular ethnic groups, such as the Zulu, Tswana, or coloureds) might provide bases for future threats to national harmony (and ANC control) if given too much independence.

Yet much has been achieved. Apartheid is gone. A constitutional court and a bill of rights protects potential victims of political abuse. The army has integrated the liberation movement forces, and the police are learning progressive, community-based methods. Young people of all races are learning about each other at school. Mandela enjoys widespread admiration as a force for interracial reconciliation, economic sanctions have ended, and South Africa is again a valued member of the international community (see Harber and Ludman, 1995).

■ CONCLUSIONS

Clearly, the difficulties involved in dismantling the legacy of apartheid and creating a truly democratic South Africa remain formidable. Over more than 300 years, the "for whites only" South African political system, economy, and racially and ethnically divided society were painstakingly constructed. Racial segregation, the encouragement of black divisions, and white supremacy were the country's foundations. Such an edifice cannot be broken down overnight, nor can the bitterness, hatreds, and prejudices of so warped a social system be easily changed.

There are real questions, even in the current climate of reform and reconciliation, concerning whether South Africa can successfully make the transition not just to a nominal majority rule, but to a lasting democracy, respectful of South Africa's diverse minorities and responsive to the still impoverished black masses. The socioeconomic problem poses an even greater challenge than constructing an acceptable political system. If the new government cannot deliver on its much-heralded Reconstruction and Development Program, South Africa's democracy will fail in a sea of poverty, disease, homelessness, unemployment, and crime.

As this chapter has shown, the problem is not only that whites monopolized political power for three centuries, but that they secured a vastly disproportionate share of the country's wealth. Most whites accept losing political control; they fear far more what they must part with for the sake of economic justice. For historical reasons, the economy still depends heavily on their skills, capital, and entrepreneurship. White business leaders therefore caution against redistributive strategies that would overburden an already narrow taxpayer base, encourage white emigration, and scare away foreign investment. In an increasingly competitive world, the low skills and productivity and endemic crime and strikes that characterize South Africa make it less attractive than many other developing economies.

At the same time, many blacks understandably fear that white insistence on "minority rights" and "free-market capitalism" are thinly disguised efforts to retain white control over the economy and land, which would make it almost impossible to improve living standards for most blacks (see Price, 1991:506, 287–289). But given the worldwide collapse of communist economic systems and the comparative success of more market-oriented emerging economies, South Africa can hardly turn to the intrusive collectivist economics that have failed elsewhere. It is these and other impasses that must be resolved before a prosperous, united, integrated, and therefore truly democratic society can emerge from the tragic history of South Africa.

■ **BIBLIOGRAPHY**

Ballard, Charles. 1986. "Drought and Economic Distress: South Africa in the 1800s." *Journal of Interdisciplinary History* 17:359–378.
————. 1989. "Traders, Trekkers and Colonists." Pp. 116–145 in Andrew Duminy and Bill Guest (eds.). *Natal and Zululand from Earliest Times to 1910: A New History.* Pietermaritzburg: University of Natal Press.
Bank, Leslie. 1994. "Between Traders and Tribalists: Implosion and the Politics of Disjuncture in a South African Homeland." *African Affairs* 93:75–98.
Barrell, Howard. 1984. "The United Democratic Front and National Forum: Their Emergence, Composition and Trends." Pp. 6–20 in *South African Review Two.* Johannesburg: Ravan.

Bhana, Surendra, and Bridglal Pachai (eds.). 1984. *A Documentary History of Indian South Africans.* Stanford, CA: Hoover Institution Press.

Bhana, Surendra, and Joy Brain. 1990. *Setting Down Roots: Indian Migrants in South Africa, 1860–1911.* Johannesburg: Witwatersrand University Press.

Bickford-Smith, Vivian. 1995. "South African Urban History, Racial Segregation and the Unique Case of Cape Town?" *Journal of Southern African Studies* 21:63–78.

Bloomberg, Charles. 1989. *Christian Nationalism and the Rise of the Afrikaner Broederbond in South Africa, 1918–1948.* Edited by Saul Dubow. Bloomington: Indiana University Press.

Bundy, Colin. 1988. *The Rise and Fall of the South African Peasantry.* London: James Currey.

Butler, Jeffrey, Robert I. Rotberg, and John Adams. 1977. *The Black Homelands of South Africa: The Political and Economic Development of Bophuthatswana and Kwazulu.* Berkeley: University of California Press.

Davenport, T. R. H. 1966. *The Afrikaner Bond: The History of a South African Political Party, 1880–1911.* Cape Town: Oxford University Press.

———. 1987. *South Africa: A Modern History.* Toronto: University of Toronto Press.

Davies, Robert, Dan O'Meara, and Sipho Dlamini. 1988. *The Struggle for South Africa: A Reference Guide to Movements, Organizations, and Institutions.* 2 vols. London: Zed.

Davis, Stephen M. 1987. *Apartheid's Rebels: Inside South Africa's Hidden War.* New Haven: Yale University Press.

Delius, Peter. 1983. *The Land Belongs to Us: The Pedi Polity, the Boers and the British in the Nineteenth Century Transvaal.* Johannesburg: Ravan.

Du Pré, Roy H. 1994. *Separate but Unequal: The "Coloured" People of South Africa—A Political History.* Johannesburg: Jonathan Ball.

Edgerton, Robert B. 1988. *Like Lions They Fought: The Zulu War and the Last Black Empire in South Africa.* New York: Free Press.

Elphick, Richard. 1985. *Khoikhoi and the Founding of White South Africa.* Johannesburg: Ravan.

Elphick, Richard, and Robert Shell. 1989. "Intergroup Relations." Pp. 184–239 in Richard Elphick and Hermann Giliomee (eds.). *The Shaping of South African Society, 1652–1840.* Middletown, CT: Wesleyan University Press.

Emmanuel, Arghiri. 1982. "White-Settler Colonialism and the Myth of Investor Imperialism." Pp. 88–106 in Hamza Alavi and Teodor Shanin (eds.) *Sociology of "Developing Societies."* New York: Monthly Review Press.

Foster, Don. 1987. *Detention and Torture in South Africa: Psychological, Legal and Historical Structures.* New York: St. Martin's Press.

Friedman, Steven (ed.). 1993. *The Long Journey: South Africa's Quest for a Negotiated Settlement.* Johannesburg: Ravan.

Friedman, Steven, and Dorren Atkinson (eds.). 1994. *South African Review 7: The Small Miracle—South Africa's Negotiated Settlement.* Johannesburg: Ravan.

Furlong, Patrick. 1991. *Between Crown and Swastika: The Impact of the Radical Right on the Afrikaner Nationalist Movement in the Fascist Era.* Hanover, NH: University Press of New England.

———. 1994. "Improper Intimacy: Afrikaans Churches, the National Party and the Anti-Miscegenation Laws." *South African Historical Journal* 31:55–79.

Galbraith, John S. 1963. *Reluctant Empire: British Policy on the South African Frontier, 1834–1854.* Berkeley: University of California Press.

————. 1974. *Crown and Charter: The Early Years of the British South Africa Company.* Berkeley: University of California Press.

Garson, Noel. 1979. "South Africa and World War I." *Journal of Imperial and Commonwealth History* 8:68–85.

Gerhart, Gail M. 1978. *Black Power in South Africa: The Evolution of an Ideology.* Berkeley: University of California Press.

Giliomee, Hermann. 1982. *The Parting of the Ways: South African Politics 1976–1982.* Cape Town: David Philip.

————. 1989. "The Beginnings of Afrikaner Ethnic Consciousness, 1850–1915." Pp. 21–54 in Leroy Vail (ed.). *The Creation of Tribalism in Southern Africa.* Berkeley: University of California Press.

Grundy, Kenneth. 1986. *The Militarization of South African Politics.* Bloomington: Indiana University Press.

Hall, Martin. 1987. *The Changing Past: Farmers, Kings and Traders in Southern Africa, 200–1860.* Cape Town: David Philip.

Hancock, W. K. 1962–1968. *Smuts.* 2 vols. Cambridge: Cambridge University Press.

Hanlon, Joseph. 1986. *Apartheid's Second Front: South Africa's War Against Its Neighbors.* Harmondsworth, England: Penguin.

Harber, Anton, and Barbara Ludman (eds.). 1995. *A-Z of South African Politics: The Essential Handbook.* Harmondsworth, England: Penguin.

Hirschmann, David. 1990. "Of Monsters and Devils, Analyses and Alternatives: Changing Black South African Perceptions of Capitalism and Socialism." *African Affairs* 89:341–369.

Hirson, Baruch. 1979. *Year of Fire, Year of Ash. The Soweto Revolt: Roots of a Revolution?* London: Zed.

Johnstone, Frederick. 1976. *Class, Race and Gold: A Study of Class Relations and Racial Discrimination in South Africa.* London: Routledge and Kegan Paul.

Kallaway, Peter (ed.). 1984. *Apartheid and Education: The Education of Black South Africans.* Johannesburg: Ravan.

Keegan, Timothy. 1988. *Facing the Storm: Portraits of Black Lives in Rural South Africa.* Athens: Ohio University Press.

Kenney, Henry. 1980. *Architect of Apartheid: Verwoerd—An Appraisal.* Johannesburg: Jonathan Ball.

————. 1991. *Power, Pride and Prejudice: The Years of Afrikaner Nationalist Rule in South Africa.* Johannesburg: Jonathan Ball.

Kotzé, Hennie, and Anneke Greyling (eds.). 1994. *Political Organisations in South Africa A-Z.* Cape Town: Tafelberg.

Lazerson, Joshua. 1994. *Against the Tide: Whites in the Struggle Against Apartheid.* Boulder: Westview.

Legassick, Martin. 1980. "The Frontier Tradition in South African Historiography." Pp. 44–79 in Shula Marks and Anthony Atmore (eds.). *Economy and Society in Pre-Industrial South Africa.* London: Longman.

————. 1989. "The Northern Frontier to c. 1840: The Rise and Decline of the Griqua People." Pp. 358–420 in Richard Elphick and Hermann Giliomee (eds.). *The Shaping of South African Society, 1652–1840.* Middletown, CT: Wesleyan University Press.

Lewis, Gavin. 1987. *Between the Wire and the Wall: A History of South African "Coloured" Politics.* New York: St. Martin's Press.

Lewis, Stephen R. 1990. *The Economics of Apartheid.* New York: Council on Foreign Relations.

Lijphart, Arend. 1985. *Power-Sharing in South Africa.* Berkeley: Institute of International Studies, University of California.

Lipton, Merle. 1986. *Capitalism and Apartheid, 1910–1986*. Aldershot, England: Wildwood House.

Lodge, Tom. 1983. *Black Politics in South Africa Since 1945*. London: Longman.

Love, Janice, and Peter Sederberg. 1990. "Black Education and the Dialectics of Transformation in South Africa, 1982–8." *Journal of Modern African Studies* 28:299–326.

Mandela, Nelson. 1994. *Long Walk to Freedom*. London: Little, Brown.

Maré, Gerhard, and Georgina Hamilton. 1987. *An Appetite for Power: Buthelezi's Inkatha and South Africa*. Bloomington: Indiana University Press.

Marx, Anthony. 1989. "South African Black Trade Unions as an Emerging Working-Class Movement." *Journal of Modern African Studies* 27:383–400.

Marx, Christoph. 1994. "The Ossewabrandwag as a Mass Movement, 1939–1941." *Journal of Southern African Studies* 20:195–219.

Maylam, Paul. 1986. *A History of the African People of South Africa*. New York: St. Martin's Press.

Meli, Francis. 1989. *South Africa Belongs to Us: A History of the ANC*. Bloomington: Indiana University Press.

Morton, Fred. 1994. "Captive Labor in the Western Transvaal after the Sand River Convention." Pp. 167–185 in Elizabeth Eldredge and Fred Morton (eds.). *Slavery in South Africa: Captive Labor on the Dutch Frontier*. Boulder: Westview Press.

Mostert, Noël. 1992. *Frontiers: The Epic of South Africa's Creation and the Tragedy of the Xhosa People*. London: Jonathan Cape.

Murray, Martin. 1987. *South Africa, Time of Agony, Time of Destiny: The Upsurge of Popular Protest*. London: Verso.

Nattrass, Nicoli. 1994. "Politics and Economics in ANC Economic Policy." *African Affairs* 93:343–359.

Omer-Cooper, J. D. 1966. *The Zulu Aftermath: A Nineteenth Century Revolution in Bantu Africa*. London: Longman.

———. 1993. "Has the Mfecane a Future? A Response to the Cobbing Critique." *Journal of Southern African Studies* 19:273–294.

Omond, Roger. 1986. *The Apartheid Handbook: A Guide to South Africa's Everyday Racial Policies*. Harmondsworth, England: Penguin.

Pakenham, Thomas. 1979. *The Boer War*. London: Weidenfeld and Nicolson.

Paton, Alan. 1964. *Hofmeyr*. Cape Town: Oxford University Press.

Peires, J. B. 1982. *The House of Phalo: A History of the Xhosa People in the Days of Their Independence*. Cambridge: Cambridge University Press.

Plaatje, Sol. 1982. *Native Life in South Africa: Before and Since the European War and the Boer Rebellion*. Johannesburg: Ravan.

Platzky, Lauren, and Cherryl Walker. 1985. *The Surplus People: Forced Removals in South Africa*. Johannesburg: Ravan.

Posel, Deborah. 1991. *The Making of Apartheid 1948–1961: Conflict and Compromise*. Oxford: Clarendon Press.

Price, Robert M. 1991. *The Apartheid State in Crisis: Political Transformation in South Africa, 1975–1990*. Oxford: Oxford University Press.

Rees, Mervyn. 1980. *Muldergate: The Story of the Info Scandal*. Johannesburg: Macmillan South Africa.

Reynolds, Andrew (ed.). 1994. *Election '94 South Africa*. New York: St. Martin's Press.

Rich, Paul. 1978. "Ministering to the White Man's Needs: The Development of Urban Segregation in South Africa 1913–1923." *African Studies* 37:177–191.

Ross, Robert. 1980. "The Rule of Law at the Cape of Good Hope in the Eighteenth Century." *Journal of Imperial and Commonwealth History* 9:5–16.

Serfontein, J. H. P. 1978. *Brotherhood of Power: An Exposé of the Secret Afrikaner Broederbond*. Bloomington: Indiana University Press.

Shell, Robert. 1994. *Children of Bondage: A Social History of the Slave Society at the Cape of Good Hope, 1652–1838*. Hanover, NH: University Press of New England.

Simons, Jack, and Ray Simons. 1983. *Class and Colour in South Africa 1850–1950*. London: International Defense and Aid Fund.

Southall, Roger. 1994. "The South African Elections of 1994: Remaking a Dominant-Party State." *Journal of Modern African Studies* 32:629–655.

Strauss, Annette. 1993. "The 1992 Referendum in South Africa." *Journal of Modern African Studies* 31:339–360.

Stultz, Newell M. 1974. *Afrikaner Politics in South Africa, 1934–1948*. Berkeley: University of California Press.

———. 1980. *South Africa's Half Loaf: Race Separatism in South Africa*. Cape Town: David Philip.

Suttner, Raymond, and Jeremy Cronin. 1986. *Thirty Years of the Freedom Charter*. Johannesburg: Ravan.

Swan, Maureen. 1985. *Gandhi: The South African Experience*. Johannesburg: Ravan.

Swanson, Maynard. 1977. "The Sanitation Syndrome: Bubonic Plague and Urban Native Policy in the Cape Colony, 1900–1909." *Journal of African History* 18:387–410.

Thompson, Leonard M. 1960. *The Unification of South Africa, 1902–1910*. Oxford: Clarendon Press.

———. 1969. "Co-operation and Conflict: The Highveld." Pp. 391–446 in Monica Wilson and Leonard Thompson (eds.). *The Oxford History of South Africa*. Vol. 1. Oxford: Oxford University Press.

———. 1971. "The Subjugation of the African Chiefdoms, 1870–1898." Pp. 245–284 in Monica Wilson and Leonard Thompson (eds.). *The Oxford History of South Africa*. Vol. 2. Oxford: Oxford University Press.

———. 1975. *Survival in Two Worlds: Moshoeshoe of Lesotho 1786–1870*. Oxford: Clarendon Press.

———. 1985. *The Political Mythology of Apartheid*. New Haven: Yale University Press.

———. 1990. *A History of South Africa*. New Haven: Yale University Press.

Torchia, Andrew. 1988. "The Business of Business: An Analysis of the Political Behaviour of the South African Manufacturing Sector Under the Nationalists." *Journal of Southern African Studies* 14:421–445.

Turrell, Rob. 1987. *Capital and Labour on the Kimberley Diamond Fields, 1871–1890*. Cambridge: Cambridge University Press.

van der Berg, Servaas. 1989. "Long Term Economic Trends and Development Prospects in South Africa." *African Affairs* 88:187–203.

Van der Ross, Richard. 1986. *The Rise and Decline of Apartheid: A Study of Political Movements Among the Coloured People of South Africa 1880–1985*. Cape Town: Tafelberg.

van Vuuren, D. J., J. Latakgomi, H. C. Marais, and L. Schlemmer (eds.). 1987. *South African Election 1987: Context, Process and Prospect*. Pinetown, South Africa: Owen Burgess Publishers.

Walker, Eric. 1960. *The Great Trek*. London: A. C. Black.

Walshe, Peter. 1970. *The Rise of African Nationalism in South Africa: The ANC 1912–1952*. London: Hurst.

Warwick, Peter. 1983. *Black People in the South African War, 1899–1902.* Cambridge: Cambridge University Press.

Watson, R. L. 1990. *The Slave Question: Liberty and Property in South Africa.* Hanover, NH: University Press of New England.

Wheatcroft, Geoffrey. 1987. *The Randlords: South Africa's Robber Barons and the Mines That Forged a Nation.* New York: Touchstone Books.

Wilson, Monica. 1969. "The Hunters and the Herders," "The Nguni People," and "The Sotho, Venda and Tsonga." Pp. 40–186 in Monica Wilson and Leonard Thompson (eds.). *The Oxford History of South Africa.* Vol. 1. Oxford: Oxford University Press.

Woods, Donald. 1987. *Biko.* New York: Henry Holt.

Worden, Nigel. 1985. *Slavery in Dutch South Africa.* Cambridge: Cambridge University Press.

Worger, William H. 1987. *South Africa's City of Diamonds: Mine Workers and Monopoly Capitalism in Kimberley, 1867–1895.* New Haven: Yale University Press.

Wright, John, and Carolyn Hamilton. 1989. "Traditions and Transformations: The Phongolo-Mzimkhulu Region in the Late Eighteenth and Early Nineteenth Centuries." Pp. 49–82 in Andrew Duminy and Bill Guest (eds.). *Natal and Zululand from Earliest Times to 1910: A New History.* Pietermaritzburg: University of Natal Press.

Yudelman, David. 1984. *The Emergence of Modern South Africa: State, Capital, and the Incorporation of Organized Labour on the South African Gold Fields, 1902–1939.* Westport, CT: Greenwood Press.

———. 1987. "State and Capital in Contemporary South Africa." Pp. 250–268 in Richard Elphick, Jeffrey Butler, and David Welsh (eds.). *Democratic Liberalism in South Africa: Its History and Prospect.* Middletown, CT: Wesleyan University Press.

▪ 14 ▪

Trends and Prospects
April A. Gordon & Donald L. Gordon

In the introduction to this book, we said that no one knows with any certitude what lies ahead for Africa. At the same time, it is important to understand what has shaped the present and to offer some considered, although certainly tentative, speculations about the future. Where does Africa appear to be heading? What do trends and policies portend for the future?

First, let's look at some of Africa's achievements since independence. Despite the problems of the continent, some important foundations have been laid that may make the future more hopeful. For one, Africa has made impressive strides in providing better health care and education for its population. While still far behind other regions of the world, life expectancy, infant mortality, and education have all improved since independence. A new generation of Africans is better prepared than its parents to tackle the challenges that lie ahead.

This is especially important with regard to African leaders. At independence, few Africans had been given access to the education, skills, or experience necessary to run the European-style nations bequeathed to them by their colonial masters. Few had traveled abroad or had experience dealing with the international community. While many African presidents were dedicated and had benefited from European schooling, educational qualifications were often quite thin as one descended the ranks of state bureaucracies or other institutions. This has certainly had a profound and negative impact on the efficiency of government and on productivity and management of the economy.

The first generation of leaders is now gone, however, dead or retired. Military and civilian governments across the continent are being challenged by the growing ranks of better-educated, technically and professionally trained younger people who were the beneficiaries of postindependence investments in schooling. Some of the newer generation have been educated or lived abroad or have worked in international business or diplomatic settings. Babacar N'Diaye, president of the African Development Bank, describes this new breed of leaders as "techno-politicians" ("A Chance," 1991:2). It is these capable leaders who are beginning to assume power in many countries in a largely peaceful revolution.

As both internal and external pressures for democracy, economic reform, and government accountability grow in Africa, even autocratic regimes are calling upon the techno-politicians. In Côte d'Ivoire, former President Houphouët-Boigny named Allasane Outtara, former governor of the Banque Centrale des Etats de l'Afrique de l'Ouest, his new prime minister. Internationally known financial figures were also appointed as prime ministers in Gabon, Mali, Senegal, Congo, Zaire, and Cameroon. In formerly Marxist Benin, Nicephore Soglo, a former World Bank official, was elected president over Mathieu Kerekou, who had ruled dictatorially for many years ("A Chance," 1991).

Unheard of a decade ago, Africa's rulers are acknowledging the urgent need for better leadership, which will entail radical democratic reforms. In May 1991, at the Kampala Forum on Security, Stability, Development, and Cooperation in Africa, delegates (including five African heads of state) agreed to the Kampala Document. This document has been described as a "blueprint for the radical transformation of the continent in the 1990s." Its proposals aim to create a democratic and economically and politically integrated Africa with responsible and accountable leadership. Human and individual rights, access to basic necessities of life for all Africans, peace, and popular participation in societal affairs must be promoted, according to the Kampala Document ("Africans Seek," 1991:8–9). Also in 1991, at the OAU meeting in Nigeria, participants backed the call for multiparty democracy, improvement in the quality of governance, and less centralized control of the economy. In a startling indirect condemnation of their own past practices, the OAU delegates concluded that democracy was necessary for development and the elimination of corruption ("Organization," 1991:10).

The need for popular participation is being applied to the economy as well as to the political system. In reality, Africa's overly centralized states have been steadily losing control since the mid-1970s. Governments have become increasingly less able to control economic activity, maintain compliance or loyalty from their citizens, or provide essential services as the economy deteriorated and structural adjustment conditionalities for loans were imposed. This situation has inadvertently promoted the growth of "civil society" in Africa as people have banded together for a variety of self-help activities (including political activism) or have done more for themselves as individuals. Ordinary people have discovered that they can (or must) do things on their own. In this environment, entrepreneurship (often in the form of illegal smuggling or black marketeering in the parallel economy), cooperatives, church groups, professional groups, informal credit unions, women's groups, and community self-help efforts have flourished. They are providing goods and services, health care, schools, water, new technologies, environmental protection, and income-generating activities, among other benefits (Hyden, 1990:46–47). In a sense, African leaders' call for popular participation amounts to validation of what already is occurring. At the same time, government support has the potential to greatly strengthen these activities if governments back their verbal approval with financial, legal, and technical assistance for private initiatives.

Despite the hardships economic reform has placed on ordinary Africans, there are indications that some countries may be beginning to show some improvement. It is too soon, however, to conclude what effect SAPs are having one way or another on economic performance, or any guarantee that such improvements will continue. Ghana has been pointed to as one possible success story, in the debate over the impact of structural adjustment. Since the beginning of structural adjustment economic reforms under World Bank/IMF auspices in 1983, Ghana's ailing economy appears to be rebounding, with GNP growth rates per year averaging 5 percent over the past decade (Matloff, 1995). Although Ghana's economy has weaknesses that may undermine its long-term recovery, its recent economic performance is a marked improvement over that of 1970–1980, when Ghana's GDP per year averaged –.1 percent (World Bank, 1995:164).

As more people in Africa and the West become caught up in the euphoria that is accompanying the movement toward democracy and economic liberalization, we must caution against the temptation to view these as panaceas for the continent's woes. Such simple conceptions overlook the weaknesses of the reform effort itself as well as the difficulty of solving Africa's manifold problems even with more democratic and effective institutions.

For one, some critics argue that claims about the positive results of current economic reforms have been highly inflated. Even where "growth" is reported, as in Ghana, most of the benefits go primarily to the wealthy, not to the poor (Morna, 1991:22); and other problems, such as unemployment, inflation, and dependence on foreign aid, may eventually bring a halt to the country's progress (Matloff, 1995). It is also noted that most countries increased output of commodities (under World Bank urging) only to find that prices fell because other Third World countries had been advised to do the same thing. Therefore, unless prices rise in the world market or Africans can diversify their economies, long-range prospects are not good for most ("A Chance," 1991:2).

Others fear that current economic reforms will make it more difficult for Africa to industrialize or produce long-term economic improvements by keeping African countries dependent on raw materials production and exposing local industry to ruinous competition from more developed countries' imports (see Riddell, 1990). This is currently a problem for Ghana, according to recent reports, as imported textiles and secondhand clothing are destroying local textile and apparel industries ("Ghana," 1991:2–3).

Africa's debt is another vexing problem that threatens to undermine current reform efforts. Bettino Craxi, the United Nations Secretary-General's special adviser on the debt crisis, warned the UN General Assembly that sub-Saharan Africa's economic problems are "insolvable" without drastically reducing their debt ("Closing," 1991:11). Africa's debt has grown from $14.8 billion in 1974 to $183.4 billion in 1992 (Callaghy, 1994:33). While smaller than Latin America's or Asia's, Africa's debt is a much larger proportion of the overall economy, and debt service takes a larger share of already poor countries' revenues ("Debt," 1991:18).

Long-range prospects for democratic political systems are also in doubt, especially if economies continue to slump, if inequality of wealth worsens, or if economic reforms exact too great a toll in the form of unemployment, inflation, and low living standards. Moreover, the extent of political (or economic) reforms may be limited if they pose a serious threat to current elites. As Tarr (1990:40–41) cautions, many African regimes are good at manipulating the desires of donor countries without actually living up to their expectations. If reforms have negative consequences for policymakers or their constituencies, they may be rejected or undermined (see Qadir et al., 1993).

An often unmentioned weakness of reforms is that while governments are forced to cut back on spending in general, military spending remains a serious drain on many countries. In Africa, spending on the military averages twice that for education and three times that for health. This wasteful use of national wealth is closely associated with other grim statistics: in 1994, sixteen countries were at war or suffering civil strife; thirteen others faced "severe political crises" (Adediji, 1995:134). Two-thirds of all the victims of war between 1980 and 1990 were African ("Recovery," 1991:6), and by 1994, Africa had more refugees than any other region in the world, largely due to political violence. In Liberia alone, nearly half of the country's 2.6 million people are now living as exiles (Kane, 1995:22–24). Peacefully overcoming ethnic, religious, and regional conflicts; encouraging respect for political and cultural pluralism; and guaranteeing human and individual rights of all Africans will be difficult goals for new and fragile democratic systems to live up to, especially in a turbulent political and economic environment.

Some are concerned that Africa's colonially drawn boundaries make it impossible to maintain stability in many countries under any kind of political system. The collapse or disintegration of many of these states is seen as a real possibility in such places as Liberia, Somalia, Angola, Sudan, and Rwanda, among others. Callaghy (1995:149–150) sees this as a disaster characterized by "war, tribute, predation, and the criminalization of economic activity as local warlords struggle to extort Africa's most useful resources for sale to the highest bidder," a scenario promoted by massive arms flows available to disgruntled and ambitious groups bent on violence.

Others, such as Nigerian Nobel laureate Wole Soyinka, see the breakdown of the nation-state in Africa as a logical and more benign death of entities constructed by foreigners that denied Africans the opportunity to define themselves (in Alpers, 1995:3–4). So far only tiny Eritrea (part of Ethiopia until 1993) has managed successfully to redraw the map of Africa, but other attempts may follow. Some observers foresee new forms of confederation, regional economic (if not political) integration, and pan-African organizations as antidotes to the current political malaise (see Alpers, 1995; Mazrui, 1995). Despite the question of the long-term viability of the nation-state in Africa, most continue to assume that for the near future democratic reforms within current boundaries offer the greatest hope for stability in most countries.

Although democracy and more market-oriented economies may be desirable, there is no assurance that a more democratic, capitalist Africa will better address such problems as environmental degradation, ethnic strife, gender and class inequality, population explosion, AIDS, or urban concentration. Indeed, a market economy (unless subject to well-formulated state regulation and planning) can be expected to exacerbate such problems if an ethos of unrestrained growth, consumerism, and private profit-seeking gains primacy and exploitation of the poor intensifies. And as Fatton (1995) cautions, the development of "civil society" associated with democracy can concentrate power in the hands of the most organized societal interest groups. These groups may not necessarily have the public good, peaceful resolution of conflict, or egalitarianism and respect for diversity on their political agendas.

With all of these uncertainties in mind, we can still be hopeful about the changes Africans are beginning to undertake on their own behalf. Perhaps because of their difficulties, Africans are realizing that they must take command of their future. This will not occur by slavishly imitating the West or by trying to recapture some idealized, mythic African past uncorrupted by the West. Africa must respond to the challenges of this century and soon the next. Scholars like Basil Davidson (1989), Ali Mazrui (1986), and others argue that Africa must find African solutions to African problems that draw on the lessons and experience of the past to create a better future. Among those lessons are African traditions of community-based rules and laws that were the results of popular participation, not dictates from above. Also widespread was the African ideal of a community in which checks and balances prevented or corrected abuses of power (Davidson, 1989:269–271). The challenge for Africa is to incorporate these traditions into modern political, social, and economic institutions suited to today's pluralistic nation-states and global political and economic environment. Building strong and stable institutions will require not only dedicated leadership but also the active involvement of ordinary Africans. As Chege (1995:194) remarks, even war-ravaged societies can rapidly rebuild themselves if political stability, the rule of law, and a hospitable economic environment allow people to exercise their talents, skills, and aspirations.

That Africa's problems must be solved by Africans does not mean that industrial nations like the United States should turn their backs on the continent. Without the Cold War to justify U.S. aid, foreign aid and development assistance are being sharply cut; they are seen as failures and a waste of money by many politicians and voters as well. The foreign aid bill approved by Congress in late 1995 would cut aid for education, health care, family planning, and environmental programs in poor nations by one-third and funds to alleviate poverty in Africa by at least 20 percent. The U.S. contribution to the World Bank's low-cost loan program for poor countries was cut by 42 percent; roughly half of these funds are allocated for sub-Saharan Africa. What is not generally understood is that aid has failed to produce development in Africa because much of it has been funneled to support corrupt and autocratic U.S. allies and U.S. foreign policy rather than to promote development. As one cynic of program cuts lamented, foreign development aid is a "little like Christianity: it's never been tried" (in Moffett, 1995).

Ironically, now is a crucial time for more aid to Africa, not less. As African governments attempt to implement economic and political reforms, financial and other kinds of assistance are needed for such vital social programs as education (especially for girls), health care (e.g., to combat AIDS), credit for entrepreneurs, family planning, and environmental protection—programs that have a long-term, positive impact on development. Other programs funded by the United States and the World Bank are devoted to promoting human rights, overhauling legal systems, demobilizing and returning military personnel to civilian life, reforming public sector bureaucracies, providing education in democracy, and monitoring elections. By rewarding reformers and helping to ensure that their reforms succeed, the West is not giving welfare "handouts"; it is promoting everyone's interests in a more peaceful, prosperous, and stable Africa (see Moffett, 1995; Guest, 1995).

After all, we must remember that many of Africa's problems are only partly of its own making; the West must face its own complicity in creating and maintaining Africa's plight. After centuries of exploiting Africa, a partnership of the West and Africa to erase the legacies of slavery, colonialism, and postcolonial domination and decay seems long overdue.

■ BIBLIOGRAPHY

"A Chance for Africa." 1991. *Africa News* 34 (May 20):1–3, 17.
"Africans Seek Homespun Remedies in Kampala." 1991. *Africa Reports* 36 (July-August):8–9.
Alpers, Edward A. 1995. "Africa Reconfigured: Presidential Address to the 1994 African Studies Association Annual Meeting." *African Studies Review* 38 (September): 1–10.

Callaghy, Thomas. 1995. "Africa: Back to the Future?" Pp. 140–152 in Larry Diamond and Marc F. Plattner (eds.). *Economic Reform and Democracy.* Baltimore: Johns Hopkins University Press.

"Closing the Debt Gap." 1991. *Africa News* 34 (July 15):11.

Chege, Michael. 1995. "What's Right with Africa?" Pp. 190–194 in F. Jeffress Ramsay. *Global Studies: Africa.* Guilford, CT: Dushkin. Reprint from *Current History,* May 1994.

Davidson, Basil. 1989. *Modern Africa: A Social and Political History.* London: Longman.

"Debt Initiative May Be Lasting Summit Legacy." 1991. *Africa News* 34 (May 20):4, 18.

Fatton, Robert, Jr. 1995. "Africa in the Age of Democratization: The Civic Limits of Civil Society." *African Studies Review* 38 (September): 67–99.

"Ghana Economy Gains Ground." 1991. *Africa News* 34 (July 29):1–3.

Guest, Ian. 1995. "'Soft' Loans Mean Better Government for Africa." *Christian Science Monitor* (November 13):19.

Hyden, Goran. 1990. "The Changing Context of Institutional Development in Sub-Saharan Africa." Pp. 43–59 in *The Long-Term Perspective Study of Sub-Saharan Africa.* Vol. 3. Washington, DC: World Bank.

Kane, Hal. 1995. *The Hour of Departure: Forces that Create Refugees and Migrants.* Worldwatch Paper 125. Washington, DC: Worldwatch Institute.

Matloff, Judith. 1995. "Ghana Seen as Showcase for Africa—in a Manner." *Christian Science Monitor* (December 20):9.

Mazrui, Ali A. 1986. *The Africans: A Triple Heritage.* London: BBC Publications.

———. 1995. "The Bondage of Boundaries: Why Africa's Maps Will Be Redrawn." Pp. 182–184 in F. Jeffress Ramsay. *Global Studies: Africa.* Guilford, CT: Dushkin. Reprint from *The Economist,* September 11–17, 1993.

Moffett, George. 1995. "Skeptical Congress Accelerates Foreign-Aid Cuts." *Christian Science Monitor* (November 30):4.

Morna, Colleen Lowe. 1991. "Ahead of the Opposition." *Africa Report* 36 (July-August):20–23.

"Organization of African Unity Faces Existential Crisis." 1991. *Africa Report* 36 (July-August):10.

Qadir, Shahid, Christopher Clapham, and Barry Gills. 1993. "Sustainable Democracy: Formalism vs. Substance." *Third World Quarterly* 14:415–422.

"Recovery from War's Trauma." 1991. *Africa News* 34 (July 15):6–7.

Riddell, Roger C. 1990. "Côte d'Ivoire." Pp. 152–205 in Roger C. Riddell (ed.). *Manufacturing Africa: Performance and Prospects of Seven Countries in Sub-Saharan Africa.* Portsmouth, NH: Heinemann.

Tarr, Byron. 1990. "Political Developments and Environment in Africa." Pp. 32–42 in *The Long-Term Perspective Study of Sub-Saharan Africa.* Vol. 3. Washington, DC: World Bank.

World Bank. 1995. *World Development Report.* New York: Oxford University Press.

■ Acronyms ■

ACM	African Common Market
AEC	African Economic Commission
AIDS	acquired immune deficiency syndrome
ANC	African National Congress
APPER	Africa's Priority Programme for Economic Recovery
AZAPO	Azanian People's Organization
CFA	Communauté Financière Africaine
CITES	Convention on International Trade in Endangered Species
CODESA	Convention for a Democratic South Africa
COSATU	Congress of South African Trade Unions
CP	Conservative Party (South Africa)
EAC	East African Community
EC	European Community
ECA	Economic Commission for Africa
ECCAS	Economic Community of Central African States
ECOWAS	Economic Community of West African States
ESF	Economic Support Funds
EU	European Union
FAL	Final Act of Lagos
FRELIMO	Frente de Libertação de Moçambique
GDP	gross domestic product
GNP	gross national product
HIV	human immunodeficiency virus
IFP	Inkatha Freedom Party
IGADD	Intergovernmental Authority on Drought and Development
ILO	International Labour Organisation
IMF	International Monetary Fund
ITCZ	Intertropical Convergence Zone
LDC	less developed country
LPA	Lagos Plan of Action
MNC	multinational corporation
MOSOP	Movement for the Survival of Ogoni People
MPLA	Movimento Popular de Libertação de Angola
NACTU	National African Confederation of Trade Unions

NAFTA	North American Free Trade Agreement
NCNC	National Council of Nigeria and the Cameroons
NCSW	National Committee on the Status of Women (Kenya)
NGO	nongovernmental organization
NLTPS	national long-term perspective study
NP	National Party (South Africa)
NPC	Northern People's Congress
OAU	Organization of African Unity
OB	Ossewabrandwag (Ox-Wagon Guard)
ODA	Official Development Assistance
OEDA	United Nations Office of Emergency Operations in Africa
OPEC	Organization of Petroleum Exporting Countries
PAC	Pan-Africanist Congress
PFP	Progressive Federal Party (South Africa)
PTA	preferential trade area
RPF	Rwandan Patriotic Front
SADCC/SADC	Southern African Development Coordination Conference. Now Southern African Development Community
SANNC	South African Natives National Congress
SAP	structural adjustment program
SD	sustainable development
SSA	sub-Saharan Africa
UAM	Union of the Arab Maghreb
UDF	United Democratic Front
UGC	General Union of Cooperatives (Mozambique)
UNDP	United Nations Development Programme
UNECA	United Nations Economic Commission for Africa
UNEP	United Nations Environmental Programme
UNESCO	United Nations Educational, Scientific, and Cultural Organization
UNFPA	United Nations Fund for Population Activities
UNHCR	United Nations High Commissioner for Refugees
UNICEF	United Nations International Children's Emergency Fund
UN-NADAF	UN New Agenda for the Development of Africa in the 1990s
UNPAAERD	United Nations Programme of Action for African Economic Recovery and Development
UPC	Union des Populations Camerounaises
USAID	U.S. Agency for International Development
WCED	World Commission on Environment and Development
WHO	World Health Organization
WID	Women in Development
ZANU-PF	Zimbabwe African National Union—Patriotic Front

▪ Glossary ▪

African Economic Community: a proposed integration of all the economies on the African continent by 2025. The idea was put forth at the Organization of African Unity (OAU) meeting in Lagos, Nigeria, in 1991.

African Independent Churches: term applied to a diverse range of Christian denominations in Africa that themselves are not part of either the Catholic church or any major Western Protestant organizational structure. As a group, these denominations generally incorporate African ceremonies, icons, and holy sites and often involve charismatic expressions of faith. A few have also had messianic leaders (people who claim to be the Second Coming of Jesus Christ). These churches have grown especially fast in southern Africa.

African Traditional Religions: a very general term given to indigenous African religious practices that predate the arrival of either Christianity or Islam in their respective areas of the continent. Most of these sets of religious practices are characterized by belief in one supreme being, belief in spirits, belief in life after death, the establishment of sacred places, plants, and/or animals, and belief in the existence of witchcraft and magic. Since the arrival of Christianity and Islam, many African Traditional Religions have blended with those faiths.

Afro-Asiatic language family: one of the four major families of African languages. This includes mainly the Semitic languages of the North African states, Somalia, and Ethiopia.

Anglo-Boer Wars: the two wars in South Africa between the British and the Afrikaners. The First Anglo-Boer War (the word "Boer" means "farmer" in the Afrikaans language) was fought in 1880 and 1881, when the Afrikaners defeated the British and reasserted control over the Transvaal region of northern South Africa. The Second Anglo-Boer War (1900–1902) was a British victory, and finally gave Great Britain total political control of all of modern-day South Africa. This war saw the killing of many Afrikaner civilians, including at least 20,000 who died of disease in concentration camps established by the British in response to the Afrikaner technique of guerrilla warfare. Much of the modern-day hostility between English- and Afrikaans-speaking white South Africans can be traced to these wars. See *Boers*.

Apartheid: Afrikaans word that means "apartness." This is the name given to the system of racial segregation and white superiority put into place in South Africa in 1948. In that year, the largely Afrikaner National Party won a whites-only election, ousting the pro-British government at the ballot box. The apartheid system, which was largely unmodified until 1990, required blacks, whites, mixed-race people, and people of Asian descent to live in separate areas, attend separate schools, and use separate public amenities. Apartheid also banned nonwhites from voting and required blacks to seek governmental permission to live in urban areas and hold urban jobs. Further, all of South Africa's rural areas were racially segregated, with whites given control of 83 percent of South Africa's farmland. The apartheid system also banned interracial marriage and intimate contact, among many other restrictions on public contact between the races and freedom of expression and movement. See *Boers*.

Authoritarianism: the political opposite of democracy. Authoritarianism is a general means of governing that does not allow meaningful choices in elections and usually restricts personal freedoms of movement, speech, and assembly. Authoritarian governments may be military governments, one-person dictatorships, one-party systems, or monarchies. Shortly after independence in the era of the late 1950s through the 1960s, most African governments were authoritarian in nature. See *Personal rule*.

Bantu language family: one of the four major families of African languages, also known as the Niger-Congo language family after its birthplace in West Africa. This is by far the largest set of African languages, spoken by the great majority of people in all regions of the African continent. See *Niger-Congo language family*.

Bantu migrations: movements of people starting about 2,500 years ago when population pressures in West Africa began to force people to slowly spread eastward and ultimately southward all across the sub-Saharan region of Africa. These largely agricultural people had developed iron spears, arrows, hoes, scythes, and axes. As a result, the Bantu migrations, which had reached all the way to the southern tip of Africa by at least 1,000 years ago, spread agriculture, iron tools, and the Bantu language family across the vast expanse of the African continent. Today, the majority of Africans are descendants of the Bantu migrations. See *Bantu language family*.

Berg Report: the colloquial name for the 1981 World Bank Report *Accelerated Development in Sub-Saharan Africa: An Agenda for Action.* Written under the supervision of economist Elliot Berg, this document called for the doubling of foreign aid to Africa. More important, it called for African nations to pursue their "comparative advantage" in the world capitalist market, i.e., the export of raw commodities. Many Africans and their governments found these recommendations unacceptable in light of their desire to industrialize and export value-added secondary commodities (e.g., the export of cotton is a primary commodity export; the production of textiles is a secondary commodity export). The Berg Report also recommended that the private sector become more involved in African economies and that the public sector take on a more "efficient" (reduced) economic role.

Berlin Conference: a meeting held in 1884 and 1885 in the German capital at which the major European powers with colonial territories in Africa (Britain, France, Germany, Portugal, Spain, and Italy) agreed on a partitioning of the continent into imperial spheres of influence. The current African map is a direct result of the Berlin Conference, whose participants drew these colonial boundaries with little knowledge of and little interest in creating ethnically homogeneous territories. Thus, many of today's African nations have boundaries that split ethnic groups between two or even several nations.

Boers: Afrikaans word meaning "farmers," another name for the Afrikaner people of South Africa, who are mainly descendants of Dutch, French, and German settlers who came to South Africa in the seventeenth and eighteenth centuries. See *Anglo-Boer Wars* and *Apartheid.*

Bourgeoisie: French word for "the middle class." Traditionally, Marxists and other social scientists have used the term to mean shopkeepers, professionals (doctors, teachers, lawyers, etc.), clerks, small- and medium-scale farmers, and small-scale capitalists. Some scholars, on the other hand, use the term as a general reference to a nation's elites.

Bridewealth: the widespread traditional practice of a husband's family compensating a wife's family with cattle or money when a marriage takes place. The theory behind the payment of bridewealth by the husband's family is that the wife's family needs to be compensated in some way for the fertility of their daughter. Only when bridewealth is paid is a marriage considered legitimate. Note how this is the opposite of the Hindu dowry, whereby the daughter's family pays the son's family to marry the woman.

Carrying capacity: a term used by geographers and other students of natural resources to refer to the ability of an ecosystem to support a certain concentration of animal life. For example, a pastureland is said to have exceeded its carrying capacity when too many cattle graze there and the grass is eaten up faster than it can be replenished. Further, both rural and urban areas are assumed to have carrying capacities for a certain number of humans, and if this quantity is exceeded, the area will soon be unable to support human life.

Clientelism: also known as "patron-client networks." Clientelism is a pattern of social interactions in which a powerful "patron" distributes economic, political, and/or social favors to a group of subordinate "clients." The relationship, however, is a two-way street, since if a patron is too harsh on his or her clients, or does not provide enough benefits in exchange for the clients' support, those people will seek a patron elsewhere, thus undercutting the ability of the original patron to wield power by passing out favors. Note that since the passing of favors and acquiescence between patron and client is a two-way relationship, this is not the same phenomenon as dictatorship or despotism.

Coup d'état: the changing of a government through means outside the electoral process. This government overthrow many be either violent (a "bloody" coup) or peaceful (a "bloodless" coup).

Dependency: term given to a relatively loose set of explanations for distorted capitalist development in Asia, Africa, and Latin America. The Dependency School was an influential movement in political economy studies in the 1970s, particularly among scholars of Latin America. According to *dependencistas,* the world capitalist economy is divided into a "core" of leading capitalist states (the United States, France, the United Kingdom, etc.) and a "periphery" of dependent client states (Brazil, Chile, Nigeria, etc.). The economies of these periphery states are mainly serving as sources of raw materials and cheap labor for worldwide capitalist industry, with the cooperation of local elites in the periphery nations who receive political and economic benefits from exploiting local labor and natural resources. This, according to the Dependency School, is why independent industrialization has remained illusory in the developing world. Critics of the dependency perspective respond that this theory cannot explain why nations such as Taiwan, South Korea, Singapore, and (more recently) Chile and Argentina have developed large industrial and technological sectors that rival the best economic outputs the "metropole" nations have to offer. See *Metropole* and *Neocolonialism.*

East African Community: attempt in the 1970s by the governments of Kenya, Tanzania, and Uganda to form a regional economic union among their three nations, with the ultimate aim of having a common currency, common international trade policies, and no tariffs on each other's goods. This attempt at regional economic integration failed because of political tensions between the three nations caused largely by the economic dominance of Kenya as compared to the relatively weaker economies of Uganda and Tanzania. A new east African community was in the process of development in 1995.

Economic Community of West African States (ECOWAS): attempt of several nations in West Africa to establish regional economic cooperation. Unlike the abortive East African Community, ECOWAS is not an attempt at full economic union among its member states, but is rather a preferential trade area (PTA) in which the participant nations agree to charge each other reduced taxes on the import of goods. ECOWAS also meets periodically to discuss environmental, military, and political issues facing its member states.

Ethnicity: one of the major social and political forces in Africa (and the entire world) and a very general term referring to shared characteristics between similar individuals. Ethnicity can be one or more of the following: a common language, common ancestral ties (bloodlines), a common culture (dress, food, social practices, etc.), a common race, or a common set of religious beliefs.

Foreign debt: debt incurred when a government borrows money from either another government or a bank in another country. The repayment of a foreign debt is usually in the currency of the lender nation. For example, if Malawi's government borrows money from Chase-Manhattan Bank in New York, the bank will expect to be repaid in U.S. dollars, not in Malawi kwatcha.

Foreign exchange: also known as "hard currency," money denominated in a currency that has worldwide acceptance due to the desirability of owning that currency. U.S. dollars, Japanese yen, German marks, French and Swiss francs, and British pounds are examples of foreign exchange. Hard currencies are crucial for African governments, because they are necessary for purchasing imports such as petroleum, automobiles, and machinery. See *Foreign debt.*

French Huguenots: Protestants from France who were persecuted by the French government in the seventeenth century. Many of these people left

France to settle mostly in the American South and in South Africa. The combination of Dutch and German settlers, along with the French Huguenots, produced the Afrikaners of South Africa. See *Boers*.

Fuelwood: wood that is harvested and burned for cooking purposes. Burning wood is still the major form of energy production in rural Africa. Population density and the cutting of wood for fuel can lead to deforestation.

Great Rift Valley: one of the most important geological features on the planet. It is an extremely long and deep fault line that bisects the entire eastern portion of the African continent. The Rift Valley is home to the major East African lakes, the Red Sea, and an abundance of wildlife unmatched anywhere on earth. Much of the soil in the valley and on its escarpments (sides) is extremely fertile.

Gross Domestic Product (GDP): measures the total output of goods and services produced by both residents and foreigners in a nation.

Gross National Product (GNP): measures the total output of goods and services produced by residents; it includes income residents receive from abroad. Measured yearly, GNP is often used as an indicator of the size of a nation's economy. Another important economic statistic, GNP per capita, is calculated by dividing a nation's GNP by its population. This indicates national income per person.

Homelands: government-designated areas, under South Africa's apartheid system, where the different ethnic groups could live. For the black ethnic groups, the apartheid regime created thirteen homelands, which were supposed to be in areas traditionally occupied by those ethnic groups. The ultimate plan, which was never fully realized, was to move all of South Africa's blacks to these homelands and grant those "nations" independence. Thus, the South Africa the architects of this system planned would ultimately have no black citizens. These homelands were almost all in agriculturally marginal areas and often were not even contiguous. The opposition to the homelands policy was a major component of antiapartheid activity in South Africa. See *Apartheid*.

Hut tax: a tax colonialists imposed on villages to acquire free labor. To provide their colonies with cheap labor, the imperial powers often taxed each village, knowing its people could not pay in currency. Thus, the colonialists "accepted" free labor as payment of the hut tax.

Import substitution: an economic strategy many developing nations follow.

The idea behind import-substitution policies is to establish local industries that produce goods that were previously imported (matches, shoes, tools, etc.). Thus, foreign exchange would be saved, since those imports would no longer be required, and hard currency would not have to be spent to acquire them. Unfortunately, when a nation has limited economic resources, following an import-substitution strategy can actually drain foreign exchange, since the focus of industrial output is to produce goods for local consumption and not for export, which could earn even more foreign currency.

Industrialization: a general economic strategy that a country may pursue, along with agriculture and postindustrialism (service and knowledge production). Most economists in the 1950s and 1960s (and even today) assumed that nations should focus their economic resources on industries (cars, textiles, furniture, steel, etc.) rather than agriculture. Unfortunately, for nations that are overwhelmingly rural and poor (the case with almost all African countries), rapid industrialization is especially difficult, and too much of a focus on industrialization can lead governments and businesses to neglect the wealth of knowledge and experience of rural producers. In the extreme, an all-out drive toward industrialization can produce a national neglect of agriculture that can lead to mass hunger and starvation.

Informal sector: general term given to business practices that are outside government regulation and thus immune to taxes. Also known as the black market, many economists estimate that some African nations' economies are taking place largely in the informal sector. While the informal sector can support many lower-middle-class traders and producers, it can also produce extremely wealthy individuals and indirectly weaken a government due to the loss of tax revenue that could otherwise be used in antipoverty and other government programs.

International Monetary Fund (IMF): loosely associated with the United Nations, a bank of last resort that lends money directly to governments, usually to either pay off private bank loans or to fund general government operations. The problem is that the IMF, as any lender would when lending money, puts restrictions on the money's use and, more important, demands that the recipient nation make macroeconomic policy changes, such as reducing the size of government and public debt and scaling back expensive social and antipoverty programs. For this reason, many governments, scholars, and civilians in Africa dislike the IMF, but many nations simply have no economic choice but to accept the IMF's restrictions and policy prescriptions in exchange for the loans.

Intertropical Convergence Zone (ITCZ): the most important meteorological phenomenon for Africa, and the primary rain producer for the continent. The ITCZ shifts seasonally around the equator, thus (ideally) creating a rainy season north of the equator around June and in the south around November. Some nations near the equator even receive two rainy seasons. When the ITCZ "misbehaves," droughts occur in the areas it fails to cover.

Khoisan language family: one of the four major families of African languages. The Khoisan group is characterized by the "click" sounds of many of its consonants. The Khoisan peoples once inhabited large stretches of eastern and southern Africa, but the Bantu migrations and European persecution have reduced the Khoisan to a few scattered pockets in southern Africa's desert regions. Almost all the cave and rock art of southern Africa is attributed to the Khoisan peoples, and their language has influenced some Bantu languages such as Zulu, Xhosa, and Ndebele, which use a subset of the Khoisan "clicks."

Kinship: an anthropological term referring to the patterns of familial relations shared by a group of people. In most African cultures, kinship goes well beyond the traditional Western concept of the "nuclear" family and even extends to the dead and unborn. Kinship is one of the fundamental social structures in sub-Saharan Africa.

Lagos Plan of Action (LPA): a set of general economic goals that most African nations are striving to achieve. Adopted by the United Nations Economic Commission for Africa in 1980, the LPA seeks food self-sufficiency; self-reliance in industry, transport, and communication; human and natural resources; and science and technology. The Lagos Plan of Action can be viewed as an outline of an African declaration of economic independence.

Levirate: a family and marriage practice common throughout Africa. Under the levirate, a man assumes responsibility for his dead brother's widow and children. Conversely, under the *sororate,* a woman takes the place of her dead or childless sister. Both these practices are designed to produce children, which is one of the primary reasons for marriage in largely agricultural Africa. Some feminists see both the levirate and the sororate as an onerous burden on women.

Matriliny: a family organization pattern largely confined to the coastal forests of west and central Africa. Under matriliny, family descent is traced through the mother, and a groom usually leaves his family to live with or near his wife's family. Resultant children are also raised with the mother's family and in the mother's village area. This is not the same as matriarchy (rule by women), since in most matrilineal societies formal positions of authority are still largely held by men. See *Patriliny.*

Metropole: an international relations term referring to either the capital city of an imperial power (London, Paris, Lisbon, etc.) or, more recently, to world financial centers of power (e.g., Toyko, New York, Geneva).

Modernization: a term given to a very broad political-economic concept popular in the 1950s and 1960s among academics and development practitioners. Under the assumptions of modernization theory, increased economic growth in Africa, particularly rapid industrialization, would inevitably lead to the creation of democracy, higher educational standards, and widespread wealth. The assumptions of modernization theory were rooted in the idea that since this was the way the Western world developed, then the same process would inevitably take place in Africa. Of course, the facts that the process of "modernization" took place in the West over a period of several centuries and largely without imperial interference were often overlooked. Still, many of the prescriptions for curing Africa's economic and political troubles still seem based on the ideas of linear development contained in modernization theory.

Multinational corporations (MNCs): a large corporation that has business operations in more than one national territory. Some very large MNCs such as Exxon and DuPont have yearly earnings that are larger than the annual economic output of several African nations. It should be no surprise that MNCs can be very powerful and persuasive economic actors in the developing world.

Nationalism: one of the most fundamental concepts in comparative politics. "Nationalism" can mean different things depending on the context in which the term is used. In the context of African politics and history, nationalism usually denotes the desire and struggle for self-determination and independence among the colonized peoples of the continent. The nationalist era in sub-Saharan Africa started after World War II. When parties and interest groups formed with the goal of full national independence for their colonies. For most countries, the nationalist era culminated in independence in the 1960s, largely under the political leadership of party and interest group heads who had lobbied London and Paris for independence or even had led armed struggles against those European powers.

Negritude: a literary movement of the 1930s among students from francophone African colonies and African Americans in exile in Paris. The

Negritude writers consciously filled their works with African motifs, thereby providing a new expression of African ideas and society in written French and English literature. See *Pan-Africanism.*

Neocolonialism: the idea that even after physical and legal colonialism ended in Africa, economic and political dependency on the former colonial power remained. For example, after legal independence in the 1960s, many former British and French colonies in Africa still found themselves in a position to purchase goods from only British and French transnational corporations. Furthermore, in the former French colonies of West Africa, most nations are still dependent on the French franc to support their own national currencies, which gives the French government and banks much economic leverage over those nations. Neocolonialism is similar to the dependency school of thought, which also sees an inexorable, cause-and-effect link between politics and economics. See *Dependency.*

Niger-Congo language family: one of the four major families of African languages. This is also known as the Bantu language family, with its origins in West Africa. As the Bantu migrations spread eastward and westward to encompass almost the entire sub-Saharan region of the continent, the Niger-Congo language family spread as well. Today the majority of Africa's people speak languages with roots in this linguistic family. See *Bantu language family.*

Nilo-Saharan language family: one of the four major families of African languages. This group is largely confined to the northeast and east-central regions of the continent. It is prevalent among the herding and fishing cultures of the area. Examples of groups whose languages have their roots in this family are the Dinka of Sudan and the Tutsi of Rwanda and Burundi.

Organization of African Unity (OAU): a regional supranational organization established in the 1960s, with headquarters in Addis Ababa, Ethiopia. The OAU is the United Nations of Africa, in that its membership now includes all the independent states on the continent. The heads of all the members come together once a year for a summit meeting, and there are several economic, environmental, and cultural committees within the OAU. Of particular note is the pledge of noninterference in the internal affairs of member nations that all participating countries take. Further, when the OAU was founded, an agreement was reached that there would be no wholesale reconfiguration of the old colonial boundaries inherited by the independent nations. The combination of these two facts, of course, hamstrings the effectiveness of the OAU as a truly pan-African entity.

Organization of Petroleum Exporting Countries (OPEC): an organization comprising the major oil exporting nations of the world. OPEC is one of the most potentially powerful economic organizations in the history of the planet, owing to industrialization's crucial need for petroleum products. Nigeria, Gabon, and Angola are the three sub-Saharan members of OPEC.

Pan-Africanism: both a literary and political term with similar meanings. In the literary usage, pan-Africanism is a writing style that reverses the late nineteenth- and early twentieth-century roles of Africans and Europeans in literature. Here, African writers and their characters critically examine European culture and identity. In the political usage, pan-Africanism can refer to any attempt at creating political solidarity or unity among either African nations or Africans on the continent and living elsewhere (the African Diaspora). Both Kwame Nkrumah, the first president of Ghana, and W. E. B. Du Bois, the African American writer and political activist, are associated with pan-Africanism. See *Negritude.*

Parastatals: government-owned or government-controlled corporations. For example, the postal service in almost all nations is a parastatal. Further, telephone, steel, and electricity-producing corporations are often government-owned or government-operated. Many economists criticize parastatals as wasteful, loss-producing entities. The World Bank and International Monetary Fund are particularly critical of parastatals.

Pastoralism: a form of social and economic organization that depends primarily on the herding of livestock (usually camels, goats, and/or cattle) rather than the cultivation of crops in a fixed area (agriculture). This livestock provides food and also stands as a measure of wealth. Pastoralists often live a seminomadic life by necessity, following shifting rainfall and grass growth patterns. Pastoralism is prevalent in the savannah grasslands and semidesert areas of eastern Africa.

Patriliny: a pattern of family organization practiced by the majority of Africa's people (and the majority of humanity, for that matter). Under patriliny, descent is traced through men, and when a bride marries she goes to live in the groom's village area. Children who are the products of patrilineal marriages are also considered to be primarily part of the father's family line. See *Matriliny.*

Personal rule: a style of authoritarian government prevalent in Africa from the late 1960s to the late 1980s. Under personal rule, the country's leader seeks to identify the state with himself, often placing his face on currency, postage stamps, and in almost every public establishment. The leader may also have stadiums, airports, streets, and schools named after himself. Furthermore, the leader will operate a system of patronage, awarding government contracts, concessions, and bureaucratic posts to his political friends, especially to members of his own ethnic group. Personal rule is a somewhat logical response to the weak state systems and relatively shallow nationalism that existed in Africa immediately after independence. With the emphasis on order rather than freedom, many personal rulers stayed in power for decades. It should be noted that not all these personal rulers were tyrants. On the contrary, the more mild-mannered personal rulers, such as Zambia's Kenneth Kaunda, stayed in power for almost thirty years. In the 1990s, personal rule started to give way to elected democratic governments, but Africa still has not seen the last of this style of authoritarianism. See *Authoritarianism.*

Poaching: the hunting or trapping of animals for food or profit that is prohibited by either national or international law.

Polygyny: the practice of having more than one wife at the same time. In societies that value the production of children, polygyny is widespread, as it is in Africa. Islam puts an upper limit of four on the number of wives one man can have at the same time.

Public sector: a general term given to a government, its employees, and any parastatals that it owns. See *Parastatals.*

Rainforests: closed forest systems that receive an abundant amount of moisture and thus provide a home to an extraordinarily high concentration and diversity of plant and animal life. Since the soil is moist and rather shallow, areas of rainforest that are clear-cut for agricultural purposes are largely unsuitable for farming within a few years. Contrary to widespread popular myth, only a small proportion of Africa is under rainforest, with these areas confined to the coastal regions of the west and to the central inland areas.

Rural sector: a general term given to public and privately held lands and productive activities that take place in rural areas; farming and ranching.

Sharpeville massacre: a seminal event in South African history, which ultimately led to the illegalization of the African National Congress and other political organizations in 1960. In this township south of Johannesburg, protestors were preparing to surrender their passbooks (internal passports people were required to carry at all times) when police opened fire, killing sixty-nine people. The massacre led to the radicalization of many antiapartheid groups.

Southern African Development Community (SADC): an alliance formerly known as the Southern African Development Coordination Conference (SADCC) that was originally founded by the nations of southern Africa in an attempt to reduce their economic dependence on the Republic of South Africa. Under British and Portuguese colonial rule, almost all the rail and road transport networks in the region ran in a north-to-south pattern to the ports on South Africa's sea coasts. In the postcolonial era, the apartheid government in South Africa could exert much political and economic leverage on its neighbors by simply threatening to cut off transport routes to the sea. The SADCC was an attempt primarily to break this transport monopoly held by South Africa and, secondarily, was an attempt at regional economic integration and the pooling of technological and educational resources. On the latter two matters it was largely successful. However, when South Africa elected a popular government in 1994, the whole raison d'être of the SADCC changed, and soon thereafter South Africa joined. It is not clear whether the new SADC will become a full-fledged economic community or a vehicle for wider South African domination of the subcontinent, albeit under a black majority government. See *East African Community* and *Economic Community of West African States.*

Soweto uprising: a protest in 1976 by schoolchildren in a township near Johannesburg. (The name Soweto is actually an acronym for Southwest Township.) The children were protesting new legislation that would require them to be instructed in Afrikaans instead of English. In response to the public protests, South African police shot at the demonstrators, ultimately killing several hundred people, almost all of them school students. This led to a further expansion of violent and nonviolent protests against apartheid within South Africa and to worldwide condemnation and limited economic sanctioning of the apartheid government.

Spirit mediums: members of a family or village who communicate with the dead. Spirit mediums are part of most African Traditional Religions and are often very powerful religious and political leaders. In some cultures, spirit mediums are also healers and tellers of the future, which gives them a revered place in public life. See *African Traditional Religions.*

Squatter settlements: urban or rural lands settled by people who do not hold title.

Structural adjustment programs (SAPs): International Monetary Fund financial assistance programs. When African governments can no longer pay their debts to either private banks or other nations, they often have little choice but to turn to the IMF for financial aid. A condition for this assistance is that the recipient nation adopt a structural adjustment program. The World Bank will sometimes give development grants only when a country agrees to implement an SAP. These economic programs, rooted in neoclassical economic assumptions about public debt, interest rates, inflation, and economic growth, require that the lendee reduce the size of the public sector, cut back on social spending, devalue its currency vis-à-vis hard foreign currencies, raise interest rates to reduce inflation, and lift import restrictions so that foreign goods are more freely available. In the short run, at least, such programs often lead to great hardships on urban dwellers and bankruptcies in the private sector. As such, they are wildly unpopular with rank-and-file citizens and governments alike. See *International Monetary Fund*.

Urban sector: a general term given to government and private institutions located in urban areas and the people who live in cities.

■ Basic Political Data ■

Country and Date of Independence	Capital City	Rulers Since Independence
Algeria 5 July 1962	Algiers	1. Ahmed Ben Bella, president, 1962–June 1965 2. Col. Houari Boumedienne, president, June 1965–December 1978 3. Col. Benjedid Chadli, president, February 1979–1992 4. Five-member High Council of State (HCS) fulfils the functions of the head of state until January 1994 5. General Liamine Zeroual, president and minister of defense—appointed 30 January 1994 6. Zeroual elected president 16 November 1995
Angola 11 November 1975	Luanda	1. Antonio Agostinho Neto, founding president, 1975–10 September 1979 2. José Eduardo dos Santos, president, 20 September 1979–
Benin 1 August 1960 (formerly Republic of Dahomey 1960–1975) 1965	Porto-Novo	1. Hubert Maga, president, 31 December 1960–28 October 1963 2. Col. (later Gen.) Christophe Soglo, president, 28 October 1963–January 1964 3. Sourou Migan Apithy, president, January 1964–29 November 1965 4. Tahirou Congacou, president, 29 November 1965–22 December 1965

5. Gen. Christophe Soglo, president, 22 December 1965–16 December 1967
6. Lt. Col. Alphonse Alley, president, 16 December 1967–July 1968
7. Emile-Derlin Zinsou, president, July 1968–10 December 1969
8. Lt. Col. Paul Emile de Souza, president, 10 December 1969–May 1970
9. Hubert Maga, president, May 1970–May 1972
10. Justin Ahomadegbé, president, May 1972–26 October 1972
11. Col. Mathieu Kerekou, president, October 1972–April 1991
12. Nicephore Soglo, president, April 1991–March 1996
13. Mathieu Kerekou, March 1996–

Botswana
30 September 1966

Gaborone

1. Sir Seretse Khama, president, 30 September 1966–13 July 1980
2. Quett Masire, president, 3 July 1980–

Burkina Faso
5 August 1960
(formerly Upper Volta; renamed Burkina Faso, August 1984)

Ouagadougou

1. Maurice Yaméogo, president, April 1959–January 1966
2. Lt. Col. Sangoulé Lamizana, president, January 1966–1980
3. Col. Sayé Zerbo, president, 1980–1982
4. NCO coup, October 1982
5. Maj. Jean Baptiste Ouedraogo, president, January 1983–August 1983
6. Capt. Thomas Sankara, president, Conseil National Révolutionaire (CNR), 1983–1987
7. Capt. Blaise Compaoré, president, CNR, 1987–

Burundi
1 July 1962

Bujumbura

1. (King) Mwami Mwambutsa II, 1915–1966. Prime ministers: André Muhirwa, 1962–1963; Pierre Ngendandumwe, 1963; Albin Nyamoya, 1964–1965; Pierre Ngendandumwe, 1965 (assassinated, January 1965); Joseph Bamina, 1965; Leopold Biha, 1965
2. Mwami Ntare V (deposes father, Mwambutsa II, as king); Capt. (later Col.) Michel Micombero, prime minister, 8 July 1966–29 November 1966
3. Micombero declares Burundi a republic, with himself as president, 29 November 1966–1 November 1976
4. Col. Jean-Baptiste Bagaza, president, November 1976–3 September 1987
5. Maj. Pierre Buyoya, chairman, Comité Militaire pour la Salvation Nationale, 1987–1993
6. Melchior Ndadaye, 1 June–21 October 1993
7. Cyprien Ntaryamire, 13 January –6 April 1994
8. Interim president Sylvestre Ntibantunganya 8 April–1 October1994, president, 1 Ocotber 1994—

Cameroon
1 January 1960

(1960–1961: Republic of East Cameroon; October 1961–1972: Federal Republic of Cameroon, composed of the East— former French trust territory—and

Yaoundé

1. Ahmadou Ahidjo, president, 5 May 1960–November 1982
2. Paul Biya, president, November 1982–

West—part of
former British trust
territory; 1972–:
United Cameroon
Republic)

Cape Verde July 1975 (in federation with Guinea-Bissau, 1975–January 1981)	Praia	1. Aristides Pereira, president, 1975–February 1991 2. Antonio Mascarenhas Monteiro, March 1991–
Central African Republic 13 August 1960 (1976–1979: Central African Empire)	Bangui	1. David Dacko (formerly prime minister), president, 17 Novem- ber 1960–31 December 1965 2. Coup led by Field Marshal Jean- Bedel Bokassa, 31 December 1965 3. Bokassa proclaimed "President for Life," 2 March 1972 4. Bokassa crowned emperor, 4 December 1977 5. Bokassa deposed in coup; David Dacko, president, 10 September 1979 6. Gen. André Kolingba establishes military regime, September 1981–1993 (chairman of Military Committee for National Recovery) 7. Ange-Félix Patassé, president, 22 October 1993–
Chad 11 August 1960	N'Djaména	1. Ngarta (formerly François) Tombalbaye, prime minister; head of state on independence; president, 22 April 1962–13 April 1975 (killed in military coup) 2. Gen. Félix Malloum, president, April 1975–1979 3. Hissene Habré, appointed prime minister, August 1978 4. Malloum and Habré resign, 23 March 1979; Transitional Government of National Unity

5. Goukouni Oueddei, president, 1979–1982
6. Hissene Habré, president, 1982–December 1990
7. Idriss Déby, December 1990–

Comoros
6 July 1975

Moroni

1. Ahmed Abdallah, president, July 1975–August 1975
2. Coup led by Ali Soilih, August, 1975; president, 1976–1978
3. Ahmed Abdallah, president, reinstated in coup by mercenaries under Bob Denard, 1978–27 November 1989 (murdered)
4. Bob Denard, 27 November 1989–15 December 1989
5. Said Djohar, 16 December 1989–1996
6. Mohamad Taki Abdoulkarim, March 1996–

Congo
15 August 1960

Brazzaville

1. Foulbert Youlou elected president under preindependence constitution, 21 November 1959
2. Military coup August 1963; Alphonse Massamba-Débat, president, 19 December 1963–4 September 1968
3. Governing National Revolutionary Council, formed 5 September 1968, chaired by Capt. Marien Ngouabi. Maj. Alfred Raoul, prime minister and temporary head of state, 5 September 1968–31 December 1968
4. Capt. Marien Ngouabi, president, December 1968–March 1977
5. Ngouabi assassinated, March 1977. Col. (later Brig. Gen.) Joachim Yhombi-Opango, president, March 1977–5 February 1979

6. Col. Denis Sassou Nguesso, president, 5 February 1979–1991
7. André Milongo, prime minister, June 1991–1992
8. Pascal Lissouba, president, 31 August 1992–

Côte d'Ivoire   Yamoussoukro
7 August 1960

1. Félix Houphouët-Boigny, prime minister, 1 May 1959; president, 27 November 1960–December 1993
2. Henri Konan Bédié, president, 7 December 1993–

Djibouti   Djibouti
27 June 1977

1. Hassan Gouled, president, 24 June 1977; reelected June 1981, April 1987, and May 1993

Arab Republic of   Cairo
Egypt
28 February 1922

1. King Farouk to 1952
2. Coup led by Col. Gamal Abdel Nasser and Abdul-al Hakim. Maj. Gen. Neguib, president, June 1953–November 1954
3. Nasser, head of state, 1954–1970 (president from 1956)
4. Col. Anwar Sadat, president, 1970–October 1981
5. Lt. Gen. Hosni Mubarak, president, 6 October 1981–

Equatorial Guinea   Malabo
12 October 1968

1. Francisco Macias Nguema, president, 29 September 1968–3 August 1979
2. Military coup led by Lt. Col. Teodoro Obiango Nguema Mbasogo, 3 August 1979
3. Lt. Col. Teodoro Obiango Nguema Mbasogo, president, 12 October 1980–1989
4. Brig. Gen. Teodoro Obiango Nguema Mbasogo, elected president 25 June 1989–

Eritrea 24 May 1993	Asmara	1. Issaias Afwerki, assumes power May 1991; elected president 8 June 1993
Ethiopia	Addis Ababa	1. Succession of emperors 2. Emperor Haile Selassie, 1930–12 September 1974 3. Lt. Gen. Aman Andom, chairman PMAC (Provisional Military Administrative Council) until November 1974 4. Brig. Gen. Teferi Banti, chairman, PMAC. Power actually held by vice chairman, Maj. (later Lt. Col.) Mengistu Haile Mariam and Lt. Col. Atnafu Abate. Banti killed, 3 February 1977 5. Mengistu Haile Mariam, chairman of PMAC, head of state, 1977–21 May 1991 6. Meles Zenawi, president, May 1991–1995 7. Ngasso Gidada, president, 22 August 1995–
Gabon 17 August 1960	Libreville	1. Leon M'Ba, president, 1961–28 November 1967 2. Omar (formerly Albert-Bernard) Bongo, president, 2 December 1967–
The Gambia 18 February 1965	Banjul	1. Constitutional monarchy with Dawda Jawara, prime minister, 1965–1970 2. The Gambia becomes a republic, April 1970. Dawda Jawara becomes first president, 24 April 1970–1994 3. Capt. Yahya A. J. J. Jammeh, proclaimed head of state, 23 July 1994, chairman of the Armed Forces Provisional Ruling Council

Ghana 6 March 1957	Accra	1. Constitutional monarchy, 1957–1960; Kwame Nkrumah, prime minister. Becomes republic, 1960; Nkrumah, president, 24 February 1966 2. Lt. Gen. Joseph Ankrah, chairman of National Liberation Council, February 1966–1969. Replaced, 1969, by Brig. Gen. Akwasi Afrifa 3. Competitive electoral politics: Kofi Busia, prime minister, September 1969–January 1972 4. Lt. Col. (later Gen.) Ignatius Kutu Acheampong, chairman, National Redemption Council, replaced by Supreme Military Council, 13 January 1972–5 July 1978 5. Lt. Gen. Frederick Akuffo, chairman, Supreme Military Council, 5 July 1978–4 June 1979 6. Flight Lt. Jerry Rawlings, chairman, Armed Forces Revolutionary Council, 4 June 1979–September 1979 7. Dr. Hilla Limann, president, September 1979–December 1981 8. Flight Lt. Jerry Rawlings, chairman, Provisional National Defence Council, December 1981; elected president 3 November 1992–
Guinea 2 October 1958	Conakry	1. Ahmed Sekou Touré, president, 1958–April 1984 2. Col. Lansana Conté, president, head of Comité Militaire de Redressement National, 1984– 3. Gen. Lansana Conté takes office 4 April 1984; elected 19 December 1993–

Guinea-Bissau   Bissau
10 September 1974

1. Luiz De Almeida Cabral, president, 1974–1980
2. Gen. João Bernardo Vieira, president, Council of State, head of government, 1980; elected president in multiparty elections 3 July and 7 August 1994–

Kenya   Nairobi
12 December 1963

1. Constitutional monarchy, 1963–1964; Jomo Kenyatta, prime minister
2. Kenyatta, president, 1964–11 August 1978
3. Succeeded by Daniel arap Moi, president, 1978–

Lesotho   Maseru
4 October 1966

1. Constitutional monarchy under King Motlotlehi Moshoeshoe II
2. Chief Leabua Jonathan seizes power in civilian coup, January 1970
3. Maj. Gen. Justin Lekhanya, chairman, Military Council, 1986–30 April 1991 (military coup)
4. Col. Elias Ramaema, chairman, Military Council, 30 April 1991–1993
5. Ntsu Mokhehle, prime minister, and King Letsie swear allegiance to the new constitution under the terms of which he remains head of state with no executive or legislative powers, 2 April–January 1995
6. King Moshoeshoe II, restored to the throne, 25 January 1995–January 1996
7. King Letsie III, February 1996–

Liberia   Monrovia
26 July 1847

1. Until 1944, eighteen presidents
2. William V. S. Tubman, president, 1944–1971
3. William R. Tolbert, 1971–12 April 1980

4. M. Sgt. Samuel K. Doe, president, People's Redemption Council, 1980–10 November 1990 (murdered)
5. Amos Sawyer, president, Interim Government of National Unity (IGNU), 1990–1995
6. Transitional executive council, comprising representatives of the former IGNU, the National Patriotic Forces of Liberia (NPFL), and the United Liberation Movement of Liberia for Democracy (ULIMO) form the Council of State headed by David D. Kpomakpor, chairman, IGNU, May 1995–

Libya Tripoli
24 December 1951
(from March 1977, named Socialist People's Libyan Arab Jamahiriya)

1. King Idris, 1951–1969
2. Col. Muammar Mohammed Qaddafi, leader of the revolution, September 1969–

Democratic Republic of Madagascar Antananarivo
26 June 1960

1. Philibert Tsiranana, president, 1960–May 1972
2. Gen. Gabriel Ramanantsoa, president, 1972–February 1975
3. Col. Ratsimandrava, February 1975 (assassinated)
4. Gen. Gilles Andria Mahazo, National Military Directorate, February 1975
5. Lt. Comdr. Didier Ratsiraka, president, March 1975–1993
6. Prof. Albert Zafy, president, elected to office 10 February 1993

Malawi Lilongwe
6 July 1964

1. Constitutional monarchy, Dr. Hastings Kamuzu Banda, prime minister, 1964–1966
2. Banda, president, 1966

3. Banda, "President for Life," July 1971–1994
4. Bakili Muluzi, president, 21 May 1994–

Mali Bamako
22 September 1960

1. Modibo Keita, president, Mali Federation; president, Soudan government, 15 April 1959; president of Mali, 1960–1968
2. Lt. (later Brig. Gen.) Moussa Traoré, chairman of Military Committee of National Liberation, November 1968–June 1979
3. Gen. Moussa Traoré, president, 19 June 1979–25 March 1991
4. Lieut. Col. Amadou Toumany Toure, acting head of state, 31 March 1991–5 April 1991
5. Soumana Sacko, prime minister, 5 April 1991–1992
6. Alpha Oumar Konare, president, 6 June 1992–

Islamic Republic Nouakchott
of Mauritania
28 November 1960

1. Mokhtar Ould Daddah, president, 1961–10 July 1978
2. Lt. Col. Mustapha Ould Mohammed Salek, president, Comité Militaire de Redressement National (CMRN), 10 July 1978–6 April 1979
3. Lt. Col. Ahmed Ould Bouceif, prime minister, 6 April 1979–27 May 1979 (assassinated)
4. Lt. Col. Mohammed Khouna Haidalla, prime minister, appointed by Salek, 31 May 1979
5. CMSN (formerly CMRN) forces Salek to resign, June 1979. Lt. Col. Mohammed Mahmoud Ould Louly, president, June 1979–January 1980
6. Haidalla ousts Louly, 4 January 1980. Becomes president, head of state, and chairman of CMSN, 1980–1984

7. Col. Maaouya Ould Sidi Ahmed Taya, chairman of the Military Committee for National Salvation, 1984–   ; elected president 24 January 1992

Mauritius Port Louis 1. Seewoosagur Ramgoolam, prime
12 March 1968 minister, 1968–1982
2. Aneerood Jugnauth, prime minister, 1982–

Morocco Rabat 1. King Mohammed V, to 1961
2 March 1956 2. King Hassan II, 3 March 1961–

Mozambique Maputo 1. Samora Moisés Machel, president, 1975–1986
25 June 1975 2. Joaquim Alberto Chissano, president, 1986–

Namibia Windhoek 1. Sam Nujoma, president;
21 March 1990 21 March 1990–

Niger Niamey 1. Hamani Diori, president, 1960–
3 August 1960 15 April 1974
2. Maj. Gen. Seyni Kountché, head of state; president, Supreme Military Council, 1974–1987
3. Col. Ali Seibou, president, Supreme Military Council; head of state, 1987–1991
4. Amadou Cheiffou, head, transitional Council of Ministers, 1991–1993
5. Mahamane Ousmane, president of republic, 16 April 1993–27 January 1996
6. Ibrahim Mainassara Bare, January 1996–

Nigeria Abuja 1. Alhaji Abubakar Tafawa Belewa,
1 October 1960 prime minister, 1960–1966; Nnamdi Azikiwe, president, 1963–1966

2. Gen. Johnson Aguiyi-Ironsi, head, Federal Military Government, January 1966–July 1966
3. Lt. Col. Yakubu Gowon, head, Federal Military Government, July 1966–29 July 1975
4. Brig. Gen. Murtala Mohammed, chief, Supreme Military Council, 29 July 1975–13 February 1976
5. Lt. Gen. Olusegun Obasanjo, 13 February 1976–October 1979
6. Alhaji Shehu Shagari, president, October 1979–December 1983
7. Maj. Gen. Mohammed Buhari, December 1983–August 1985
8. Maj. Gen. Ibrahim Babangida, president, August 1985–1993
9. Chief Ernest Adegunle Shonekan, head of government, 2 January 1993–November 1993
10. Gen. Sani Abacha, head of government and commander in chief of the armed forces, 17 November 1993–

Rwanda
1 July 1962

Kigali

1. Grégoire Kayibanda, president, 1961–5 July 1973
2. Maj. Gen. Juvénal Habyarimana, president, 5 July 1973–April 1994
3. Dr. Theodore Sindikubwabo, interim president of republic, April 1994–July 1994
4. Pasteur Bizimungu, president, 19 July 1994–

Saharan Arab Democratic Republic (SADR) (Western Sahara) February 1982 (admitted as fifty-first member of OAU)

Not applicable

1. Mohammed Abdelaziz, president, 1982–

São Tomé and Principe 12 July 1975	São Tomé	1. Dr. Manuel Pinto da Costa, president, 1975–April 1991 2. Miguel Trovoada, president, 3 April 1991–
Senegal 20 August 1960 (14 April 1959– 20 August 1960: Mali Federation)	Dakar	1. Léopold Sédar Senghor, president, 1960–January 1981 2. Abdou Diouf, president, January 1981–
Seychelles 29 June 1976	Victoria	1. James Mancham, president, June 1976–June 1977 2. Albert René, president, June 1977–
Sierra Leone 27 April 1961	Freetown	1. Sir Milton Margai, prime minister, 1961–1964 2. Sir Albert Margai, prime minister, 1964–1967 3. Lt. Col. Andrew Juxon-Smith, chairman, National Reformation Council, March 1967–April 1968 4. Siaka Probyn Stevens, prime minister, April 1968 5. Stevens, president of republic, April 1971–October 1985 6. Maj. Gen. Dr. Joseph Saidu Momoh, president, 1985– 7. Capt. Valentine E. M. Strasser, chairman, Supreme Council of State, 6 May 1992–January 1996 8. Brig. Gen. Julius Maada Bio, January 1996–March 1996 9. Ahmad Tejan Kabbah, March 1996–
Somalia 1 July 1960	Mogadishu	1. Aden Abdulla Osman, president, 1960–1967; Abdirashid Ali Shirmarke, prime minister, 1960–1964; Abdirazak Hussein, prime minister, 1964–1967

2. Abdirashid Ali Shirmarke, president, 1967–1969; Mohammed Ibrahim Egal, prime minister, 1967–1969
3. Maj. Gen. Mohammed Siad Barre, president, 1969–27 January 1991
4. Ali Mahdi Mohammed, president, 29 January 1991–1993
5. No functional government 1993–

South Africa Pretoria
31 May 1961

1. Dr. Hendrik Verwoerd, prime minister, 1958–1966
2. B. J. Vorster, president and prime minister, 1966–1978
3. Pieter W. Botha, prime minister, then president, 1978–1989
4. Chris Heunis, acting president, January–September 1989
5. Frederik de Klerk, president, 14 September 1989–May 1994
6. Nelson Rolihlahla Mandela, president, 10 May 1994–

Sudan Khartoum
1 January 1956

1. Ismail al-Azhari, prime minister, 1956
2. Abdulla Khalil, prime minister, 1956–1958
3. Lt. Gen. Ibrahim Abboud, prime minister, 1958–1964
4. Sir el-Khatim el-Khalifah, prime minister, 1964–1965
5. Muhammed Ahmad Mahgoub, prime minister, 1965–1966
6. Sayed Sadiq el-Mahdi, prime minister, 1966–1967
7. Muhammed Ahmad Mahgoub, prime minister, 1967–1969
8. Abubakr Awadallah, prime minister, 1969
9. Field Marshal Gaafar Mohammed Nimeiri, president, May 1969–April 1985

10. Coup, 6 April 1985. Lt. Gen.
Abdel Rahman Swar al Dahab,
chairman, Transitional Military
Council
11. Ahmed Ali el-Mirghani, president, Supreme Council
1986–30 June 1989 (military
coup)
12. Lt. General Omar Hassan Ahmed
al-Bashir, prime minister, 30
June 1989–; appointed president
16 Ocober 1993

Swaziland   Mbabane
6 September 1968

1. King Sobhuza II, 1922–
September 1982; Queen Mother
Dzeliwe, regent, September
1982. Deposed August 1983.
Prince Makosetive named as
future king, King Mswati III,
1986

Tanzania   Dodoma
9 December 1962
(of Tanganyika)
10 December 1963
(of Zanzibar)
(Tanganyika joins
with Zanzibar to
form United
Republic of Tanzania
in April 1964.)

1. Julius Nyerere, prime minister,
December 1961–January 1962
2. Rashidi M. Kawawa, prime minister, January 1962–December
1962
3. Tanganyika becomes a republic,
December 1962; Julius Nyerere,
president, December 1962–
November 1985
4. Ali Hassan Mwinyi, president,
1985–November 1995
5. Benjamin Mkapa, president, 17
November 1995–

Togo   Lomé
27 April 1960

1. Sylvanus Olympio, president
1960–13 January 1963
2. Military coup, January 1963, led
by Sgt. (later Gen.) Etienne
Eyadema. Nicholas Grunitzky,
president, 1963–January 1967

3. Col. Kleber Dadjo, chairman, Comité de Réconciliation Nationale (CRN), January–April 1967 (bloodless coup)
4. Gen. Gnassingbé Eyadema, president, April 1967–

Tunisia
20 March 1956

Tunis

1. Habib Bourguiba, prime minister, 1956–July 1957
2. July 1957, becomes a republic. Habib Bourguiba, president, 1957–1987
3. November 1987, Zine El-Abidine Ben Ali accedes to the presidency, November 1987–

Uganda
9 October 1962

Kampala

1. Apollo Milton Obote, 1962–1971 (prime minister until 1966; then president)
2. Maj. Gen. Idi Amin, president, 1971–April 1979
3. Yusuf Lule, president, Provisional Government, April–June 1979
4. Godfrey Binaisa, chairman, Military Commission of Uganda National Liberation Front (UNLF) and president, June 1979–May 1980
5. Paulo Mwanga, chairman, UNLF, May–December 1980
6. Obote, president, December 1980–July 1985
7. Coup led by Lt. Gen. Tito Okello of Uganda National Liberation Army; president, July 1985–January 1986
8. Yoweri Museveni, National Resistance Army (NRA), president, 29 January 1986–

Zaire
30 June 1960
(formerly Congo-
Kinshasa; named

Kinshasa

1. Patrice Lumumba, prime minister, June–September 1960; Joseph Kasavubu, president, 1960–1965

Zaire in October
1971)

2. Col. Joseph Mobutu suspends
   constitution, September 1960.
   College of Commissioners rules
   until February 1961
3. Joseph Ileo, prime minister,
   February–August 1961
4. Cyrille Adoula, prime minister,
   August 1961–July 1964
5. Moise Tshombe, prime minister,
   July 1964–October 1965
6. Evariste Kimba, prime minister,
   October–November 1965
7. Military coup led by Gen.
   Mobutu Sese Seko, president,
   1965–

Zambia   Lusaka
24 October 1964

1. Kenneth Kaunda, president
   1964–31 October 1991
2. Frederick Chiluba, president, 2
   November 1991–

Zimbabwe   Harare
18 April 1980

1. Canaan Banana, president and
   head of state, 1980–1988; Robert
   Mugabe, prime minister,
   1980–1988
2. Robert Mugabe, president,1988–

Sources: Africa South of the Sahara, 1990 (London: Europa Publications, 1989); *Africa Research Bulletin: Political Series* (Exeter: Africa Research, January–September 1991); *Keesing Record of World Events* (London: Longman, January–December 1990 and January–April 1991); *Sub-Saharan Africa, Daily Report* (Washington, DC: Government Printing Office, April 1–November 27 1991); *Africa South of the Sahara 1995, Twenty-Fourth Edition Europa Publications Limited* (London: Europa Publications, 1994); *The Europa World Year Book 1995* (London: Europa Publications, 1995); *Financial Times International* 18 March 1996 © 1996 Financial Times Limited; "Benin Vote Surprise," by Nicholas Phythian, Reuters 1996 © 1996 Reuters; "Abdoulkarim is elected," by Annie Thomas, Agence France-Presse 1996 © 1996 Agence France-Presse; *Political Handbook of the World 1995–1996* (Binghamton University State University of New York: CSA Publications, 1996).

Note: The Basic Political Data appendix is based on information gathered from a variety of sources. It should be noted that obtaining completely accurate data on African political events is difficult. Incomplete and conflicting accounts of government actions and dates are common among standard sources, and although all information on independence and on periods of political leadership was corroborated by three or more sources, readers may occasionally find discrepancies in other sources.

▪ About the Authors ▪

Virginia DeLancey is assistant director of the African Studies program at Indiana University.

Patrick J. Furlong is assistant professor of history at Alma College, in Michigan.

April A. Gordon is director of women's studies and associate professor of sociology at Winthrop University, in South Carolina.

Donald L. Gordon is professor and chair of political science and director of the African-Asian program at Furman University, in South Carolina.

George Joseph is associate professor of languages and literature at Hobart and William Smith Colleges, in New York State.

Ambrose Moyo is senior lecturer and chair of the Religious Studies Department at the University of Zimbabwe, Harare.

Jeffrey W. Neff is associate professor of geography and chair of the Department of Geosciences and Anthropology at Western Carolina University, in North Carolina.

Julius E. Nyang'oro is professor and chair of African and Afro-American Studies at the University of North Carolina at Chapel Hill.

Thomas O'Toole is professor of history in the Department of Sociology and Anthropology at St. Cloud State University, in Minnesota.

Peter Schraeder is associate professor of political science at Loyola University, in Chicago.

Brian Siegel is associate professor of anthropology in the Department of Sociology at Furman University, in South Carolina.

■ OTHER CONTRIBUTORS

Kevin A. Hill is assistant professor of political science at Florida International University.

Mary Spear is assistant professor of political science at Nebraska Wesleyan University.

▪ Index ▪

▪ About the Book ▪

Understanding Contemporary Africa is an up-to-date, multidisciplinary book that can be used as a core text in "Introduction to Africa" courses and also as a supplemental reader in various discipline-oriented courses.

The authors concentrate on the crucial issues facing Africa in the 1990s: there is a thorough treatment not only of politics, economics, and history, but also of women and development, the family, population and urbanization, the environment, religion, and literature. Each topic is covered in depth and on the basis of the latest available scholarship.

Showing how Africa's past has shaped its present and examining the major forces now shaping the Africa of the next century, *Understanding Contemporary Africa* focuses on the themes most vital to an awareness of the African experience in all its diversity and complexity.